W9-BTT-062

Adventure Guide to

Hawaii
The Big Island

Bryan Fryklund & Jen Reeder

HUNTER

HUNTER PUBLISHING, INC.
130 Campus Drive, Edison, NJ 08818-7816
☎ 732-225-1900 / 800-255-0343 / fax 732-417-1744
www.hunterpublishing.com
E-mail comments@hunterpublishing.com

IN CANADA:
Ulysses Travel Publications
4176 Saint-Denis, Montréal, Québec, Canada H2W 2M5
☎ 514-843-9882 ext. 2232 / fax 514-843-9448

IN THE UNITED KINGDOM:
Windsor Books International
5, Castle End Park, Castle End Rd, Ruscombe
Berkshire, RG10 9XQ England, ☎ 01189-346-367/fax 01189-346-368

ISBN 978-1-58843-625-2

Index by Nancy Wolff

4 3 2 1

Contents

Acknowledgements

Researching and writing this book was a massive undertaking, and we have a lot of people to thank: Michael Hunter, of course; Keely Baribeau at Novom Marketing; and Jeannette Vidgen at *Current Events*. We owe a debt of gratitude to James L. Wing of Dolphin Dreams Images, for allowing us to include his spectacular underwater photos, and to *Hawaii Forest and Trail* for use of their *`I`iwi* photo. We really appreciate Boyd Bond taking the time to talk story with us about his ancestors and North Kohala.

Tom Reeder proofread the entire manuscript (and has offered insights into many of Jen's writing projects since she learned to hold a pen) – we owe you big time. Les Charles gets a shout out for his extensive research and input on most of the golf courses on the island – your notes (some of which we repeated verbatim) came at a time when the Big Island was starting to seem especially big.

Thank you to Charles T. Hua, park ranger at Pu`uhonua o Honaunau National Historical Park, for not only sharing his knowledge of traditional Hawaiian culture, but for demonstrating how to play the nose flute while cracking up, and to Kaipo from Tow Guys in Waimea, for valiant efforts to resuscitate an island beater with over 230,000 miles on it when a deadline was looming.

Our friends and family are the rocks in our lives. Lots of love and appreciation to George and Lori Fryklund, Tom and Sally Reeder, Les and Zora Charles, Harrison and Doris Stephens, Lillian Morgan, Sophie Fryklund, Shelly and Tom Rose, Marcia and Chris Elvidge, Brian Reeder and Heidi Campbell, and all the members of our big, beautiful extended family; Steve Ellison, Cheryl Wiederspohn and our handsome shave ice model Julius; Christina and Matt Jackson; the Suraci family; our *ohana* in Durango, Colorado and the *Durango Telegraph*; Colleen Dunn Bates, for advice on freelancing and mentorship over the years; Michael Martone, our favorite English professor (we still can't believe Syracuse let you slip away to Alabama); the staff of *Louisiana Cookin'* magazine and our friends working to rebuild New Orleans – we love you.

Finally, a huge *mahalo* to the people of the Big Island, many of whom expressed enthusiasm and support for a guidebook that would attract visitors who were both adventurous *and* considerate (i.e., "cool"). And to you, our readers, for your love of adventure, whatever form it may take.

"The world is a book, and those who do not travel read only a page." – St. Augustine of Hippo

Dedication

This book is dedicated to our awesome nephews and nieces – Collin, Mitchell, Brendan, Morgan, Ashley and our beautiful goddaughter Maddy.

We hope your lives are filled with the joy of adventure.

About the Authors

Bryan Fryklund and Jen Reeder have been writing and traveling together since they graduated with English degrees from Syracuse University in 1994. Nomadic by nature, they have lived in Hawaii (Maui and the Big Island), Australia, Taiwan, California, Washington, DC, Seattle, New Orleans and Durango, Colorado, their home base on the mainland. They have traveled extensively in Mexico, Central and South America, Southeast Asia, the Philippines, Australia, New Zealand, and the United States. They moved back to Hawaii after Hurricane Katrina blew them out of New Orleans, and currently reside in Kailua-Kona on the Big Island.

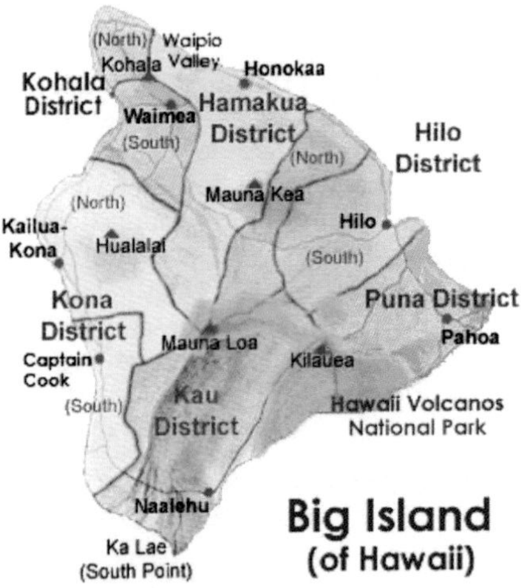

Introduction

O Hawaii no ka `aina maikai.
"After all, Hawaii is the best land." – Hawaiian proverb

IN THIS CHAPTER

There's no place like the Big Island of Hawaii. Nearly twice the size of the other Hawaiian Islands combined, it is a land of superlatives. It is home to Mauna Kea, a dormant volcano that towers over the Hawaiian Islands at 13,796 feet – and is Earth's tallest mountain when measured from its base on the ocean floor. It is also one of the world's best sites for astronomy; 13 telescopes representing nine countries cluster at its summit, observing 90% of the universe's visible stars. Another Big Island volcano, Kilauea, has been continuously erupting since 1983, making it the most active volcano on our planet.

The Big Island's Ka Lae is the southernmost point in the United States, and Parker Ranch is one of the largest privately owned ranches in America. Hilo is the country's rainiest city, which creates ideal growing conditions for crops like macadamia nuts and orchids – the Big Island is the worldwide leader in harvesting them. Kona is the only place in the US where gourmet coffee is grown, and is reputed to have the best scuba diving in Hawaii.

Its history is bold, too: the Big Island is the birthplace of King Kamehameha the Great, who united all of the Hawaiian Islands under his rule, and the final resting place of the great explorer Captain James Cook, who was killed here by native Hawaiians in 1779 (the snorkeling near his monument is some of the best in the Islands).

But there's more to it than such tangible facts. The Big Island is more off the beaten tourist path (though word is getting

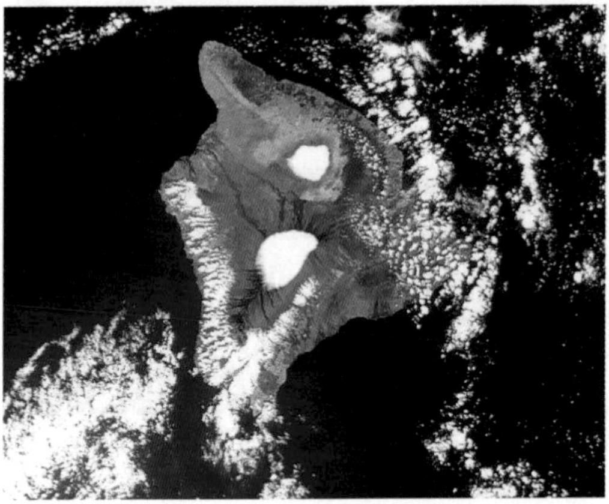
Mauna Kea and Mauna Loa from space

out) than elsewhere in the state, and has maintained a slower pace of life – it's known for its mellow vibe. It is common here to see cars with bumper stickers that read "Live Aloha," and love and caring are indeed an integral part of life on the island. The people are as beautiful as their natural surroundings – sometimes hilariously funny, sometimes deeply sensitive, but always pretty darn happy to be living in such a special place. The lush tropical forests, the expansive lava flow deserts, the sun-drenched beaches, the *ono* (delicious) cuisine, the fiery sunsets, the towering mountains and the idyllic weather make it impossible to be unaffected by the Big Island.

BONUS MATERIALS ONLINE

Not every detail could be included in this guide. You'll find all sorts of bonus materials at www.bigislandadventurefuide.com, including descriptions of additional restaurants, accommodations, shops, sights and even some adventures.

The range of climates and activities on the "Orchid Isle" means you can custom-tailor a vacation to suit your heart's desire. We've included detailed information about adventure opportunities around the island, keeping in mind that, just as "Beauty is in the eye of the beholder," adventure is very subjective. To the exhausted executive, it might be finding the perfect beach, golf course or mai tai. To others, it might be snorkeling in a coral garden, swimming with dolphins, night diving with manta rays, hiking to a waterfall, horseback riding through Paniolo Country, taking a helicopter ride over Hawai`i Volcanoes National Park, examining petroglyphs, skiing down Mauna Kea, surfing, kayaking, whale-watching, stargazing or learning to dance the hula. The Big Island has "adventures" that will appeal to everyone, and help you return home refreshed, invigorated and relaxed. Best of all, you can always come back. Aloha!

TOP BIG ISLAND ADVENTURES

- Boogie boarding at Hapuna Beach (p. 244)
- Manta ray night dive/snorkel (p. 45-46)
- Kayaking/snorkeling Kealakekua Bay (p. 164)
- Exploring Waipi'o Valley (p. 388)
- Place of Refuge (p. 176-78)
- Helicopter flight over Kilauea (p. 431-32)
- Kilauea Iki Trail (p. 346)
- Driving the Hamakua Coast (p. 376)

Having spent over half a year researching this book full-time, we can promise that you will not run out of things to see or do on the Big Island. There are so many amazing places and adventure opportunities that you really can't go wrong. So keep this in mind when we mention the highlights of each region – it's often better to spend more time really getting to know one area than trying to cram in too much. Our job is to give you as many options as possible, and let you "choose your own adventure." Have fun!

HIGHLIGHT OF EACH REGION

- Kona – Manta ray night dive/snorkel (p. 45-46)
- South Kohala – Hapuna Beach (p. 244)
- North Kohala – Pololu Valley (p. 282)
- Waimea/Mauna Kea – Stargazing at Mauna Kea (p. 312)
- Hamakua Coast – Waipi`o Valley (p. 388)
- Hilo – Rainbow Falls (p. 444)
- Puna – Red Road (p. 462)
- Ka`u – Green Sands Beach (p. 485)
- And the highlight of the entire island – Hawai`i Volcanoes National Park (p. 323)

History

Pre-Contact

The Big Island

Long before western sailors were equipped to venture more than a short distance from land, Polynesians were confidently criss-crossing the Pacific in double-hulled sailing canoes. They relied on an incredibly nuanced navigation system that was passed down from generation to generation, calling on knowledge of the stars, currents, winds – as well as the *look* and the *taste* of the water, among other things – to successfully voyage from place to place. They brought their lifestyles with them when they went, stuffing the canoes with pigs and dogs, live banana trees, *ti*, taro, coconut and sugar cane. It was in this way that voyagers from the Marquesas Islands (French Polynesia, today) first arrived in Hawaii, coming ashore near South Point on the Big Island sometime between the third and fifth centuries AD. In Hawaii they found a virgin land, where they and the species they introduced thrived.

It has long been thought that a second wave of migration occurred around 1000 AD from Tahiti, and that these people conquered and displaced the existing population, imposing the rigid societal restrictions that came to define pre-contact Hawaii. However, recent archeological evidence casts doubt on this theory, and it now appears that there was simply a steady stream of migration until it ceased several centuries prior to European contact.

For centuries, Hawaii was ruled by the *kapu* system, which not only stratified society, but also dictated what people could do and when they could do it. It was a harsh system, and breaking a *kapu* meant death. The idea of *mana*, or spiritual power, was fiercely guarded by *kapu*, and any commoner whose shadow fell across a chief was in danger of stealing the superior's *mana*. Such breaches of *kapu* were punishable by death. While it may have been a convenient way for the ruling class to retain power, it also appears to have been widely accepted by everyone, and the thought was that if a *kapu* was broken, the gods would be angered and would dole out retribution to all.

Kapu means "forbidden" or "no traspassing"

It was certainly a brutal system, but it was also very successful at regulating natural resources. For instance, fishing was subject to *kapu*, which dictated when and where the people could fish, and prevented the depletion of the fisheries, thereby ensuring the health of the ecosystem. However, *kapu* also meant a strict social hierarchy, whereby the ruling class (*ali`i*) maintained dominion over the other classes: the *kahuna*, who were the professional class at everything including religion; the *maka`ainana*, who were the commoners, doing all of the "blue-collar" work, such as agriculture and fishing; and the *kauwa*, or slave class, who were outcasts and often used as human sacrifices. There was, essentially, a feudal system in place, whereby commoners were allowed to work land owned by *ali`i*, but were required to provide them with a large quantity of what they produced. Another aspect of the *kapu* system was that men and women were forbidden to eat together. This was the system that was in full swing when the arrival of a foreigner set in motion a chain of events that changed Hawaii forever.

Even today, if you see a sign marked "Kapu," it means "no trespassing." Please respect these signs.

Captain Cook

Captain James Cook was on the third of his legendary voyages, and had sailed the vast majority of the 200,000-plus miles he was to sail in his lifetime (a distance roughly equivalent to sailing to the moon), when he stumbled upon the Hawaiian Islands. Though he had mapped a massive amount

Captain Cook

of Pacific territory for the English crown (including New Zealand and Easter Island), Cook wasn't looking for any islands in January of 1778. He was on his way northeast, with his sights set on the much-sought-after Northwest Passage that Europeans hoped linked the Pacific and Atlantic Oceans. While what transpired is the source of endless debate, the prevailing opinion is as follows.

Cook and his men happened to arrive at the Big Island at the time of the annual Makahiki festival, which was a time of sporting events, feasting and peace in honor of Lono, the god of fertility (among other things). Lono, it was said, would one day return with "trees that would move over the seas." Cook's ships, with their high masts and sails, bore a striking resemblance to the traditional icon of Lono that was carried in an annual procession around the island. Additionally, Cook circled the island in a clockwise direction, the same direction as the procession, before anchoring at Kealakekua Bay, the symbolic home to Lono. His most ardent followers lived in villages here, and had erected a *heiau* (temple) to him.

The journals of Captain Cook

The Hawaiians thought Cook was Lono, and welcomed him as a god. He and his crew were enthusiastically supplied with everything they needed, after which they left, pushing on to the west coast of the Americas. A year later, however, they returned, again during the Makahiki festival, and this time the locals' hospitality quickly wore thin. Despite his best efforts to prevent it on the previous voyage, Cook's sailors had infected the local women with syphilis and the disease had spread throughout Hawaii. The islanders treated them tolerably well, but were pleased when they made preparations to depart. Unfortunately, they hit harsh seas between the Big

Island and Maui, and were forced to return to Kealakekua Bay to repair the *Resolution*, Cook's ship.

Cook Point at the entrance to Kealakekua Bay (Hawaiian Images)

This was a fatal mistake: the Makahiki festival had ended and the Hawaiians had entered the season of Ku, the god of war. As repairs to the ship began, several petty thefts occurred that strained relations with the islanders. Then a Hawaiian stole a cutter in the middle of the night. Cook planned to retrieve his boat by kidnapping the high chief and holding him for ransom until the cutter was returned. This had worked for him in other islands in the Pacific, but it wouldn't this time. Armed Hawaiians gathered to protect the chief. Cook pulled his gun and shot an islander, but the birdshot didn't penetrate the warrior's protective clothing. Emboldened, they advanced on Cook. His men were retreating into boats just a short distance offshore, but, ironically, one of the greatest sea captains in history had never learned to swim, and was stuck. One warrior hit the captain in the back of the head with a club, while another stabbed him between the shoulder blades. He was then surrounded and stabbed repeatedly, with the Hawaiians taking turns sharing in the kill.

Captain Cook named Hawaii the Sandwich Islands after one of his patrons, the fourth Earl of Sandwich. The Earl has been immortalized by the food he insisted on being served while gambling: meat served between two pieces of bread.

Kamehameha the Great

According to some, there on the rocks the day Cook was killed, was a tall, broad-shouldered chief who is said to have made off with the captain's hair. This man, born Pai`ea in the district of North Kohala in the year 1758, would soon move to fulfill the prophecy told prior to his birth, that a man born while a light blazed across the sky would conquer the islands and unite the people under one rule. When Kamehameha was born with Halley's Comet in the sky, he was hidden away in Waipi`o Valley and raised under a different name. By the time Cook arrived in the Islands, the young man, now called Kamehameha, had a reputation as an especially skilled warrior who hungered for more power.

Kamehameha the Great

Less than a year after the death of Cook, the existing high chief of the Big Island, withered and palsied by abuse of *`awa* (kava), saw his own death approaching. He willed his political position to his son, but to his nephew, Kamehameha, he gave his war god, Ku, a fierce-looking image infused with the power of war. This set the stage for a violent power play, and upon the old chief's death, Kamehameha and the heir battled, with the future king of Hawaii the victor. However, Keoua, the younger brother of the heir, escaped.

After the death of Captain Cook, his crew sailed back to England, and the world learned of the existence of Hawaii. Traders soon flocked to the islands, and the wisest of the *ali`i*, Kamehameha among them, took the opportunity to trade for weapons. Before long, Kamehameha took possession of a western ship, the first of his many warships. He used his new ship to attack Maui, despite the fact that he hadn't yet fully conquered his home island.

LAW OF THE SPLINTERED PADDLE

"Let every elderly person, woman and child lie by the roadside in safety."

This edict by Kamehameha I has become one of the guiding principles of human rights law concerning non-combatants in modern warfare. It is said that Kamehameha was hit in the back of the head with a canoe paddle by a commoner who was trying to save his family from the fierce warrior during a battle on the Big Island of Hawaii, and that the future king concluded that civilians should not be targets during war.

Soon after, a *kahuna* told Kamehameha that if he built a *heiau*, or temple, at Pu`ukohola (whale hill) near Kawaihae in the district of Kohala and dedicated it to the war god, Ku, then he would fulfill his destiny and conquer all of the Hawaiian Islands. When the temple was completed, he invited his last enemy to a parley. When the rival showed up with his men, one of Kamehameha's chiefs took him down with a spear, and his enemy became the first sacrifice to the new temple.

Close-up of the heiau

With his home island in hand, Kamehameha went on to take the other islands by force, capturing O`ahu in a bloody battle in 1795. Several times he planned to take Kaua`i, even building a massive fleet of war canoes, but he was repeatedly turned back, once by a huge storm and another time by an outbreak of disease. The king of Kaua`i became a vassal to Kamehameha, ceding the island and Ni`ihau by treaty in 1810, thereby finally making him the supreme ruler of the islands.

Queen Ka`ahumanu

With his favorite wife, Queen Ka`ahumanu at his side, Kamehameha ushered in the modern era to Hawaii. While he used the taxes he collected to promote outside trade, especially with the US and Europe, and allowed foreigners to exert influence (though largely for his own military gains, to further his ultimate ends), he put forth an edict that allowed only Hawaiians to own land, thereby ensuring the independence of the island chain long after other Pacific islands had submitted to foreign powers.

Following the death of Kamehameha the Great in 1819, his eldest son Liholiho ascended the throne as King Kamehameha II. However, his power was limited from the beginning. Ka`ahumanu asserted that her dead husband's last wish was that she share in the governance of Hawaii. Parliament agreed to this, and made her *kuhina nui*, with power equivalent to that of a Prime Minister. She began exerting her will over the new king immediately, and only six months into his reign (and following a two-day drinking binge) the king agreed to sit down with her publicly and break bread, a serious breach of *kapu*. This single, staged act kicked the legs out from under the entire *kapu* system, and the very foundations of Hawaiian society crumbled nearly overnight.

Did you know? The Hawaiian flag is the only state flag of the US to display the Union Jack, or flag of the United Kingdom. This is due to the historic relationship of the Kingdom of Hawaii with the UK.

Missionaries & Whalers

Not only did the destruction of the *kapu* system result in unprecedented social upheaval, but it left a religious vacuum that fate was about to fill. In 1820, Calvinist missionaries out of Boston landed on the Big Island on the brig *Thaddeus*, and a religion that would have found very little social traction only a year before was now easily spread. It became even easier when Ka`ahumanu, who had previously disdained the missionaries and made things politically difficult for them, fell seriously ill and was nursed back to health by a missionary's wife. Ka`ahumanu emerged from her sickness with a new religious zeal, which greatly facilitated the newcomers' mission. Missionaries set up the first schools in Hawaii, gave sermons and sang hymns in Hawaiian, and forced clothes upon the lightly-dressed natives, most of whom were converted to Christianity.

Early whaling

Missionaries and traders were not the only ones who found Hawaii an attractive destination in the middle of the vast Pacific. Whalers discovered that Hawaii was ideal for their purposes. They came in droves, most from far-away New England. At the height of Pacific whaling in 1846, nearly 600 whaling ships anchored in Hawaiian waters. Despite the fact that humpback whales flock to Hawaii in huge numbers in winter, this is not what drove the Hawaiian whaling industry. Humpbacks have an inferior oil content to other whales, and they tend to dive deep when harpooned, which ships in the mid-1800s were not equipped to handle. Rather, Hawaii was used for rest and relaxation for sailors and to provision ships headed to Japan and the Arctic to hunt sperm, right and blue whales, since Japanese shores were closed to foreign whalers in those days. Whalers were rough men who enjoyed drinking rum and carousing with island women when they weren't at sea, and this often brought them into conflict with the missionaries. In one notable event, whalers blasted cannons at the homes of missionaries who were trying to close brothels in Lahaina on Maui, a not-so-subtle tactic that succeeded in keeping the doors of the brothels open.

Sugar

Missionaries believed that Hawaii needed a stabilizing industry not subject to the whims of nature and vagaries of the soul as whaling was. They decided on sugar. But there was an obstacle to this massive agricultural undertaking: King Kamehameha I's decree that only Hawaiians could own land. Foreigners and children of missionaries – with dollar signs in their eyes – exerted pressure on King Kamehameha III, a socialite who was open to suggestion. In 1848, he decreed the Great Mahele, which made it legal for non-Hawaiians to own land, while at the same time doling out thousands of acres of land to native Hawaiians. However, it's clear that few commoners understood the concept of land ownership, and they were eventually conned or swindled out of their land by the plantation owners.

While some investors were looking to cash in, others, like Reverend Elias Bond, were simply looking for an economic opportunity for the locals in their district. He created the Kohala Sugar Company in 1863, and many other ventures in the area soon followed. This was the beginning of an industry that would drive the economy on the Big Island for over 100 years before going bust due to cheaper foreign labor in the late 20th century. The five major sugar barons of the 1800s came to be known as the "Big Five," and have a legacy around the islands as opportunists who stopped at nothing to consolidate their power, which meant steering Hawaii toward the United States, first as a free-trade partner, later as a territory and, eventually, a state.

King Kalakaua & Queen Lili`uokalani

King Kalakaua

King Kalakaua came to power in 1874 following the short reign of King Lunalilo, who was appointed king after the death of King Kamehameha V ended the reign of the Kamehameha line. He would come to be known as the Merrie Monarch due to his enjoyment of the finer aspects of life, and it was during his rule that the art of hula made a strong resurgence. Unfortunately, not all things during his reign were so positive. Soon after assuming the throne, he signed a reciprocity agreement with the US, allowing some Hawaiian products, mainly sugar, to enter America duty free. In 1884, he extended the reciprocity agreement for seven years, allowing the US to use Pearl Harbor as a naval base. In 1887, despite his best intentions for the people of Hawaii, he was forced, under threat of arms, to sign what is known as the Bayonet Constitution. The new constitution stripped the monarchy of much of its power, gave European and American immigrants the right to vote and barred most native Hawaiians from the polls by imposing economic and literacy standards on voter eligibility.

Kalakaua's travels: When King Kalakaua traveled around the world to visit with other heads of state in 1881, he became history's first monarch to circumnavigate the globe.

Kalakaua grew ill, and died in 1891. With no children, the throne fell to his sister, Queen Lili`uokalani, who soon attempted to invalidate the Bayonet Constitution. Despite a poll that showed native Hawaiians were overwhelmingly in support of overturning the constitution, the powerful business interests who initiated it had no intention of letting their power be stripped away. In what is now considered an illegal coup, the Hawaiian monarchy was overthrown by the Committee of Safety, a confederation of sugar planters backed by the American Consul and American marines. Queen Lili`uokalani was deposed and put under house arrest in `Iolani Palace for eight months. They drafted a new constitution soon after and declared the "Republic of Hawaii" on, ironically, July 4, 1894.

Queen Lili`uokalani

Annexation

With the election of Republican William McKinley in 1896, the annexation of Hawaii was seriously considered. American expansionists had the ear of the president, and when the Spanish-American War broke out in 1898 the importance of the naval base at Pearl Harbor became abundantly clear. In response to the annexation proposal there were numerous protests in Hawaii. Over 21,000 people, which was more than half the population of native Hawaiians, signed an anti-annexation petition. However, this document was ignored by Washington, and President McKinley signed a joint congressional resolution formally annexing Hawaii. This petition, as well as the fact that the US Constitution doesn't allow for independent countries to be annexed through congressional resolution, is one of the cornerstones of the modern Hawaiian sovereignty movement.

Statehood

Hawaii endured over 60 years of territorial status, with no voting rights for its citizens, until 1959 when it was welcomed as the 50th state in the union. The Big Five conspired to keep down those who opposed them, though as the 20th century wore on, labor unions took hold and grew mightily, allegedly becoming one of the reasons that the US took so long to warm to the idea of Hawaiian statehood.

Today, the Aloha State's main industry is tourism, with over seven million visitors a year.

Geography

"Hawaii has always been a very pivotal role in the Pacific. It is in the Pacific. It is a part of the United States that is an island that is right here." – Dan Quayle

The Big Island is the youngest of the Hawaiian Islands, situated at the southern end of the archipelago in the middle of the Pacific Ocean, 2,400 miles west of California. Because of the nature of the volcanic islands, Hawai`i's geography is tied to its geology.

Each of the Hawaiian Islands was formed as the Pacific Plate of the Earth's surface drifted northwest over a "hotspot," essentially a source of a volcanic eruption in the Earth's mantle. The first major island to form – 3.8 million to 5.6 million years ago – was Kaua`i, an underwater volcano that erupted and accumulated land mass until it breached the ocean's surface and continued to grow into an island. As the plate drifted northwest over millions of years, other volcanoes formed the other principal islands: O`ahu, Moloka`i, Maui and, less than a million years ago, Hawai`i. The Big Island is still partially over the hot plate, and its Kilauea volcano is the world's most active, adding roughly 550 acres of new land since it began continuously erupting in 1983.

But the plate continues to drift to the northwest a few inches each year, and the "Hawaiian hotspot" is forming a new island beneath the ocean called Lo`ihi, which rises 10,100 feet from the ocean floor. Lo`ihi is 18 miles off the southern coast of the Big Island and in a few tens of thousands of years it will rise above sea level and merge with the Big Island to form a sixth volcano for the island.

Until that time, the Big Island has a land mass of roughly 4,030 square miles, which continues to grow each day. Presently there are 266 miles of coastline. Five shield volcanoes make up the Big Island. The oldest is the extinct Kohala Volcano, the dormant Mauna Kea and Hualalai, the active Mauna Loa and the very active Kilauea.

The Big Island may be the largest of the Hawaiian Islands, but it is relatively small when compared to a US state. The Big Island is closest in size to Connecticut (though it's not quite that big yet). It is 95 miles from the northern tip to the southernmost point, and about 80 miles across.

Climate

"Sunshine is delicious, rain is refreshing, wind braces us up, snow is exhilarating; there is really no such thing as bad weather, only different kinds of good weather."
– John Ruskin

Of the 13 climate zones on Earth, the Big Island is missing only two: the Arctic and the Saharan. You'll be amazed by the striking contrasts in the environment around the island, from lava deserts to rainforests, black sand beaches to snowy mountain peaks. The average temperature ranges from 71 to 77°F, though this can be misleading, aside from the indication that the temperature doesn't fluctuate much (in fact, it is hard to date trees here because, with so little change, they don't form "tree rings"). The most obvious sign of winter is the arrival of the humpback whales, who grace Hawaiian waters from late November through March.

Temperatures, in fact, vary significantly according to different locations around the island. Along the Kona and Kohala coasts, conditions are balmier than elsewhere, usually lingering between the high 70s and high 80s. Things are cooler at higher elevations, such as Waimea, which ranges between 62 and 66°F at 2,760 feet. You'll need a sweater, raingear and shorts at Hawai`i Volcanoes National Park – the visitor center at 4,000 feet is much cooler (57 to 63°F) than the coastal areas of the park, which are comparable to the Kona Coast.

Rainfall is another consideration. As mentioned above, Hilo is the country's rainiest city, recording an average rainfall of 129 inches each year. Hilo and the rest of the windward side are covered with luxuriant rainforests that sparkle when the sun makes an appearance, usually in the mornings before the afternoon clouds roll in. By contrast, some of the coastal areas on the leeward side often receive less than seven inches of rain per year, making for sunny skies nearly every day (and many more hotels on this side of the Big Island).

The temperature of the water is always refreshing, reaching an average of 72° in February and rising to around 78° in August. Surfers don't need wetsuits, but divers will want a short suit at the least.

With such little climatic fluctuation, the Big Island is a fabulous place to visit year-round. The ocean is calmer in the summer than the winter, so if you're a surfer, you'll want to come in winter. If you're a diver or kayaker, summer is slightly better (but these sports are still amazing in winter). Otherwise, come when you can!

Early bird gets the worm: The typical weather pattern on the Big Island is sunny skies in the morning, with clouds rolling in during the afternoon. So even if you're a night owl, you'll want to hope your jet lag gets you out of bed and into the early morning sunshine!

Hawaiian Culture

Ua mauke ea o ka `aina i ka pono.
"The life of the land is perpetuated by righteousness."
– Hawaii state motto

People

The Big Island had a total population of 148,677 at last census, and 42,288 (28.4%) are descended from two or more races in this unique melting pot. Most single-race residents are white (31.5%), Asian (26.7%), and Native Hawaiian or other Pacific Islander (11.2%). Hispanic or Latino residents make up 9.5%.

The Big Island spans 4,028 square miles (and still growing), but it is much less populous than the other major islands, creating more room for everyone to stretch out and enjoy the land. Residents tend to be laid-back, not given to honking horns or other symptoms of road rage. This is the place where the slow pace of "Hawaiian Time" rules.

BE COOL

It goes without saying that visitors should remember to treat Hawaiians with respect. The reasons for this extend beyond good manners and common decency. Hawaii, America's 50th state, was once a sovereign nation until a group backed by agents of the US government deposed Queen Lili`uokalani in 1893. Hawaiian culture was suppressed until the cultural renaissance in the 1970s, which led the military to stop test bombing the now-uninhabitable Hawaiian Island of Kaho`olawe in 1978. As such, there is sometimes resentment towards mainland haoles (foreigners), though it is less intense on the Big Island than on other islands like O`ahu. Still, you may notice "Free Hawaii" signs, and Hawaiian flags hanging upside down, the international symbol for a nation in distress.

Please treat locals with the respect they deserve. Don't snap your fingers for your waiter, or order people around. Do not trespass onto a property if you see a sign marked "Kapu," which literally means "forbidden," or "no trespassing." Smile, and say thank you (or mahalo). Remember, most locals are not wealthy, and often cannot afford homes because the cost of real estate has been driven up by mainland haoles buying vacation homes here. Yes, Hawaii is an American state, but it has a unique history and culture, and even US citizens should remember that they are still visitors to this unusual place. Be cool, and people will be cool to you. Tourism is the lifeblood of the economy, after all, and Hawaiians are usually extremely proud to share their island and culture with people who visit with respect.

So that's it. Just relax and enjoy the hospitality of your gracious hosts. After all, this is the land of aloha.

"In what other land save this one is the commonest form of greeting not 'Goodday,' nor 'How d'ye do,' but 'Love'? That greeting is 'Aloha': Love, I love you, my love to you... It is a positive affirmation of the warmth of one's own heart-giving." – Jack London

What to Wear

Hawaii's unofficial state motto is "Hang Loose," so leave your neckties and pantyhose at home (unless you really love them). The fanciest dress code you'll find on island is in the resorts of South Kohala, where the best fine-dining restaurants may request "Resort Attire." This basically means "Look kinda nice – not a bathing suit." If you want to do what the locals do, wear comfortable clothes that make you feel good. Seriously, no ties – Hawaiian men wear aloha shirts for dressy occasions.

Remove your shoes: It's customary in just about every Hawaiian household – and many B&Bs – to remove one's shoes before entering. Hawaiians are usually amiable and won't mention it, but if you see a line of shoes near the door, follow suit and remove your own. Your hosts will appreciate it!

Language

Ua ola no i ka pane a ke aloha.
"There is life in a kindly reply." – Hawaiian proverb

Language is a complex issue in Hawaii for both the Hawaiian language (`Olelo Hawai`i) and Hawaiian Pidgin English ("Hawaiian creole"), simply called Pidgin in the islands.

In 1896, shortly after the queen was deposed, a law was passed banning Hawaiian – and all languages other than English – from being taught in public and private schools. Children were punished for speaking Hawaiian at school and often at home, since parents were told that speaking Hawaiian would harm their children's future chances of success. By the 1920s, very few Hawaiian children could speak their native tongue.

Meanwhile, a different language was evolving on sugar plantations. The influx of immigrants from Portugal, Japan, China, the Philippines, Korea, Puerto Rico and other countries who came to work on Hawaii's sugar plantations in the 1800s led to the evolution of a common language that combined words from many cultures: Pidgin.

Thanks to the Hawaiian cultural renaissance of the 1970s, Hawaiian joined English as the official language of the Aloha State, making Hawaii the only US state with two official languages. Hawaiian is now taught both at the university level and at some immersion schools, where all subjects are taught in Hawaiian. But Pidgin remains the unofficial language, and you'll hear it every day of your vacation (provided you leave your hotel). There is a movement calling for its acceptance as a legitimate language, rather than "bad English," which faces opposition similar to the Ebonics movement on the mainland.

MARY KAWENA PUKUI

Hawaiians credit the efforts of one woman, Mary Kawena Pukui, as crucial to the preservation of the Hawaiian language and culture. Born on the Big Island in Ka`u in 1895, Pukui had a deep interest in hula and the Hawaiian language, and began recording stories and sayings she overheard in the community as a teenager. In 1928, she translated the Hawaiian stories and sayings into English for the Bishop Museum, and co-authored the *Hawaiian Dictionary* in 1957. She wrote and edited Hawaiian chants and songs with composers, and was a Kumu Hula, or teacher of the dance. She passed away in 1986 but, thanks in part to her efforts, the Hawaiian language lives on.

Hawaiian was originally an oral language, but missionaries created an alphabet based on the sounds they heard. The Hawaiian language has only 12 letters, and five of them are vowels. Because syllables never have more than one consonant and always end in a vowel, it is a melodious language befitting the island's natural beauty.

The Hawaiian alphabet is: a, e, i, o, u, h, k, l, m, n, p, w.

The consonants – except w – are pronounced like their English counterparts, but vowels are pronounced as though spoken in Spanish:

A – "ah" – like father
E – "eh" – like egg
I – "ee" – like ski
O – "oh" – like choke
U – "oo" – like glue

"W" is sometimes pronounced like a "v." You'll even hear some people pronounce Hawaii with a "v." That's because if the "w" follows the letter "a," it can be pronounced either way – though usually one becomes common usage. If "w" follows "o" or "u," it is pronounced like an English "w." But if it follows "e" or "i," it assumes the "v" sound.

To complicate things, there's the `okina, or glottal stop. It looks like a backwards apostrophe `. The glottal stop is the signal to make a break into another syllable – if you see the word for jagged lava, a`a, you pronounce it "ah-ah," instead of one long "aah."

**Hawaii vs. Hawai`i:** In this book, we use the traditional spelling of Hawai`i when we write about the Big Island. When we spell it without the glottal stop, we're referring to the entire state.

There's a symbol called a macron, which looks like the horizontal bar over a vowel you'll see in English books to denote a long vowel. It has become uncommon in general print around the islands, and we have not used it in the book because of accuracy concerns. If you do see it, it indicates that the vowel has more emphasis.

We have included a Hawaiian glossary in the appendix of this book.

WHICH BATHROOM?

Many restaurants on the Big Island use the Hawaiian words to show the men's and women's restrooms. Restaurant employees will be thrilled (and able to get your food to you faster) if you learn these words and don't have to ask them.

The easiest way to remember is that the Hawaiian word for "woman," wahine ("wah-HEE-nay"), also starts with a "W." Kane ("KAH-nay") means man.

Learning some Pidgin terms might prove even more helpful; here is a "cheat sheet" to help you sound cool – or at least be able to understand what's being said. We've included some Hawaiian expressions that are commonly used, as well.

Any kine . . . . any kind
Auwi! (Ow-EE) . . . . Ouch!
Braddah . . . . brother
Brah . . . . short for braddah; friend
Broke da mout . . . . delicious
Bummahs . . . . bummer

Chicken skin . . . . goose bumps
Da . . . . the
Da kine . . . . anything to which you're referring
Grind . . . . eat
Grinds . . . . food
Hana hou (HA-nah HO) . . . . Do it again; encore
Haole (HOW-lee) . . . . white person
Howzit? . . . . How's it going?
In deep kimchee . . . . in big trouble
Kaukau (cow-cow) . . . . food
Kokua (koh-KOO-ah) . . . . help
Mo bettah . . . . much better
No can . . . . not possible, cannot
Okole maluna (oh-KOH-lay mah-LOO-nah)
. . . . Bottoms up, cheers
Pau hana (pow HA-nuh) . . . . done with work
Pupus (POO-poos) . . . . appetizers
Slippahs . . . . rubber slippers, aka flip flops
Stink eye . . . . mean look, glare
Talk story . . . . have a conversation, chat
Tanks . . . . Thanks
To da max . . . . all the way
Tutu . . . . grandmother, older woman

THE LETTER "S"

The letter "S" does not exist in the Hawaiian alphabet, so the same word applies for singular or plural meanings. You might notice that we have taken some poetic license in creating our own sort of pidgin as many other locals do, by adding an "S" out of habit to words to make them plural, as in "It's a good place to buy leis and `ukuleles." However, if the entire sentence were in Hawaiian, we would preface the word with "na" to make it plural, like "na lei."

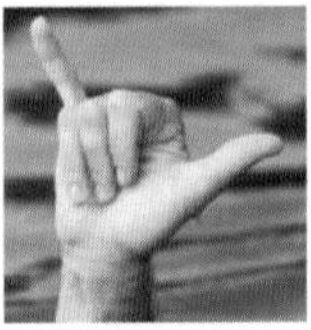

Shaka: The shaka sign is a common greeting in Hawaii and in parts of Polynesia, done by extending the thumb and pinkie finger and giving a little shake with the palm towards your body. It's also a gesture akin to "Cool!" or "Right on!"

Music

The first thing you should do when you get into your rental car and drive away from the airport is set your radio to a station playing island tunes, like KAPA (100.3 FM in Hilo; 99.1 FM in Kona). Hawaiian music epitomizes the relaxing vibe of the islands and the soothing affect of the natural environment on the nervous system. Listening to it will help you adjust to the slower pace of "Hawaiian time" (plus the DJs are usually really funny).

The two main genres of Hawaiian music are the legendary falsetto singers, with their sweet voices reaching to the skies and usually accompanied by an `ukulele, and the slack key guitarists, who fingerpick acoustic guitars with strings "slacked" from standard tuning. You'll have the opportunity to hear falsetto singers perform at restaurants and hotels on the Big Island, as well as hear recordings on the radio or in public malls. The most famous Hawaiian falsetto singer is probably the late Israel Kamakawiwo`ole, known as Iz, whose lovely cover of *Somewhere Over the Rainbow* can moisten the eyes of even the most hardened cynic.

Slack key guitar (Ki ho`alu) is a Hawaiian style of playing that has recently garnered acclaim at the national level through pianist George Winston's label, Dancing Cat Records, which has released and promoted over 35 albums featuring the music. In 2005, a Grammy award was created for Best Hawaiian Album, and in 2006, Dancing Cat's *Hawaiian Slack Key Guitar Masters, Vol. 1* won. Some of the famous Hawaiian slack key guitarists include brothers Keola and Kapono

Beamer, Ray Kane, Sonny Chillingworth, George Kahumoko, Jr., Gabby Pahinui and his son Cyril, and John Keawe. Hawaiian hip hop and "Jawaiian," a Hawaiian form of reggae, have also gained popularity in recent years.

`UKULELE

The name *`ukulele* (often mispronounced "YOU-kah-LAY-lee" instead of "OO-koo-LEH-leh") comes from two words – *`uku*, which means "jumping," and *lele*, meaning "flea." It was developed in Hawaii in the 1880s, after the ship *Ravenscrag* carried Portuguese immigrants to O`ahu in 1879. When Hawaiians saw some of the Portuguese men playing small, four-stringed guitars (braguinhas), they thought their fingers moved so fast that they were like a "jumping flea," and the name *`ukulele* was born.

Hula

`A `a i ka hula, waiho ka hilahila i ka hale. "When one wants to dance the hula, bashfulness should be left at home."
– Hawaiian proverb

True hula is a far cry from the campy portrayal of grass-skirted women shaking their hips in Elvis movies. Hula and mele, the chants that dancers interpret with their movements, have played a crucial role in Hawaii's oral tradition, particularly important since the Hawaiian language had no written form until the 1800s. This oral tradition recorded the creation myth (which is very similar to modern scientists' Big Bang and evolution theories), stories of Hawaiian gods, royalty and genealogies. It was considered unlucky to make a mistake while dancing the hula, and students placed themselves under the protection of Laka, the patron goddess of hula, who some traditions believe gave birth to the dance on the island of Moloka`i.

The missionaries considered hula immoral, and had it banned after their arrival in 1820. Hula practitioners were forced underground, where their commitment in a time of cultural suppression – this is the same time that English supplanted the Hawaiian language – preserved the oral tradition. King David Kalakaua, also known as the Merrie Monarch, was a supporter of Hawaiian arts, and he is credited with hula's revival in the 1870s. The annual Merrie Monarch Festival in Hilo is the world's largest hula competition.

Today there are two distinct forms of hula. Hula Kahiko is the ancient form, in which practitioners chant sacred mele and are accompanied by traditional percussive instruments like the ipu, a drum made from a gourd. Hula `Auana is the modern form brought about by Western influences, and employs softer movements accompanied by musical instruments, such as the `ukulele, and song. Both have been embraced since the Hawaiian Cultural Renaissance of the 1970s.

"I believe Hawaii is the most precious jewel in the world." – Don Ho

■ Food

The food in Hawaii is delicious for two primary reasons: fresh fish and fresh produce. There are a lot of farmers on the island, growing everything from organic greens to macadamia nuts. Fruit trees are everywhere; the fruit is so sweet and juicy that you might not want to return to the mainland once you've tasted it. Don't ignore the papayas and mangos, either!

You'll want to sample the fresh fish while you're on the Big Island, but you might need some guidance in choosing the one that's right for you. **Mahi mahi**, shown above, also known as dolphin fish (not Flipper), is probably the most famous of the Hawaiian fish, with pale, pink flesh and a mild, slightly sweet flavor that is great with any preparation. **Opakapaka**, or pink snapper, is one of the finest fish in the world, with firm, pink flesh and a mild, subtle flavor that is best when sautéed, broiled, poached, or served as sushi. **Ono**, or wahoo, also has a mild flavor and firm texture, and is so good that the Hawaiians made it their word for "delicious." **Ahi**, or yellowfin tuna, has a tender, meaty texture and blood-red flesh when raw (sold as sashimi, a type of sushi). *Ahi* is best when grilled or seared and cooked rare to medium rare, as overcooking destroys its wonderful flavor. It is often used in poke, a salad of cubed raw fish, seaweed, soy sauce and other ingredients.

Asian influence in the food reflects the diverse population, such as Japanese, Korean, Chinese and Filipino. One native Hawaiian told us that, growing up in Kona, if they didn't catch fish, her family ate white rice and shoyu (soy sauce) for dinner. Another international influence is apparent in the prevalence of Portuguese bean soup and Portuguese sausage on menus around the island. And everyone loves malasadas, or Portuguese donuts.

Inexpensive local food, often found at a "drive-in," includes a Hawaiian noodle soup called **saimin**, which is in a chicken or fish stock base, topped with fish cake. **Loco moco** is another standard, and consists of a piece of meat like hamburger or Spam on a bowl of rice, topped with gravy and a fried egg. **Mixed plate** usually has "two scoop rice," potato-macaroni salad, and a meat, anything from teriyaki beef or chicken skewers to grilled fresh fish like mahi mahi. You can usually also find cheap burgers, fries and breakfasts at these places.

At the other end of the spectrum is "**Hawaii Regional Cuisine**," or fine dining. Pioneering Hawaiian chefs like Roy Yamaguchi, Peter Merriman, Sam Choy and Alan Wong have put Hawaii on the culinary map with this fusion cuisine that makes return visitors drool just thinking about it. As always, fresh, local ingredients are the core. A dish that exemplifies this sort of food is found at Roy's in South Kohala: the roasted macadamia nut mahi mahi in lobster butter sauce. Are you listening, foodies?

TOP 10 UPSCALE RESTAURANTS

- Kaikodo (p. 441)
- Roy's (p. 228)
- Donatoni's (p. 229)
- Bamboo (p. 274)
- Brown's Beach House (p. 242)
- Canoe House (p. 241)
- Daniel Thiebaut Restaurant (p. 304)
- Jackie Rey's Ohana Grill – not super-upscale, but a favorite nonetheless (p. 123)
- Alan Wong's (p. 208)
- Hilo Bay Café (p. 441)

COOL OFF WITH SHAVE ICE

Shave ice is a Hawaiian version of the snow cone, but the ice is shaved from a block for a light, dissolve-on-the-tongue texture. Nothing hits the spot like shave ice on a sunny day. Syrup flavors range from traditional favorites like lime and strawberry to tropical ones like mango and coconut. You can usually add ice cream or sweet azuki beans to the bottom for an extra touch of decadence.

Best Pizza Places on the Big Island

Kona Brewing Co.	(p. 125)
Kiawe Kitchen	(p. 368)
Waimea Ranch House	(p. 303)
Solimene's	(p. 302)
Café Pesto	(p. 259 and p. 439)
Aloha Luigi	(p. 440)
Big Island Pizza	(p. 437)
Café il Mondo	(p. 378)

Luaus

Many resorts offer an evening luau, or Hawaiian feast. These are often fairly cheesy affairs that have become almost a rite of passage for first-timers to the Islands – people either love them or hate them. The traditional centerpiece of the luau is the slow-roasted pig, which cooks in an underground oven called an imu. Often the public can watch the pig "planted" in the oven on the hotel grounds around 9 am the morning of the luau. Before dinner, there's

an *imu* ceremony where people gather around to watch a pig that has disintegrated into kalua pork emerge from the dirt oven. There's also an all-you-can-eat buffet and open bar (with bottom shelf booze, of course). An emcee makes jokes and teaches the audience how to say "aloha" (by mispronouncing it with a shout at the end).

After sunset and dinner, there's a Polynesian show, typically with fire twirlers, dancing and costumes. Instead of focusing on Hawaiian culture, most luaus showcase songs and cultures from the Polynesian Triangle (formed by Hawaii, Easter Island and New Zealand). The Maori haka of New Zealand may not have much to do with the Aloha State, but it's still something you don't see every day. The bottom line is that the shows are entertaining – kids love the fire dancers – and, though an inauthentic cultural experience, they're a fun way to spend an evening.

"I never drink water. I'm afraid it will become habit-forming." – W.C. Fields

MAI TAI

While Hawaiians are more likely to be found drinking Steinlager beer than mai tais, the rum-based concoction has retained an almost legendary status in Hawaiian restaurants and resorts. We've bought into the craze whole-heartedly, since few libations conjure up images of tropical bliss like rum and fruit juice. There's a bit of a debate over the actual recipe for a mai tai, and we can't approve of the ones that include sour mix. But you'll know the bartender is on the right track if he combines white rum with fruit juices like guava and passion fruit, then tops it off with a hefty dark rum float. Sipping a mai tai at sunset is a sure-fire way to feel you're on vacation in Hawaii.

Vegetarians

It is not difficult to be a vegetarian in Hawaii, thanks to all of the Asian influences in the cuisine. Almost all restaurants offer a vegetarian option on their menu and, if you ask, they might have additional offerings. That said, Hawaiians are very adventurous eaters – they may not have a problem eating tofu, but Hawaii is also the American state that consumes the most Spam. (Seriously – McDonald's has Spam on the menu in Hawaii.) Try to be as open-minded about their dietary choices as they are of yours.

■ Flora

O`hia

The stunning beauty of Big Island foliage is something we have never gotten used to, whether it's the brilliance of flowering trees beside a waterfall or the landscaping in someone's front yard. Plants love the mineral-rich volcanic soil and the balmy weather and they thrive here. Even in lava deserts, **o`hia**, the Big Island's tree, establishes forests of gnarled branches sometimes blooming with red bottlebrushes, the lehua flower.

Banyan

The Big Island has all of the tropical trees you'd expect to find in Hawaii – **coconut palms**, **bamboo** and an abundance of luscious fruit trees, including **mango**, **papaya**, **banana**, **avocado**, **guava**, **breadfruit**, **noni**, **macadamia nut** and coffee trees.

You'll find the striking **travelers palm**, reaching heights of 30 feet, with its branches splayed like a fan. Native hardwoods like **koa**, with its sickle leaves, have been harvested for canoes, bowls and furniture, but can still be found growing in protected areas like Hawai`i Volcanoes National Park. The twisting branches of the **kiawe**, with its sharp thorns, are a common sight in South Kohala – it is a mesquite tree traditionally used to smoke foods like kalua pork.

Banyan trees are always amazing, with their aerial roots allowing them to expand in width – one in Kea`au in Puna has a diameter of 95 feet! Hilo's Banyan Drive, the "main drag" for the town's hotels, is lined with banyan trees planted in the last century by local and national celebrities, including Amelia Earhart. There are several near the Kailua Pier in Kona that offer shade for those waiting to take a boat tour.

Monkepod tree

One of our favorite trees is the **monkeypod**, easily identified by its large umbrella shape. Locals love to tell the story that the beloved shade tree was introduced to the Big Island by Mark Twain, who planted one in Ka`u "as a gift to the people of Hawai`i." (Sources differ on the actual person who introduced the tree.)

The **kukui**, or candlenut tree, is the state tree of Hawaii. This makes sense because it had so many uses for ancient Hawaiians – the oil in the nuts burned slowly, creating candles (you'll find their ashes in caves on the island); it was also used for dye, as a laxative, for waterproofing, for spreading on water to create a "window" when fishing, for making leis and many other practical and ornamental uses. In fact, the

Plumeria

Hibiscus

Polynesians who settled Hawaii carried kukui on their voyaging canoes to the archipelago because of its many uses.

Then there are all of the flowering trees. **Plumeria** is the most famous, the tree with clusters of fragrant yellow, white or red flowers used in leis. **African tulip trees** bloom year-round, adding splashes of orange to rainforest settings, particularly along the Hamakua Coast. In spring in the lush areas of south Kona, you can see the golden bottlebrushes of the **silver oak** complementing the purple blooms of the **jacaranda**, and shopping malls brighten with the purple blossoms of **Hong Kong orchid trees** (Ali`i Gardens Marketplace and Keauhou Shopping Center are two good examples). You'll know you're looking at an **octopus tree** when you see the "tentacles" covered with tiny crimson flowers that look like suction cups.

Hong Kong orchid tree blossom

These are just a few of the diverse trees – there are also myriad tropical plants and flowers. The Big Island is nicknamed the Orchid Isle, since it is one of the world's leading producers of the intricate flowers. You'll often find them on tables in restaurants, or for sale (cheap!) at farmers' markets. **Akatsuka Orchid Gardens**, on the road to Volcano, is a must-stop if you want to take some home with you (see p. 472).

With flowers blooming year-round in Hawaii, it's like a constant spring. As one visitor gushed, "Hawaii – where indoor plants grow outside!" **Hibiscus**, with their colorful petals and phallic stamen, flourish here, along with the tropical flowers that have helped make Hawaii famous: **protea**, **anthurium**, **heliconia**, **ginger** and **bird of paradise**. Fuchsia **bougainvillea** light up the stark lava landscape of South Kohala. Gardens are full of **tiare**, a Tahitian gardenia, with its fragrant white petals. The air in such places really is scented. There are dramatic flowers like the **angel's trumpet**, **cup of gold**, and **golden dewdrop** – in fact, there are so many beautiful flowers here that they could fill an entire book on their own. We highly recommend two such books in the "Pocket Guide" series: ***Tropical Trees of Hawai`i*** and ***Flowers and Plants of Hawai`i***, both written by Paul Wood and photographed by Ron Dahlquist. We also recommend that nature fans head to the breathtaking **Hawaii Tropical Botanical Garden** on the Hamakua Coast (see p. 406).

Tiare flowers

Wild ginger

The flower behind the ear: Many people in Hawaii enjoy placing a fragrant flower behind their ear, but visitors don't always know that the choice of which ear has traditional meaning. Flower placement is like a wedding ring: If you are "available," put a flower behind your right ear. If you are "taken," place it behind the left.

Fauna

"Animals are such agreeable friends – they ask no questions, they pass no criticisms." – George Eliot

Geckos

Gecko

How cool are geckos? They flit, they flirt, they leap, they use their tongues to slurp up tiny bugs or nectar, they shake their booties as they climb headfirst down walls – they symbolize the tropics. The beauties of the Big Island are the **gold dust day geckos**, fluorescent green lizards up to five inches long, with pink splotches on their backs and noses, electric blue shading around their eyes, and the gold speckles that give them their name. Spectacular! They're common in homes and businesses Kona-side. It is possible to waste hours watching or photographing them.

A gold dust gecko

Birds

`I`iwi (Hawaii Forest & Trail)

Hawaii is a special place for birdwatchers, as well as anyone who delights in brightly colored birds and their songs. The native Hawaiian songbirds – the ones that have survived Western contact and the introduction of mosquitoes – fill the mountain forests of the Big Island (up where there are fewer mosquitoes). The most famous are Hawaiian honeycreepers such as the scarlet red **`i`iwi** with its curved beak for sucking nectar from flowers; the bright red **`apapane** with white feathers under its tail; and the yellow **`amakihi**. The feathers of these birds were used to make capes worn in the past by Hawaiian royalty, and their standards (kahili). A walk through the forests in Hawai`i Volcanoes National Park is a great way to get to know these little guys.

`Apapane (Hawaii Forest & Trail)

The park also offers a chance to see the endangered **nene**, the Hawaii state bird.

`Amakihi (Hawaii Forest & Trail)

The nene is a Hawaiian goose, a relative of the Canadian goose, but with reduced webbing on its feet (an adaptation to walking on lava). Because these endemic birds were saved from the brink of extinction – there were only about 30 alive in 1952 because of introduced predators like the mongoose and feral pig – seeing them is deeply satisfying (plus their honks sound startlingly like Chewbacca from *Star Wars*). There are several hundred nene alive today, but it is still the world's rarest goose. You'll see numerous signs in the park reminding you to drive slowly in areas the birds frequent, and that "a fed nene is a dead nene."

Nene

Kona-side is home to some very common but very pretty little birds. Two of our favorites – and ones you'll probably see while you're eating lunch in a grassy area – are South American transplants. The **saffron finch** is a bright yellow bird with an orange head, and the **yellow-billed cardinal** is easily recognized by its scarlet head atop a charcoal body

Palila *(Hawaii Forest & Trail)*

with a white chest (and, of course, the yellow bill). You'll also probably see their neighbors the **zebra dove** (look for stripes and listen for cooing) and the aggressive **common myna**, with yellow spots around their eyes. If you spend any time on golf courses, you're sure to encounter **gray francolins**, goofy partridges that are actually brown.

Elepaio *(Hawaii Forest & Trail)*

More elusive residents are the **`io**, or Hawaiian hawk, and the **pueo**, or short-eared owl. For much more comprehensive information about Big Island birds, including shore and wetland birds, we recommend ***A Pocket Guide to Hawai`i's Birds***, written by H. Douglas Pratt and photographed by the author and Jack Jeffrey.

Did you know? Over 90% of Hawaii's native flora and fauna is found nowhere else on earth.

Land Mammals

Hawaiian bat

The only native land mammal in Hawaii is the **`ope`ape`a**, or Hawaiian bat. Since "native mammals" are those that weren't brought here by humans, it makes sense that the only native mammals swam or flew. Many of the non-native mammals have become introduced pests.

Feral goats on the lava fields of North Kona

The most infamous pest is the **mongoose**, introduced in 1883 with the hope that it would eat the rats in cane fields. It turns out that the rats are nocturnal so, instead of preying on the rodents, the mongoose rapidly decimated the native songbird population by eating their eggs. You'll see a lot of these predators skulking across roads. They look like brown weasels.

Feral pigs haven't done any favors for the native songbirds and habitats either, uprooting vegetation and creating troughs where stagnant water pools and mosquitoes breed (and then kill the defenseless birds). There are few restrictions on hunting them.

A wild horse in the Waipi`o Valley

Domestic animals like cattle and sheep are fairly well maintained (since the first paniolos arrived here from Mexico to get the rampaging cattle under control), but you'll see **wild goats** in the lava fields of South Kohala. "Kona Nightingales," the **donkeys** originally used to transport coffee cherries, were once a common sight, but they ventured onto the highway too often and their numbers have been drastically reduced. **Wild horses** and **ponies** still roam free in the Waipi`o Valley.

Under the Sea

"All of the animals except for man know that the principle business of life is to enjoy it." – Samuel Butler

Dolphins

Spinner dolphin (James L. Wing)

Over 15 species of dolphins inhabit Hawaiian waters, and the acrobatic **spinner dolphins** are particularly common around the Big Island. In fact, there's a group of over a thousand spinners that live around kua Bay in South Kona. Spinner dolphins get their name because they leap out of the ocean and spin. Their bellies are usually white, but turn pink when they are active or excited.

Spinner dolphins are nocturnal, hunting in the open ocean at night. If you see spinners while you are swimming during the day (a truly awesome experience), remember that many of them are resting, and be sure to give them room. In case you need more of an incentive, keep in mind that it is illegal to harass, hunt, capture or confine them. The rule of thumb is "let marine animals decide how close they want to get to you."

Turtles

Honu

We mention *honu* frequently in this book, and that's because **green sea turtles** love the Big Island. These Hawaiian natives bob in the water, sometimes heading toward your mask as you snorkel or dive, surfacing to gulp the air before they placidly glide away over the reef. Or you'll be strolling the beach – day or night – and realize you almost stepped on several basking turtles. By State and Federal law, humans must keep 15-20 feet from these threatened creatures. The endangered **hawksbill turtle** (honu `ea) has been reduced to only around 30 nesting turtles (remember the "tortoise shell" craze?), but some of them come ashore on the Big Island to lay their eggs.

Whales

Hawaii's official state mammal is the humpback whale, and an estimated 5,000 of these majestic behemoths grace our waters from December to April, having migrated here from Alaska to birth their babies (and get in a little mating, too). Though the "best" island from which to see humpbacks is Maui, since the waters between Maui, Moloka`i, Lana`i and Kaho`olawe are particularly shallow and warm, the Big Island is also a great viewing spot. As one dive instructor enthused, "We get the party animals!" They tail slap, breach (heave their entire bodies out of the water), and sound (diving down for seven-12 minutes – a prime opportunity to see the fluke, or tail). Look for puffs of water as they exhale and create steam. If you're snorkeling, dive down and listen to their ethereal songs. Other species of whales like **pilot**, **sperm**, **orca**, **beaked**, and **melon-headed** frequent Big Island waters year-round.

Sperm whale

ADOPT A HAWAIIAN WHALE

As kids, we both adopted whales and looked forward to receiving photos and information about our whales ("Half-Moon" and "Midnight"). The tradition continues in Hawaii at the Pacific Whale Foundation, a Maui-based nonprofit founded in 1980 to save whales from extinction and protect them in Hawaii. Through their website at www.pacificwhale.org, you can adopt a Hawaiian whale for $35, earning you a color photo of their fluke, an adoption certificate, information about your whale, an "I Love Whales" bumpersticker, newsletters and action alerts – plus the knowledge that you're helping to protect these beautiful animals.

Tropical Fish

Twenty-five years ago, it was hard to see very far in Hawaiian waters because there were so many brilliant tropical fish swarming in front of your face. This isn't the case anymore, as over half a million tropical fish are snatched from Hawaii's reefs each year to sell for aquariums. Local groups have successfully lobbied for the creation of some marine sanctuaries in the Big Island, allowing the fish to reestablish themselves, so you're sure to see enough fish to stimulate your imagination on the reefs around the island.

Yellow tang

Looking at the ocean from shore, you'll usually see flashes of yellow glistening just beneath the surface. These are **yellow tangs**, members of the surgeonfish family. When viewing them underwater, note the white scalpel on their dorsal (rear) fin, which will cut you if it's touched. The rainbow-colored members of the **parrotfish** family use their beaks to chomp on coral, eating the algae and then releasing the ingested coral as sand (a Kona tour guide explained, "the white sand beaches here are parrotfish poo poo."). The unofficial state fish, the **Picasso triggerfish**, comes up a lot because of its long Hawaiian name humuhumunukunukuapua`a (HOO-moo-HOO-moo-NOO-koo-NOO-koo-AH-poo-AH-ah). The repetition of words means the Hawaiians who named the fish really thought it had a nose like a pig. If you see a pair of brightly colored fish swimming together, they are probably one of the 24 species of **butterflyfish** that live in Hawaii – they mate for life.

Picasso triggerfish

There are many more tropical fish (several identification cards and books are sold around the Big Island), as well as larger critters that are fun to see. **Eels** (they're not snakes!) often gape from rock crevices with their mouths open, or even better, wriggle their way across the coral gardens looking for a new hiding spot. For obvious reasons, don't stick your fingers too close to an eel's mouth. They seem to have a friendship with **peacock groupers**, a species introduced for their beauty (that has unfortunately also decimated the native fish on the reef, chomping on yellow tangs like it's Sunday Brunch at the Hilton). If you see one of the large, purple groupers with bright blue spots, check the coral heads around it for eels.

Rainforest of the Sea: Hawaii's reef ecosystem, known as the "rainforest of the sea," contains over 7,000 species of marine plants and animals. Over 25% of our planet's marine life is endemic to Hawaii.

Graceful **rays** also live in Hawaii, and the beauty of a spotted eagle ray "flying" through the water may make you forget to breathe. Swimming with manta rays at night while they feed on plankton is one of the best adventures on the island (see *Adventures*). In fact, the Travel Channel named it one of the "Top 10 Things To Do In Your Life." How's that for a recommendation?

Manta ray night dive (James L. Wing)

Thanks to the movie *Jaws*, many people are terrified of sharks. While **sharks** do inhabit Hawaii – most commonly white-tipped reef sharks (the tips of their fins are white) – they will most likely be more scared of you and swim in the opposite direction. Though there are freak accidents and tiger, hammerhead and great white sharks do swim in Hawaii, the odds are small that you will be attacked (if you are, hit the shark's nose). One statistic popular with dive instructors is, "The odds of being bitten by a shark are less than being killed by a coconut." (Of course, with all of the coconut palms on the island, your odds increase here for that as well.)

Coral

Living corals (William Rafti)

Though it may look like a really cool rock formation, coral is actually a living organism, composed of tiny polyps that deposit a calcium carbonate exoskeleton. The nocturnal polyps are only a few millimeters long, and resemble minuscule sea anemones – they're in the same class. Growth rates vary, but it is always very slow, sometimes as little as a quarter of an inch a year, which is why we'll remind you never to touch, walk on or break off coral.

■ Books

A Narrative of an 1823 Tour through Hawai`i: Journal of William Ellis, by William Ellis – View the Big Island through the eyes of a Westerner only 44 years after the death of Captain Cook.

Letters from Hawaii, by Mark Twain – The witty observations of a cub reporter's visit to Hawaii, including the Big Island, in 1866.

A Pocket Guide to Hawai`i's Birds, by H. Douglas Pratt

Flowers and Plants of Hawai`i, by Paul Wood

Tropical Trees of Hawai`i, by Paul Wood

Hawaii's Fishes: A Guide for Snorkelers, Divers and Aquarists, by John P. Hoover – The best guide for identifying tropical fish in Hawaii unfortunately also details how to capture and raise them for aquariums (even Hoover expresses reservations about the practice in the current edition).

Kohala `Aina: A History of North Kohala, by Sophia V. Schweitzer – A gorgeous coffee table book full of historic photographs and information about North Kohala.

Myths and Legends of Hawai`i, by William D. Westervelt

Shoal of Time: A History of the Hawaiian Islands, by Gavan Daws – The definitive history of Hawaii from the time of Cook through statehood.

Pele: Goddess of Hawai`i's Volcanoes, by Herb Kawainui Kane – Stories about Pele recounted by Herb Kane, author, artist-historian, Polynesian Voyaging Society co-founder and "living treasure of Hawaii."

Exploring the Hamakua Coast: A Pictorial Guide to the Plantation Era, by Ken Okimoto – The book combines old photos and captions to paint a picture of the historic Hamakua Coast.

The Parker Ranch of Hawai`i: The Saga of a Ranch and a Dynasty, by Joseph Brennan – The authorized story of Parker Ranch.

Living Pidgin, Contemplations on Pidgin Culture, by Lee A. Tonouchi ("Da Pidgin Guerrilla") – A book written in Pidgin, extolling its virtues and describing challenges it faces for acceptance as a legitimate language.

Blue Latitudes, by Tony Horwitz – Part-history, part-travel narrative, Horwitz traces the journey of Captain James Cook, who met his end on the Big Island.

A Cup of Aloha: The Kona Coffee Epic, by Gerald Y. Kinro – A beautifully written and designed book that chronicles the story of one of the world's finest coffees.

■ Adventures

"Life is either a daring adventure or nothing." – Helen Keller

The Big Island tends to attract visitors with a curious, adventurous nature. There's a reason for it: the Orchid Isle has adventures for every taste and desire. The more you explore, the greater your reward. And the possibilities for adventure are endless. Have fun!

> We've made mention of a few challenging adventures like backcountry hikes, but those we've detailed here can be enjoyed by everyone. Still, know your limits, and use caution when trying something new. Getting hurt can ruin any vacation!

On the Beach

As the youngest Hawaiian Island, the Big Island still has lots of lava outcroppings that haven't been transformed into sand yet. But it also has some of the most beautiful beaches in the entire state, from black sand frequented by turtles, to white sand with aquamarine water, to vast expanses of sand backed by hotels and amenities, to little isolated coves that seem reserved for lovers. There are even green sand beaches in the southernmost region of the island, made of tiny pale-green peridots, the birthstone for August.

TOP 10 BIG ISLAND BEACHES	
Kua	(p. 201)
Hapuna	(p. 244)
Green Sand s	(p. 485)
Makalawena	(p. 200-201)
69s	(p. 246)
Kehena	(p. 466)
`Anaeho`omalu Bay	(p. 217)
Punalu`u	(p. 492)
Mauna Kea	(p. 244)
Waipi`o	(p. 384)

On Water

Swimming at Beaches

The classic Hawaiian beaches – palm trees, white sand, and sunsets – are on the Kona-side of the Big Island, primarily in Kona and South Kohala. The green sand and black sand beaches of Ka`u are more unusual destinations, sublimely beautiful. There are also beaches in Hilo, Puna, and the Hamakua Coast, though they usually have rougher swimming conditions. Pay attention to signs warning of strong currents, high surf or other hazards, even if there is a lifeguard on duty. And always remember the number one rule: Never turn your back on the ocean! There are *honu* (green sea turtles) on most of the beaches, so remember the other rule: always stay 15-20 feet away from the protected turtles.

Snorkeling

Having had the good fortune to become snorkeling addicts at early ages, we sometimes forget that not everyone is familiar with this popular pastime. It is fun, easy and extremely affordable, so why not give it a try? You'll probably be hooked in the first few minutes.

To snorkel, you basically float on your stomach and gaze down at fish and coral beneath you. Your mask provides visibility (there are prescription masks available at quality outfitters like Snorkel Bob's) and your snorkel is the tube that feeds you air, so that you can breathe with your face in the water and not have to stop looking at the cute angelfish swirling near your nose, or the parrotfish chomping on coral. To swim, you don't really move your arms, just kick your legs – keep them straight – and the fins will do all the work for you.

A couple of tips: Put your fins on in the water. Walking around in them on the beach makes you look very silly, particularly if you trip and fall on your face, which is likely (plus they'll fill with sand and rub, creating cuts or blisters).

Check to see if your mask fits by pressing it to your face – if suction makes it stick, it fits. Be sure to keep stray hairs out of the mask, which compromises the seal. If you do not have some sort of anti-fog lubricant for your mask (available at all outfitters), try spitting in it – the more phlegm, the better – to keep it from fogging.

To dive down for a closer look, plug the snorkel with your tongue (you won't need to with the newer models) and pinch your nose to equalize your ears (like "popping" them on an airplane) as you descend.

There are a plethora of great snorkel trips on boats that leave from Honokohau Harbor (p. 186), and Kailua (p. 92) and Keauhou (p. 132) piers.

REEF ETIQUETTE

The most important rule of the ocean (well, besides "never turn your back on the ocean") is that you should never, ever stand on or otherwise break off coral (it can give nasty cuts that tend to get infected, anyway). Coral takes a very long time to grow, so tramping it is incredibly damaging to the ecosystem. Another rule is to avoid touching or feeding fish, no matter how cute they are. And if you should be lucky enough to swim with turtles or dolphins, remember to give them at least 15 feet of space – let them decide how close they want to get to you (they can be very curious!).

TOP 5 BIG ISLAND SNORKEL SPOTS	
Pawai Bay	(p. 187)
Kealakekua Bay	(p. 164)
Puako	(p. 242-43)
Place of Refuge	(p. 178)
Kapoho Tide Pools	(p. 464)

"All serious daring starts from within." – Eudora Welty

Swimming with Dolphins

Spinner dolphin

Spinner dolphins frequent the waters around the Big Island, and it is always a thrill to see them leaping from the ocean and spinning in the air. Many unscrupulous "guides" have popped up around Kona in recent years in an attempt to capitalize on people's love of dolphins by offering to take them snorkeling with wild dolphins. This has negatively impacted the local pods of dolphins because they are sometimes approached while in sleep mode (if they aren't frolicking, they're probably sleeping). We've heard it compared to having a bedroom light switched on every 10 minutes while you're trying to sleep. So go with a sensitive tour guide, and remember not to chase dolphins if you see them in the ocean. The rule of thumb that you'll hear repeatedly is "let them decide how close they want to get to you." You can volunteer or intern with Dolphin Dreams Images to learn how to film them (p. 109). An alternative to trying to swim with dolphins in the wild is visiting the Hilton's dolphin lagoon, or swimming and working with them through the Hilton's DolphinQuest program (p. 220).

Scuba Diving

"The best way to observe a fish is to become a fish."
– Jacques Cousteau

The Kona Coast is a scuba diving mecca, with some of the best visibility and features in the entire Hawaiian archipelago. It is awe-inspiring to be neutrally buoyant and floating through a lava tube, or watching eels free-swimming next to a brilliant peacock grouper across coral fields, or circling a lava pinnacle where *honu* (green sea turtles) like to hang out. If it is your first time diving in Kona, you might want to request a visit to Turtle Pinnacle or, if you are more advanced, a "long-range" dive to the south to explore the grand Au`au Canyon. And the manta ray night dive is a must for any scuba diver visiting the Big Island (see below).

KONA'S ULTIMATE ADVENTURE

Manta ray

The Kona coast is host to a pod of about 100 manta rays, the filter-feeding cousins to sharks. Because they feed on plankton attracted to bright lights, there are two areas in Kona where some of the mantas show up to feed almost every night – one company even guarantees a sighting or you can come back until you do see them.

The manta ray adventure needs to be experienced to fully appreciate it. Photographer Jim Wing has an apt description of the mantas as "giant, gaping rib cages on wings." Then those rib cages – whose wingspans can reach up to 20 feet – put on a show while they feed in the plankton attracted to your lights. Imagine a creature like that gliding right for your head, then veering up at the last minute so that you can see the pink of its gill slits – just inches from your face – before gracefully somersaulting through the water and coming back at you for more. This is a life experience that you will never forget.

Adventurous snorkelers can float above the "campfire ring" of the divers' lights, getting a show of their own as the mantas pass under them, sometimes stomach-to-stomach. This is also a one-of-a-kind adventure that is pure exhilaration.

Because manta rays are attracted to plankton that are in turn attracted to lights, you have a better chance of seeing them during a new moon when the sky is darker. During a full moon, there is light everywhere, and the mantas have more ease in finding the plankton. There's a discrepancy about where to go see the manta rays – many dive shop operators prefer the old airport area, where there are occasional reports of over 25 manta rays at once. Still, you may share them with 10 other boats of divers and snorkelers. Trips to the south in Keauhou, where the Sheraton shines a spotlight in the water specifically to attract the mantas, may have fewer mantas but there are also fewer people in the water to knock into one another. The bottom line is that you only need to see one manta ray to make the experience one of the most memorable of your life. Most dive shops offer a manta ray tour (p. 45-46).

Manta Ray Conservation

Manta Pacific Research Foundation is a Kona-based nonprofit focused on manta ray research, education and conservation. In addition to waging an ongoing battle to pass legislation for protecting Hawaiian manta rays before they are slaughtered, as they have been elsewhere in the world, the foundation distributed a list of guidelines to dive shops to minimize the impact on the "charismatic megafauna." A few crucial rules are that humans should never touch mantas, as it removes their protective mucus coating, snorkelers should stay on the surface instead of diving into the midst of feeding mantas, and divers should remain on the bottom in a semicircle so that the mantas have an open area, or "column," in which to maneuver. For more information about manta rays, visit www.mantapacific.org.

TOP 10 BIG ISLAND SUNSET SPOTS	
Mahukona Beach Park	(p. 266)
Kapa`a Beach Park	(p. 269)
`A Bay	(p. 217)

Holoholokai Beach Park	(p. 255)
Alii Drive seawall	(p. 94-95)
Huggo's on the Rocks	(p. 118)
The Copper Bar at the Mauna Kea	(p. 251)
Beach Tree Bar & Grill	(p. x)
Harbor House	(p. 193)
Crystal Blue Lounge	(p. 138)

Snuba

To be honest, we don't really get snuba. It's essentially training wheels for people who might like to try scuba diving but haven't been certified; instead of strapping air tanks onto your back so that you can freely swim, you breathe through a tube that leads to the floating tanks on the surface. One time when we were snorkeling in Kealakekua Bay, we came across five snuba divers swimming in a circle, essentially tethered, unable to free dive or travel more than 20 feet from the centrally located tanks. It was one of the silliest things we've seen. Snorkeling is more fun and much cheaper. Still, never say never, right?

Boogie Boarding

Want a glimpse of why surfers are so "stoked"? Catch a wave on the surfboard's little brother, the boogie board. Also known as a "body board" or "sponge" (because of the board's typical foam composition), this is a cheap, silly way to give yourself a thrill. You'll know you're stoked when you get ahead of the wave's whitewater, skimming across the surface of the water. It's like flying!

A few tips: attach your leash to your wrist, not your ankle (as surfers do). To catch a wave, get as close as you can to its break – it will have more power to push you. If you're having trouble getting a long ride, try putting more weight toward the front of the board, maybe even put a hand on the top to help you steer. The only protocol of sponging is that you shouldn't position yourself behind another sponger – they might run into you. And don't be afraid to laugh your brains out!

"Dream as if you'll live forever, live as if you'll die today."
– James Dean

Surfing

The Big Island isn't known for its waves like the North Shore of O`ahu is, but there are still plenty of places to surf. Many first-timers take lessons at Kahalu`u Beach or elsewhere in Kona from Kona Beach Boys (p. 98), while experienced surfers head to Pine Trees in Kona (p. 189), Honoli`i in Hilo (p. 429), and the Waipi`o Valley (p. 388), a spot for advanced surfers in one of the world's most gorgeous places.

You can check current surf conditions at the **Surf News Network** by calling ☎ 596-SURF, or www.surfnewsnetwork.com. Keep in mind that the Hawaiian scale measures wave heights differently than on the mainland – about half of the face height, measured from crest to trough. So what mainland surfers call "head-high" (about six feet) would be called "three foot waves" in Hawaii. It's thought this system of downplaying the height of waves was an attempt by surfers and lifeguards to keep the number of people competing for choice waves to a minimum.

Did you know? An estimated one out of every 10 people in Hawaii surfs.

Kayaking

Kayaking around the Kona coast of the Big Island is easier than paddling on the mainland, particularly because the water is protected – there are no open crossings or narrow passes. And the water is nice and warm.

The most popular kayak adventure – and one of the best on the island – is renting a boat and paddling to Kealakekua Bay to go snorkeling. The half-hour paddle to the bay often is enhanced by the presence of spinner dolphins, which frequent the area. Kayak rental shops abound in the stretch of highway near the launch area (p. 164-65)

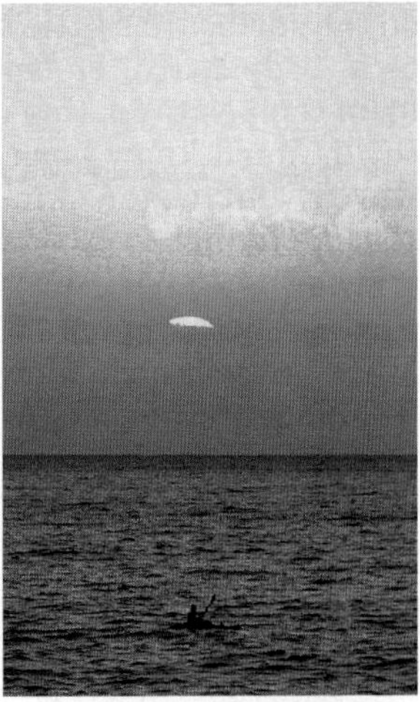

Sunset kayaking

If you want to do a half-day or multi-day kayak trip, the ecotourism company, **Hawaii Pack and Paddle** (p. 169), has knowledgeable guides that will lead to you astonishing areas along the coast or around the entire island.

Thermal Pools

Thanks to its proximity to Kilauea, the Puna district has volcanically heated thermal pools where you can soak away your worries. Champagne Pond (p. 463) and the "hot ponds" at Alahanui Beach Park (p. x) are local favorites.

Tide Pools

While you'll find tide pools during low tide in many rocky coastlines around the Big Island, the Kapoho Tide Pools in Puna (p. 464) are something special. The network of shallow pools contains what some locals consider the best snorkeling on the island.

Fishing

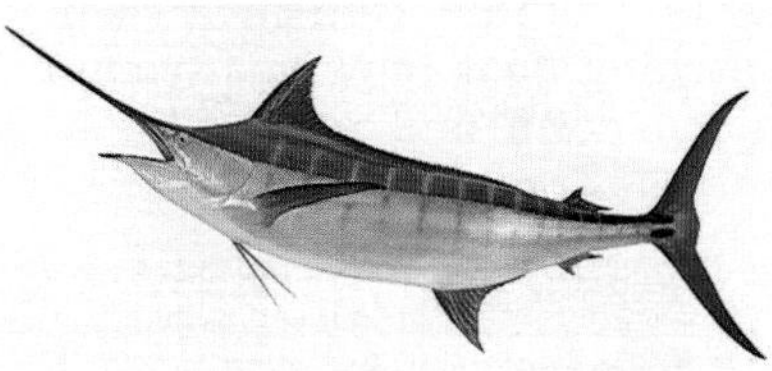

Pacific blue marlin

Kona is blessed with some of the finest fishing "grounds" in the world. Huge marlin are regularly caught just a short boat ride from the harbor. This is due to the dramatic drop-off from shore to the deep blue, as well as the intense concentration of aquatic species that create a healthy food chain from the bottom up. Most charter boats leave from Honokohau Harbor on the Kona coast, just south of the airport. Charters are expensive, but the size of the quarry and the frequency of catches means most boats stay busy year-round. The most sought-after prey is Pacific blue marlin. These behemoths can tilt the scales at well over 1,000 lbs. Some more of the other usual suspects include striped marlin, spearfish, mahi mahi (dolphin fish), *ono* (wahoo), and *ahi* (yellowfin tuna).

Whale-Watching

Humpback whale

Few things lift the spirit like seeing a humpback whale shoot out of the ocean, splashing down with up to 40 tons of body weight in a dramatic breach. From shore, we've seen whales breaching in every coastal region of the Big Island, but obviously it's even more thrilling to be closer to them in a boat. By law, boats must stay a minimum of 100 yards from the endangered mammals, but once they cut their motors and drift, the whales sometimes swim closer, leading to some awesome displays. Many dive boats and other excursions include a humpback whale watch option for non-divers from December 15 to March 15, and these sightings are a bonus for regular participants. Captain Dan McSweeney (see p. 190) leads whale-watching boat trips year-round, as other whales (including pilot, sperm and pygmy killer whales) frequent Hawaiian waters throughout the year.

WHEN ANIMALS ATTACK

Remember the video clip of a female snorkeler touching and trying to ride a pilot whale, and then being dragged below the surface by a protective bull? That happened in Kona! The word around town is that the woman and her husband sold the video for $10,000 to the TV show, but were fined $20,000 for harassing marine life when officials saw the tape. Fines and possible death are just two more reasons to abide by the rule of never touching or harassing wildlife. Always let marine animals decide how close they want to get to you.

Booze Cruises

"Where I go I hope there's rum!" – Jimmy Buffett

Though usually called "dinner cruises" or "sunset sails," these floating parties are known by their repeat guests as "booze cruises." The reigning champion of the booze cruise circuit is undoubtedly Captain Bean's dinner cruise in Kona (p. 127), which is essentially a luau at sea, where dancing takes place on the dinner tables. But now the ticket price only includes one cocktail (they blame it on some Homeland Security regulation), instead of the open bar that made the cruise infamous. Or there are the sunset sails of South Kohala, much more relaxing affairs with open bars and mai tais with two kinds of rum instead of just juice with a wimpy dark rum float. The boats are smaller, and the entertainment consists of wind-filled sails, a fiery sunset, pupus, and in winter, breaching whales.

TOP 5 BIG ISLAND WATERING HOLES	
Kona Brewing Co.	(p. 125)
Nichols Public House	(p. 438)
Lulu's	(p. 119)
Mixx Bistro Bar	(p. 127)
Kaikodo	(p. 441)

On Foot

"Great ideas originate in the muscles." – Thomas Edison

Hiking

Hiking can greatly enhance your appreciation of the Big Island. Some hikes lead through rainforest to waterfalls, others pass over lava flows for views of volcanic mountains and craters. Most hikes will inspire you to book your next trip to the Big Island, or even move here.

Of course, you should always stay on designated trails to avoid damaging the ecosystem. When hiking over lava in places like Hawai`i Volcanoes National Park or Saddle Road, remember to follow the rock piles, or *ahu*, which mark the trail. The weather changes rapidly on the Big Island, so in addition to water and sunscreen, always carry wet weather gear like a waterproof jacket (layering your clothing is always smart). Because of lightning, metal hiking poles are obviously a bad idea in exposed lava areas. Most hiking trails are prone to flash floods, so pay attention to the weather and don't cross streams that seem to be rising. Lava can cut you, so always hike in closed-toe shoes, preferably hiking boots.

The Pololu Valley area

We've listed fantastic hikes in every chapter of this book, with a quick reference list of the distance, time, type of trail and difficulty level to help you choose one that fits your skill level and taste. In particular, we strongly recommend hiking in Hawai`i Volcanoes National Park (pp. 343 ff) and the spectacular hike into and beyond the Pololu Valley (p. 284). See the *Ecotourism* section below for several outstanding companies that lead hikes on private land. At press time several hiking trails were closed due to the October 2006 earthquake. They should be open again by time pf publication, but you can find the details at www.bigislandadventureguide.com.

Na Ala Hele (☎ 974-4217, www.hawaiitrails.org) is the state's Trail and Access Program. You'll see their name on brown and yellow signs at many trailheads. Visit their website for a list of trails they maintain.

"Wipe out wilderness and the world's a cage." – David Brower

Camping

Though camping is an inexpensive option, you might not get a lot of sleep, particularly on weekends when locals gather to party. You'll probably sleep best at the volcano, or at Spencer Beach Park in South Kohala; it's the largest campground, and has a strict noise, alcohol and drug policy. A guard checks a permit list for anyone entering the campground after sunset, and the gate is locked from 11 pm to 6 am.

Camping at either of the campgrounds of Hawai`i Volcanoes National Park is free to anyone who purchases the $10 vehicle pass to the park, with a maximum stay of seven days. Permits and payment are needed to camp at county and state parks.

Thanks to the Internet, county permits are much easier to obtain than state ones because you can go online to check campsite availability, purchase a permit with a credit card and print it out at http://co.hawaii.hi.us. You can also call ☎ 961-8311 and arrange to mail in a permit to the Dept. of Parks and Recreation at 101 Pauahi St, Ste. 6, Hilo, HI 96720. There is a $1 a day extra charge to use the online service for adults, or 25¢ a day for kids 13-17. Rates are $5 a day for adults, $2 a day for juniors (aged 13-17), and $1 a day for children (12 and under).

County camping permits are issued for:

- Punalu`u Black Sand Beach Park
- Whittington Beach Park
- Laupahoehoe Point Beach Park
- Kolekole Gulch Park
- Kapa`a Beach Park
- Mahukona Beach Park
- Isaac Hale Memorial Park
- Spencer Park at Ohai`ula Beach
- Ho`okena Beach Park
- Miloli`i Beach Park

State permits require more hoop jumping, thanks to the infamous Hawaiian bureaucracy. They do not accept credit cards, and there are rules about when personal checks are accepted (30 days before the date). Cash and money orders are the easiest payment methods. The cost is $5 per site, per day. They encourage potential campers to call and check availability before applying for a permit at ☎ 587-0300.

You can print out a permit found online at www.hawaii.gov/dlnr/dsp/index.html. Send the permit and payment to the Hawai`i District Division of State Parks office: PO Box 936, Hilo, HI 96721. (The direct line is ☎ 974-6200). Still, priority is given to walk-ins at 75 Apuni St, #204 in Hilo.

State camping permits are issued for:

- Kalopa State Recreation Area
- MacKenzie State Recreation Area
- Manuka State Wayside Park

They also issue permits for the shelters at Hapuna ($20/night for four people) and the cabins at Kalopa ($55/night for up to eight people) and Mauna Kea ($35/night for four people, $5 extra for fifth and sixth campers). The Hapuna shelters consist of four wooden platforms, so you'll need to bring your own bedding. The Kalopa cabins hold eight bunk beds, with a separate mess hall where you can cook (bring your own gear). They recently underwent ADA upgrades. The Mauna Kea cabins are only open Fri-Sun, and have no water other than that which flushes the toilets. Again, you'll need to bring your own cooking equipment.

Caving

One of the most interesting by-products of a heavily vulcanized island is the prevalence of lava tubes. Once these tubes have drained and cooled, they make for fascinating exploring, with features such as lava falls, plunge pools, skylights and lavacicles. **Kazumura Cave** (p. 472), in Glenwood near the national park, is the longest lava tube in the world at over 40 miles, and is also the deepest cave of any kind, in the world. Additionally, try the guided explorations at **Kula Kai** (p. 479), or give it a go yourself at **Emesine Cave** (p. 319) off Saddle Road or **Kaumana Cave** (p. 445-46) near Hilo.

You can also scuba dive lava tubes, and it's a thrill to be able to float to the top of a cave. Popular sites are **Suck Em Up** near Kailua-Kona and **Three Room Cave** along the South Kona Coast.

Golf

The Big Island is known as the "Golf Capital of Hawaii," with over 20 courses in spectacular settings. With brilliant coastline, sunny days and the trademark lava hazards, it's hard to beat a day on the links here. The best golfing is definitely on the leeward coast, with the courses of South Kohala costing top dollar, but offering the quintessential golfing experience. However, don't

The gray francolin is a common sight on golf courses

miss the upcountry Kona courses, or the opportunity to golf just a few good drives from Hawai`i Volcanoes National Park. And, of course, if you get lucky with the weather, or you don't mind dodging raindrops, you can get in some inexpensive links time in Hilo.

TOP 5 BIG ISLAND GOLF COURSES	
Mauna Kea	(p. 246)
Mauna Lani North	(p. 237)
Waikoloa Kings' Course	(p. 222)
Big Island Country Club	(p. 191)
Hualalai	(p. 204)

Snow Skiing

Yup, it snows on the Big Island, mainly on Mauna Kea. Though there are no commercial ski operators on the mountain, many people like to thrash their skis on "pineapple powder" just to say they did. But keep in mind that because it is a sacred mountain to native Hawaiians, and a fragile environment, this type of recreation on the mountain is frowned upon. You might want to settle for a snowball fight.

Hawai`i Volcanoes National Park

This is one of the most unusual parks in America's already stunning National Park system – it is home to the world's most active volcano, after all. A drive around the Crater Rim Drive and to the end of Chain of Craters Road to see the lava enter the ocean is impressive, but true adventurers will allow more than just a few hours for this. There are over 150 miles of hiking trails – many with very little elevation gain, since you might be trekking across a steaming crater floor – that are

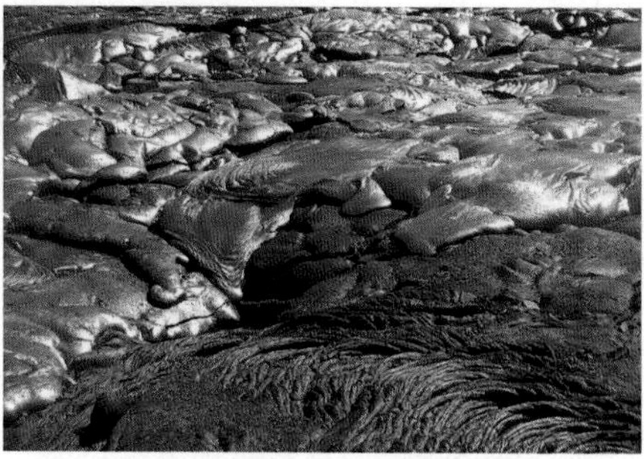

Molten lava in Hawai`i Volcanoes National Park

sure to inspire even the most jaded of hearts. From lava deserts to rainforests, petroglyphs to steam vents, ocean views to an erupting volcano, this park has endless opportunities for exploration and adventure.

Top Five Hikes at Hawai`i Volcanoes National Park

Kilauea Iki Trail . . . . (p. 346)
Crater Rim Trail . . . . (p. 348)
Napau Crater Trail . . . . (p. 354)
Pu`u Loa Petroglyphs . . . . (p. 358)
End of the Road . . . . (p. 341)

"To the dull mind nature is leaden. To the illuminated mind the whole world burns and sparkles with light."
– Ralph Waldo Emerson

Stargazing

The highest place in the most isolated land mass on Earth – Hawaii's Mauna Kea – has the clearest skies in the world, and is a world center for astronomy. The Big Island helps telescope observations by using sodium lights to prevent "light pollution."

Observatories cluster at the summit of Mauna Kea

Whether you're strolling on a beach at night with a lover, or staring through a telescope on Mauna Kea, the night skies will dazzle you with their brilliance. During the annual Leonid meteor shower each November, the sky is filled with shooting stars (and the visitor center at Mauna Kea is the place to be!).

On Horseback

With so much wide-open space, the Big Island is a terrific place to indulge in the freedom of riding a horse. There are tours to suit every skill level, from nose-to-tail walks to tours for experienced riders with nonstop gallops across private ranches.

The most obvious place to ride a horse is in **Paniolo Country**, home to Hawaiian cowboys. The epicenter of Paniolo Country is in Waimea at **Parker Ranch**, one of the country's largest privately owned ranches – over 175,000 acres.

Horses at Parker Ranch

The original *paniolos* were three cowboys from Mexico who New Englander John Palmer Parker hired to help King Kamehameha I control the wild cattle population (which had grown from the original cattle Captain George Vancouver gave the king in 1793). Out of friendship and gratitude, King Kamehameha III rewarded Parker with land, and the rest is history. Parker Ranch (p. 292) offers a number of tours of the ranch, including horseback riding and kiddie wagon rides.

The **Waipi`o Valley** is one of the island's natural treasures, and several companies offer nose-to-tail rides on the verdant valley floor and to taro farms. This is a peaceful way to explore the rich foliage and waterfall-covered *palis* (cliffs) of the "Valley of Kings."

Tours of the **Kohala Mountains** (p. 389) are the choice for experienced riders, who can gallop across open fields with views of mountains, the coastline and even neighboring Maui on clear days. The companies also offer tours for novices.

On Wheels

Scenic Drives

Top Five Big Island Waterfalls

Akaka Falls . . . . (p. 402)
Rainbow Falls . . . . (p. 444)
Umauma Falls . . . . (not free – p. 398)
Hi`ilawe Falls . . . . (p. 383)
Kaluahina Falls . . . . (p. 385)

The Big Island has such rich and varied topography that virtually any time you get in the car you're rewarded with breathtaking views – you may find yourself pulling over for a "Kodak moment" quite often! There are no billboards on the Big Island (yeah!), though in South Kohala it's a challenge to avoid reading the "eco-graffiti" locals make by using white coral to write phrases like "Aloha Auntie" or "J + B" that stand out against the black lava fields.

There is startling rainforest scenery along the 40-mile stretch of the **Hamakua Coast**, and sidetrips to the **Waipi`o Lookout** (p. 380), **Akaka Falls** (p. 402), **Hawaii Tropical Botanical Garden** (p. 406) and the **Pepe`ekeo Four-Mile Scenic Drive** (p. 403) are musts. There are scenic drives in **Hawai`i Volcanoes National Park**, with numerous stops at vantage points of craters, cinder cones, lava fields, rainforest and the "End of the Road," where lava flowed over the road.

If you have a 4WD vehicle, you'll be able to drive to the summit of **Mauna Kea** (p. 309), the valley floor of the **Waipi`o Valley** (p. 386), birdwatch on **Mana Road** (p. 319-20) and reach otherwise inaccessible beaches. It is pointless and dangerous to attempt these drives with 2WD.

Another option is to take an ATV tour in North Kohala (p. 279) or on Parker Ranch (p. 298).

Authors' Tip: Don't forget to roll up your vehicle's windows – front and back – before you drive though a large puddle (the ruts on some 4WD roads fill in like lakes!). We seem to always forget the rear windows, and end up splashing the inside of our car with mud!

Cycling

The Big Island has many more opportunities for road cyclists than mountain bikers. But, because it is the largest of the Hawaiian Islands and has such diverse topography, road riding can be extremely fulfilling. Day-trips can be arranged with **Kona Coast Cycling Tours** (p. 100), and **Orchid Isle Bicycling** (p. 100) offers multi-day bike tours. There are rental shops in Kailua-Kona, where the annual Ironman Competition starts and finishes, and you can have your bike shipped and stored at one of them (p. x). Keep in mind that there are few areas with designated bike lanes; be sure to wear a helmet.

Ecotourism

"Study nature, love nature, stay close to nature. It will never fail you." – Frank Lloyd Wright

A Hawaii Forest & Trail walking tour

The breathtaking beauty of the environment is why most people visit Hawaii, and ecotour guides love to share their passion and knowledge of it with adventurous visitors. There are several excellent ecotour companies on the Big Island, with knowledge of the local environment and culture to help enhance your experience.

Hawaii Forest & Trail (p. 101) is the largest of the ecotourism companies, with eight "Nature Adventures" to different parts of the island for hikers, birdwatchers, and off-road enthusiasts. **Hawaiian Walkways** (p. 388) leads hikes into the Waipi`o Valley and other areas from its base on the Hamakua Coast. **Native Guide Hawaii** (p. 331) offers the best tour of Hawai`i Volcanoes National Park. **Hawaii Pack and Paddle** (p. 169) conducts half-day and multi-day kayak and snorkel tours of the island, with the longer trips incorporating hiking and camping. All four companies are outstanding.

In Air

Helicopter Tours

Waipio Valley from a helicopter

Locals may get a tad annoyed with the overhead buzzing of "lava flies." We've always been skeptical of helicopter tours, since hiking, picnicking or horseback riding, where you can smell the flowers, touch the trees, hear the birds, and see the fine details, is more intimate and rewarding than flying over it in a noisy machine.

Then we took a helicopter tour over the eruption at Pu`u O`o in Hawai`i Volcanoes National Park and were left speechless: what a spectacular display of the power of nature and the birth of land in one of the Earth's most geologically active environments. Red lava bubbles in pits, gas bellows out of fissures, and you're right over it all. It's an experience that cannot be attained by hiking, driving or any other means – you have to be able to fly.

We still think that the hundreds of dollars – each – that you'd spend on a helicopter flight over the Hamakua Coast, North Kohala or other green spots on the Big Island could be better spent elsewhere, such as an eco-tour on the ground or boat trip on the water. But a flight over the erupting volcano is truly phenomenal.

Helicopter tours over Hawai`i Volcanoes National Park are listed in the Hilo chapter (p. 431). Many of the companies also offer other tours to other parts of the island from heliports in South Kohala.

"It is the greatest shot of adrenaline to be doing what you've wanted to do so badly. You almost feel like you could fly without the plane." – Charles Lindbergh

Parasailing

UFO Parasail

There's more to parasailing then meets the eye. From shore, it looks like a colorful parachute behind a person gliding through the air while a speedboat circles below. But if you are that person, with only the sound of wind in your hair and the sparkling sea to distract you, it is hard to feel worried about, say, paying bills or how your team is doing in the playoffs. Tandem flights are quite romantic, and a great way to get on Hawaiian time. **UFO Parasail** offers trips several times a day from the Kailua Pier in Kona (p. 97).

In Culture

There are some scenic and captivating cultural parks on the Big Island for visitors interested in ancient Hawaii. South Kohala's **Pu`ukohola Heiau** (p. 253) is a temple built by King Kamehameha the Great to fulfill a prophecy, and a nearby *heiau* to the shark gods is frequented by black-tipped reef sharks to this day. In North Kohala, **Lapakahi State Historical Park** (p. 265) has an interpretive trail though an ancient Hawaiian fishing village in a visually stunning setting. Because of its remote location in North Kohala, few visitors venture to **Mo`okini Luakini Heiau** (p. 269), a temple to the war god Ku and site of thousands of human sacrifices near the *heiau* that marks the probable location of King Kamehameha's birth. There are no signs or amenities at these places, just a chance to sense the *mana* (spiritual power) of two of Hawai`i's sacred sites.

Pu`uhonua o Honaunau tiki wood carvings

**Pu`uhonua o Honaunau** (p. 176), or "Place of Refuge," is a National Historical Park that no visitor to Kona should miss. Aside from the chance to take pictures of carved statues (*ki`i*) and learn about ancient games like *konane*, or Hawaiian checkers, it's a way to imagine the elation a condemned man would feel when he successfully swam to absolution at the safe haven. These days, turtles and snorkelers swim in the bay around the park; this is one of the best snorkel spots in Kona.

Hilo is home to many quality museums with a focus on Hawaiian history and culture, including the **Lyman Museum** and the state-of-the-art **`Imiloa Astronomy Center of Hawai`i**. Both are full of interactive displays and screen films about ancient Hawaii, as do the visitor centers at Mauna Kea and Hawai`i Volcanoes National Park. To have a chance to learn about Hawaiian culture from native Hawaiians, you can take a guided tour of Puna or Hawai`i Volcanoes National Park with **Native Guide Hawaii** (p. 331), or a walking tour of Kailua-Kona with the **Kona Historical Society** (p. 88).

To explore a more recent cultural tradition, you can tour coffee farms in **Kona Coffee Country** (p. 148), usually for free. All of the farms offer free samples, and we've included a special section for readers who'd like to go on a coffee-tasting tour of some of the area's finest farms.

Hula

Though the hula schools on the Big Island are reserved for serious scholars of the dance, many resorts, luaus and even shopping malls, like the Kings' Shops in South Kohala (p. 227), offer demonstrations and sometimes classes for interested visitors. The **Merrie Monarch Festival**, held in Hilo each spring, is the world's largest gathering of hula and is known as "The Olympics of hula."

Hawaiian Quilting

Hawaiian quilting is an unusual art form, different from traditional quilting, because it uses only two colors – one for the background and one for the design (which is cut from one piece of cloth) – and the entire quilt is hand-appliqued. The designs incorporate Hawaiian images like flowers or dolphins in a kaleidoscopic way. They're beautiful.

The oldest Hawaiian quilt club, Ka hui kappa apana O Waimea, meets the last Saturday of every month in Waimea from 9 am-noon. Visitors are welcome to join the women, who as Auntie Dorothy Badua says, "just quilt, talk story, laugh and eat." They create quilts from many traditions, including Hawaiian. For more information, ☎ 775-9894.

Petroglyphs

There is something about petroglyphs that excites the imagination at a primal level. Because we know so little about the meaning of these vivid, ancient symbols etched in lava stone, seeing them in the stunning Hawaiian setting is an incredible experience. The best areas for petroglyph viewing are at **Puako** (p. 236) and **Hawai`i Volcanoes National Park** (p. 358).

Relaxation

Spas

If you've come to Hawaii with some residual stress, we suggest that you treat yourself to some time at a spa on your first day. This is guaranteed to slow your blood pressure down to "Hawaiian time" and set the tone for the rest of your trip. Most high-end resorts in Kona and South Kohala have spas that offer a range of treatments, from couples massage to seaweed wraps to facials. *Lomi lomi* is a Hawaiian form of massage that literally means "to stir" – ancient Hawaiians used sticks in the practice, though now practitioners knead the stress out of your body in a stirring motion. As a bonus, there are usually steam rooms and soaking pools in beautifully landscaped resting areas to help you really relax and get into vacation mode. We had a couples' massage at a Hawaiian spa the day before we were married and nothing else could have removed every last trace of pre-wedding stress (if you've been married, you know what we're talking about!). Warning: you may become such a relaxed noodle that you can no longer perform simple math.

Retreats

The beauty of Hawai`i attracts New Age practitioners, some of whom have combined accommodation with other services like yoga or meditation classes. The Puna district is the center for these sorts of activities, with particularly desirable facilities at **Yoga Oasis** (p. 470), **Steam Vent Inn** (p. 461), and **Kalani Oceanside Retreat** (p. 470), as well as community events with a similar sensibility. The nearby **Volcano Rainforest Retreat** in Volcano Village (p. 366) offers a range of classes and services.

Volcano Rainforest Retreat

Buddhists will enjoy the serene environment at **Wood Valley Temple** in Ka`u (p. 493), and **Akiko's Buddhist B&B** in the Hamakua Coast (p. 400). The rainbow labyrinth at South Kona's **Dragonfly Ranch** (p. 180) is unique to the island.

"Sometimes your joy is the source of your smile, but sometimes your smile can be the source of your joy."
– Thich Nhat Hanh

Practicalities

When to Go

The Big Island has minor climatic changes, so the best time to come is whenever you can! The busiest tourist season is winter – from November to March. Winter is also the time to see humpback whales or to go surfing. May and June are the slowest months while families wait for school to let out, and this is a great time to find lodging deals. Many of the brilliant flowers of tropical trees start blooming in this season, so it's also a terrific time to visit. Otherwise, you might want to plan your trip around one of the island's big events, like the Ironman Competition or Merrie Monarch Festival. It's up to you!

Time Difference: Remember when you're calculating the time difference to call loved ones on the mainland – or making reservations – that Hawaii doesn't observe Daylight Savings Time (the weather here is just right year-round). So during Daylight Savings Time, Hawaii is two hours ahead of the Pacific time zone instead of three (i.e., if it's 8 pm in California, it is 6 pm in Hawaii).

Costs

"When preparing to travel, lay out all your clothes and all your money. Then take half the clothes and twice the money."
– Susan Heller

Lodging

The chart at right is a key to the hotel price codes used throughout this guide. Accommodation options on the Big Island run the gamut, from free camping at Hawai`i Volcanoes National Park, to cheap hostels around $50 a night, from intimate B&Bs in the $150 range, to basic hotels between $100 and $200 a night, or even resort suites and bungalows

HOTEL PRICE CHART	
Cost per night for two before tax	
$	Under $70
$$	$70-$125
$$$	$125-$250
$$$$	Over $250

costing thousands of dollars (there are more of these than the cheap hostels, if that tells you anything). Many visitors book condos or vacation rentals with kitchens in order to save money by cooking in their rooms.

You'll spend more money on sunny Kona-side than the rainy windward side, since this area is more popular. In each section, we've included lodging options for all available price brackets, but on average you can expect to spend $150-$200 a night. Keep in mind that there are often discounted rates and packages available online, so check your hotel's website before you book a room (this is particularly true of the big resorts of South Kohala).

B&BS

Many bed & breakfasts require that guests stay a minimum number of nights (usually two), and offer discounts for longer stays. There is often a nominal extra charge for more than two occupants. Almost all are nonsmoking, and some are filled with cats. Be sure to ask when you make your reservation.

Because there are so many B&Bs on the Big Island, and because many of them have just a room or two, we've only included some of them, particularly in areas without hotels or comparable accommodation. For a complete list of B&Bs, visit the Hawaii Island Bed & Breakfast Association's website at www.stayhawaii.com.

Read the fine print: Before you make a reservation at a resort or hotel, check with the booking agent for hidden fees so that there are no surprises when it comes time to check out. Some charge a "resort fee" for things like use of the tennis courts and fitness room (even if you won't use these facilities), or for parking.

Dining

There's no doubt that food is more expensive in Hawaii than the mainland – it costs more to ship it here, after all. There's a mark-up in grocery stores ($4 for a loaf of bread seems normal now), though deals abound at farmers' markets and at Costco in Kailua-Kona. Restaurants are more expensive ($10 for a burger or omelette is typical, and a steak under $30 is a bargain!) as well. You can spend a lot of money on fine dining, or make sandwiches or barbecue at your hotel for much less. Local restaurants are super-cheap. If you see "Drive In" in the name, that's the signal for $2 burgers and other inexpensive fare.

DINING PRICE CHART	
Price per person for an entrée, not including beverage, tax or tip	
$	Under $7
$$	$7-$15
$$$	$15-$25
$$$$	Over $25

The chart above is a key to the restaurant price codes in this guide.

As is the case with lodging, gas and everything else, Kona-side is more expensive for food than elsewhere on the island, and there are some terrific, reasonably priced restaurants in Waimea, Pahoa, Hawi, Honoka`a and elsewhere. Essentially, South Kohala prices are exorbitant compared to the rest of the Big Island (not counting the town of Kawaihae, another great restaurant community). But if you love fresh fish and fresh produce, you may find the splurge well worth it.

Note: The prices we've listed do not include tax unless noted.

Shopping

There are a range of shopping opportunities around the Big Island, from *koa* rocking chairs worth thousands of dollars to shell necklaces sold three for a dollar.

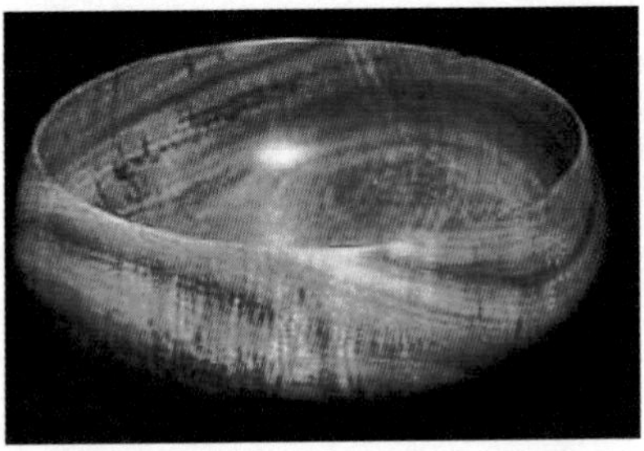

Koa wood bowl *(Volcano Gallery)*

The diverse beauty of the Big Island inspires local artists, and that inspiration often shines in their paintings, ceramics and photography. You will find artists and art galleries in virtually every part of the island. If you are interested in buying a piece of Hawaiian art – or even just want to see the cool stuff – steer clear of South Kohala; its outrageous markups extend to the art world as well. If you are staying in South Kohala, head north to the galleries of

Waimea or **North Kohala**, or south to the artistic community of **Holualoa**. If you find yourself on the windward side of the island, you can find outstanding art galleries in **Hilo**, **Volcano**, and the **Hamakua Coast**.

The Big Island is home to many master woodturners, artists who carve bowls from Hawaiian hardwoods like *koa*. Because their bowls can cost thousands of dollars, they usually also offer less expensive items like bookmarks, hairclips, wine stands, frames, and crosses. If you hear of an exhibition or competition in wood-turning, go – their creations are amazing.

Wild ginger quilt design (quilts-shop.com)

Traditional Hawaiian quilts are another high-quality souvenir. The patterns are reminiscent of snowflakes, but incorporate Hawaiian images like tropical flowers, turtles and dolphins. Usually the "snowflake" is one color and set against a different solid color background. If you are a quilter, or shopping for a quilt, you can purchase a pattern, the fabric, a book on the art form, and quilt your own.

Musicians might want to invest in an `ukulele, and music lovers have the opportunity to buy CDs of Hawaiian falsetto singers and slack key guitarists in gift shops and grocery stores.

Gardeners love the orchids, plumeria and other tropical flowers and trees that they can take home. Just remember: these plants might not flourish as well on the mainland as they do in Hawaii!

Tip: If you're planning to take a helicopter ride or dive with the manta rays, you might want to budget for a video of the experience. These trips are once-in-a-lifetime adventures and you'll probably be so pumped when you're done that you'll fork over whatever they ask for a video tape or DVD of your flight or dive, which usually costs around $50.

Everybody loves Kona coffee's smooth flavor. Just be sure to buy a bag marked "100% Kona Coffee" or you'll end up with 10% Kona coffee, and 90% inferior product. Another perennial favorite is macadamia nuts, whether plain or dipped in chocolate, combined with caramel and chocolate, covered in toffee, sprinkled with garlic salt, etc. Jams and jellies made from Hawaiian tropical fruit are delicious – and something called "Lilikoi Butter" is a sinful passion fruit concoction some people serve on cream cheese or pancakes.

Aloha shirt from Hilo Hattie

Aloha shirts and dresses can be tasteful and cool – something locals wear on dressy occasions – but they can also be obnoxious and over-the-top. Either buy from a stylish store like **Sig Zane's** in Hilo, or stop into a **Hilo Hattie** in Kona or Hilo and purposely buy the most outrageous matching outfits you can find – this makes for a great couples' Halloween costume.

Farmers' markets are an inexpensive place to find authentic goods, from handmade Samoan war clubs to *lauhala* hats, mats and drink cozies – these woven goods are a dying art. There are several outdoor markets in Kona as well.

Then there are the cheap and tacky but always classic souvenirs like plastic leis filled with miniature bottles of rum, *puka* shell necklaces, and picture frames painted with turtles or sunsets. Lotions scented with tropical flowers like *pikake* (jasmine) are divine. You'll find many of these items at **Whalers'** and **ABC Stores** in South Kohala and Kona. These general merchandise stores are also good places to hit when you first arrive on island, in case you need to buy an inflatable raft, sunscreen or a cold drink.

Puka ("POO-kuh") means "hole" in Hawaiian, and you'll hear it used to describe everything from a giant lava cave to the tiny holes of the shells used in *puka* shell necklaces.

Festivals & Events

"You can discover more about a person in an hour of play than in a year of conversation." – Plato

January

Kona: **MasterCard Championship** at Hualalai (☎ 325-8000, www.pgatour.com/tournaments/s524). Each year the **PGA Champions Tour** (aka "Seniors Tour") kicks off at the Four Seasons Hualalai, offering a chance to try to improve your golf game by watching these living legends swing the wrenches.

February

Waimea: **Waimea Cherry Blossom Heritage Festival** (☎ 961-8706). This is a fun event because not only are the cherry blossoms blooming, there are booths with food and crafts and live performances.

Hilo: **Hilo Chinese New Year Festival** (☎ 933-9772). Ring in the **Lunar New Year** by celebrating Chinese culture at Kalakaua Park.

March

Kona Brewers Festival

Kona: **Kona Brewers Festival** (☎ 331-3033, www.konabrewersfestival.com). We're partial to this one – a fiesta of craft beer and food from numerous local restaurants that raises money for local environmental and children's causes. This is a party you don't want to miss!

Kona: **Kona Chocolate Festival** (☎ 937-7596, www.konachocolatefestival.com). Each year chocoholics swarm the Outrigger Keauhou Beach Resort to sample chocolate created by island chefs, drink wine and beer, dance to live music and raise money to fund a local school.

April

Hilo: **Merrie Monarch Hula Festival** (☎ 882-7218, www.merriemonarchfestival.org). Each year, Easter Sunday kicks off this, the world's biggest hula festival. The aroma of flowered *lei*, the skill of the dancers, the parade, the crowning of Miss Aloha, art and cultural exhibits, the competitions and general celebration of hula make tickets to this event hard to get – ticket requests (only two) must be postmarked Dec. 26. Most events are broadcast on a local television station.

Merrie Monarch Hula Festival

May

Statewide: **May Day** is Lei Day in Hawaii – give someone you love a *lei*!

Hamakua Coast: **Hamakua Music Festival** (☎ 775-3378, www.hamakuamusicfestival.org). The main "festival" events happen in May and October in Honoka`a, but this is an organization that hosts concerts – primarily jazz, Hawaiian and classical – sporadically throughout the year to raise money for scholarships and music workshops for students on the island, and to put music teachers back in public schools. Hooray!

South Kohala: **Big Island Film Festival** (☎ 557-5200, www.bigislandfilmfestival.com). This event kicked off in 2006, with the usual filmmaker parties and so on, but also a golf tournament to raise money for Project ALS and, in true Hawaiian style, two of the screening venues are outdoors so you can watch the flicks under the stars.

June

North Kohala: **King Kamehameha Day** on June 11 (☎ 889-0169, www.kamehamehadaycelebration.org). Though King Kamehameha Day is a state holiday celebrated throughout Hawaii, the largest celebration is at his birthplace in North Kohala. There is a parade and daylong festival celebrating Hawaiian culture in Kapa`au, and the statue of King Kamehameha the Great is covered with fragrant *leis*, many of which are over 20 feet long!

July

Waimea: **Parker Ranch Fourth of July Rodeo** (☎ 885-7655, www.parkerranch.com). Who better to host a rodeo on the Big Island for over 40 years than the *paniolos* (Hawaiian cowboys) at Parker Ranch? Kids under 10 are free, and they can enjoy pony and wagon rides.

Hilo: **Big Island Hawaiian Music Festival** (☎ 961-5711, www.ehcc.org). The big guns come out for this weekend of Hawaiian music, including slack key, `ukulele, steel guitar and those soaring falsettos.

Kona: **Hawaiian International Billfish Tournament** (☎ 329-6155, http://hibtfishing.com). Bigshot anglers from around the world have been flocking to Kona for nearly 50 years for the "Grandfather of All Big Game Fishing Tournaments." To get an idea of the size of the marlin caught during the tournament, check out the giants in the lobby of the King Kamehameha Hotel near the Kailua Pier.

August

Statewide: **Aloha Festivals** (toll free ☎ 800-852-7690, www.alohafestivals.com). For two months, over 30,000 volunteers help stage events throughout Hawaii to celebrate Hawaiian culture, including art, music, dance and history. Check the website for Big Island events during your visit.

September

Hilo: **Queen Lili`uokalani Canoe Races** (☎ 331-8849, www.kaiopua.org). Attention paddlers: this is the largest long-distance canoe race in the world. It's fitting that the Labor Day weekend races are hosted by the Kai `Opua Canoe Club, one of Hawaii's oldest outrigger canoe clubs.

October

Kona: **Ironman Triathlon** (☎ 329-0063, www.ironmanlive.com). These crazy nuts swim 2.4 miles in the ocean, ride their bikes for 112 miles and then run 26.2 miles. The start and finish line is at Kailua Pier, so this is a wild day to be in Kailua-Kona, with around 25,000 people screaming at the finish line.

November

Kona Coffee Cultural Festival (☎ 326-7820, www.konacoffeefest.com). There's over a week of activities celebrating not only Kona coffee itself, but also the culture and community surrounding it. In addition to coffee tastings, bean-picking competitions and the cupping contest to decide Kona's current top coffee farm, there are parades, displays, workshops, hula and *lauhala* weaving classes, a foot race, a golf tournament, `ukulele jam sessions, plays, a quilt competition, and recipe contests.

December

Island-wide: **Christmas** and **New Year's Eve** celebrations. A complete list of festivals and dates is available at www.bigisland.org.

Getting Here & Getting Around

Airports

Odds are that your first stop on the Big Island will be to an airport, either the **Hilo International Airport** (ITO; ☎ 935-5707, http://www.hawaii.gov/dot/airports/hawaii/ito/) or **Kona International Airport** at Keahole (KOA; ☎ 329-3423, http://www.hawaii.gov/dot/airports/hawaii/koa/). It's such a good feeling to know you've landed in Hawaii that often some passengers cheer!

Airlines

You can usually find good deals online with websites that compare prices, dates and times of flights from the mainland for different airlines at sites like Expedia.com, Travelocity.com, and Orbitz.com. Inter-island flights used to be dominated by Hawaiian Airlines and Aloha Airlines, but in June of 2006 a new airline company called go!, a division of Arizona-based Mesa Air Group, sparked heated fare wars by offering $39 inter-island tickets. Island Air flies at lower altitudes than jets for the best views.

Aloha Airlines (☎ 800-367-5250, www.alohaairlines.com)

go! (☎ 888-IFLYGO2, www.iflygo.com)

Hawaiian Airlines (☎ 800-367-5320, www.hawaiianairlines.com)

Island Air (☎ 800-323-3345, www.islandair.com)

Online deals: Some airlines offer online deals that are not available by phone. These deals are only sold via the Internet.

Ground Transportation

Because the Big Island is so big and has so many pockets to explore, and because bus service is on the flakey side, you'll probably want to rent a car from one of the companies at the airport. You can book directly with one of the companies, or look for deals online (what would we do without the Internet?).

Alamo (☎ 800-327-9633, www.alamo.com)
Avis (☎ 800-331-1212, www.avis.com)
Budget (☎ 800-527-0700, www.budget.com)
Dollar (☎ 800-800-4000, www.dollar.com)
Harper Car & Truck Rental (☎ 800-852-9993; free shuttle service to off-site locations, www.harpershawaii.com)
Hertz (☎ 800-654-3011, www.hertz.com)
National (☎ 888-868-6207, www.nationalcar.com)
Thrifty (☎ 800-847-4389, www.thrifty.com)

Note: Many rental car companies place restrictions on travel, commonly prohibiting trips to Saddle Road and 4WD locations. Keep in mind that venturing into off-limits areas can void your insurance.

TRAVEL TIMES & DISTANCES

Kailua-Kona to:	Distance (miles)	Drive time (minutes)
Hawi	53	75
Hilo	90	135
Honoka`a	50	75
Kawaihae	35	50
Pahoa	110	165
Volcano	99	150
Waimea	39	55

Directional info: When giving directions, we will refer to *mauka* ("MAO-kuh" – toward the mountains) and *makai* ("muh-KAI" – toward the ocean) so that you will know which way to turn no matter which direction you are headed.

"I never travel without my diary. One should always have something sensational to read on the train." – Oscar Wilde

Buses

Hele-On Bus (☎ 961-8744) has daily stops around the island, though they are infrequent, unreliable and hard to know where to get on. Some locals suggest standing outside and waving if you see it come by. Still, it's free! (Each piece of luggage is $1, and surfboards are not allowed.) The main terminal is in Hilo – Mo`oheau bus terminal (see *Hilo* for map). Bus schedules available at www.co.hawaii.hi.us.

Taxis

Both airports have at least a dozen taxi companies hoping to drive new arrivals to their hotels. They are scarcer elsewhere, only available in Kailua-Kona and Hilo. Locals rarely use them, and it can be hard to find one late at night when you really want one. If you need a late night pick-up, you'll want to make an advance reservation. In fact, you have to call at any time for pick-up; taxis don't cruise the streets looking for fares. Here are a few of the taxicab companies; see the local phone book for a comprehensive list.

Kona:

Aloha Taxi (☎ 329-7779, late service by request)

Cruz'n Taxi (☎ 325-1234, 24 hours with advance reservations)

D&E Taxi (☎ 329-4279, until 9 pm with exceptions for airport runs)

Hilo:

Ace One Taxi (☎ 935-8303, 24 hours)

Percy's Taxi (☎ 969-7060, 6 am-6 pm)

Health & Happiness

Sunburn can ruin a vacation, or at least put a serious damper on it. Hawaii's proximity to the equator means that the ultraviolet rays are more intense here. Apply sunscreen before you go outside, with at least a 15 SPF for your face (you'll probably want a hat or visor, too). If you use waterproof sunscreen, let it soak into your skin for at least 15 minutes before you go frolic in the ocean. And when you get out, reapply it (and every hour or so while you're at the beach, particularly during what Southern California teens refer to as "PTT" – Prime Tanning Time – between 10 am and 2 pm). Your skin will thank you.

Dehydration (and its more serious cousin, heat exhaustion) is no fun – remember to drink plenty of water (at least 8-10 cups a day). Bringing a collapsible cooler from home, filling it with ice and bottles of water, and keeping it in your car is a great way to be sure you never go thirsty.

It probably goes without saying that, no matter how thirsty you do get, you should never drink untreated water from a river or stream since you don't want to get giardiasis or leptospirosis. Animals pee and poop in rivers, after all, and drinking it is clearly a bad idea. But people continue to die from this every year, so we repeat the warning here. Watch your open sores when wading, too. There aren't always symptoms of giardiasis, though they sometimes include fatigue and "foul smelling stools." Leptospirosis symptoms include fever, headache, chills, pink eye, and vomiting. You'll want to see a doctor if any of these crop up.

> The **emergency phone number** is the same in Hawaii as it is on the mainland: **911**. We've also included the phone numbers to local emergency rooms in the *Practicalities* sections.

Mosquitoes were absent from Hawaii until they made their way here as stowaways in water barrels on whaling ships. In rainforested areas, they are voracious – keep insect repellent in your car at all times. Some companies offer sunscreen with insect repellent, though we usually find it's too diluted.

Sea stings can be painful, whether attained by stepping on a sea urchin or brushing against a jellyfish. It may sound gross, but the path to quick relief is to douse the sting with urine. Soaking the sting in vinegar works, too, but it takes a heck of a lot longer. Opinions vary on the subject of how to deal with the sting of Portuguese man-of-wars, but urine apparently doesn't work. Pick off the stingers (with gloves, a rock or any other method that doesn't involve skin), and use a cold compress. You'll hear about any infestation of man-of wars from locals, or see them on the beach, since they tend to get washed ashore en masse.

Altitude sickness crops up for some visitors to the summit of Mauna Kea (climbing from sea level to nearly 14,000 feet will do that), and it is nothing to be trifled with. Be sure to acclimatize at the visitor center for at least 45 minutes, drink lots of water, and be willing to descend if you feel nausea, dizziness, or fatigue. The only cure is to descend to a lower elevation. Scuba divers should avoid ascending Mauna Kea – or flying – for 24 hours after their last dive.

The Big Island has an active volcano, so residents and visitors have to occasionally deal with "vog," a volcanic smog composed of water vapor, sulfur dioxide and carbon dioxide. The tradewinds then wrap the haze around the southern point of the island, dispersing it over Kona, where it sometimes hangs like a blanket, causing problems for people with respiratory problems, or extremely sensitive contact lens users. The State Department of Health has a Vog Index hotline for Kona at ☎ 885-7143. (Contrary to the Bo Derek movie, "10" is bad and "0" is best.) The hotline recommends drinking water, avoiding physical exertion, and consulting a doctor if you have complications.

TSUNAMIS

The sirens you see around the Big Island (and the rest of Hawaii) are tsunami warnings. A tsunami is a series of waves usually triggered by earthquakes. They are often deadly, and occur in all of the world's oceans. A tsunami in 1946 killed 159 people in Hawaii, and a one in 1960 killed 61 people in Hilo. Though there haven't been any catastrophic tsunamis on the Big Island in the past 30 years, it never hurts to know what to do in the event of one.

If you hear a siren's alarm, head inland (preferably) or evacuate as high as you can in a concrete building. (If it occurs at 11:45 am on the first business day of the month, turn on the TV or radio to make sure it's not just the monthly test.) Evacuation routes for the larger towns are listed in the front pages of the phone book. You'll want to bring water, food (a cooler is a good idea), prescription medicine, flashlights or candles and matches, cash, blankets, books for your kids, and other necessities.

If you are at the beach and feel an earthquake or see the ocean suddenly recede, head for higher ground immediately. Do not attempt to drive a car. If a tsunami is generated locally, it can reach the coastline in minutes. Tsunami waves in the open ocean can travel faster than 500 miles an hour, crossing the Pacific Ocean in a day.

Since we had to evacuate New Orleans for Hurricane Katrina, we take comfort in the fact that in December of 2005, the National Weather Service declared that Hawaii is the first state in the nation to be both storm- and tsunami-ready. You should be ready too. Take it from us: heed the warnings and evacuate!

Temperatures range from super-hot in beach areas to super-cold atop Mauna Kea – and both extremes occur in Hawai`i Volcanoes National Park. It's a good idea to layer your clothing (it can be cool in the evening, particularly in places like Waimea), and pack a waterproof jacket.

With so many steep cliffs in the rain-soaked valleys, flash floods can quickly swell streams and rivers. Do not cross swollen streams until the water drops (usually after a few hours).

On a final note, theft is a problem in Hawaii as much as it is on the mainland, so don't leave valuables in your car, including the trunk – we hear those rental car trunks can be easily pried open with a butter knife. You'll want to leave someone on the beach with your camera, purses or any other valuables if the rest of the group decides to go for a swim (or leave that stuff in the hotel!).

Hawaii is a beautiful place, full of environmental wonders and culturally significant structures. Be sure to practice the "leave no trace" philosophy while visiting Hawaii: "Leave nothing but footprints, take nothing but pictures, kill nothing but time." Mahalo!

Tipping

We always tip at least 20%, though technically 15% is acceptable. Just as the cost of vacationing in Hawaii is expensive, the cost of living in Hawaii is expensive. Electricity, food, gas and rent are much higher than prices on the mainland. So when the boat crew mentions the tip jar, feel free to leave around $5 for each member of your party (or more). If someone valet-parks your car or carries your bags to your room, you'll want to grease their palm, too. The tourist industry is the lifeblood of the economy and everyone is dependent on – and extremely grateful for – you!

"We make a living by what we get, but we make a life by what we give." – Winston Churchill

Information Sources

Big Island Visitors Bureau (☎ 961-5797) is online at www.gohawaii.com/bigisland.

A site dedicated to eco-cultural tourism, **www.alternative-hawaii.com** has links to accommodation, activities and other like-minded businesses.

Hawaii Ecotourism Association has a comprehensive listing of their members at www.hawaiiecotourism.org.

The **Coral Reef Outreach Network** has information about Hawaii's reef life and a downloadable public service announcement about reef etiquette available at www.hawaiireef.org.

Travel with Keiki (Children)

It's simple: kids love the beach. Bring some plastic shovels and buckets for the little ones, rent boogie boards and snorkels for the older ones, and they'll be happy for hours. Boat rides are always a hit, too. Tours of coffee country... not so much.

Many resorts have babysitting services or day camps if you need some time alone, or want to explore more adult activities. **Sitters Unlimited of Hawaii** (☎ 674-8440, http://sittershawaii.com) is an O`ahu-based childcare company with rigorous standards for their employees, including background checks and CPR certification.

Gay Travelers

Gay travelers should feel welcome on the Big Island, and many B&Bs, restaurants and companies have gay owners. There isn't much in the way of nightlife – gay and straight revelers head to Waikiki on O`ahu for that purpose – but there's plenty in the way of daytime adventures and romantic evenings.

There's a list of gay-friendly accommodation at **www.purpleroofs.com**, as well as commitment ceremony officiants.

Travelers with Disabilities

Though the Big Island has a reputation as the least accessible of the Hawaiian Islands, it's still true that travelers with disabilities can have a fabulous time on the Big Island. You'll need to make advance inquiries and reservations to ensure the best service. For example, normally dogs entering Hawaii must be quarantined in O`ahu for 120 days (to prevent the introduction of rabies), but blind visitors with guide dogs are not subject to the rule so long as they qualify (and do some hoop-jumping) with the Animal Quarantine Facility (☎ 483-7151, http://www.hawaiiag.org/hdoa/ai_aqs_guidedog.htm). You must arrive though O`ahu.

For information about travel around the world and in Hawaii, visit **www.access-able.com**, a website with information about the Big Island's accessible attractions and adventures.

Access Aloha Travel (toll free ☎ 800-480-1143) is an O`ahu-based travel agency specializing in vacations for people with disabilities, though they subcontract for the Big Island. They recommend **Polynesian Adventure Tours** (☎ 833-3000, toll free ☎ 800-622-3011, www.polyad.com) for their ADA buses and sensitivity to travelers with disabilities. **Roberts Hawaii** (☎ 539-9400, toll free ☎ 800-831-5541, www.robertshawaii.com) also has wheelchair-accessible buses that tour the Big Island. Both companies request advance reservations.

If you would like to rent a hand-controlled car, you can make a reservation about a week in advance from the Kona International Airport branches of Dollar Rent-A-Car (toll free ☎ 800-342-7398) or Thrifty Rent-A-Car (toll free ☎ 800-367-5238).

Weddings

I ho`okahi kahi ke aloha. "Be one in love."
– Hawaiian proverb

Can there be any better place to start a marriage than Hawaii? The sounds of the ocean, the aroma of tropical flowers draped around your neck, the beauty of the sunsets – it doesn't get more romantic than this.

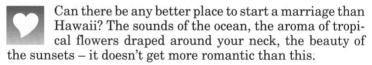

Many of the Big Island resorts have on-site wedding coordinators if you're looking for a lavish affair. Another option – the one we chose – is to hire a private wedding coordinator, since they have contacts with private homeowners for more intimate ceremonies. These folks are great because they make all the arrangements through local companies about which you know nothing, so when you arrive from the mainland, all you have to do is get a quick tan, without burning! There are lists of Big Island wedding coordinators through links at www.alternative-hawaii.com, www.gohawaii.com, www.thebigday.com, and www.theknot.com.

Yet another option is to get married on a sailboat with one of the companies that offers sunset sails, like **Ocean Sports** (p. 219, 221) or **Kamanu** (p. 187). This can be an affordable and peaceful option for small wedding parties.

Kona sunset

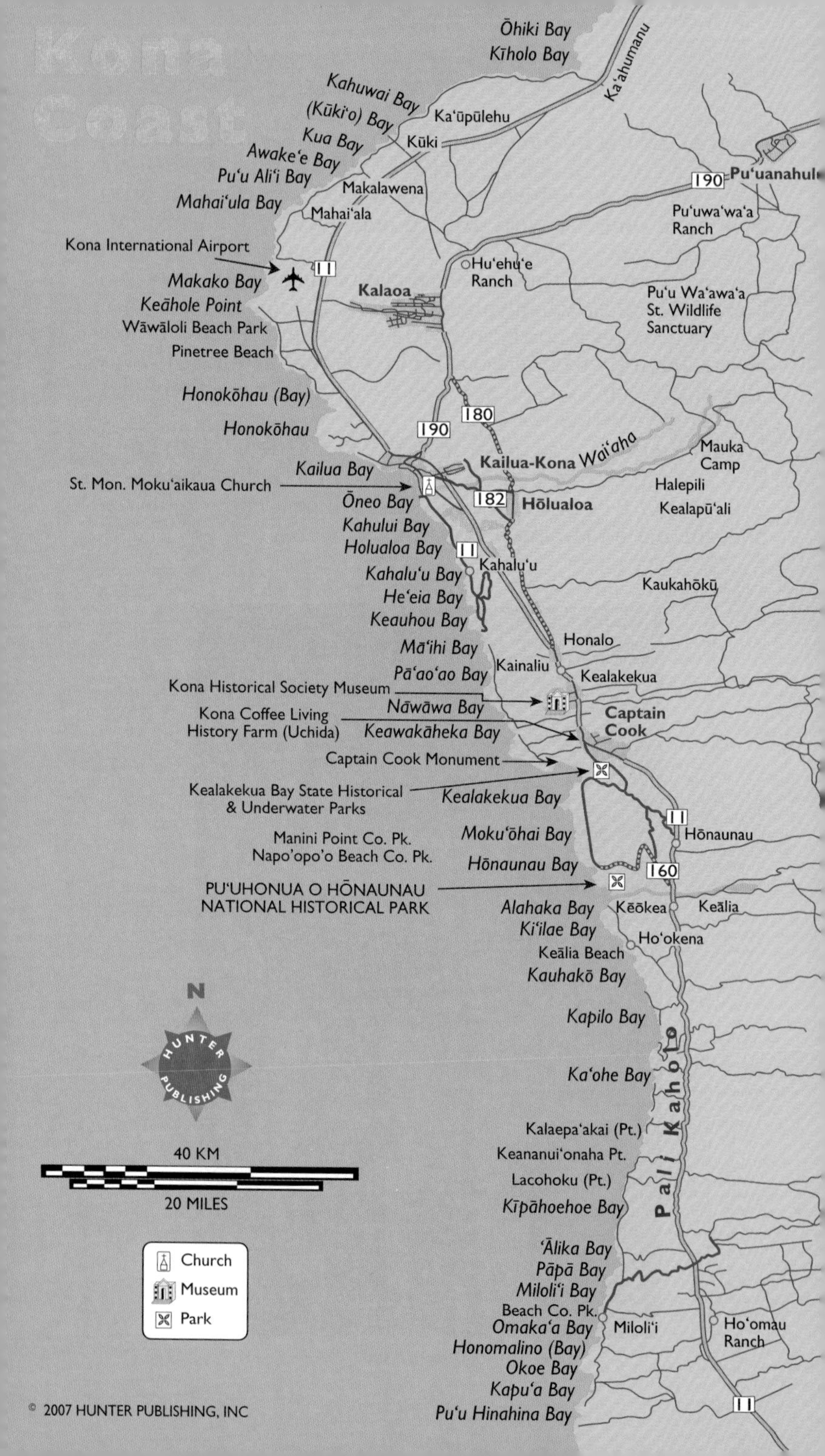
Kona Coast
Ōhiki Bay
Kīholo Bay
Ka'ahumanu
Kahuwai Bay
(Kūki'o) Bay
Kua Bay
Awake'e Bay
Pu'u Ali'i Bay
Mahai'ula Bay
Ka'ūpūlehu
Kūki
Makalawena
Mahai'ala
190
Pu'uanahulu
Pu'uwa'wa'a Ranch
Kona International Airport
11
Hu'ehu'e Ranch
Makako Bay
Keāhole Point
Kalaoa
Wāwāloli Beach Park
Pinetree Beach
Pu'u Wa'awa'a St. Wildlife Sanctuary
Honokōhau (Bay)
Honokōhau
180
190
Kailua-Kona
Wai'aha
Mauka Camp
Kailua Bay
St. Mon. Moku'aikaua Church
Ōneo Bay
182
Hōlualoa
Halepili
Kealapū'ali
Kahului Bay
Holualoa Bay
11
Kahalu'u
Kahalu'u Bay
He'eia Bay
Keauhou Bay
Kaukahōkū
Honalo
Mā'ihi Bay
Kainaliu
Pā'ao'ao Bay
Kealakekua
Kona Historical Society Museum
Nāwāwa Bay
Kona Coffee Living History Farm (Uchida)
Keawakāheka Bay
Captain Cook
Captain Cook Monument
Kealakekua Bay State Historical & Underwater Parks
Kealakekua Bay
11
Hōnaunau
Manini Point Co. Pk.
Napo'opo'o Beach Co. Pk.
Moku'ōhai Bay
Hōnaunau Bay
160
PU'UHONUA O HŌNAUNAU NATIONAL HISTORICAL PARK
Alahaka Bay
Kēōkea
Keālia
Ki'ilae Bay
Ho'okena
Keālia Beach
Kauhakō Bay
Kapilo Bay
Ka'ohe Bay
Pali Kaholo
Kalaepa'akai (Pt.)
Keananui'onaha Pt.
Lacohoku (Pt.)
Kīpāhoehoe Bay
'Ālika Bay
Pāpā Bay
Miloli'i Bay
Beach Co. Pk.
Omaka'a Bay
Miloli'i
Ho'omau Ranch
Honomalino (Bay)
Okoe Bay
Kapu'a Bay
Pu'u Hinahina Bay
11
N
HUNTER PUBLISHING
40 KM
20 MILES
Church
Museum
Park

Kona

`Oi kau ka la, e hana i ola honua.
"While the sun still shines, do all you can."
– Hawaiian proverb

IN THIS CHAPTER

Kona is the heart of the sunny side of the Big Island. It's a historic region promising balmy weather, white sand beaches, Kona coffee country, tropical flowers and trees, fantastic snorkeling and diving and countless other adventure opportunities. Hualalai, an 8,271-foot dormant volcano, towers above it all.

Three distinct areas comprise the Kona district: North Kona, South Kona, and the "big city" of **Kailua-Kona**. The bustling commercial hub was the capital of Hawaii from 1812 to 1819, when King Kamehameha the Great lived out his life at Ahu`ena Heiau near the Kailua Pier. Nearby **Hulihe`e Palace** was a retreat for generations of Hawaiian royalty, or *ali`i*, and in honor of this legacy, the main street in Kailua-Kona is named **Alii Drive**. Today, Alii Drive is an oceanfront boulevard teeming with tourists visiting the strip's lively restaurants, shops and art galleries.

Kailua Pier is another link between the past and the present, situated alongside Hawaii's Plymouth Rock, where the first missionaries set foot on the Big Island in 1820. Now it is the departure point for many boat trips, such as parasailing, glassbottom boat rides, and snorkel tours. It is also the starting point for the annual Ironman Triathlon, a grueling endurance race combining swimming, running and cycling that floods downtown with over 25,000 spectators each October.

The rest of Kona has a much slower pace. The artistic community of **Holualoa** is perched above Kailua-Kona at 1,500 feet, offering visitors the chance to browse its galleries while gazing at the expanse of shoreline and ocean below. It's an ideal place to begin a tour of the coffee farms in **Kona Coffee Country**, a belt of land that runs 20 miles between 1,000 and 2,500 feet, where the rich volcanic soil, sunshine and moisture create perfect growing conditions for the acclaimed coffee beans.

In addition to the Kona coffee belt, South Kona has small towns, lush surroundings, waters frequented by spinner dolphins, and two of the best snorkeling sites on the island. The spectacular coral gardens and underwater life at Kealakekua Bay are particularly good in front of the monument to explorer James Cook, who was killed here by Hawaiians in 1779. Farther south, **Pu`uhonua o Honaunau National Historical Park**, or "Place of Refuge," offers a chance to snorkel with *honu* (turtles), and to explore a fascinating cultural park that was once a royal residence for ancient Hawaiians.

North Kona has some of the island's best beaches, sometimes requiring a hike but always worth the extra effort for the powdery white sand and lack of crowds. Turtles cluster at beautiful **Kiholo Bay**, while surfers flock to **Pine Trees**, one of the most popular surf spots on the Big Island. **Kaloko-Honokohau National Historical Park** has beaches, birding, hiking and ancient fishponds for hours of exploring.

Honokohau Harbor is the jumping-off point for all sorts of boating adventures, such as fishing, diving, sunset sails and whale-watching. Some boats head to **Pawai Bay**, a dramatic snorkel site accessible only by boat. Others are full of fishermen hoping to land a thousand-pound marlin; the annual Hawaiian International Billfish Tournament, the "Grandfather of All Big Game Fishing Tournaments," takes place here each July. Dolphins, turtles and whales are often in the vicinity of the harbor, the icing on the cake for a day spent on the water. Two ultra-deluxe resorts cap the district in the north, the "Fantasy Island"-esque **Kona Village Resort**, and the

Four Seasons Hualalai (Hawaiian Images)

Four Seasons Hualalai, consistently rated as one of the best resorts in the world.

The waters of the entire Kona Coast are renowned as a mecca for scuba divers. With incredible visibility at about 75 dive sites that have underwater features like lava caves, arches, pinnacles and canyons and a diversity of marine life, most divers consider this the best in Hawaii. The manta ray night dive, the ultimate adventure on the island, erases any doubt – it is the experience of a lifetime. You haven't really seen the Big Island until you've seen its underwater world, and Kona is the place to do it. Its beauty both above and below the ocean is breathtaking.

"We live in a wonderful world that is full of beauty, charm and adventure. There is no end to the adventures that we can have if only we seek them with our eyes open."
– Jawaharlal Nehru

Kailua-Kona

Alii Drive, Kailua-Kona's main street (HTJ)

Residents of other districts on the Big Island often compare Kailua-Kona to O`ahu's Waikiki, criticizing the traffic and sizeable population (a "whopping" 9,870 people at last census). But everything is relative, and Kailua-Kona is a far cry from the neon glitz, crowds and skyscrapers of Waikiki. It's an actual community where people live, and the natural beauty, particularly along Alii Drive, is undeniable.

Orientation

There are three main thoroughfares through Kailua-Kona, and they're all roughly parallel. Queen Ka`ahumanu Highway is the upper road, connecting North and South Kona through Kailua-Kona. In the north it is Highway 19, which south of Palani Road becomes Highway 11. Kuakini Highway is the main road through town. The waterfront avenue is Alii Drive, where cars tend to inch along while the drivers gape at the sensational views of the ocean.

Directional info: We've written the directions the way they're given on the Big Island: *mauka* and *makai*. Turn *mauka* means "toward the mountain," *makai* means "toward the ocean." This way you'll make sure to turn the correct way no matter which direction you're headed.

Practicalities

Don't forget: There is only one area code for the entire island: 808.

The section of Alii Drive that runs though downtown Kailua-Kona has multiple ATM machines, but strip malls off the main drag have most of the town's basic services and box stores.

Makalapua Shopping Center, on Makala Blvd. *makai* of Queen Ka`ahumanu Hwy, has a Macy's, Kmart, and a movie theater. It also has tremendous sunset views from the parking lot.

Crossroads Shopping Center, above Walmart on Henry Street, has a Safeway, Denny's, Mailboxes Business Center, several eateries and Kona Natural Foods, a natural grocery store.

The **Lanihau Shopping Center**, on Palani Road, has a Sack N Save grocery store, Longs Drugs, First Hawaiian Bank, GNC, several inexpensive restaurants like L&L Drive-Inn, and the Kailua Kona Post Office (open 8:30 am-4:30 pm Mon-Fri, 9:30 am-1:30 pm Sat).

The **Kona Coast Shopping Center** has a Tesoro Gas (open 5 am-10 pm daily), KTA Super Store, Payless, Radio Shack, Blockbuster, and ethnic restaurants (including Ba-Le, our

Opposite: Kailua-Kona from the air (Vlad Turchenko, Dreamstime.com)

favorite Vietnamese noodle soup place). The outdoor "food court," with tables and a public restroom, closes at 10 pm.

King Kamehameha Mall on Kuakini Highway has shops, a tattoo parlor, restaurants and public restrooms.

Hualalai Urgent Care (Crossroads Emergency Center, ☎ 808-327-4357) is the town's emergency room. It is on Henry St across from the Safeway Mall, near Quizno's.

> **Cheap Gas:** The cheapest gas in Kona (and most other places) is at **Costco** (73-5600 Maiau St, ☎ 331-4880). If you have a Costco card, you can buy gas at the heavily used pumps – sometimes for up to 40¢ less than elsewhere. Payment is by debit and credit card only. Pumps are open 6 am-9:30 pm Mon-Fri, 6 am-8 pm Sat, and 6 am-7 pm Sun. Expect long lines no matter when you go.

Sights

Kona Historical Society's Historic Kailua Village Walking Tour

A walking tour with Kona Historical Society (☎ 323-3222) is highly recommended, as it will enhance your experience exponentially. Essentially, it is a two-hour crash course in Hawaiian language, culture, history, traditions, art, flora and fauna, local sights and even the sovereignty movement. These Hawaiian guides know their stuff. Donna is usually the guide for independent travelers, and she fires off information like a machine gun, peppering it with lots of jokes. It was impressive to watch her engage three generations of the same family, kids, parents and grandparents. "I doubt I'll remember it all, but I'm sure enjoying it!" the grandmother said.

The tour starts near the Kailua Pier, heading to Ahu`ena Heiau, then looping back to the air-conditioned lobby of the King Kamehameha Hotel (the hotel also has a tour of the art and historical artifacts there). The group heads to Moku`aikaua Church and the grounds of Hulihe`e Palace (there is an additional charge to enter the palace).

If you want to enhance your vacation with cultural understanding, take this tour and support a group striving to preserve knowledge and spread awareness of Kona and Hawaii. Tours are $20, and reservations are required (call at least 24 hours in advance), as there must be at least three participants to a tour. Times vary.

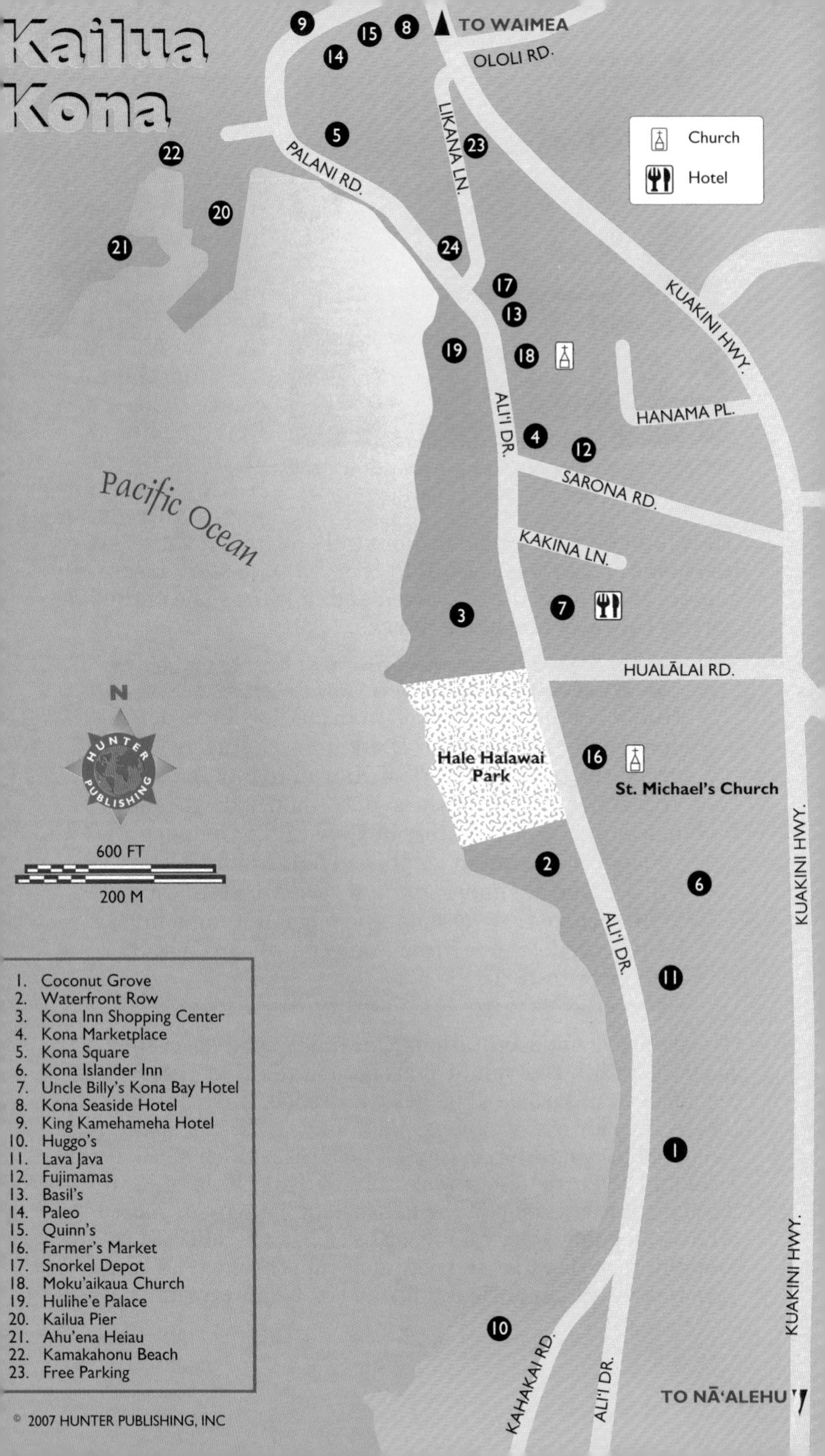
Kailua Kona
TO WAIMEA
OLOLI RD.
LIKANA LN.
PALANI RD.
Church
Hotel
KUAKINI HWY.
HANAMA PL.
ALI'I DR.
SARONA RD.
KAKINA LN.
Pacific Ocean
HUALĀLAI RD.
Hale Halawai Park
St. Michael's Church
N
HUNTER PUBLISHING
600 FT
200 M
KUAKINI HWY.
ALI'I DR.
KAHAKAI RD.
ALI'I DR.
KUAKINI HWY.
TO NĀ'ALEHU
1. Coconut Grove
2. Waterfront Row
3. Kona Inn Shopping Center
4. Kona Marketplace
5. Kona Square
6. Kona Islander Inn
7. Uncle Billy's Kona Bay Hotel
8. Kona Seaside Hotel
9. King Kamehameha Hotel
10. Huggo's
11. Lava Java
12. Fujimamas
13. Basil's
14. Paleo
15. Quinn's
16. Farmer's Market
17. Snorkel Depot
18. Moku'aikaua Church
19. Hulihe'e Palace
20. Kailua Pier
21. Ahu'ena Heiau
22. Kamakahonu Beach
23. Free Parking
© 2007 HUNTER PUBLISHING, INC

Hulihe`e Palace

Hulihe`e Palace (*Eric Guinther*)

(75-5718 Alii Dr, ☎ 329-1877, www.huliheepalace.org). Many visitors probably pass through Kailua-Kona without realizing that there is a palace right on Alii Drive. This is a shame, because Hulihe`e Palace was a retreat for Hawaiian royalty for generations (ali`i means "royalty," hence the name of the street). Built in 1838, the two-story palace is a chance to see how the *ali`i* lived and to learn some of the history of Hawaii's kings and queens.

DAUGHTERS OF HAWAII

Hulihe`e Palace was saved from possible hotel development in 1925 by the Daughters of Hawaii, who urged the then Territory of Hawaii to buy the property and lease it to them so they could operate it as a museum. The Daughters of Hawaii was founded in 1903 with the intent to preserve Hawaiian history, culture and language pronunciation before annexation occurred. To become a member, a woman must be directly descended from someone who lived in Hawaii prior to 1880.

The palace is not ostentatious, but full of symbols of the past, such as kahili, the yellow feathered staffs that acted as the royalty's standard; a flag bearer carried them into battle. There are several weapons, including a 22-foot spear that belonged to King Kamehameha the Great. Much of the furniture and other artifacts were sold by King Kalakaua in the 1880s, but the women of the house kept meticulous records of what was being sold, and most have been recollected by the Daughters of Hawaii, who now maintain the museum and can give interesting historical talks as you begin your tour.

In addition to a view of Kailua Bay from the lanai, the second story has perhaps the most impressive furniture in the palace, like the *koa* bed frame, and a table with stars inlaid with 20 different Hawaiian woods that was handmade for Queen Lili`uokalani. This is a worthy stop that costs less than the price of a frozen daiquiri, so have a look! Admission $6, seniors $4. Open 9 am-4 pm Mon-Fri, 10 am-4 pm Sat-Sun

Moku`aikaua Church

Moku`aikaua Church (HTJ)

(75-5713 Alii Dr across from Hulihe`e Palace, ☎ 329-1589, www.mokuaikaua.org). Founded in April of 1820, this was the first Christian church in the state. It's an arresting stone edifice – lava and mortar – with a steeple 112 feet high, making it the tallest structure in Kailua-Kona (as we said, it's a far cry from the skyscrapers of Waikiki). Visiting the church is free, and worth a stop to enjoy the native wood interior (o`hia pillars and *koa* pews), with simple ceiling fans and a few displays in the back. One is a model of the brig *Thaddeus*, the 85-foot ship that carried the church's founding missionaries from Boston, on a 163-day journey around Cape Horn. Talk about close quarters! There's also a fascinating "Micronesian Stick Chart," an ancient navigational aid that shows currents, swell patterns and drift lines around the Marshall Islands. On either side of the altar are kahili, the feather standards used for Hawaiian *ali`i* (royalty). This usage symbolizes "Jesus is king." The church still holds Sunday services at 8 am and 10:30 am (the latter features the choir). Hymns are sung in Hawaiian.

"If you reject the food, ignore the customs, fear the religion and avoid the people, you might better stay home."
– James Michener

Ahu`ena Heiau

The rock walls and replicated thatch hut and *ki`i* statues at Ahu`ena Heiau, across from Kailua Pier, mark the settlement

Ahu`ena Heiau

where King Kamehameha lived at the end of his life, from 1812 to 1819. Because it was home to the king, it was the capital of Hawaii during those years as well. When he died, a *kahuna* secretly disposed of his remains, then killed himself, leaving the king's last resting place a mystery. Admission is free.

Kailua Pier

The town pier is the departure point for a variety of water tours, like boat trips and parasailing. The lava flat that runs near and just to the right of the pier is Hawaii's "Plymouth Rock," where missionaries first landed on April 4, 1820. Today, the pier area is the start and finish line for the Ironman Triathlon. It's also the unloading point for the hordes of cruise ship visitors that arrive at least twice a week.

AVOIDING SEASICKNESS

Getting seasick is a drag, as anyone who's experienced it knows. To avoid this nauseating condition, try these tips:

- Do not go indoors or below deck, where the air is stale.
- Look at the horizon (you'll want to scan the water for dolphins and whales, anyway!).
- Sit in the stern of the boat, where there is less motion.
- If you have to vomit, do it over the side of the boat instead of in the bathroom, which will make you feel even sicker.

Where to Shop

Alii Drive

Alii Drive

Alii Drive is chock full of shops, from several ABC Stores selling *puka* shell necklaces, macadamia nuts and coffee, fake leis and other knickknacks, to jewelry, clothing and art stores. Shopaholics will be able to browse for hours. We've included a few of the more distinctive shops here.

TIMESHARE BOOTHS

You'll notice many booths and shops along the Alii Strip advertising discounted luaus, boat trips and helicopter tours under banners like "Activity Discount Headquarters" and "Volcano Information." These are actually the offices of timeshare salesmen – to get a discounted trip, you'll have to endure several hours of a sales pitch trying to get you to buy into a timeshare vacation home. Whether the discounted ticket is worth the price of losing several hours of your vacation is up to you.

Pearl Factory (75-5719 Alii Dr, Kona Marketplace, ☎ 327-1749, www.pearl-factory.com). This jewelry store has a fun gimmick: for $14, you can pry open a live oyster and keep the pearl inside. Then you can select a ring or other piece of jewelry and, for an additional charge, they'll mount your pearl in it right then and there. Little girls love this. Open 9 am-9 pm daily.

TAKE A BREATHER

The main shopping malls on the *makai* (ocean) side of Alii are the **Kona Inn Shopping Center**, anchored by the Kona Inn Restaurant, and the blue-roofed **Waterfront Row**. Both have nice ocean views; Waterfront has chairs near a railing, and there is an expansive public lawn and sea wall in front of the Kona Inn Restaurant. Both offer a chance to give your feet a rest while enjoying ocean breezes and aquamarine waters. Of course, there are also places to sit on the seawall or the beach along the strip as well.

Bad Ass Coffee Co. (75-5770 Alii Dr, Waterfront Row, ☎ 326-4637, toll free ☎ 800-252-7468, www.badasscoffee.com). Tucked in the back of Waterfront Row you'll find Bad Ass Coffee, a franchise that started in Hawaii but is now run from Salt Lake City, Utah. In addition to 100% Kona coffee (they ship to the mainland), ice cream and merchandise with their oh-so-catchy name and logo, this Bad Ass has an Oxygen Bar. There are different oxygen menus depending on your ailments, so by sticking a tube up your nose, you can diminish your migrane headache, PMS symptoms, sore throat, sinus infection, hangover or other irritant to your vacation. "It's a natural high," enthused an employee. Oxygen treatments last 10 minutes ($10), 15 minutes ($12) or 30 minutes ($18). Open 9 am-9 pm.

Off the Strip

Kona Wine Market (75-5626 Kuakini Hwy, King Kamehameha Mall, ☎ 329-9400, toll free ☎ 800-613-3983, www.konawine-market.com). To paraphrase Jane Austen, it is a truth universally acknowledged that every town needs a wine store with gourmet cheeses and other temptations for romantic evenings and sunsets. In Kailua-Kona, it's Kona Wine Market. It has a deli case with imported cheeses, gourmet meats, fresh tomatoes and even $6 baguettes imported

from Quebec. The owner, Howard Burford, is very knowledgeable about wines, and he has a fairly extensive selection, as well as liquor and beer of the non-Budweiser variety. He also carries cigars, and gifts like Hula Girl Hot Sauce or Hawaiian-themed wine glass decorations. In a nod to tourists, they deliver gourmet gift baskets to hotels and condos. There are free wine tastings Fridays from 3-7 pm. It's easy to spend money here, and worth it. Open 9 am-8 pm Mon-Sat, 10 am-6 pm Sun.

Quilting Good Luck: Local lore contends that if your first Hawaiian quilt has `ulu, or breadfruit, in its design, you will have a long and prosperous quilting life.

Quilt Passions (75-5626 Kuakini Hwy, King Kamehameha Mall, ☎ 329-7475). The quilter in our life always makes a stop at this store when she's in town. Quilt Passions is small, but has beautiful fabrics – mostly batiks – for a quilt with colors to remind you of the Islands when you return home. In addition to fabric and lots of fat quarters, owner Katy sells quilting supplies and books for traditional Hawaiian quilts as well as mainland styles. She also has some handmade coconut buttons for a special touch. Open 10:30 am-4:30 pm Mon-Fri.

Soundwave Music (75-5599 Luhia St, ☎ 326-2297). Musicians looking to buy, sell or trade an instrument will want to visit Soundwave, next door to Hula Lamps in the Old Industrial Area. It has a good selection of `ukuleles, as well as guitars, drums, and amps. Open 10:30 am-6 pm Mon-Fri, until 5 pm Sat.

Markets

Ali`i Gardens Marketplace. Hong Kong Orchid Trees line the entrance to this open-air market, south of the two-mile marker on Alii Drive. Individual vendors sell their wares from shady, permanent *hales* (houses) offering tropical clothing, art, jewelry (from gold and pearls to beads and shells), 100% Kona coffee, soaps and lotions, fruit, vegetables, flowers, cold drinks, shave ice and food. There's a relaxed feel to this market, probably because it's on fragrant Alii Drive, away from the business of downtown. Open 9 am-5 pm Thurs-Sun.

Kailua Village Farmers Market. This market, right in the heart of Kailua-Kona on Alii Drive at Hualalai, has a large selection of produce and flowers, as well as knicknacks, clothing, sunhats, soaps, coffee, sunglasses, drums, `ukuleles, food and drinks (there's usually a taco wagon here), and sometimes live music from a local musician trying to sell CDs. Open roughly 9 am-5 pm Wed-Sun.

Kona International Marketplace. This is a new endeavor near the old industrial area on Luhia St There are numerous permanent stalls in the open-air market selling pottery, t-shirts, shells, jewelry, bags, hula girl dolls, wind chimes, kids' stuffed-animal backpacks, wood vases, produce, macadamia nut butter, flowers and so on. There's an indoor food court, ATM and public restrooms.

"No poem was ever written by a drinker of water." – Horace

Adventures

On the Beach

Kamakahonu Bay, next to the Kailua Pier, is a little swath of beach in the heart of town. The Ahu`ena Heiau is in plain view, a reminder that King Kamehameha the Great used to live here. More recently, it's where local families used to picnic and play after church on Sundays, until the 5 o'clock bell at Moku`aikaua Church signaled that it was time to head home. Now the locals are joined by guests at King Kamehameha's Kona Beach Hotel.

Old Kona Airport beach *(shorediving.com)*

Old Kona Airport Marine Life Conservation District. This is more of a picnic area than a swimming beach (lots of lava), but it is so large that it can be a relaxing place to find some space. There are many picnic tables scattered throughout tidy beach heliotrope trees, tide pools and public restrooms. It's fun to drive to the beach along the old runway. You'll see lots of dive boats offshore at the nearby Garden Eel Cove. To get here, follow

Kuakini Hwy north through Kailua-Kona until it leads onto the runway.

Airport beach aerial (shorediving.com)

White Sands Beach Park (aka La`aloa Bay, Magic Sands, Disappearing Sands). La`aloa translates to "very sacred" in Hawaiian, but this place doesn't look very sacred anymore. While it certainly has the whitest sand in Kailua-Kona, this beach is wildly popular with locals who flock into the water with boogie boards, competing with 20 others for space on a wave. Its prime location on Alii Drive means a lot of tourists come here too, but they're outnumbered by local dudes drinking beer and playing horseshoes. That said, the lively scene makes for some colorful people-watching. There is a lifeguard on duty here, and public restrooms.

White Sands Beach

Coconut Grove Beach Volleyball Court. One of the most popular beach destinations in Kona is man-made, surrounded by shops and restaurants, and right on the Alii strip. This free, lighted beach volleyball court is nearly always swinging. Tourists and locals stop and watch the more intense matches, usually two-on-two. You're welcome to try it yourself!

"The time you enjoy wasting is not wasted time."
– Bertrand Russell

In Air

UFO Parasail (☎ 325-5836, toll free ☎ 888-359-4836, www.ufoparasailing.com). Gazing out at the water in Kailua-Kona, you'll often see a boat towing a person flying though the air while harnessed to a rainbow (or smiley-face) parachute. This is parasailing. Its detractors will tell you that parasailing is very expensive (it's best not to calculate the cost per minute of

the 7- to 10-minute ride). Still, it's really fun. UFO Parasail flights launch from a boat, and one or two people can go up at a time (tandem is romantic). This has the added value of a harbor cruise while other group members (up to six on a boat) are having their turn in the air. But the ride is obviously the best part. You get strapped into the parachute's harness and up you go to 400 feet (seven minutes, $60), or 10 minutes for higher flights to 800 ($70) or 1,200 feet ($80). These include a freefall (we were sure our feet would hit the water but we flew back in the air at the last minute – a great effect). The time you are suspended in air is as close as you'll come to flying – it's noiseless, the water glitters in the sunlight, the waves and lava formations far below instill a sense of peace. It's a big deep breath. Call ahead for reservations (7:30 am-3 pm) and to find out when to meet the boat at the Kailua Pier. There's an 8 am "early bird" flight that saves you $5.

On Water

***Body Glove* Cruises** (☎ 326-7122, toll free ☎ 800-551-8911, www.snorkelkona.com). *Body Glove* packs in the crowds and cruises up to the outstanding snorkeling site at Pawai Bay, which is essentially accessible only by boat. The boat trip includes snorkel gear and a lunch buffet, and a scuba upgrade is available. There's a fun 15-foot slide. The 4½-hour morning tour ($105, kids $65, children under five free) leaves at 9 am from Kailua Pier, and the three-hour afternoon tour departs at 2 pm ($66, kids $44). Locals tend to feel pity for the people who seem crammed onto the 51-foot boat; for a smaller group both on the boat and in the water (and a lower price), try the *Kamanu*, which sails from Honokohau (see p. 187).

Kona Beach Boys (☎ 326-7686). Located in a thatched-roof hut near Kailua Pier, Kona Beach Boys offers several adventure opportunities with a focus on Hawaiian culture; owner and Big Island native Kalani Nakoa wants visitors to have fun while learning about Old Hawai`i. So his surf classes ($119) include not only 15 minutes on land learning about safety, but also a Hawaiian history of "the sport of kings" (and two hours in the water or "until your arms fall off!"). His outrigger canoe ride up the coast of Kona ($38/pp) involves paddling, but also includes a guide who paints a picture of the coastline before development, with myths and stories learned by listening to local *kapuna*. Kona Beach Boys rents kayaks ($20/hour) and snorkel gear ($10/day or $50/week), and can arrange for scuba and snuba trips. Kalani has plans to start renting out a 19-foot Ferrari deck boat with fishing rods in the future.

Underwater

Atlantis Submarines (☎ 329-6626, www.atlantis-adventures.com). Submarine tours with Atlantis are good for kids and people who don't snorkel or dive – it's a way to drop to 100 feet below sea level without getting wet. There's a theme park vibe to the excursion – guides snap photos of guests posing with a life preserver on the pier before they leave (for sale at the end of the tour, of course), and the submarine is air-conditioned and plays Enya music.

Though there are large portholes for every two people, the seats – plastic indentations – are only a little over a foot wide, so there's a lot of flesh-pressing going on, a chance to experience the American obesity epidemic first-hand.

Tours leave daily at 10 am, 11:30 am, 1 pm and sometimes 2:30 pm; they cost $84 for adults or $42 for children 12 and under. Children must be at least 36 inches tall. Be sure to call and make reservations, as the boats often run at capacity.

Kailua Bay Charter Co. (☎ 324-1749, www.konaglassbottomboat.com). For a more comfortable and much less expensive experience, you can take a ride on a 36-foot glassbottom boat. It's a big hit with kids. With comfortable padded benches and salt-air breezes, up to 24 people cruise

Kailua Bay while gazing through glass viewing boxes. Trips leave Kailua Pier every hour starting at 10:30 am. The boat is also available for private parties. Tickets are $30 for adults, $15 for kids 12 and under.

On Wheels

The Big Island may not have much in the way of mountain biking (lava and mud will do that), but road bikes are another story. There are a slew of mainland companies offering all-inclusive tours of the Big Island, but why not support the local ones who have first-hand knowledge of the island?

Kona Coast Cycling Tours (☎ 327-1133, toll free ☎ 877-592-BIKE, www.cyclekona.com). Kona Coast Cycling offers daily bike tours Monday through Saturday. Participants don't need to be experts – these folks think the best way to experience a new place is on the seat of a bicycle. Their tours are mostly downhill and "van supported," so if you need a breather and want to ride in the van for awhile, you can. They offer several tours, including the popular "Kona Coffee Express" through coffee country ($80). There is a two-person minimum for tours, which include bikes and helmets. Closed-toe shoes are required.

Orchid Isle Bicycling (☎ 327-0087, toll free ☎ 800-219-2324, www.orchidislebicycling.com). Orchid Isle, another locally owned company, offers multi-day bike tours of the Big Island, such as the Kona Coast tour ($1,995), a seven-day excursion that covers the route of the Iron Man triathlon, or the Tour de Paradise ($2,495), a nine-day jaunt around the entire island. Prices are per-person and include guide, bike, helmet, breakfast, lunch, repair services, airport pick-up and hotel shuttle. There is a minimum of two participants per tour, though single riders can pay more for an individual tour.

On Surfboards

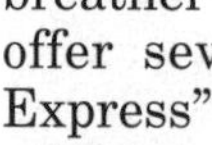

Banyans. The fiercest surfing in town happens at Banyans, just north of the three-mile marker on Alii Drive. The wave is quick and hollow, but competition and vibes from the local boys make it a challenge to drop into one.

Kahalu`u

**Kahalu`u**. Even when the sea is dead flat you'll still see a lineup at the break at Kahalu`u. This is where most surf lessons take place, and when there's a cruise ship (or two or three) in town they'll show up here whether it's breaking or not. However, if there's a swell from any direction, waves and surfers stack up at the northern point of the bay. It's a forgiving wave that closes out when the waves get *too* big. Locals flock here, too, so you'll often see pros and complete novices hanging in the same lineup. Beware an occasional nasty rip.

Ecotourism

"My father considered a walk among the mountains as the equivalent of churchgoing." – Aldous Huxley

Hawaii Forest and Trail (Queen Ka`ahumanu Hwy, ☎ 331-8505, toll free ☎ 800-464-1993, www.hawaii-forest.com). Hawaii Forest and Trail is the premier ecotourism company on the island, with eight distinctive "Nature Adventures" to different regions of the island, as well as custom tours. The Kona-based company was founded in 1993 by naturalist Rob Pacheco and his wife Cindy with the vision of sharing knowledge of the natural Hawaiian environment with visitors. The organization has expanded from the couple and a single van to 35 employees, a fleet of 4WD vans and Pinzgauer vehicles, and an outfitting store. This is the kind of company that gives back to the community; among other good deeds, they lead schoolchildren on free field trips. They were named the 2006

Ecotour Operator of the Year by the Hawaii Ecotourism Association.

Hawaii Forest and Trail's niche is that its knowledgeable guides can lead the public onto private lands for which they have special-access permits, so you can see parts of the Big Island that are otherwise off-limits. Tours include hikes to waterfalls in the Pololu Valley ($125) and the Kohala Countryside ($109); birdwatching adventures to a private section of Hakalau Forest National Wildlife Refuge ($155) and the "Rainforest and Dry Forest Adventure" ($159); Kilauea Volcano ($149); the "Mauna Kea Summit and Stars Adventure" ($165); and off-road Pinzgauer trips up Hualalai Mountain and to a lush, remote area of the Polulu Valley, with a swim in a mountain pool. See the website for details.

Kohala Wai off-road Pinzgauer Trek

Adventure Rental Shops

"We cannot discover new oceans until we have the courage to let go of the shore." – Muriel Chen

Snorkel Bob's (75-5831 Kahakai St, ☎ 329-0770, www.snorkelbob.com). If you're looking for a bargain, Snorkel Bob's has inexpensive yet quality snorkel gear – this is where people "in the know" go (it's next to Huggo's). The store rents a variety of snorkel gear (packages are $2.50-$12 a day), as well as prescription masks, boogie boards and other gear for watersports. Snorkel Bob's has locations throughout Hawaii, and you can rent gear from a store on one island and return it at no charge to a store on a different island.

The business's slogan is "Snorkel Bob Cares." This isn't some hollow marketing campaign by a faceless corporation – Snorkel Bob, aka Robert Wintner, was born on Maui and became a snorkeling fanatic at the ripe old age of four. Though his stores are fun and his marketing whimsical (he uses the phrase, "I, Snorkel Bob" a lot), he is passionate about marine conservation, from donating $45,000 of snorkeling equipment to help the people of Vanuatu protect the reefs, to writing articulate letters to the local newspaper about resource mismanagement at places like Kahalu`u Beach Park. In fact, he's the director of the Snorkel Bob Foundation, a nonprofit organization dedicated to international reef defense. Go, Bob, Go! Open 8 am-5 pm daily.

World Core Surf Shop (75-5744 Alii Dr, Kona Inn Shopping Center, ☎ 329-8825). Next to the "surf museum" in the entrance to the Kona Inn Restaurant, World Core shapes and sells boards, and rents them for $25 a day. You can also rent "softies," which are beginner surfboards, for $20. Boogie board rentals are $10 a day. They also sell t-shirts, board shorts, rash guards and other gear. They have two other stores in California. Open 9 am-9 pm daily.

HP Bike Works (Hale Hana Centre, 74-5583 Luhia St, ☎ 326-2453, www.hawaiianpedals.com). This is the hardcore sister store to Alii Drive's Hawaiian Pedals, with performance mountain bikes and road bikes for rent (starting at $35/day) or sale, as well as repair services, tunes and other assistance for serious bikers. Bike Works has information on their website about how to ship your bike to the Big Island (you can ship it direct to them) and other services like storing your bike box while you visit. Open 9 am-6 pm Mon-Sat.

Kona Harley Davidson (74-5615 E. Luhia St, ☎ 326-9887, toll free ☎ 866-326-9887, www.konaharleydavidson.com). This authorized Harley dealer sells bikes, parts, accessories and requisite Harley gear like headbands and leather jackets. They also have a rental kiosk in the store, with several bikes available for rent. Rates start at $100 for a half-day (4½ hours), $125 for a full day (nine hours) and range up to $750 for a week. Riders must have a motorcycle license or certificate and are required to wear a helmet, despite Hawaii not having a helmet law. Open 8 am-6 pm Mon-Sat, 8 am-4 pm Sun.

Dive Shops

Kona is reputed to have the best visibility – typically at least 100 feet – and diving in Hawaii. While we also love diving in other parts of the state, there's no denying the clarity of the Big Island waters or the splendor of the roughly 75 dive sites along the coast. The manta ray night dive seals the deal – watching their underwater ballet is a truly phenomenal experience. We'd been diving in the Big Island for over a decade before we tried the manta dive, and we've been wondering why we waited ever since. There's simply nothing like it.

"From birth, man carries the weight of gravity on his shoulders. He is bolted to the earth. But man has only to sink beneath the surface and he is free. Buoyed by water, he can fly in any direction – up, down, sideways – by merely flipping his hand. Underwater, man becomes an archangel." – Jacques Cousteau

Safety Reminder: Don't forget that for 24 hours after your last dive, you shouldn't fly or even drive to higher elevations, like Saddle Road or Mauna Kea.

Sandwich Isle Divers (75-5729 Alii Dr, ☎ 329-9188, www.sandwichisledivers.com). You've gotta love the little guys with big hearts, and that's Sandwich Isle Divers. This is a very professional yet personal mom-and-pop store run by Steve and Lara Myklebust, who limit groups to six divers (probably because the boat couldn't possibly fit more). They like to stay shallow so that dives can last an hour, another nice trait, and both have been diving in Kona for years; Captain Steve has logged over 12,000 dives in the past 25 years, and has a degree in marine biology. They purposely want to stay small – quality over quantity. Two-tank dives, including gear, are $115. They do some manta ray dives ($125 incl. gear and light), and night dives ($85 for one tank and gear). They also have certification classes and gear rentals (or sales) – even you snorkelers can rent snorkel gear for only $8, or boogie boards for $8.50. Open 8 am-6 pm daily.

Your weight belt: You'll want to ask for additional weights (we like at least four extra pounds) for the manta ray night dive. The dive is usually only 30 feet deep or shallower, and you're pretty much stationary for the entire dive. The last thing you want to worry about is being blown around by surge while the mantas are somersaulting overhead.

LONG RANGE BOAT DIVE

Some dive companies offer a "long range boat dive." This usually involves three dives in the southern section of the coast, including a trip to the amazing **Au`au ("ow-ow") Canyon**. Other nearby sites are **Paradise Pinnacles**, where you explore the coral, fish, eels and other life around two lava pillars, one of which is over 80 feet tall, and **Three Room Cave**, a chance to float through a lava tube consisting of three major rooms filled with brilliant lobsters and Spanish dancers. If you have the time and extra money, we highly recommend this trip to some of the best dive sites on the island.

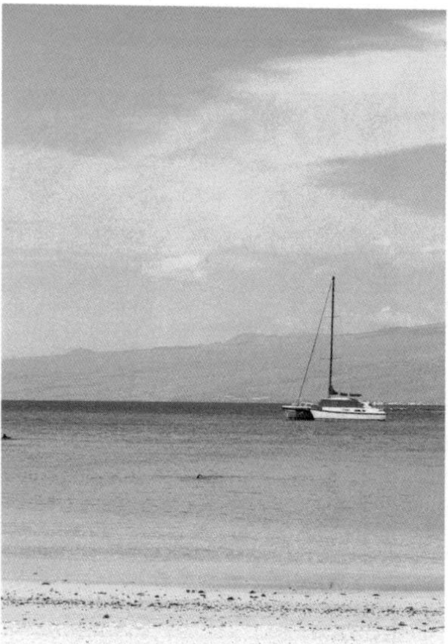

Jack's Dive Locker (75-5813 Alii Dr, ☎ 329-7585, www.jacksdivinglocker.com). These days, Jack's is the biggest scuba company in town, having expanded a shop to include a training pool with a window, so the public can watch scuba certification classes aquarium-style. They have four boats and over 40 employees, usually taking groups of 12-14 divers (though they can take up to 23). Smaller dive shops around town (and many divers) cringe at how many people they'll take on a dive, and vow to avoid letting what happened to Jack's happen to them.

Jack's was a small operation when it started in 1981, with a staff of laid-back divers. We used to dive only with Jack's. But we just can't bring ourselves to do it anymore – got a case of the "good ole days," and things just ain't the same. We miss the small boats and the mellow vibe. Still, it's a professionally run outfit with all kinds of dives (two-tank morning dive $99, advanced two-tank $145, two-tank sunset and manta $115) and certification classes (open water $425). The price to rent their "state-of-the-art" equipment is high – regulator $15, wetsuit (per piece) $10, BC $15, weight belt $6, mask and fins $7.50. Open 8 am-9 pm daily.

"Inspiration – move me brightly." – Grateful Dead lyric

GRATEFUL DIVER

It will interest our Deadhead readers to know that toward the end of his life, Grateful Dead guitarist Jerry Garcia got certified with Jack's – he liked to say that scuba diving filled the space drugs once had. Jack's had all kinds of "Grateful Diver" stickers, hats and other merchandise (these are gone now), and stories about how Jerry had the record for the longest dive, at 103 minutes.

AUTHOR'S CHOICE ★

Dive Tek Hawaii (☎ 329-1004, toll free ☎ 877-885-DIVE, www.divetekhawaii.com). There are a lot of positive attributes that make Dive Tek Hawaii stand out, and that have won them excellent word of mouth among locals. Owner Keith Keizer customizes each dive trip to the needs and tastes of his guests, from separating advanced and beginning divers into different groups instead of sending them all down with one dive master (even if there are only two in a group!), to asking what you'd like to see or photograph on your dives, to whether you want sushi or deli sandwiches for lunch. One extremely unusual feature is that Dive Tek is kid-friendly – kids are allowed to ride along, which is not permitted by most other companies – and they can arrange for onboard child care.

Frog fish (*Dive Tek*)

The company's 36-foot boat is large – and equipped with a bathroom, another excellent attribute. Groups usually consist of two-eight divers (though private groups of up to 22 people

Dive Tek boat

can be accommodated). Keith still employs the original three full-time staff members he hired when the company opened in 1996; his dive guides are extremely experienced and highly certified. They will find marine life – from eels and lionfish to rare butterfly fish and Spanish dancers. Despite all of their knowledge and experience, they don't have the all-too-common attitude of many dive guides that lets you know they think they're cooler than you. They love diving in Kona and want to share it with others.

Lion fish (*Dive Tek*)

Because Dive Tek customizes tours for each guest, prices are not listed on the website. Their prices are generally a little higher than other companies, but you get what you pay for, especially if you are an advanced diver. A standard two-tank, open water dive generally costs $130, and the manta ray night dive is $99 for one tank, $130 for two tanks, and $79 for snorkelers. The cost of gear rental is only $15. We joined them

Whale Shark (*Claudia Christman - Dive Tek*)

Whale Shark (*Claudia Christman - Dive Tek*)

for a three-tank, long range dive ($225) and it was one of the best days of our lives. The captain told us to keep our snorkels attached to our masks on the trip down in case we found sharks or whales. Sure enough, he found a pod of pilot whales, and we jumped in the water. Seven of the behemoths swam right by us, then sounded beneath us, disappearing into the deep blue. Dive Tek also offers a lot of certification classes, from advanced levels such as trimix and rebreathers all the way down to intro dives (for people who don't have the time for a cert class). There are discounts for members of the military, groups of six or more, and people who dive for three days or more.

Bottom Time Hawaii (☎ 331-1858, toll free ☎ 866-GO-DIVE-N, www.bottomtimehawaii.com). This is one of the newest dive shops, and they're passionate about scuba. They are conscientious about trying to group divers (six to a guide) by experience level, and allow buddies to do their own dives if they like. Depth is usually limited to 60 feet for longer bottom times. Between dives they serve sandwiches (including veggie ones), sodas and "clean, dry towels." A two-tank dive is $120, gear rental is $30, intro dives are $130, and manta ray night dives are $119 for two tanks. Bottom Time also offers all the usual PADI courses, and even an internship for dive masters.

On a dive with Live/Dive Pacific

Live/Dive Pacific (74-5626 Alapa St Bldg. A-6, ☎ 329-8182, ☎ 800-344-5662, www.aggressor.com). The *Kona Aggressor II* is the company's 80-foot live-aboard boat, which departs Kailua-Kona at the pier. If

Kona Aggressor II

you're looking for a week of immersing yourself in scuba diving and living on the water, this is it. The *Aggressor* takes 14 passengers from Saturday to Saturday, providing 5½ days of diving, usually with five dives each day. There are five deluxe staterooms with queen beds (and a single berth overhead), private head and shower, and one quad that sleeps four. There's a saloon area for dinner, and an adjacent entertainment center with a television and stereo. But it's all about being on deck, either at the staging area on the dive deck or relaxing in a lounge on the sundeck, in the hot tub, or at the bar (wine and beer are included in the rates). The *Kona Aggressor II* trips received a five-star rating from the Handicapped Scuba Association, and many doorways are wide enough for wheelchairs. The deluxe rate is $2,195, and the quad rate is $1,995.

"Life itself is the most wonderful fairy tale."
– Hans Christian Andersen

UNDERWATER INTERNSHIP

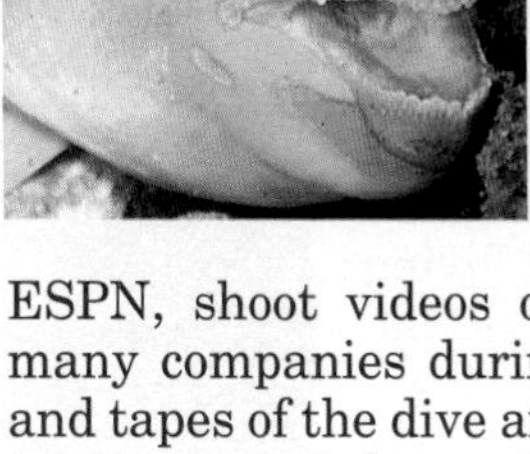

Dolphin Dreams Images (☎ 987-8660, www.dolphindreams.com). We met Jim and Martina Wing, owners of Dolphin Dreams Images, when they were filming us during manta ray night dives. The underwater photographers/videographers, whose credits include the Discovery Channel and ESPN, shoot videos of divers and snorkelers for many companies during their tours, selling DVDs and tapes of the dive afterward. Because of their extensive knowledge and experience, they also lead educational talks about manta rays at the Sheraton several times a week around dusk.

The Wings offer internship and volunteer programs for anyone over the age of 18 who is interested in underwater photography. Since their specialty is filming mantas, dolphins, and turtles on the Kona coast, this is a unique opportunity. The internship program (for which college credit is available) includes subjects like video production, underwater photography and videography, scuba diving, photo editing and web design (you don't have to scuba dive for the internship, but come on! Go for it!). Interns work fulltime for eight- to 10-hour days over four-12 weeks. There is no charge, though there is an option to live "on campus" (they feed and house you) that starts at $2,500 for four weeks. There is a $20/day charge for scuba gear if you don't have your own. The volunteer program focuses less on training and more on underwater experience. A week of living "on campus" costs $1,000. Visit the Dolphin Dreams website for more information.

In Relaxation

Kailua-Kona Day Spa (75-5725 Alii Dr, Kona Marketplace, ☎ 329-5048). It's hard to believe this spa is just off the bustle of Alii Drive. The day spa offers a range of treatments, such as massage, facials, body wraps and waxing services. Use of an infrared sauna, steam room and the Jacuzzis on the back lanai is included with treatments lasting at least 55 minutes, or separately at $29 for two hours. The bargain here is the $45 student massage, or $55 with an advanced apprentice. Call ahead for availability. Open 8 am-8 pm daily.

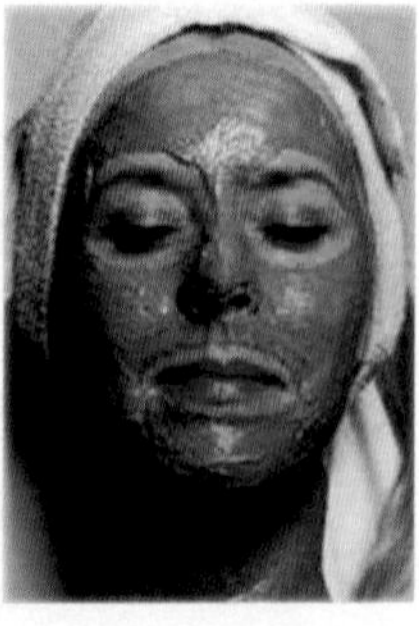

Hawaii Healing Ohana (75-5799 Alii Dr, Alii Sunset Plaza, ☎ 331-1050, www.hawaiihealingohana.com). This new "holistic health spa and natural living center" uses language like "massage modalities," "alternative health disciplines," and "our patent pending products are free of parabens." In laymen's terms, they offer acupuncture, massages like hot stone massage, scrubs with deep sea salt or raw island sugar, body wraps, facials, waxing, foot and hand reflexology and aroma steam therapy. One employee said that a 30-minute session in the infrared sauna burns 900 calories (so you can eat outside at Lava Java guilt-free afterward). They also offer QiGong, Vinyasa yoga and Pilates classes for $14. Open 9 am-6 pm Mon-Fri, 9 am-5 pm Sat, 10 am-4 pm Sun.

Clairvoyant Center of Hawaii (75-5909 Alii Dr, ☎ 329-ROSE, www.clairvoyanthawaii.com). Located a few blocks south of the Alii strip, the Clairvoyant Center of Hawaii specializes in "spiritual training, healing and wellness." There are free spiritual healings Mondays from 5-6 pm and Saturdays from 1-3 pm. On the fourth Tuesday of each month there is a clairvoyant abilities demonstration from 7-9 pm. There are also massage treatments, guided meditations and clairvoyant readings.

Where to Stay

"He that can take rest is greater than he that can take cities."
– Benjamin Franklin

There are a number of "vacation rentals" on the Alii strip, usually condominiums owned by mainlanders and managed by local companies (we rent one ourselves). Because owners decorate their own home, and some management companies pay better attention to the quality of the rentals than others, accommodation can vary widely. Be sure to ask if there is an additional "cleaning fee," usually around $75, so there are no surprises when it's time to settle up.

One testament to how many vacation rentals line Alii Drive is how many people you'll see taking morning walks along the tree- and flower-filled road.

Here are some of the Kailua-Kona property management companies:

Abbey Vacation Rentals (☎ 331-8878, toll free ☎ 866-456-4252, www.konarentals.net)

ATR Properties (☎ 329-6020, toll free ☎ 888-311-6020, www.konacondo.com)

Hawaiibeach.com (☎ 327-KONA, toll free ☎ 800-588-2800, www.hawaiibeach.com)

Hawaii Resort Management (☎ 329-3333, toll free ☎ 800-BIG ISLAND, www.konahawaii.com)

Knutson & Associates (☎ 329-6311, toll free ☎ 800-800-6202, www.konahawaiirentals.com)

Property Network (☎ 329-7977, toll free ☎ 800-358-7977, www.hawaii-kona.com)

Resort Quest (toll free ☎ 800-321-2558, www.resortquesthawaii.com)

SunQuest Vacations (☎ 329-6438, toll free ☎ 800-367-5168, www.sunquest-hawaii.com)

West Hawaii Properties (☎ 322-6696, toll free ☎ 800-799-KONA, www.konarentals.com)

See page 65 for an explanation of the hotel $ price codes given below.

Kona Tiki Hotel

GOOD VALUE ★ **Kona Tiki Hotel** (75-5968 Alii Dr, ☎ 329-1425, www.konatiki.com, 15 units, $65-$88). A little white and blue hotel built in 1955, the Kona Tiki has a sweet location right on the ocean. As one guest said of the pool, "If it was any closer, it would be *in* the ocean." All of the clean, simple rooms have ocean-facing lanais, and many guests like to leave the sliding door open so they can fall asleep to the sound of the waves crashing on the lava below. There are no TVs, phones or A/C in rooms, but they all have a refrigerator and some have kitchenettes. All rooms have at least a queen bed and a twin. Rates include a continental breakfast. Parking is tight, but the managers will double-park cars to make sure everyone fits at night. The grounds are landscaped to include a small tropical garden, and there is a ceremonial tiki torch lighting every evening. This is a great budget option. $

Kona Islander Inn (75-5776 Kuakini Hwy, ☎ 329-9393, 154 rooms, $80-$90, weekly $445-$495 high season). Because Kona Islander Inn has weekly rates and a location in the

View from Kona Islander Inn

heart of Kailua-Kona, this is where a lot of people "live" until they find their own apartment when they first move to town. It's a budget condominium complex run like a hotel and managed by Hawaii Resort Management, but because there are different owners, room decorations vary – some are much nicer than others. There are no kitchens, though all rooms have a microwave, A/C, mini-fridge, TV, and coffee pot. The rooms are small and reminiscent of a motel, with a TV directly across from the bed in the room. There is a pool, hot tub (the kind with contoured seats and jets that massage your back), and two outdoor grills. The lush grounds, filled with ginger, palms, plumeria and *ti*, help compensate for the drab mint green walls, floors and railings, but there probably isn't anything to compensate for the noise and derelicts that waft in from Alii. Lock your doors here. $$

Kona Islander Inn pool

Uncle Billy's Kona Bay Hotel

Uncle Billy's Kona Bay Hotel (75-5739 Alii Dr, ☎ 329-1393, toll free ☎ 800-367-5102, www.unclebilly.com, 123 rooms, $99-$110). Uncle Billy bought his hotel back in the early '70s, and it's retained an Old Hawaii feel ever since. The lobby has the same thatch lampshades on shell chandeliers, and piped in Hawaiian music that the sister hotel in Hilo has. With comparably low prices and a prime location right on the Alii strip, this is a deal, if you don't mind that the property is on the worn side (all sorts of renovations, like replacing the carpets and drapes, are in the works). Rooms are clean, and have central air conditioning, TVs, mini-fridges, phones and blow dryers. Most have lanais. Deluxe rooms also have irons and coffee makers. Parking is $5 a day, and there are coin-op laundry machines and a swimming pool. There are usually discounted rates at the website. $$

Kona Seaside Hotel (75-5646 Palani Rd, ☎ 329-2455, toll free ☎ 800-560-5558, www.konaseasidehotel.com, 240 rooms, $88-$108). Though the lobby of this network of buildings is a block off Alii on Palani, there are two large decks (one is above a fish-and-chips joint) that overlook the Alii strip and Kailua Pier. This is a budget accommodation with a great location, just a few minutes' walk to the pier. Rooms are basic, with TV, A/C, phone, mini-fridge, and bright blue carpet. Some have kitchenettes and lanais (sometimes with an ocean view). There are two pools, one for children. The lobby has Hawaiian quilts and an authentic Hawaiian vibe. $$

Kona Seaside Hotel

Kona Seaside Hotel pool area

"To awaken alone in a strange town is one of the pleasantest sensations in the world." – Freya Stark

Royal Sea-Cliff Resort Condominium (75-6040 Alii Dr, ☎ 334-3117, www.outrigger.com, 154 units, of which 63 are managed by Outrigger Hotels and Resorts, $159-$305). The Royal Sea-Cliff is a commanding white building on Alii Drive, with a sculpture of a humpback whale attached to the front wall. The lobby area has a lush central atrium with ginger, croton, ferns and banana trees around a small fountain.

Though the rooms are independently owned, Outrigger runs the property like a hotel, and owners must meet their standards (the other rooms are time-share units). There is a free parking garage with more spaces than rooms – a rarity – as well as a bellman and daily housekeeping. There are two pools on the property, one saltwater and one freshwater. There are also tennis courts (balls and racquets available for $5), outdoor grills, and free weekly functions like the "Aloha Party," a Hawaiian show with live music, dancing and complimentary *pupus*. There is some variation in décor, but all rooms have lanais, full kitchens, central air, washer/dryers, and TVs, and range from studios to two-bedrooms that have two lanais with views of the surf crashing on lava below. A large common area on the fifth floor overlooks the ocean and the tops of palm trees. All units are non-smoking. Check for attractive deals online and at websites like Expedia.com. $$$-$$$$

Royal Sea-Cliff Resort (Hawaiian Images)

Room in Royal Sea-Cliff Resort

King Kamehameha's Kona Beach Hotel (75-5660 Palani Rd, ☎ 329-2911, toll free ☎ 800-367-2111, www.konabeachhotel.com, 460 rooms, $170-$250). The King Kamehameha opened in 1975 in a prime location in Kailua-Kona, right on the water at Kamakahonu Bay. A sense of Hawaiian history and tradition pervades the hotel, not just in its largely native Hawaiian staff, who wear alohawear, but with its portraits of Hawaiian kings and queens hung on lava rock walls, feather standards, and other displays about

Kona

King Kamehameha Kona Beach Hotel

Hawaiian culture. The hotel offers guided tours of the displays in its air-conditioned lobby – the only one in Kona – and the nearby Ahu`ena Heiau. The hotel is nothing fancy, but it's comfortable. Air-conditioned, "family-style" rooms have either two double beds or a king and a twin, as well as mini-refrigerators, TVs, blow dryers, coffee makers, irons, pool towels and lanais. (The mint-green carpets are another reminder of days gone by.) The big selling point for the hotel is its exceptional location right in town, at the pier; many guests who stay here save money by not having to rent a car (though there is an on-site car rental company for people who want to drive to places like Volcanoes for the day). This is the hotel headquarters for the Ironman Competition, since the start/finish line is right out front. There's an oceanfront pool, and the luau is so popular that it takes place five nights a week (see *Entertainment*). The hotel's **Kona Beach Restaurant**, with its huge window overlooking Kailua Bay, has a breakfast buffet and weekend prime rib and seafood buffet. This is a chance to get a feel for Old Hawaii right in town. $$$

Royal Kona Resort (Hawaiian Images)

Royal Kona Resort (75-5852 Alii Dr, ☎ 329-3111, toll free ☎ 800-919-8333, www.royalkona.com, 436 rooms, $230-$650). Built in 1967, Royal Kona Resort is in the midst of a multi-million dollar renovation. The former Kona Hilton still has a sort of grand '70s feel, with pillars supporting the open-air lobby, a Hawaiian mural on the wall behind the front desk, and lamps filled with coral and shells. The new look will feature new tile floors in the lobby, an exterior facelift, and a tropical décor in rooms. Most rooms have lanais with at least a partial ocean view (otherwise it's a mountain view), and all have TVs, mini-fridges, A/C, coffee makers and other standard comforts.

Located next to Huggo's, the resort has a prime location right on the edge of town that leads to all the other Alii accommodations. As the new slogan says, "an oceanfront landmark in the heart of Kailua-Kona." There is an ocean-side pool with thatch umbrellas, and a small, private lagoon. The bar and restaurant (**Don the Beachcomber**) have incredible views of Kailua Bay, and fun *tiki* decorations. There is a full-service spa, wireless Internet access in the lobby, and $10 daily parking. No resort fee. $$$-$$$$

Kona by the Sea (Hawaiian Images)

Kona by the Sea (75-6106 Alii Dr, ☎ 327-2300, toll free ☎ 800-321-2558, www.resortquesthawaii.com, 74 rental units in an 86-unit building, $270-$445). This condo complex, run like a hotel by Resort Quest, is popular for an attribute that sets it apart from most: it has a beach. It may be artificial, and a seawall prevents you from accessing the rocky shore, but hey – you can walk barefoot on the sand at sunset. There are tables on the beach near the four grills available to guests, and a swimming pool. Rooms are large (one and two bedrooms available), well-furnished with full kitchens, and there are lanais with partial to oceanfront views. Friends of ours stayed here and loved it, calling it clean, quiet and "minimalist – they let the ocean speak for itself." $$$$

Where to Eat

"Never trust a skinny chef." – Sam Choy

Huggo's (75-5828 Kahakai Road, ☎ 329-1493, www.huggos.com). Everyone can agree that Huggo's has great atmosphere: oceanside tables, torches, and contemporary island décor. The casual elegance of this fresh seafood and prime rib restaurant – which has been around for over 35 years – is undeniable. But the food and service tend to receive mixed reviews. For our part, we love it. The mushroom appetizer of shittake and button mushrooms sautéed in soy sauce, ginger, oyster sauce and butter, served sizzling fajita-style, is fantastic (and if you're a vegetarian or a mushroom fanatic, you can get a similar pasta dish as your entrée). Our non-vegetarian author loves the New York strip. We've never had an issue with service, but then again, we always request the energetic and entertaining "Island Johnny" as our server. Having spent some time working in restaurants ourselves, we're also fans of the open kitchen. Open for lunch 11:30 am-2:30 pm Mon-Fri, dinner 5:30-9:30 pm nightly. $$$$

For an explanation of the restaurant $ price codes, see page 66.

A NOTE TO ROMANTICS

In restaurants and bars around the Kona coast, you'll see women with flowered necklaces called *leis* draped on their arms circulating through the room, usually selling them for $10. Your companion may claim she/he doesn't want one, but why not buy one anyway? A *lei* is a symbol of love, often traded in Hawaiian wedding ceremonies – plus it is intoxicating to have your head and neck surrounded by the fragrance of plumeria or tuberose. *Leis* are yet another beautiful Hawaiian way to spread aloha. Speaking of aloha, don't forget to tip the gal who sells it to you.

Huggo's on the Rocks (75-5828 Kahakai Rd, ☎ 329-1493). The bar adjacent to Huggo's has live music nightly and overpriced drinks. Still, sometimes you just want to enjoy a tropical drink next to the ocean with your feet in the sand, and this is the place to do it. The sandy area of the bar has a pleasant ambiance and an "Exotic Potions" menu; the Rocks Jungle Juice (strawberries, mangoes and guava blended with light rum) is refreshing, if a little weak on the booze for $8, though you get to keep the coconut cup as a consolation prize. Some of the *pupus*, like the pizzas, are downright bad. Still, visitors love the live hula and Hawaiian music from 6-8:30 pm, and the rock on weekends. Open for lunch 11:30 am-5:30 pm, dinner 5:30-10 pm daily. $$

HOT SPOT ★ **Lulu's** (75-5819 Alii Dr, Coconut Grove Marketplace, ☎ 331-2633). We have a neighbor who works at Lulu's; she says tourists often complain that the utility wires spoil the view of the ocean at sunset, and suggest that the city pool its resources to move the offending wires underground. Whatever. It's a fun, open-air spot with a somewhat irreverent attitude – the walls and ceiling are covered with dollar bills signed by former patrons – and boozy, 22-oz. slush drinks (though the margaritas are a better way to go). A lot of people staying in South Kohala make pilgrimages to Lulu's "because it's a real bar" – and burgers are $8 instead of $12 or even $16. You'll find all the usual bar food here. The rail seats on this second floor establishment are prime people-watching seats. Open for lunch 11 am-9:30 pm, bar 10:30 am-1:30 am $$

TOURIST TRAP ★ **Pancho & Lefty's Cantina and Restaurante** (75-5719 Alii Dr, ☎ 326-2171). "Don't go!" a friend implored when we ran into her on the way to Pancho and Lefty's, echoing a familiar sentiment in town. But there are always long lines to get into the Mexican restaurant on the Alii strip, so we thought we should see for ourselves. It's a large restaurant with dirty silverware and the greasiest tortilla chips we've ever been served – and two waiters (including a blond with a hacking cough) confirmed that they are always like that. It's a food tragedy because the salsa is pretty good – you'll want to slather it over the food if you do eat here for some reason, but it won't improve things much. Combination plates (i.e., a dish that includes rice and beans) are buried in the right hand corner of the menu and are $16, a rip-off any way you slice it. The enchilada sauce is bland and thick as gravy. This restaurant's popularity proves the real estate axiom that location is everything. Happy hour 3-6 pm with $4 margaritas. Don't forget that it's not that far to Tres Hombres (see below). Open for breakfast 8-11:30 am, lunch 11:30 am-10 pm. $$$

"The poets have been mysteriously silent on the subject of cheese." – G.K. Chesterton

Tres Hombres Steak and Seafood Cantina (75-5864 Walua Road, ☎ 329-2173). This is a much better option for Mexican food than Alii Drive's Pancho and Lefty's (though for the most authentic and inexpensive grinds, we love Habanero's in Keauhou) – good enough to warrant a second location in Kawaihae. Tres Hombres, just off Alii Drive, heading south, serves the usual Mexican staples like tacos and burritos. Try the quesadilla de ajo (garlic) for an inspired twist on a classic. It's also nice that they have three sizes of nacho platters, so you may still have room for your entrée. Open 11:30 am-9 pm daily. $$

Fujimamas Restaurant (75-5719 Alii Dr, ☎ 327-2125). This fusion Japanese restaurant is a fabulous place to indulge your inner yuppie, and pretty much the only place to do so on Alii Drive. This is where to come for designer $10 martinis and "saketinis," to sit at the sushi bar, in a candlelit *tatami*-style room, or out on the expansive lanai. Meals are not as overpriced as the drinks, and lack the outrageous mark-up so prevalent on Alii Drive – a $20 rib-eye steak with miso mashed potatoes and shiitake mushrooms? This is a downright bargain in Kona. Meals start with complimentary hummus, cucumbers and pita, but you'll probably be tempted by the *pupus* – we love the corn, avocado and jalapeno quesadilla with Asian tomato salsa. Noodle lovers should not miss the handmade Chinese noodles with wild mushrooms and truffle oil. The desserts are equally scrumptious, like the hot chocolate and walnut waffle with white chocolate ice cream. The original Fujimamas is in Tokyo. Open for lunch 11:30 am-2:30 pm, dinner 5-10 pm Tues-Sun. $$$

La Bourgogne French Restaurant (77-6400 Nalani, ☎ 329-6711). Offering French food in a fine dining atmosphere, La Bourgogne is one of Kona's better splurge options. You wouldn't know you were in Hawaii if you suddenly found yourself transported to La Bourgogne... there's no trace of Hawaiiana in the restaurant's décor. An added quirk is that the chef and his wife do all the serving – have you ever had the chef deliver your drinks before? The food is pretty good (it depends on what you order), with ample portions. The perfectly cooked duck with raspberry sauce deserves the raves it consistently garners, and the brie baked into a puff pastry is pure indulgence. Also, the wine list has a good selection at lower prices than the resorts in South Kohala. The chef can make a few vegetarian dishes that aren't on the menu, such as vegetarian bouillabaisse. Open 6-10 pm Tues-Sat. $$$$

BEST VEGETARIAN CUISINE ★ **O's Bistro** (75-1027 Henry St, Crossroads Shopping Center, ☎ 327-6565, www.osbistro.com). This is the best option for vegetarian food on the island. Vegetarians will understand how unusual it is to have an entire page of a menu dedicated to over 25 meat-free offerings, aka "Food without Faces." Wow – choice! Formerly the beloved "Oodles of Noodles," O's Bistro has Asian and Italian dishes, and options for carnivores too (fish, steak, duck, chicken – all the usual suspects). Chef/owner Amy Ferguson, a James Beard award nominee, was the first woman to be named executive chef of a major luxury resort in the United States (Ritz-Carlton Mauna Lani). Her food is healthy but, better yet, delicious.

You'll want to make a reservation to sit inside, which is chic, instead of outside, which is a a strip mall sidewalk. The spinach and tofu potstickers are incredible, the noodle soups are savory, the eggplant parmesan and grilled vegetable lasagna (three cheese with sun-dried tomato) are divine. Many dishes are available with tofu or tempeh. Lunch features grilled foccacia sandwiches. You'll want to try one of the desserts, like the chocolate decadence (OK, not everything is healthy.) As the restaurant motto says, "Oh so good." Beer and wine are served. Open for late breakfast 10 am-noon Mon-Fri and until 2 pm weekends; lunch 10 am-4 pm, dinner 4-9 pm. $$$

Basil's (75-5707 Alii Dr, ☎ 326-7836). If you aren't a pizza snob, you might like Basil's. There's a faded restaurant review posted outside with Billy Crystal proclaiming Basil's "a great pizza place." It's always seemed solidly mediocre to us in terms of both food and service. Kids under 12 eat pizza or pasta free. Open 11 am-9 pm daily. $$

LOCAL'S PICK ★ **Lava Java** (75-5799 Alii Dr, ☎ 327-2161). It always seems to be packed at Lava Java, and that's because of the great food at great prices for breakfast, lunch and dinner. Order at the counter and they'll serve your food to you on the sidewalk tables along the Alii strip – so people-watching is great here, too. This is our favorite breakfast spot in town. They have fluffy three-egg (or egg-white) omelettes served with breakfast potatoes and bacon or Portuguese sausage, a short stack breakfast of two giant pancakes, fresh squeezed and whipped juices, and Kona coffee. We also love lunches here: the Portobello mushroom sandwich, grilled and topped with gorgonzola butter and roasted red pepper dressing, the salads with organic greens, and the creative burgers ($9 for beef, chicken and veggie, with combos like Teriyaki grilled pineapple and Swiss, or jalapeño and blue cheese). Casual dinners are delicious if you don't mind the fact that there's no wine to accompany the grilled artichoke, butternut squash and rosemary lasagna, or grilled fresh fish tacos. Open for breakfast 6-11:30 am, lunch 10:30 am-4:30 pm, dinner 4:30-9 pm daily. $$

Kona Taeng-On Thai (75-5744 Alii Dr, ☎ 329-1994). A Thai girlfriend of ours thinks Taeng-On Thai serves the best Thai food in Kailua-Kona (apart from her own restaurant), which is obviously a sound endorsement. We like it a lot, too. It has a lively atmosphere, is right on the Alii strip, and the food is yummy. The Panang Curry is beautifully spiced for plenty of flavor without the heat, and the Pad Thai is some of the best we've had – savory goodness. Special dishes like the Volcano Shrimp, broiled in butter, topped with a spicy sauce and served on a sizzling hot plate, offer a Hawaiian twist on the more traditional dishes. Open 10 am-9:30 pm daily. $$

LOCAL'S SECRET ★ **Quinn's Almost by the Sea** (75-5655 Palani Rd, ☎ 329-3822). Quinn's is unpretentious and very popular with locals and tourists alike, probably because the prices don't have the typical markup you'll find in Kona and the resorts, and the servings are generous. The food is fun for families – giant fried onion rings, calamari and chips, catch of the day, sandwiches. The fish is overcooked, the beef tenderloin less than tender, but what are you going to do? It's Quinn's. The bar area is a great place to wait for your table; they don't take reservations for parties of fewer than eight people. One tip: If you don't like mayo, be sure to tell the waiter when you order your sandwich or it will be smeared on both pieces of bread. Open lunch 11 am-5 pm, dinner 5-11 pm. $$-$$$

The quaint green building that houses Quinn's was once the town post office, located next to a Bank of Hawaii. In 1972, a waterspout (like a tornado) twisted its way through town and hit the post office and bank, scattering mail and money everywhere. Local lore contends that every single bit of paper – green or otherwise – was returned to the businesses.

Jackie Rey's Ohana Grill (75-5995 Kuakini Hwy, ☎ 327-0209). Jackie Rey's may be off the tourist path because it's up on Kuakini, but it's squarely on the locals' path – this place is usually packed. For a special dinner in Kona, this is a solid bet (unless you're one of those people who only eats at waterfront restaurants in Hawaii). The atmosphere is open and friendly, with wooden ceiling fans, bright yellow, green and red walls, white fairy lights, a long rattan bar and vintage Hawaiiana posters. There are crayons at each table so you can get silly on the paper tablecloths, possibly after a mai tai at happy hour (they're respectable here).

The service is friendly, and the food is delicious and reasonably priced. *Pupus* are great for sharing, like the shrimp and vegetable tempura ($9.50) with a soy-based dipping sauce. The dinner rolls are of the sweet Hawaiian variety, with a touch of coconut. Entrées include the Seafood Trio with the grilled catch of the day, crispy wontons, shrimp kabob and a Thai coconut sauce, not to mention the grilled chicken breast with rice, grilled vegetables and papaya sauce. It's also a delicious lunch option, with salads, burgers and sandwiches a cut above what you'll find on Alii. Open for lunch 11 am-2 pm Mon-Fri, happy hour 3-5 pm (*pupus* available) Mon-Fri, dinner 5-9 pm daily. $$$

LEARN THE LINGO

`Ohana is the Hawaiian word for "family." In the context of Hawaii, it has a richer meaning because it also refers to an extended family that may not be related. So a child might refer to his mother's best friend as "Auntie" because she emotionally feels like family, despite not being an actual blood relative. It's an example of the kind of close-knit community that exists in the Aloha State.

AUTHOR'S CHOICE

Oceans Sports Bar and Grill (rear of the Coconut Grove Marketplace, ☎ 327-9494). Here's the most important thing you need to know: Oceans serves *pupus* till midnight. If your airplane doesn't land until 10 pm, or if you're full of rum and craving a late-night snack, head to Oceans – this is the only place open to grind. The *pupu* menu is quite extensive, including teriyaki beef skewers, blackened *ahi* sashimi, macadamia nut crab wonton and the usual pub grub like jalapeno poppers, hot wings and curly fries. The bar screens surf videos and "Sports Center," and has two blue felt pool tables, pinball, foosball, a basketball game and, best of all, about 20 beers on tap. There is a terrace outside for a more intimate atmosphere, with dinner items like burgers, sandwiches and pastas. Open 11 am-1:30 am daily. $$

AUTHOR'S FAVORITE

Paleo Lounge Bar and Grill (75-5663 Alii Dr, Kona Seaside Mall, ☎ 329-5550). Paleo is our favorite spot in Kailua-Kona for happy hour, but no one else seems to have discovered it yet. The second-story, open-air establishment overlooks Kailua Bay and is filled with ocean breezes and rows of orchids. The stately wooden bar is backed by mirrors, and the staff is friendly and welcoming. *Pupus* are half-price during the three-hour happy hour; dinner is excellent and much more reasonable than the famous waterfront restaurants like Huggo's and Jameson's – good steak, good tofu steak. Another significant attribute of this place is the smoking section. Normally smokers are shunted aside, but here the smoking section, aka "Hookah Lounge," consists of overstuffed reclining chairs next to a bookshelf. Leaning back, you are treated to views of palm trees. Almost wish we were still smokers. Open for lunch 11 am-3 pm, happy hour 3-5 pm, dinner 5-9 pm Mon-Sat. $$$

Jameson's by the Sea (77-6452 Alii Drive, ☎ 329-3195) is one of those restaurants that's been around so long, and is ostensibly a fine-dining restaurant on the water, that many visitors dine there. But the service and food quality has taken a nosedive; locals know to stay away, but plenty of tourists still leave with lighter wallets and a deep sense of disappointment. We hope they get their act back together in the future. Open for lunch 11 am-2:30 pm Mon-Fri, dinner 5-9 pm nightly. $$$$

Ba-Le Kona Restaurant (75-5588 Palani Road, Kona Coast Shopping Center, ☎ 327-1212). Finding this Vietnamese restaurant was a pleasant surprise for us, and we eat here a lot. The veg-head was overjoyed to finally be able to eat "Pho," the noodle soup of Vietnam, because they can make it at Ba-Le with mushroom broth instead of beef marrow broth. There are all sorts of savory noodle dishes here, as well as sandwiches made with the French rolls or fresh baked croissants typical in Vietnam. This is a no-frills establishment without table service or alcohol – just *onoliciousness*. Open 10 am-9 pm Mon-Sat, 11 am-7 pm. $-$$

Wasabi's (75-5803 Alii Dr, ☎ 326-2352). Wasabi's serves respectable Japanese food and tasty sushi for lunch and dinner in the Coconut Grove Marketplace. It's the usual fare with a few special surprises like tempura Maui onion rings. Open 10:30 am-9:30 pm daily. $$

"I generally avoid temptation unless I can't resist it."
– Mae West

Kona Brewing Co. (75-5629 Kuakini Highway, ☎ 334-BREW, www.konabrewingco.com). We visited Kona Brewing Co. in 1995, the year it opened, and asked to take a tour of the microbrewery, the source of one of our favorite beers, Fire Rock Pale Ale. Instead, we were told we could come in and drink free beer with the brewers, who were knocking off work. After a few pints, the sociable fellows did give us a "tour" by pointing at a vat. These days, Kona Brewing Co. has grown into a full-fledged restaurant with award-winning microbrews and awesome pub grub. They even have a satellite location in Honolulu! Their bottled beer is available around the Islands – look at the underside of the bottle cap to learn a Hawaiian word and its English translation.

Terrace at Kona Brewing Co.
(Starbulletin.com, Craig T. Kojima)

The roasted garlic with focaccia and gorgonzola spread or the strawberry spinach salad should let you know this is more than a pub with chili – these folks have style. The pizzas are great – try the wild mushroom, or have it converted into a puffy calzone for an extra $2. You can eat inside or outside on the large lanai. Reservations are a good idea because this place is usually hopping (pun intended). The service could probably use a little tune-up, so order a high octane beer from the bar before you sit down and you won't mind any delays.

Beer lovers will be in heaven. We acquired a taste for hops when we lived in the Pacific Northwest, so the India Pale Ale is our favorite, but lots of locals are faithful to the *liliko`i* (passion fruit) wheat – though they go through spells when they're out of it. Try a sampler and decide which you like best, or take one of the daily tours at 10 am or 3 pm. Open 11 am-9 pm Sun-Thurs (bar till 10 pm), 11 am-10 pm (bar till 11 pm) Fri-Sat. $$

"He was a wise man who invented beer." – Plato

Cassandra's (75-5669 Alii Dr, ☎ 334-1066). If you're craving Greek food, head to Cassandra's. This is Kona's Greek place, with yummy humus and a fantastic dip called kafteri, which is feta, roasted red peppers, garlic and chili peppers blended with olive oil and served with pita. It has all the standards like moussaka, lamb chops, and steaks and seafood. Lunch has the expected sandwiches like gyros. As you enter the second-story restaurant from the stairs, you encounter the pool table in the bar area. This is where karaoke can be pleasant or obnoxious, depending. Open for lunch 11 am-4 pm, dinner 4 pm-close. $$$

GOOD VALUE ★ **Pot Belli Deli** (74-5543 Kaiwi St, ☎ 329-9454), a small, somewhat out-of-the-way deli, gets crammed with local folks on lunch break from businesses in the old industrial area, but it's catching on with tourists too. They serve quick, over-stuffed deli sandwiches for less money than you'll find in tourist quarters. The Classic Reuben is a favorite, with pastrami, sauerkraut and Russian dressing on toasted rye. Others to look for are Mom's Meatloaf Sandwich and the Veggie Burger. They also serve up breakfast sandwiches and burritos before lunch. Open 7:30 am-3 pm Mon-Fri. $-$$

Mahina Pizza (Alii Dr, ☎ 326-1577). This new pizza place, upstairs on Alii next to Taeng On Thai, has a primo location yet inexpensive prices – the house salad is only $3! The pizza is the best on Alii, with a crust that remains mercifully ungreasy and unsoggy. You can order a specialty pizza like the Poi Dog with Italian sausage, pepperoni, mushrooms, black olives, onions and fresh garlic, or build your own, starting with a small (10-inch), large (14-inch) or extra-large (18-inch) – the large cheese is only $10. There are seats along the railing so you can look down on the Strip, or tables where you can enjoy the surfer motif. This is the new location for what was a popular local place near a laundromat, so owner Darcy must be on to something! BYO at the moment (another way to keep your meal cost down), and cash only. Open 11 am-9 pm Mon-Sat. $-$$

Mahina ("mah-HEE-nah") is the Hawaiian word for "moon."

There are several national chain restaurants on Alii, including a Hard Rock Café, Bubba Gump Shrimp Co. and Outback Steakhouse. You know what to expect. Many more options are online at www.bigislandadventureguide.com.

Entertainment

TOP FIVE KONA HAPPY HOUR SPOTS

Paleo . . . . (p. 124)
Harbor House . . . . (p. 193)
Lulu's . . . . (p. 119)
Huggo's on the Rocks. . . . . (p. 118)
Kona Brewing Co. . . . . (p. 125)

Mixx Bistro Bar

Mixx Bistro Bar (King Kamehameha Mall, ☎ 329-7334 www.konawinemarket.com/mixx.shtml). This is currently the "It" bar for singles and other boisterous partiers looking for nightlife. There is entertainment each night on the 150-seat outdoor lanai, such as salsa dancing Thursday nights. The interior bar is air-conditioned and serves 20 wines by the glass, club drinks like mojitos, and tapas. Open daily "lunch to late."

The Dinner Cruise

Captain Bean's Dinner Cruise (☎ 329-2955, www.robertshawaii.com). Captain Bean's is essentially a floating luau, with a sunset dinner and a Polynesian show. The cheese meter rating is high here, so come with the proper attitude – expect silliness and kitsch – and you'll have a blast.

After the captain snaps a photo of your group (available for $20 later), you climb aboard the *Tamure*, a large double hulled "canoe." Entering the boat, it's hard not to notice that the waitstaff consists of young people in traditional Polynesian attire, such as hula dresses for the girls, and *ti* leaf leis around ankles, heads, etc. These are the folks that energetically dance on the sunken tables around which dinner guests are seated, while an emcee modeled after Don Ho sings (yup, "Tiny Bubbles" is one of the first numbers) and narrates the show. He'll rev up the crowd by teaching them to yell "Aloha" at him, or proposing a toast with *Okole maluna* ("Bottoms up"). You may wish that your ticket got you more than one free drink, but there is a cash bar after you've downed your weak mai tai (just fruit juice with a dark rum float).

Hula dancer on the cruise

After dining on garlic bread, salad, teriyaki beef and the sort of rubbery chicken made infamous by wedding receptions, the party really starts cranking – the dancers pull up members of the audience to dance with them on tables to Polynesian classics like "YMCA" and "Car Wash." There are occasionally slow songs for couples, providing the bizarre opportunity to dance on a table alongside one's parents.

The fringe benefit of a cruise with Bean's is that, during the winter, it doubles as a whale-watching cruise. Grab a spot at the rail and you might see numerous whales breaching, tail slapping and spouting. That's the real show!

Captain Bean's Dinner Cruise sails daily except Monday. Tickets are $65.62 (tax incl.), and $37. 50 for kids four-11. A free shuttle to and from the pier is available from most hotels.

At the luau

King Kamehameha's Kona Beach Hotel (☎ 329-2911) offers one of the island's more unusual luaus, with performers portraying Hawaiian royalty arriving at the luau in outrigger canoes. The hotel has such an emphasis on Hawaiian culture and history, evident in its museum-like lobby, that this is one of the more authentic luaus on the Big Island. The luau has the usual staples like an *imu* ceremony, Hawaiian buffet, singing and dancing. It is so popular that it takes place five nights a week on Tues-Fri and on Sunday. Tickets are $65, or $29 for kids five-12.

Royal Kona Resort (☎ 329-3111) hosts a luau called "Lava, Legends and Legacies" each Monday, Wednesday and Friday, including the traditional *imu* ceremony, open bar, all-you-can-eat buffet, and Polynesian revue capped by the requisite fire-twirling. Adults $72 (show only $39), kids six-11 $27, five and under free.

Kona Bowl (75-5591 Palani Rd, ☎ 326-BOWL). If it's raining, or you're just looking for a bit of fun at a bowling alley, head to Kona Bowl! The alley has 24 lanes with automatic scoring, an attached diner and a cocktail lounge with a karaoke machine (if you aren't into karaoke, you can take your drinks back into the bowling area). There's also a small video arcade. Games are usually $4 for adults with a $2.75 shoe rental, but there are specials, such as buy two games, get one free on Tuesdays. Friday and Saturday nights, the "family entertainment center" hosts Cosmic Bowling starting at 9:30 pm Fridays and 8 pm Saturdays, with music and disco lights. (Then you pay by the hour – call ahead to reserve a lane for up to six people.) Open 9 am-10 pm Mon, Wed, Thurs, Sun, 9 am-11 pm Tues, 9 am-12:30 am Fri-Sat.

"One good thing about music, when it hits you, you feel no pain." – Bob Marley

Swing Zone (74-5562 Makala Boulevard, ☎ 334-1211). The only driving range in Kailua-Kona (though a municipal range is in the planning stages) also boasts batting cages, miniature golf, a putting green and six full golf holes. It's an economical place to brush up on your golf game before heading to the Kohala courses and dropping some big coin. Open daily, 8 am-9 pm.

Makalapua Stadium Cinemas shows first-run Hollywood films in the Makalapua Shopping Center at Makala and Queen Ka`ahumanu. Showtimes at ☎ 329-4461.

■ Keauhou

Keauhou is a sleepy tourist enclave a few miles south of downtown Kailua-Kona, accessed via Alii Drive or Queen Ka`ahumanu Hwy. A drive to Keauhou along Alii is worthwhile in and of itself because of the tropical landscaping in front yards and sandy beaches along the way. The Keauhou Pier is a launch area for a number of fabulous boat trips and adventures (see below).

Practicalities

Keauhou Shopping Center

Keauhou Shopping Center is the area's commercial hub, with a **Longs Drug Store** (☎ 322-5122, open 8 am-9 pm Sun-Thurs, until 6 pm Fri-Sat); grocery store **KTA** (☎ 322-2311, open 7 am-10 pm daily); movie theater (**Keauhou Cinemas**, 800-FANDANGO, enter zip code 96740 for movie listings); **post office** (open 9 am-4 pm Mon-Fri, 10 am-3 pm Sat); a natural grocery store and deli called **Kona Natural Foods** (☎ 322-1800, open 9 am-7 pm Mon-Sat, 10 am-5 pm Sun); ATMs; acupuncture services; a hardware store; shops selling clothing, jewelry, flowers and souvenirs; restaurants; and, most importantly, public restrooms.

The **Keauhou Farmers Market** is a good place to find inexpensive fruit, vegetables and tropical flowers grown by local farmers. It takes place 8 am-noon on Saturdays at the corner of the Keauhou Shopping Center near the movie theater.

Keauhou Bay (Hawaiian Images)

Sights

St Peter's Catholic Church

It's hard to pass teeny tiny St Peter's without saying, "Aw, what a cute church!" The little white church with aqua trim is situated right on the water near Kahalu`u Beach Park, a stunning setting that makes it a favorite for weddings. (A minister told us it is the most popular place in Kona with Japanese couples.) There is a Catholic mass here Saturday mornings at 7:30 am.

Kahalu`u Beach Park

Kahalu`u Beach Park (Shorediving.com)

Oh, Kahalu`u. What a heartbreaker. This once fantastic snorkeling spot has been extremely degraded by overuse – though tourist throngs, often delivered straight from cruise ships, still crowd onto the small beach and into the ocean, walking on the reef and bumping into each other. Most *Adventure Guide* readers will find it overcrowded, with at least 50 people in the water even on "slow" days, snorkeling or taking surf lessons (even when there aren't any waves!). There are lots of amenities catering to the masses, such as a life guard, restrooms, snorkel and gear rental, a large picnic pavilion, and showers, and it's a short walk to the **Outrigger's Kalanikai Bar & Grill**, which has burgers, sandwiches and a full bar.

Kahalu`u Beach Park (Hawaiian Images)

It is possible to see some coral if you swim quite a ways from shore, and probably the best snorkeling feature is the oversized fish – the parrotfish here are huge! Still, it is odd to feel claustrophobic in the ocean. Turtles sometimes come into the bay and are quickly surrounded by people, and the poor creatures try to escape. For truly amazing snorkeling, head to protected areas like **kua** (p. 164) or **Place of Refuge** (p. 178). Boat trips to these places leave from the Keauhou Pier (see below).

Place of Refuge (Shorediving.com)

REEF REMINDERS

Since tour operators don't seem inclined to do so at Kahalu`u, and life guards aren't allowed to because it could distract them from saving lives, feel free to help other people learn about reef etiquette, as in not walking on or breaking off coral, touching or feeding fish, and allowing turtles at least 15 feet of space. One resident – actually, Snorkel Bob – wrote to the local paper about a cruise ship passenger at Kahalu`u picking up a turtle and smashing it on a rock. When asked why, the man said, "I've always wanted to do that" and disappeared into the crowd. This kind of behavior is obviously bewildering (and appalling) to local residents. So don't be afraid to clue people in!

Adventures

On Water

"If one way is better than another, that you may be sure is nature's way." – Aristotle

Keauhou Pier is adjacent to the Sheraton, so a lot of people park at the hotel and walk to their boat trip at the pier. There might be a closer spot if you arrive early enough.

Fair Wind (☎ 322-2788, toll free ☎ 800-677-9461, www.fair-wind.com). Fair Wind has been running catamaran snorkel

tours to Kealakekua Bay since 1971. Because they established their mooring just before the area was designated a marine life sanctuary, they are the only large boat that sails into the bay (the boat can accommodate up to 104 people). The crew is good about explaining reef etiquette, and ways to minimize the tour's impact on the pristine reef environment (Rule No. 1: don't touch anything).

This is a great tour for beginning snorkelers, as the crew carefully explains how to use the gear and enter the water. There is also a snorkeling class for first-timers. The boat has two staircases that enter the water for easy access. The crew even provides inner tubes and "view boxes" for non-swimmers. Most importantly, the phenomenal beauty of the coral gardens and fish below – yellow tangs are everywhere! – will make instant snorkeling fanatics out of everyone. As a bonus, there is a fast, 15-foot slide and a high dive platform (watch your bikini top!). Spinner dolphins sometimes surf the waves of the *Fair Wind* as it returns to Keauhou, the icing on the cake.

Yellow tang (*Bryce Groark for Fair Wind*)

The company's main boat, the *Fair Wind II*, sails twice daily. The morning tour ($99 adults, $59 kids) is longer, has a better chance of sunny weather and serves a lunch of burgers and gardenburgers. The afternoon tour ($69 adults, $43 kids) has snacks like fresh fruit and chips. Both cruises have beer, mai tais (tasty ones) and other cocktails available for purchase after the snorkel is done. Snuba

Fair Wind II

upgrades are available for $69. The *Hula Kai*, the company's newer, faster "luxury catamaran," has deluxe tours to two snorkel sites usually near Miloli`i ($139) and offers scuba upgrades. The company also offers whale-watching tours from Dec. 15 to March 15.

Sea Quest (☎ 329-RAFT, www.seaquesthawaii.com). We'd heard from a former travel agent that all her clients loved Sea Quest tours, so we thought we'd check it out when some family members were in town. Turns out, she was right. Essentially, it's a snorkel tour on an inflatable raft to two of the best snorkel spots on the island, Kealakekua Bay and Place of Refuge. But while these sites are accessible on your own, Sea Quest throws in the thrill of exploring sea caves, blow holes and lava tubes. The boats will zip along the water as the surf pounds the lava shoreline, then wait between sets to enter a cave, check out the spray of water erupting through a "blow hole," then head off to another *puka* (hole) to watch the water create a cascading waterfall through an arch. My mom was whooping and squealing like a schoolgirl. Good stuff. The morning tour (four hours, adults $85, kids $72) includes both sites, while the afternoon tour (three hours, adults $64, kids $54) only goes to Kealakekua Bay. There are usually coupons on the Sea Quest website. A similar tour run by Captain Zodiac leaves from Honokohau Harbor (see p. 188).

On a Sea Quest tour

Guaranteed Manta Rays/Sea Paradise (☎ 322-2500, toll free ☎ 800-322-KONA, www.seaparadise.com). You'll see leaflets around Kona promoting a manta ray night dive with a guarantee: see at least one manta ray when you snorkel or dive with Sea Paradise or you can return again for the next

Sea Paradise

seven days until you do. This makes the risk of the splurge for the night dive much easier to rationalize ($79 snorkelers, $89 plus $15 gear rental for divers). Dive groups are limited to six people, though snorkelers can number over 40 (a potential zoo). There's not much of a sail on the 46-foot catamaran *Hokuhele*, since it's less than 10 minutes to motor from Keauhou pier to the mooring off the Sheraton. The crew is friendly, and there's often a half-hour manta ray briefing with videographers Jim or Martina Wing (you can purchase a video or DVD of your underwater encounter from them after the dive – we're proud owners of one). The bar is open after the dive and the tap beer is free, though you can't drink too much in the 10-minute trip back to shore. The company offers daytime snorkel tours to Kealakekua Bay (adults $95, kids under 12 are $59).

On the Links

Kona Country Club (78-7000 Alii Dr, ☎ 322-2595, www.konagolf.com). The two courses here are fun and a good test. The fairways are generally wide, but the greens can be beguiling. There isn't as much lava as you'll find up the coast, but that's not a bad thing. Also, the winds are less intense here than farther north, making it a great option when the winds won't stop howling on the Kohala coast.

Kona Country Club Ocean Course
(Teetimeshawaii.com)

The Ocean Course ($160, $145 after 12 pm) was designed by William Bell and has several holes right on the water, including the 13th, whose tee box is a few yards away from a lava blow hole that usually erupts in the middle of your back swing. The signature holes, No. 3 and No. 12, offer great views of the ocean, where you might spy humpback whales during the winter, and the 17th is a short par 3 over some intimidating lava.

On the Mountain Course
(Teetimeshawaii.com)

The Mountain Course ($145, $125 after 12 pm) is a bit more difficult due to the many elevation changes and side hill lies. It also requires more strategic planning than the lower course, and has several holes where water figures into the equation. The 8th is a gently curving par 4 with an approach shot over a lake, and the 17th is a par 3 over a lava-rimmed lake with a shallow green backed by bunkers. The Mountain Course relies on broad panoramas for its scenic thrills rather than direct oceanfront interaction, which means that it is often less crowded than the Ocean Course.

The full-price greens fees seem high for what you get here, but there are often special deals offered, making it more reasonable. The club also has a very good restaurant, open for breakfast, lunch and dinner.

Where to Stay

See page 65 for an explanation of the $ price codes given for each hotel below.

Outrigger Keauhou Beach Resort (78-6740 Alii Dr, ☎ 322-3441, toll free ☎ 877-KEAUHOU, www.outriggerkeauhoubeach.com, 309 rooms incl. three suites, $209-$449). The best thing the Outrigger Keauhou has going for it is

King bedroom at the Outrigger

its location. It's adjacent to Kahalu`u, the town's "best" snorkel beach; it's close to the Kona Country Club, the town's only golf club; and its location on Alii Drive is relatively close to town but removed from its traffic. Aside from room service, it has most of the amenities you'd expect from a hotel with "resort" in its name, such as a pool, restaurants, bar, tennis courts, exercise room, small spa (no extras with treatments, such as steam rooms or a lounge area), retail shops and large lobby area. Still, it's high-end prices for mid-range accommodation. Rooms are plain and have a TV, mini-fridge, coffee maker, safe, iron and ironing board, and lanai. Wireless Internet is available in the lobby. There is a daily $5 fee for self- or valet parking. $$$-$$$$

Outrigger Keauhou Beach Resort
(Hawaiian Images)

The outrigger canoe, or *wa`a*, is a canoe fitted with at least one stabilizing float – the long "pole" you'll see alongside canoes in Hawaii, called an "outrigger." Polynesian settlers navigated outrigger canoes when they migrated to Hawaii. Outriggers are still used for ocean journeys by the Polynesian Voyaging Society, and in racing.

Sheraton Keauhou Bay Resort and Spa (78-128 Ehukai St, ☎ 930-4900, toll free ☎ 888-488-3535, www.sheraton-keauhou.com, 521 rooms, incl. 10 suites, $325-$2,000, for suites). The former Kona Surf (built in 1972) was vacant for five years until the Sheraton bought the property and gave it a $70 million face lift in 2004. Actually, it was more than a face lift – even the rebar was replaced. The result is a resort

Kona

The pool at Sheraton Keauhou Bay

attempting to compete with the ones in South Kohala. Seventy percent of the hotel looks at the ocean (though there is no beach, a shuttle transports guests to Kahalu`u), and the rooms feature "Sweet Sleeper" beds that are very comfortable, as well as lanais, two phones (one wireless), room service, coffee makers, mini-fridges, full cable for TVs and gaming systems like Nintendo, robes, ironing boards, hair dryers, in-room safes designed to hold laptop computers, and wireless internet access ($10 for 24 hours).

The property has a 24-hour fitness center with a giant window facing the ocean – though treadmills and stairmasters have individual TVs if you need more distraction. There are several restaurants on the property, with live nightly entertainment at the **Crystal Blue Lounge**. Two spotlights near the lounge beam into the surf below to attract plankton and

Sheraton Keauhou Bay (Hawaiian Images)

the manta rays that feed on them – you'll see the glow of divers' flashlights drawn to the area for manta ray night dives. (Three evenings a week speakers from Dolphin Dreams Images, an underwater photography company, give talks here about manta rays.) There is a wedding chapel and a wedding planner, aka "Director of Love," on the property. The pool has a 200-foot slide that is fun for kids and adults – when our family stayed here, we went on the slide so many times that other people followed suit to see what all the whooping was about. Adults who want a break from their kids (or vice versa) can enroll them in the Keiki Club, which has a children's play area with movies, foosball, ping pong, an arts and crafts room and planned activities.

The Sheraton sees a lot of groups come through, thanks to the 10,000-square-foot convention center and lawn area events like a "plumeria drop," when a helicopter dumps a load of plumeria flowers on the people below. There are retail stores, a rental car company, the Ho`oloa Spa with an oceanfront salon, business center services through the concierge, a convenience store with snacks and alcohol (unusual in resorts), and basketball, volleyball and tennis courts. Be sure to check online for packages and significantly discounted rates. $$$$

Where to Eat

"I want a sandwich named after me." – Jon Stewart

Keauhou Shopping Center

Rocky's Pizza and Family Dining (☎ 322-3223) has decent pizza and often frantic service. They also serve hearty pasta dishes like lasagna and eggplant parmesan (both dishes $8.45 à la carte, or $12.45 to include soup or garden salad and doughy focaccia bread), salads, sandwiches and barbecue. Portions are definitely big here. There's a small bar with sports on TV where regulars get pretty sloshed. We found out the hard way that this is a bad place to have your wallet slip out of your pocket; it was returned minus the cash. Open 11 am-9 pm. $$

For an explanation of the restaurant $ price codes, see page 66.

GOOD VALUE ★ **Habaneros** (☎ 324-HOTT) is a locals' favorite, featuring authentic and delicious Mexican fare like burritos, tacos and enchiladas, a fresh salsa bar and great prices. They also serve breakfast (*huevos rancheros*, breakfast burritos) until 11:30 am, and Mexican beer and margaritas. It's a small, festively decorated *taqueria* without table service (you order at the register), and is often packed. They are cash only, but this is supposed to change at some point in the future. We love this place. Open 9 am-9 pm Mon-Sat. $

Drysdale's Two (☎ 322-0070) is a sports bar with lots of neon, big screen TVs, inflatable Bud balloon blimps and the typical greasy grub you tend to expect: burgers, sandwiches, fried calamari, chili, potato skins, fried zucchini and so on. You might have to wait awhile before you see your server. There's a nice big bar here. Officially, they serve food until they close, but we've been hurried out as early as 8:30 pm. Open 11 am-11:30 pm (sometimes earlier if it's slow). $$

Kenichi (☎ 322-6400), with two other locations in Aspen CO and Austin TX, serves sushi and fusion cuisine that's a definite step above the usual fare in Kona. For that reason, they have very positive word of mouth among locals. Aside from delicious, melt-in-your-mouth sushi, Kenichi has intriguing dishes like fresh lobster summer rolls, lemongrass ahi, macadamia-crusted lamb with taro risotto, and pan-roasted mahimahi with eggplant mousse, hearts of palm, asparagus and a miso beurre blanc sauce. Yum! The Wafu Pasta is a "foodgasm" of mushrooms. The restaurant has an Asian-themed, urban loft feel with subtle touches like black paper napkins, and serves sake, beer and wine. Open 11:30 am-1:30 pm Tues-Fri, nightly 5-9 pm. $$$

Entertainment

Outrigger Keauhou Beach Resort (☎ 324-2509) has a new "cultural show and dinner" (technically not a luau, since there's no slow-roasted pig in an *imu*) on Thursdays and Saturdays ($80).

The **Sheraton** (☎ 930-4900) hosts "The Origins Luau," with two tiers of tickets: the "Alii" offers preferred seating by the stage and "family-style" table service, while the "Traditional" does not include an open bar, and guests serve themselves from a buffet. Both include a *lei* greeting, cocktail hour, and a Polynesian show with the standard fire twirling and dancing. Alii tickets cost $79, or $39.50 for kids six-12, children five and under free. Traditional tickets cost $65, or $32.50 for kids six-12.

Holualoa

Perched above Kona at about 1,500 feet, Holualoa seems more than just 10 minutes away from the hustle and bustle of Kailua-Kona. The former sugar town – the only one in Kona – is now a community of artists and coffee farmers that has a pleasant run-down authenticity. The town has lots of funky art galleries, lush tropical surroundings, views of the town and bay below, and the refreshing pace of Old Hawai`i.

Holualoa (*Hawaiian Images*)

To get to Holualoa from Kailua-Kona, turn *makai* onto Hualalai Road between mile markers 120 and 121 on Hwy 11 just south of town. The road climbs through the forest before intersecting with Hwy 180 just south of Holualoa. Turn north (left) to reach Holualoa in about a mile.

The **post office** is open 8:30 am-4 pm Mon-Fri (closed from 11 am-11:45 am), 8:30 am-11 am Sat.

Where to Shop

Holualoa Gallery (76-5921 Mamalahoa Hwy, ☎ 322-8484, www.lovein.com). There's a fun, energetic vibe at Holualoa Gallery, which sells whimsical paintings, glass sculpture, silver jewelry, photography, prints, cards and other art by owner/artists Matt and Mary Lovein and other Big Island artists. It's hard not to like Mary Lovein's *Why is this woman smiling?* – a painting of the Mona Lisa with a vibrant Jackson's chameleon on her arm (Lovein has extensively photographed the chameleon and is working with publishers on a book about them.) Open 10 am-5 pm Tues-Sat.

Ipu Hale Gallery (76-5893 Mamalahoa Hwy, ☎ 322-9069). This gallery has a selection of decorative gourds created using ancient techniques from Ni`ihau, the privately owned island near Kaua`i. Co-owner/artist Michael Harburg is passionate about the art form and can demonstrate how gourds are designed by using coffee or other dyes to create the unusual art. The store also sells Asian beaded jewelry crafted by local artists. Open 10 am-4 pm Tues-Sat.

"Art does not reproduce what we see; rather, it makes us see."
– Paul Klee

AUTHOR'S CHOICE ★ **Kimura Lauhala Shop** (Mamalahoa Hwy, ☎ 324-0053). Want a taste of Old Hawaii? Visit Kimura Lauhala Shop, which has been run by the Kimura family since Grandfather Yoshimatsu Kimura built it in 1914. He and his wife originally opened it as a general store, and ladies in the early 1900s traded their handmade *lauhala* hats – woven hats made with *hala* leaves – for merchandise. The hats became a hit with local plantation workers. The store has stayed in the family for "almost five" generations, and now Tsuruyo Kimura talks story with friends or sings and hums while visitors browse not only goods made from *lauhala*, such as placemats, tissue box covers, beverage holders and, of course, hats, but *koa* wine stoppers, hair clips shaped like whales, Hawaiian hardwood bracelets, carved canes and other made-in-Hawaii souvenirs. She might even offer you a chocolate-covered coffee bean from her private stash! Open 9 am-5 pm Mon-Fri, until 4 pm Sat.

Kimura Lauhala Shop

Holualoa Ukulele Gallery (photo by KarlJ)

Holualoa Ukulele Gallery (Mamalahoa Hwy, ☎ 324-4100) is in the old post office. Gallery owner Sam Rosen sells his handcrafted instruments, works as a goldsmith, and will discuss the history of Holualoa with anyone who's interested. There's an interesting display in the front of his store with old pictures of the Holualoa community taken around 1900. Open 10:30 am-4:30 pm Tues-Fri, noon-4:30 pm Sat.

Studio 7 Gallery (Mamalahoa Hwy, ☎ 324-1335) feels more like a museum than a gallery because of the high quality of the contemporary art it showcases, such as woodcut prints; a shoe constructed of dollar bills, dimes, a bullet, canvas and leather; and sculptures reminiscent of installation exhibits. The gallery feels like walking through an installation, actually, as the floors of some rooms consist of lava gravel, with wooden steps creating a path for visitors. This is a gallery of serious art, a change from the broader appeal of "tourist art" found throughout Hawaii (though we like plenty of that, too!). One way or another, Studio 7 is a must for art aficionados. Open 11 am-5 pm Tues-Sat, though best to call first.

Kona

Dovetail Gallery (76-5942 Mamalahoa Hwy, ☎ 322-4046) has an eclectic selection of high-end wood products, glass art, paintings, jewelry and bags. Items are thoughtfully arranged in a small but interesting space. There's a phenomenal view over Kailua-Kona from the lanai in the back, providing an excellent reason to stop by and browse. Open 10 am-4 pm Tues-Sat.

AUTHOR'S CHOICE ★ **Shelly Maudsley White Gallery** (76-5894 Mamalahoa Hwy, ☎ 322-5220, www.shellymaudsleywhite.com). You have to appreciate galleries that go out of their way to make you feel comfortable while you're on a gallery crawl. The Shelly Maudsley White Gallery offers cushy couches and overstuffed chairs to rest your tired feet while you admire Shelly's bright, vivid art. Her mixed-media images and paintings are inspired by Hawaiian subject matter, including colorful banana flowers, Kona coast houses nestled in verdant jungle and *honu* (sea turtles) basking in the sun. Her tropical fish series is visually stunning and amusingly conceived, with names like *Much Humu About Nothing* and *Pride and Pufferfish*. The gallery

Oh No!!

offers originals, lithographs and giclée, which is a high-end ink jet printing process. Much of the work is framed in highly polished *koa* wood frames. The gallery director is friendly, the amenities are plush, and the art is sure to bring a smile to your face. Open 10 am-5 pm Tues-Sat.

Coconuts

Paul's Place (76-9524 Mamalahoa Hwy, ☎ 324-4702). What appears to be a run-of-the-mill Hawaiian general store is actually a repository for fine spirits! Paul's Place has a surprising selection of single-malt scotches, tequilas, rums and top-shelf vodkas. Their wine selection isn't too bad either, and it breaks up the string of art galleries nicely. Another plus: the community bulletin board outside is a great place to find out the local haps. Open daily 8 am-8 pm.

"When you take a flower in your hand and really look at it, it's your world for the moment." – Georgia O'Keefe

Esther Shimazu teaches sculpture at Donkey Mill Art Center

Donkey Mill Art Center (78-6670 Mamalahoa Hwy, ☎ 322-3362, www.donkeymillart-center.org) is the studio for the Holualoa Foundation for Arts and Culture, which seeks to encourage art education for people of all skills and ages. Donkey Mill began as a coffee farmers' co-op in the 1940s, but these days offers workshops and classes in a variety of traditions; watercolor painting, *lauhala* weaving, ceramics, yoga and `ukulele and slack key guitar for beginners illustrate the range of offerings. There is usually an art exhibit open to the public. Open 10 am-4 pm Tues-Sat.

Where to Stay

Holualoa Inn B&B (☎ 324-1121, toll free ☎ 800-392-1812, www.holualoainn.com, six rooms, $245-$290). Based on the price, you'd expect the Holualoa Inn to be exceptional – and it is.

Lounge

Though the sweeping views of Kailua-Kona could probably justify the price, this B&B also has a touch of elegance, with gleaming eucalyptus floors and lush grounds – the driveway is lined with torch ginger and palms, the pool with plumeria trees. Furniture from Bali and Thailand gives the common areas a sense of tropical luxury, and each room has a king-size bed. The big hot tub in the garden, the cushy lounge area and the telescope in the "tower" are a few of the accents that make this a highly acclaimed accommodation. The lavish breakfast includes treats like *liliko`i* butter over German cheese. The only TV is in the family room, a common area with books, games and a DVD and video collection near the grill, microwave, and refrigerator, all of which are available to guests. There are three Wi-Fi access points as well. $$$$

The Balinese Suite

See page 65 for an explanation of the $ price codes given for hotels.

Where to Eat

Holuakoa Café (Mamalahoa Hwy, ☎ 322-2233). The only food in town is served in this small, unassuming café. They have both indoor and outdoor tables and serve a few basic sandwiches and wraps, such as roast turkey, cheddar and avocado, as well as a variety of sweets. Due to their location in the heart of Kona coffee country, they also serve fantastic coffee. They have an array of unique gifts for sale inside, including locally-made candles and jewelry. A new, full-service restaurant next door is slated to open at some point in the future. Open 6:30 am-3 pm Mon-Fri. $-$$

For an explanation of the restaurant $ price codes, see page 66.

The South Kona Coast *(Vlad Turchenko, Dreamstime.com)*

South Kona

South Kona may not be far from Kailua-Kona, but it has a rhythm and pace that's far slower than its bustling neighbor to the north. It is also far more verdant than North Kona, largely due to the rich volcanic soil and the dependable mix of morning sun and afternoon rain. There has also been an absence of recent large-scale lava flows, which has allowed the vegetation to grow abundantly. The Kona coffee belt runs through this area, thriving on the slopes of Hualalai and Mauna Loa. You'll notice the signs for farms and smell the slightly acrid scent of roasting coffee in the air.

Highway 11, the Mamalahoa Highway, runs straight north and south through the area. It passes through a series of small settlements that are close together and don't really have much in the way of distinguishing characteristics. From north to south they are: Honalo, Kainaliu, Kealakekua, Cap-

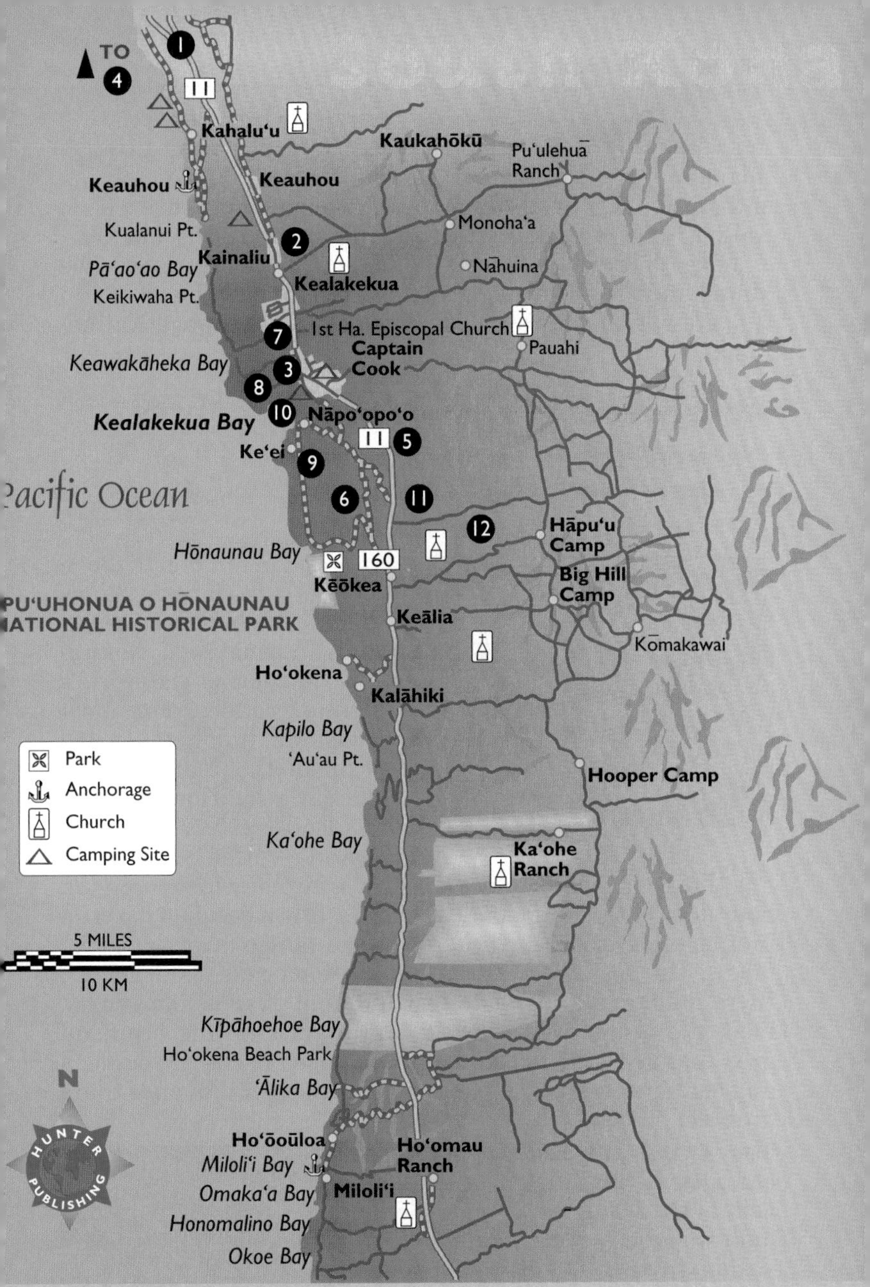

1. Kona Blue Sky Coffee
2. Kona Joe
3. Greenwell Farms
4. Ueshima Coffee Company
5. Royal Kona Coffee
6. Bay View Farms
7. The Kona Coffee Living History Farm
8. Nāpo'opo'o Wharf
9. Manini Beach
10. Captain Cook Monument Trailhead
11. Honaunau
12. The Painted Church

tain Cook and Honaunau. It is best to avoid going through this area during rush hour, especially north in the morning and south in the evening, as it can take an hour to drive from Kailua-Kona to Captain Cook during the evening commute – a drive that would normally take only 20 minutes. The Mamalahoa Highway continues north along Highway 180 in Honalo when Highway 11 diverts northwest toward Kailua-Kona.

Adventures in Kona Coffee Country

"Kona coffee has a richer flavor than any other, be it grown where it may and call it by what name you please."
– Mark Twain

Kona coffee cherries

You don't have to be a snooty barista to know that Kona coffee enjoys an international reputation as one of the world's finest coffees. For most visitors, it only takes one sip of the real thing to know why. However, few know exactly what makes Kona coffee so special. For those who want to dedicate an entire day (or merely an hour or two) to finding out, what follows is a detailed description of some of our favorite (and one not-so-favorite) coffee farms. The best way to get a feel for Kona coffee is to get out there and sample it, taste-test different grades and roasts, meet the people who grow it, and experience the beautiful area that gives life to these highly praised beans. If you need any more incentive, keep in mind that most of the coffee tours are free.

The size of the Kona coffee belt changes depending on who you ask, but it's roughly 20 miles long and two miles wide, ranging in elevation from 1,000 to 2,500 feet. Excellent Kona coffee can be grown around the margins, at higher or lower elevations, or a few miles north or south, but if you venture too far away it is no longer Kona coffee. We met a guy on the island who grows coffee in Ocean View, around the southern tip of the island in the district of Ka`u, who told us he goes to Lake Tahoe every summer and sells his beans as "Kona coffee" for $25 a pound!

Visiting Kona coffee farms, you will learn that there's nothing mysterious about the "secret" to Kona coffee: rich volcanic soil, a mix of morning sun and evening cloud cover, ample precipitation, proper elevation and a high quality *arabica* coffee plant. All of these elements result in a cup that is most often described as "smooth" and "balanced" with a low to medium acidity, which, to the layperson, means it's downright drinkable.

WARNING: 10% KONA COFFEE

Much of the less expensive coffee you'll see for sale in discount stores is actually a 10% "blend," meaning only 10% of the coffee is from Kona, and the rest is low-grade filler, usually from a much inferior coffee growing region, like Brazil. There is little value to this method. It is like adding a few drops of Château Rothschild to a bottle of Ripple and marketing it as a gourmet wine blend. If you want the real deal, be sure that the label says "100% Kona Coffee."

Kona Blue Sky Coffee (Holualoa, ☎ 322-1700, toll free ☎ 877-322-1700, www.konablueskycoffee.com) is the brand name of the coffee grown on the Twigg-Smith estate, a 500-acre spread that ranks as the third-largest coffee farm in Kona. The visitor center is staffed by friendly workers who gladly steep visitors in information. They offer their finest grades of coffee for tasting and provide a brief, fun walking tour that includes a short ramble through some coffee and fruit trees, a demonstration of how coffee cherry is harvested, a peek at the roasting room, and a seven-minute orientation video. Unlike many other producers, Kona Blue Sky Coffee applies both a medium and dark roast to each grade of coffee, which is then clearly marked on the bags for sale in the gift shop. This makes selecting your preferred combination of grade and roast a snap.

The Twigg-Smith estate coffee orchards lie between 1,400 and 3,500 feet. Their Estate Reserve, composed entirely of Extra Fancy grade beans, is competitively priced at $26 per pound.

The **Kona Blue Sky Coffee Visitor Center** is just south of Holualoa on Hwy 182 near the intersection with Hwy 180. Tours are offered 9 am-3:30 pm Mon-Sat.

FYI: GRADES OF BEANS

Kona coffee beans are graded on their size and density, which affect the taste of the bean. The top two grades are the most desirable for regular coffee, while the lower grades are most often used for decaf and flavored coffees. From best to still-good-but-not-the-best, the grades of coffee are: Kona Extra Fancy, Kona Fancy, Kona Number One, and Kona Prime.

To complicate things, there's the wild-card, Peaberry. While standard coffee cherries contain two seeds, approximately 5% of coffee cherries produce a single, round seed, called Peaberry, which some believe has a better flavor than standard beans. Kona Peaberry is separated into two grades: the higher quality is Kona Number One Peaberry and the lower quality is Kona Peaberry Prime.

Kona Joe (79-7346 Mamalahoa Hwy, Kainaliu, ☎ 322-2100, toll free ☎ 866-KONA-JOE, www.konajoe.com). With an array of shady couches and a rough-hewn plank bar overlooking the kind of mountain-to-sea view that will make you swoon, Kona Joe offers a stylish and relaxing place to put on a hard-core caffeine buzz. The modern headquarters of this budding Kona coffee empire allows visitors to observe the milling and roasting processes, all performed by shiny, clean machines, while they suck down gourmet shot drinks from the espresso bar and pile up a hefty credit card bill investing in t-shirts, chocolate-covered java beans, and, of course, coffee.

While most Kona coffee farms don't provide anywhere near the level of amenities that Kona Joe does, it's their coffee production technique that truly sets them apart. Kona Joe proprietor Joe Alban has pioneered a revolutionary system in which he "opens" the coffee trees along wire trellises and "trains" them to grow along the trellises through a tireless pruning regimen, in much the same way wine grapes are produced. This process achieves more consistent sun exposure and a more even ripening of the beans, resulting in a 35% higher yield and a sweeter, more intense flavor.

Mature, unroasted beans (cherries)

Kona Joe maintains 20 acres of coffee growing at 1,000 to 1,400 feet elevation in Kainaliu, the heart of Kona coffee country. Free tours are available Monday through Friday at 10 am, 12, 2 and 4 pm **A pound of their "Trellis Reserve," a blend of extra-fancy and fancy grade beans, will run you $38, the priciest beans to be found in the region.**

Kona Joe is at the northern edge of the town of Kainaliu. Turn *makai* between the **113 and 114** mile markers on Hwy 11. Open 9 am-5 pm Mon-Fri

Kona

WHY IS KONA COFFEE SO EXPENSIVE?

The answer is simple: everything is expensive in Hawaii (and it's so good, of course). From gas to real estate to food and basic necessities, everyone who lives in Hawaii pays higher prices than people on the mainland, and this is reflected in the prices of their products. Few of the 600 coffee farmers in Kona are getting rich, and most are just barely getting by, operating their farms as a labor of love rather than a get-rich venture.

Greenwell Farms (81-6581 Mamalahoa Hwy, Kealakekua, ☎ 323-2275, toll free ☎ 888-592-5662, www.greenwellfarms.com). One of the largest coffee producers in the area, the Greenwells trace their lineage back to Henry Greenwell, who in the mid-1800s was responsible for making Kona coffee internationally famous, when his coffee was officially recognized at the Kaiser's Exposition during the 1873 World's Fair in Vienna, Austria. The fourth generation of Greenwells continues that tradition today. Their farm and processing facili-

Coffee flowers, called snow

ties are adjacent to the homestead and general store that Henry Greenwell opened in 1875, which is now the site of the Kona Historical Society Museum. The Greenwells provide a pleasant, open-air tasting and retail area located above their orchard. They keep 10 piping-hot coffees out for tasting, which runs the entire spectrum of their products from their Private Reserve and Peaberry, all the way down to their chocolate macadamia nut. It's easy to drop a lot of time here taste-testing the various beans against each other, despite the fact that they use styrofoam cups, which not only adversely affect health and the environment, but also pass on a strange taste and smell to the coffee that slightly sullies the flavor. A free 20-minute tour departs regularly, encompassing a small orchard of 100-year-old coffee trees and the coffee processing facility. The knowledgeable tour guides should be able to answer any coffee-related question you can muster, and will likely brag that their experienced pickers can each harvest 500-700 pounds per day. Considering that most professional pickers clear 100 pounds per day, that is an impressive amount.

Coffee farm

Greenwell Farms is made up of a total of 200 acres, with over 25,000 coffee trees that lie between 1,000 and 1,700 feet elevation. The Greenwell Estate Reserve is made from Extra Fancy grade beans, is roasted to Full City (a medium dark roast), and currently runs at $30 per pound.

Greenwell Farms is at the northern edge of Kealakekua, *makai* between mile markers 111 and 112. They're open 8 am-5 pm Mon-Sat.

DID YOU KNOW? COFFEE ROASTING

Roasting

The goal of coffee roasting is to coax the ideal flavor from the bean, while leaving some room for the subjective taste of the consumer. The lighter the roast, the more of the beans' inherent characteristics remain. For this reason, most top-grade Kona coffee beans are roasted in the medium range, while lower-grade beans are roasted darker, which imparts more intensity and bite to the final product. From lightest to darkest, roasts range as follows: Cinnamon, American, Medium, Full City, French, Espresso and Italian.

Contrary to commonly-held perceptions, the darker the roast, the less caffeine remains in the bean. Specifically, there are about 75 mg of caffeine in a shot of espresso (one of the darkest roasts), versus 225 mg of caffeine in an 8 oz cup of light roast drip coffee. Think of the money you'll save eschewing a quad-shot latte for the grande drip during your next Starbucks run!

Ueshima (UCC) Coffee Company (82-5810 Napoopoo Rd, Captain Cook, ☎ 328-5662, toll free ☎ 888-822-5662, www.ucc-hawaii.com). This Japanese mega-giant (recognized in Japan by its motto "Good Coffee Smile") has owned and operated its own Kona coffee farm and processing facility since 1989. The main thing it has going for it is the prime location of its visitor center on Napoopoo Road, on the way to

Kealakekua Bay. The word from a former employee is that they ship *all* of their Extra Fancy grade beans back to Japan, which means the coffee they sell on the island is inferior to that of other farms. But their unique offering is the Roastmaster Tour. Now, to be honest, it's a little on the pricey side, and seems mainly to be targeted to the Japanese tourists who recognize the brand from home, but it really is jolly good fun.

You'll receive eight ounces of green Fancy grade coffee beans, endure a tortured English/Japanese orientation on the basic theory of roasting, and then are closely guided as you dump your beans into the small-batch, propane-fueled roaster. Coffee beans can go through a total of two "pops," a time when the beans begin to ping like popcorn against the roaster, the first of which indicates the beginning of the acceptable roast zone. A second pop occurs right around the Espresso roast level, at which time the beans are really too burned to be enjoyed as a brewed cup. The target level is somewhere in between, with a good standard for higher grade Kona beans being a Medium to Full City roast. You'll receive a wooden spoon to insert into your roaster to pull out a few beans and evaluate the progress of your roast. When you are ready, and the coach begins gesturing wildly, it's time to dump your beans into a screen box and transfer them to a cooling fan to stop the roast. To add kitsch to the experience, you'll be provided with a couple of coffee bags and personalized labels with your photo and name digitally printed on them.

Roastmaster Tours cost $30 and take place several times daily. Reservations are required. Ueshima Coffee Co. is close to the eight-mile marker on Napoopoo Road in lower Captain Cook.

Did you know? Coffee is the second-most traded commodity in the world, trailing only oil.

The Kona Coffee Living History Farm (Captain Cook, ☎ 323-2006, www.konahistorical.org/tours/coffeefarm.shtml). First homesteaded in 1900, this working coffee farm provides a fascinating peek into the lives of a typical immigrant family whose days revolved around the production of Kona coffee. This tour is an interesting supplement to a day of touring coffee farms, as it provides some historical context for the region and culture of Kona coffee.

The Japanese were the second wave of immigrant coffee pickers (following the Chinese) brought in by the owners to work their land. Eventually, some of these workers were allowed to homestead and toil for their own profit, though they often didn't own the land they were working. One of these families was the Uchida family, whose seven-acre farm is the subject of the tour and is composed of coffee, macadamia and papaya trees, as well as vegetable gardens, the homestead, and the coffee mill.

If you have already been to some other farms and seen enough of the processing mills to understand the milling process, then you can't help but find the nearly hundred-year-old mill on the property absolutely captivating. It performs all of the functions that today's equipment does, but with a series of belts run by a three-horse-power, one-cylinder gas engine of the vintage that has great nicknames like "one-lunger," "donkey engine," and "hit-and-miss." Once the beans are processed, they are laid out on the adjacent Hoshidano, a long deck with a retractable roof that can be rolled over the beans when it rains. During harvest season, visitors have a chance to see the harvesting and drying process, and may even strap on a picking basket and see just how difficult it is to fill one.

The Uchida's home is equally interesting, and has been restored to its early 1900s appearance. Many family belongings remain, which gives authenticity to the home tour. Knowledgeable docents point out fascinating details like the empty sardine cans that were filled with kerosene and placed under each leg of the table in the pantry to keep ants out of the food. There's a Japanese bathhouse out back with a wood-fired hot tub.

Kids will enjoy the two "Kona nightingales" on the property, donkeys whose ancestors were once used to transport coffee beans before the advent of the Jeep. Tours can be specifically skewed to the *keiki* (children) by teaching traditional Japanese games, or involving a hands-on demonstration in which kids can wash clothes "the old fashioned way."

Like all good coffee tours in the area, there are free samples of the product available. They offer medium and dark roasts for their collection of Extra Fancy and Fancy grades. The price is very reasonable at $22 per pound.

The Kona Coffee Living History Farm is just north of Captain Cook. Turn *makai* at the sign slightly north of mile marker 110 on Hwy 11. The hour-long tours cost $15 and leave on the hour between 9 am and 1 pm, Monday through Friday.

STEPS IN COFFEE PROCESSING

Milling – This strips the fruit membrane off of the coffee "cherry."

Fermentation – The stripped beans are dumped into a water tank to soak out the sugars that, if left intact, would cause rotting.

Drying – Most coffee processors in Kona use the Hoshidana drying process in which the beans are sun-dried on a flat surface, such as a roof.

Parchment – In this step, the paper-like parchment layer is milled off of the beans, leaving the "green" bean.

Grading – A vibration table is used to sort the beans through holes into their specific grades.

Shipping – At this point, 95% of Kona beans are shipped out, still in their "green" phase, to be roasted by the purchasing company.

Roasting – Roasting still takes place in many processing facilities in Kona to sell retail on the island or online.

Did you know? A single coffee tree provides enough coffee each season for about 50 cups of brewed coffee.

Bay View Farms (Painted Church Rd, Honaunau, ☎ 328-9658, toll free ☎ 800-662-5880, www.bayviewfarmcoffees.com) consistently produces one of the most highly rated cups on the island. The 30-acre estate sits at about 850 feet, a rather low elevation for coffee production, but that doesn't seem to affect the quality. They specialize in Extra Fancy and Peaberry grade beans, and have quickly made a name for themselves in the tight Kona coffee market. A breezy little veranda serves as their retail outlet and tasting room, with a stunning view over Kealakekua Bay. Their staff is friendly and they love to chat about coffee. They offer a free tour of their facilities, which will take you through the entire process, from growing to milling to roasting and packaging.

One of the most laudable aspects of Bay View Farms is that they are the only farm on the island that decaffeinates their own coffee. Most other farmers must outsource their beans to British Colombia, where the coffee is Swiss Water Processed, a procedure in which the beans are immersed in water and the caffeine is soaked out of them. Bay View uses the more expensive CO^2 method of decaffeination, in which the beans are exposed to a carbon dioxide/water mix and subjected to high temperature and pressure. The process is chemical-free and retains more flavor than in Swiss Water Processing or solvent extraction.

A pound of Bay View Extra Fancy grade beans runs $22 for a medium or dark roast, while their prized Peaberry is a little more, but still very reasonably priced at $26. Bay View Farms is on Painted Church Road, just a half-mile north of the Painted Church. Look *makai* for the gazebo.

Ke kope ho`ohia`a maka o Kona. "The coffee of Kona keeps the eyes from sleeping." – Hawaiian saying

■ Honalo

Honalo is the first of a series of small settlements running south along Mamalahoa Highway (Hwy 11). As mentioned above, it can be a challenge to determine where one ends and the next begins.

The Shell gas station in Honalo, next to Teshima's, is open 24 hours.

Where to Eat

Teshima Restaurant (79-7251 Mamalahoa Hwy, ☎ 322-9140), run by "Mama" Teshima since the 1940s, is a local favorite for authentic Japanese food. It's a brightly lit, casual restaurant with excellent value; most meals include miso soup, rice, tsukemono (salted and pressed cabbage), sunomono (flavored cucumbers) and hot tea. Hot sake, beer and cocktails are also available, as well as sandwiches for less adventurous eaters. The tempura here is fantastic. Teshima's doesn't accept credit cards, but there is an ATM machine in the doorway. Open for breakfast 6:30 am-11 am, lunch 11 am-1:45 pm, and dinner 5-9 pm daily. $$

■ Kainaliu

"Let us be grateful to people who make us happy; they are the charming gardeners who make our souls blossom."
– Marcel Proust

Kainaliu (*Hawaiian Images*)

Where to Shop

Keoki's Surfin' Ass Coffee (79-7411 Mamalahoa Hwy, ☎ 324-7733, toll free ☎ 800-416-7770). While the coffee's not out of this world, they do provide a full spectrum of roasts to fit your taste. They used to roast right on the premises, but something popped and they've been forced to cook 'em elsewhere. What they really have going for themselves are the addicting, and imminently marketable, Donkey Balls. They make these chocolate covered macadamia nuts right in the store, and explore an array of bawdy iterations, such as Salty Balls (mac nuts covered with milk chocolate and dusted with sea salt) or Dingle Berries (milk chocolate-covered strawberries). These make for great gifts, provided you can get them home without finishing them off on the plane. Open 7 am-7 pm Mon-Sat, until 6 pm Sun.

Conscious Riddems (79-7430 Mamalahoa Hwy, Kainaliu Center, ☎ 322-2628). Our DJ friends love this place. It's a reggae store with vinyl records and turntables, hemp clothes and bags, t-shirts that urge "Listen to Bob Marley," roots and dancehall CDs, glass, and incense. Open 10 am-5 pm Mon-Sat.

Where to Eat

"If you are ever at a loss to support a flagging conversation, introduce the subject of eating." – James Henry Leigh Hunt

Evie's Organic Café (79-7460 Mamalahoa Hwy, ☎ 322-0739) is a small natural food grocery store with a deli on the back lanai that serves healthy food (often vegan), such as fish tacos, spelt crust pizzas, fake "riblet" sandwiches, veggie soups, egg or tofu scrambles, waffles, "fakin' bacon" and organic smoothies. The views of the greenery leading to the ocean are wonderful. Open for breakfast 9-11:30 am, lunch 11:30 am-7 pm daily. $-$$

For an explanation of the restaurant $ price codes, see page 66.

AUTHOR'S CHOICE ★ **Aloha Angel Café and Aloha Theatre** (79-7384 Mamalahoa Hwy, café ☎ 322-3383, box office ☎ 322-2122, www.alohatheatre.com) combines food and entertainment in a gorgeous setting. It's a great place for a scrumptious breakfast out on the lanai that overlooks a gigantic avocado tree. (If there are just two in your party, try for the table at the end overlooking the ocean.) It's a relaxed place that also serves homemade baked goods like ginger snaps and mac-nut turtles. Omelettes cost about $10, and veggie sausage is available, or you can add tofu for $1. One complaint about breakfast: despite the fact that they're in the heart of Kona coffee country, their drip coffee is Yuban. Stick with their espresso drinks, which use 100% Kona coffee.

Lunch overlaps with breakfast and dinner, so you can tailor your meal to your appetite, a nice touch. Lunch includes sandwiches, wraps, burgers and salads, and you can add chicken, tofu or fresh fish to several items. Dinner entrées are fancier, such as the taro crusted fresh catch with lemon caper beurre blanc. The big secret is the bar in the dining room, probably the best place to grab a happy hour cocktail in South Kona.

Aloha Theatre and Café

The **Aloha Theatre** shares the building; it screens movies and hosts concerts, plays and other

Kona

special events, like *kapuna* (elders) describing life in Old Kona. It's one-stop-shopping for a perfect date of dinner and a movie (or theater). Generally open for breakfast and lunch 7:30 am-2:30 pm, lunch and dinner 2:30-8 pm, dinner till 9 pm on event nights. $$-$$$

Ke`ei Café (75-7511 Mamalahoa Hwy, ☎ 322-9992) grew from good local word of mouth, which was based on its food and nothing else. The new location is even better, an open-air room with ceiling fans, earth-tone painted walls adorned with Hawaiian art, wood tables that are tablecloth-free, and a bar cut from a tree trunk, with some rough edges left so the wood can speak for itself. It's moderately priced for the quality of the food. Starters include salads, black bean soup, and eggplant rolled around couscous. Entrées range from the fresh catch of the day done in various ways (can also be made with tofu), pastas, fajitas and steaks – the chef certainly doesn't feel limited to one genre. Ke`ei Café doesn't accept credit cards, so be sure to hit an ATM before you come. It's south of mile marker 113 on the Mamalahoa Highway. Open for lunch 10:30 am-2 pm Mon-Fri, dinner 5-9 pm Tues-Sat. $$$

Kealakekua Bay (Vlad Turchenko, Dreamstime.com)

Kealakekua

Where to Shop

Discovery Antiques and Ice Cream (Mamalahoa Hwy, ☎ 323-2239) is a quirky, somewhat claustrophobic antique store with great old gas pumps outside, and delicious Tropical Dreams ice cream inside. The store is crammed with old bottles, jewelry, dishes and the usual antique fare. Open 11:30 am-5 pm Tues-Fri.

DID YOU KNOW? KONA HERITAGE STORES

South Kona is home to a number of Kona Heritage Stores, general merchandise stores that have been open for over 50 years. Many of them have stayed within the families that started them, and survived by accepting trade as payment, such as *lauhala* hats or Kona coffee, for which Honolulu merchants would trade. Though some are on the weathered side, these mom-and-pops add to the charm of the area.

Kealakekua's Grass Shack (Mamalahoa Hwy, ☎ 323-2877). Wanna get back to that little grass shack in Kealakekua, Hawaii? You can hit this Kona Heritage Store that opened in 1930. It has souvenirs like *lauhala* hats, *koa* bowls (but not the high-end ones), jewelry, and oddities like a Wedgewood dish with the bust of Captain Cook. It's famous for being famous. Open 10 am-4:30 pm Mon-Sat.

Adventures Underwater

"Life loves the liver of it." – Maya Angelou

South Kona Scuba (79-7539 Mamalahoa Hwy, ☎ 322-5012). Owner Tim Folden touts himself as one of the only Hawaiian dive shop owners on the Big Island, at least the only one with an actual shop. Sharing space with Kona Boys in Captain Cook, Tim offers shore dives with local style. As he says, "I'm a fun guy but I'm a safe guy." He rents and sells dive gear, teaches certification classes, and leads mainly shore dives at $100 for a two-tank dive. Divers who are feeling rusty can come for an update here. Open 7:30 am-5 pm "usually."

Relaxation

The Hawaiian Islands School of Massage (81-6587 Mamalahoa Hwy, Pualani Terrace, ☎ 323-3800, www.hawaiianmassageschool.com) is the place to come for affordable spa treatments, like an hour of *lomi lomi* massage for only $60, aromatherapy treatment for $65, and body wraps for $85. But if you still have trouble pampering yourself, keep this in mind: Student massages here are only $30! Call ahead to schedule an appointment.

Where to Stay

Pineapple Park (81-6363 Mamalahoa Hwy, toll free ☎ 877-800-3800, www.pineapple-park.com, 12 rooms incl. 18 dorm beds, private rooms $65-$85 or $25 dorm beds). This is where we lived when we first moved to the Big Island, having rented kayaks here while on vacation earlier that year and noticing (and remembering) that they were also a hostel. Pineapple Park is owned by Doc Holliday and Annie Park, who, as Doc lovingly says, "rules the place with an iron fist." She has a soft side too, usually shown to people who pay their rent on time, and was kind enough to let us list her on our apartment application as a local resident who would vouch for us. Rooms are very basic, essentially a box with a bed, table and, mercifully, an air conditioner. The common areas are more comfortable, with book swaps, TVs, and couches. The second-story lanai has distant ocean views, a terrific place to watch the sunset. The lower level has a share kitchen, bathrooms, coin-op laundry machines and a covered area for smokers. Guests are usually backpackers and people moving to the island, so you'll meet an interesting mix of people. There are discounted rates after a week. $

Bedroom at Pineapple Park

Where to Eat

Nasturtium Café (79-7491 Mamalahoa Hwy, Kealakekua, ☎ 322-5083, www.nasturtiumcafe.com) is a vegetarian-friendly café with a focus on healthy food, serving dishes like eggplant and hummus wraps, roasted red pepper soup, and tempeh reubens, plus free range, hormone-free buffalo, turkey and ostrich dishes. The lemongrass iced tea is unusual and delicious. The ambiance is inviting, as the former mechanic's shop is brightened by purple and red paint, colorful art, and stained glass window hangings. BYO without a corkage fee. They also have a booth at the Alii Gardens Marketplace. Open 11 am-7:30 pm Tues-Fri. $$

Nasturtium Café

Uncle Inbea's Steakhouse (Mamalahoa Hwy, ☎ 323-2595). With an unassuming atmosphere and local-style friendliness, this place can give you a red meat heart attack the old fashioned way: with arteriosclerosis, rather than a $55 price tag on an 8 oz filet. All your old friends are here: New York strip, rib eye, T-bone, prime rib, and even a 10 oz filet mignon for under $20. With a supporting cast of pork, chicken and seafood for the less hell-bound in your group, this is a solid place on Kona's south side. You'll have to bring in your own wine, but you can pick it up from the convenience mart right next door. Uncle Inbea's is *mauka* just south of mile marker 111 on Hwy 11 in Kealakekua. Open for lunch 11 am-3 pm Mon-Fri, and for dinner 3-9 pm Mon-Sat. $$

Chris' Bakery (81-6598 Mamalahoa Hwy, ☎ 323-3717). West-side locals agree: *the* place for malasadas in Kona is Chris'. It will only take a quick stop for you to feel the same way. There aren't any tables, bells or whistles, but in one bite you'll know why we've directed you here. The malasadas, or Portuguese donuts, are light, airy and glistening with granulated sugar. They seem to know the secret to leaving the grease in the pot. They also have an array of doughnuts and other tasties, such as cream-filled "Long Johns." This is a cheap place to pack on the calories, with a malasada and a cup of joe for $1. Open 6 am-3 pm daily. $

Captain Cook

"What we see depends mainly on what we look for."
– John Lubbock

There's a shopping mall called the **Kealakekua Ranch Center** that is anchored by **Choice Mart** (☎ 323-3994, open 6 am-9 pm Mon-Sat, until 8:30 pm Sun), a grocery store with an especially good selection of Mexican food products. The mall also has an **Ace Hardware** and some casual eateries with local food, Chinese food, and the popular Mexican food at **Adriana's**, the new home for what used to be a famous food wagon around the coast (open "Hawaiian Time" 10 am-5 pm Mon-Fri, "sometimes" Sat or Sun).

The Captain Cook **post office** is in town right on the Mamalahoa Highway, and is open 8 am-4 pm Mon-Fri, 9 am-noon Sat.

The Captain Cook **police station** is also on the Mamalahoa Highway, right across from the Keawekaheka Plaza.

The **gas station** in Captain Cook (diagonally across from Antiques & Orchids) is open 6 am-10 pm daily.

Where to Shop

Kona Chips (Mamalahoa Hwy, ☎ 323-3785) sells potato chips that they make fresh daily – crisp, salty and good. They have a "special" technique that makes them less greasy than other brands. You can buy them by the bucket if you like, including the four-gallon size. There are some other munchies like crackseed on sale with their other label "Petroglyphs in Paradise." Kona Chips has a unique gift idea: they can make personalized labels for you. Who wouldn't want a potato chip named after them? Open 9 am-5 pm Mon-Fri, until 3 pm Wed and 2 pm Sat.

Adventures in Water

Kealakekua Bay

DON'T MISS! ★

Here's the adventure you've all been waiting for – at least you water babies. Kealakekua Bay is a glittering, underwater paradise of coral and tropical fish, with crystal-clear water in a breathtaking setting. The snorkeling here is some of the best in the state, and stands a chance of staying that way because you have to work to get here. You can hike down (and up) a very steep, challenging trail; you can pay for a tour on a raft trip that leaves from Keauhou; or you can rent a kayak and paddle an easy mile to the Captain Cook Monument, that big white obelisk beckoning to you from across a bay fringed with steep green *palis* (cliffs) and often inhabited by spinner dolphins.

Kealakekua Bay (*Hawaiian Images*)

The drive to the kayak launch pad for Kealakekua Bay at Napo`opo`o Wharf is down a winding 4½ mile road. The road is always beautifully colored with bright flowers and inviting mango trees – as with most homes in Hawaii, people have fun with their gardens here – but it's a treat in early spring when the jacaranda trees are filled with purple blossoms. There are many fragrant plumeria trees at the base of the road, where locals sometimes sell fresh *leis* for under $5. Five bucks will also buy you help from a local guy getting into or out of the water, which is money well spent if the tide is low, or the surge is high. Word is out about how spectacular the snorkeling is, so parking can be tight, especially on weekends. There are portable toilets here. Don't forget to bring water and sunscreen!

CAPTAIN JAMES COOK

The great explorer James Cook is to Australia what Christopher Columbus is to America. When we lived Down Under in our early 20s, we took an admittedly childish delight in taunting some of our Australian friends with the fact that Captain Cook was killed in Hawaii (and by extension, America). "That's not true!" they protested. "He was killed in the Sandwich Islands!" Then we would reveal, to their horror, that "Sandwich Islands" was the name Cook gave the Hawaiian Islands when he "discovered" them (in honor of John Montagu, Fourth Earl of Sandwich, one of his sponsors).

The Death of Captain Cook (by George Carter, 1791)

On a serious note, Captain Cook's arrival in 1778 at Kealakekua Bay – and the introduction of Westerners to the sovereign kingdom of Hawaii – is still very controversial today. The Captain Cook monument in the bay is sometimes vandalized (as well as repainted) by Hawaiians who perceive Cook as a symbol of the end of "pre-contact" Hawaii. It is undeniable that the introduction of Europeans led to decimation of the population and suppression of the traditional culture. Some historians, such as Tony Horwitz in the book *Blue Latitudes*, believe Cock's legacy has been somewhat distorted, as Cook respected indigenous cultures and tried to prevent his men from inappropriate activities, like spreading syphilis to villages by sleeping with local women (unfortunately, he didn't have much success with that). But whatever your position on Cook, the fact remains that he was one of the world's great adventurers. That he was killed on the Big Island by Hawaiians in Kealakekua Bay just adds to his legend.

Kealakekua Bay State Historical Park

To the right of the boat launch area is a beach park area with public restrooms, showers and a picnic pavilion. What was once a sandy beach is now a boulder-strewn area, though

This is where you'll be diving, to the right of the entry point (shorediving.com)

there is sand at the break and kids still like to boogie board here. The views of the white obelisk across the bay are one reminder of where you are, as well as the Hikiau Heiau, a temple of lava rock walls, where a plaque marks the site of the first Christian service held in the Hawaiian Islands. It was a funeral for one of Captain Cook's seamen, William Chatman, and Cook himself led the service. There is a $50 fine for launching kayaks here.

Kealakekua Bay (shorediving.com)

Manini Beach

To the left of the boat launch area, a right turn on Manini Beach Road takes you to – you guessed it! – Manini Beach, traditionally called Kapahukapa. The site of a sacred community gathering place, today the beach is a quiet park with picnic tables and stunning views of the *palis* (cliffs) that help make Kealakekua Bay so lovely. There is a small area to the right of the beach where you can enter the water through the lava for great snorkeling. There are no facilities except a portable toilet with its own little enclosure. The parking lot is a small area just after the robin's egg blue house and a sign

Manini Beach

that says "No launching of rental kayaks at Manini Beach." The park is open from 6 am-8 pm daily.

Kayak Rental Shops

"I confess my own leisure to be spent entirely in search of adventure, without regard to prudence, profit, self-improvement, learning, or any other serious thing."
– Aldo Leopold

Adventures in Paradise (81-6367 Mamalahoa Hwy, Kealakekua, ☎ 323-3005, toll free ☎ 824-2337, www.bigislandkayak.com). This is a professional kayak outfit that offers quality gear and information to help you enjoy Kealakekua Bay. In addition to a board with updated information about the tides, sunrise/sunset times and marine life, the staff gives customers a map of the area, and screens a 10-minute instructional video about what to do if you capsize, how to get into and out of the water, and tips for unloading gear. Kayak rentals ($30/person) include life jackets, padded seats, mesh bags, soft coolers and ice, and plastic bags to help you pack out your garbage. If you also need snorkel gear, it is available for $5. Open 8 am-4:30 pm daily.

Kona Boys (79-7539 Mamalahoa Hwy, Kealakekua, ☎ 328-1234, www.konaboys.com). These surfer dudes started their shop in 1995, and have been promoting educated kayaking to Kealakekua Bay ever since. Their shop not only rents kayaks (double $67) and snorkel gear ($7), but sells sunglasses, rash guards, swim suits, skateboards and used surfboards. Their slogan is "You deserve a good paddling." They also offer tips like "Remember that paddles don't float!" Open 7:30 am-5 pm daily.

Aloha Kayak Co. (Honalo, ☎ 322-2868, toll free ☎ 877-322-1444, www.alohakayak.com), owned by native Hawaiian and kayak fanatic Iwa Tolleson, offers kayak and snorkel rentals ($6) as well as guided kayaking tours to Kealakekua and Keauhou bays ($75-$129) and can arrange for surf lessons. Kayak rental is by the half-day (double $45), or full day (double $60). Special clear-bottom kayaks rent for $90 a day. Open 8 am-5 pm daily.

KAYAK ALLIANCE OF THE ISLANDS

The aforementioned kayak rental companies have recently joined forces with eco-tour company Hawaii Pack and Paddle (see below) to form a nonprofit group called K.A.I., the Kayak Alliance of the Islands. With the goal to protect Kealakekua Bay's marine environment from degradation, the group plans to establish and staff an educational kiosk at the bay with information about the reef and how to visit responsibly. They will also be a voice in meetings that impact the future of the bay.

Hawaii Pack and Paddle (87-3187 Honu Moe Rd, Captain Cook, ☎ 328-8911, www.hawaiipackandpaddle.com) offers fantastic kayak tours with a focus on ecotourism. In fact, owner Betsy Morrigan is a founding member of the Hawaii EcoTourism Association. She and her guides love to paddle, and can gear trips to all skill levels; they are patient in teaching paddling and snorkeling skills to their guests.

The company offers half-day tours along the Kona Coast. The standard tour is the "Ho`okena Beach Day Paddle," which starts at a beach frequented by dolphins and continues south to the outstanding snorkeling at Pu`uhonua o Honaunau National Historical Park. It's a six-mile paddle, but the trip can be shortened if you like. The cost is $91.25, or half-price for children three-12.

The longer trips are really special, combining paddling, hiking, camping and snorkeling for four- and seven-day "multisport" trips. This is a unique way to visit the Big Island, paddling into sea caves – the tour hugs the shore for easy paddling – hiking to scenic areas, popping into the water to check out the underwater scenery, and eating gourmet camp food prepared by the guides each night, usually fresh fish, fresh fruit and organic produce from local farmers. These two tours usually run once a month, so check the website calendar to schedule your vacation dates if this appeals to you. The four-day tours are $235/day, and the seven-day tours are $245/day, with a four-person minimum. There are discounts for larger groups. Hawaii Pack and Paddle is a terrific outfit.

Adventures on Foot

Captain Cook Monument Trail

Rating: Strenuous
Distance and type: 3.7 miles total, up-and-back
Time: 2-3 hours

As an alternative to renting a kayak or booking a snorkel cruise, visitors can follow the old jeep road down to Captain Cook Monument to experience some extraordinary snorkeling. It's a steep hike, dropping over 1,250 feet in under two miles. Additionally, the trail is rocky and rough in places, meaning it will punish your ankles and knees on the way down as much as it will test your heart and lungs on the trip back up. On top of that, for most of the way the trail is sandwiched between high hedges of grass and *kiawe* trees that limit the view. Still, it's better than swimming the whole way over from the Napo`opo`o Wharf, which is what a couple we met on our last trip down the trail had done. No matter that we described the hike back up as hot, dusty and painful; they still would have preferred it to the long swim back across the bay.

About three-quarters of the way down the path, the trail swings sharply to the south. This is the best vantage point of the hike, with views down to the sea cliffs below. From here the trail drops another 350 feet to the bay. To your left along this stretch, tucked into the cliffs above the bay, are numerous cave openings that are visible through the trees. This is where the *ali`i* (Hawaiian royalty) were often buried, their remains hidden away by commoners suspended on ropes who were cut loose and fell to their deaths once they had completed their task. It was thought that the bones of the *ali`i* contained their *mana* (spiritual power) and thieves would attempt to capture the bones if they knew the location, hence the importance of secrecy.

Just before the trail intersects the bay, there is a spur trail that leads to the Captain Cook Monument. If you continue straight, you will find the landing area for kayaks at Napo`opo`o Wharf. There is a small plaque here in shallow water, tucked into some trees, that marks the place where Cook was actually killed.

The trail is on Napoopoo Road, a tenth of a mile from the turn-off of Hwy11 on the right side. It's an unpaved jeep road that drops steeply into the grass. You'll likely see other vehicles crammed onto the shoulder. You'll know that you're on the correct path when you pass a massive mango tree about 100 yards down the trail. In the late spring and summer you may get lucky and find some low hanging fruit to enjoy on the hike down.

"Freedom lies in being bold." – Robert Frost

Where to Stay

Manago Hotel (Hwy 11, Captain Cook, ☎ 323-2642, www.managohotel.com, 42 hotel rooms, $54-$59, 22 rooms with shared bath, $33). Opened in 1917 by Kinzo and Osame Manago, this old-fashioned hotel provides one of the few budget accommodations on the island. Now run by the third generation of the Manago family, the tradition of providing no-frills lodgings at affordable rates continues. A three-story structure attached to the main building by an elevated catwalk contains the private, hotel-style rooms. The rooms are simple and a little threadbare, with no TV or A/C, but they are kept clean, and the views are great from the top-floor private lanais. The original building houses the **Manago Restaurant** and older rooms with shared bath for much lower prices. The Manago Hotel is a world away from the luxury Kohala resorts, a nightmare for some and a breath of fresh air for others. $

Cedar House B&B (Captain Cook, toll free ☎ 866-328-8829, www.cedarhouse-hawaii.com, two rooms, two suites, one cottage, $110-$135). With a location at 2,200 feet on three acres of coffee orchard, a stay at the Cedar House is a coffee lover's dream. As an added bonus, it's a great deal. The house is a large, cedar structure (as the name suggests), which looks as if it would be more at home in the Rocky Mountains, but it fits in just fine on the cool, wet slopes of South Kona.

The main house has four spacious guest rooms, but they also offer a separate "suite" (really more of a small house) and an original coffee cottage, both of which are perfect for families. The "Hibiscus Suite" is a two-story complex with a kitchenette, private bath, hardwood floors, living area and a funky little extra bedroom for the kids. The coffee cottage is tucked right up against the coffee trees set off from the main house. It includes a full kitchen, two bedrooms, living area, TV/VCR, a double futon and a covered lanai. There is a two-night minimum stay for the rooms, and a four-night minimum for the suite and cottage. Rates include breakfast for all accommodations except the cottage, for which food is provided but not prepared. All in all, this is a great, reasonably-priced and relaxing place to stay smack in the middle of the coffee belt. Their coffee is processed at a local co-op; they serve it for breakfast and have whole beans for sale. Wi-fi Internet access is available throughout the inn.

"Sometimes the most urgent and vital thing you can possibly do is take a complete rest." – Ashleigh Brilliant

Areca Palms Estate Bed and Breakfast (Captain Cook, ☎ 323-2276, toll free ☎ 800-545-4390, www.konabedandbreakfast.com, four rooms $110-$145). With a large common area, open kitchen, attractive beamed ceiling and a wonderful lanai looking out over the immaculately sculpted grounds, this small B&B is

owned by the friendly Janice and Steve Glass. Each guest room is decorated with country-style floral prints and includes private baths, fresh flower arrangements, TVs and bathrobes, a very nice touch that makes nighttime excursions out to the Jacuzzi in the chilly night air a little more comfortable. The Lanai Room, downstairs, features, as you might guess, the only private lanai in the house, and is popular with honeymooners. The hosts provide everything guests need for a trip to the beach, including coolers, beach towels and snorkel gear. The inn is in the heart of Kona coffee country, with some of the best soil in the world, which the innkeepers utilize to grow loads of fruit trees, hundreds of palms and gorgeous tropical flowers that they use in their fresh floral arrangements. Rates include an inventive, full breakfast. $$

Where to Eat

The Coffee Shack (Mamalahoa Hwy, ☎ 328-9795, www.coffeeshack.com). This restaurant and bakery serves tasty food and fantastic coffee, but be warned: it gets jam-packed. Expect a wait, and feel lucky if you don't get one. The parking lot holds only a few spaces right off the highway and, in the morning parking frenzy, we're always amazed at the number of near-accidents we see. So what is all the fuss about? In an area of the island without much in the way of restaurants, the Coffee Shack offers omelettes with fresh veggies, egg sandwiches, thick French toast slices, and lunch all day. They serve gourmet pizzas on house-baked crust with fresh, unique toppings. Try the Luau Pizza, with ham, pineapple, mozzarella and provolone, or one of the sandwiches served on big slices of freshly baked bread. The coffee is grown right on the property, so you can't expect to find fresher coffee anywhere. You might want to pick up a bag of beans while you're here. They also serve an array of soups, salads, and daily specials. If the wait is too long for you to bear, just pick up one of their muffins and a cup of coffee and get on your way.

View from the Coffee Shack's lanai

The Coffee Shack is south of Captain Cook between mile markers 108 and 109. Open 8 am to 3 pm daily. $-$$

For an explanation of the restaurant $ price codes, see page 66.

Señor Billy's Cantina (82-6123 Mamalahoa Hwy, ☎ 323-2012). Señor Billy's reopened under new management early in 2006, offering healthy Mexican food in a casual restaurant with a surfer vibe. The homemade chips with guacamole (pure avocado, no mayo) are a great way to start the meal, or go straight for the nachos with pinto beans (no lard), jack and cheddar cheese, tomatoes, onions, olives, jalapeños, sour cream and that delicious guacamole. The enchiladas are small enough to warrant eating two ($9) or three ($11) on a combo plate. They have Trivial Pursuit cards at tables if you want to quiz yourselves while you sip beer or a margarita, or passion fruit juice. The only bit of warning: they don't have chile rellenos, so get your appetite up for something else. It's better for you anyway (at least, that's what we keep telling ourselves). Open 11 am-9 pm daily. $$

Honaunau

"The love for all living creatures is the most noble attribute of man." – Charles Darwin

Sights

The Painted Church (84-5140 Painted Church Rd, ☎ 328-2227). Established in 1899, the Painted Church hosts thousands of visitors each year, who come to see this unique Catholic church (also known as St Benedict Church). The views from the church of a garden, cemetery and the ocean below are noteworthy, but the obvious draw is the interior for which the church is named. Slightly faded paintings (they are over a century old, after all) wash the walls and ceiling with color; lamps are surrounded by con-

The Painted Church (Joan McCandlish)

centric circles, palm trees seemingly sprout from the tops of pillars. Father John Berchmans Velge, a self-taught artist, also painted Biblical scenes on the walls as a way of educating native Hawaiians about Christianity – his interpretation of Hell is pretty disturbing.

Outside, there are public bathrooms and a walk through the stations of the cross to a statue of a Pietà. This church, on the National Register of Historic Places, will either delight or mortify lapsed Catholics. If you feel a rush of that famous guilt coming on, you can attend Mass on Saturdays at 4 pm, Sundays at 7:15 am, and Tuesdays, Thursdays, and Fridays at 7 am. Every second Sunday, the mass is Hawaiian. To get here, turn *mauka* from Highway 160 onto Painted Church Road.

Where to Shop

Bong Brothers (84-5227 Mamalahoa Hwy, ☎ 328-9289). Contrary to the name, Bong Brothers is not a head shop. It's a tiny natural health food store with a few vegetarian dishes like burritos made fresh daily, as well as smoothies. They also sell store t-shirts, as well as a women's line of "Bong Sistahs." There's a "free" shelf outside. Open 9 am-6 pm Mon-Fri, 10 am-5 pm Sun.

Macadamia nuts

Kona Coast Macadamia Nut and Candy Factory (Mamalahoa Hwy, ☎ 328-8141, toll free ☎ 800-242-NUTS, www.konaoftheworld.com). Some may call it corny, but the big draw here is an old-fashioned macadamia nutcracker, with which guests can try to crack open the farm's mac nuts – and then eat them, of course. (If you are allergic to some nuts but usually not to roasted macadamia nuts, you might want to avoid this, since the raw nuts can induce a sudden reaction.) Located in a funky old farmhouse, this is a quaint stop where you can buy mac-nut cookies, mac-nut oil ("the healthiest oil in the world"), chocolate-covered mac nuts, and 100% Kona coffee. At the corner of Highway 11 and Middle Keei Road in Honaunau. Open roughly 8 am-4 pm Mon-Sat at 10 am Sun.

Did you know? It takes 300 lbs. of pressure to crack the hard shell of a macadamia nut.

Kona Seafood Market (Mamalahoa Hwy, ☎ 328-9777). This out-of-the-way market is reputed to have the freshest seafood on the island. Whether that is literally true or not is entirely unimportant, since they are sure to have a sensational array of blood-red, sashimi-grade *ahi* (yellow-fin tuna), *ono*, shrimp and other selections like *kimchee* and *poke* available. If you're on your way back from the volcano and have the facilities for a cookout, you'll want to stop here and pick up some of the best fish to be found anywhere. They also sell beer and wine, so it's one-stop-shopping for your island BBQ. Open 10 am-6:30 pm Mon-Fri, 10 am-5 pm Sat-Sun.

Adventures in Culture

I ka nana no a `iki. "By observing, one learns."
– Hawaiian wisdom

Haulu (hut) used in the ancient fishing method of hukilau to attract fish to a shoal (HTJ)

**Pu`uhonua o Honaunau National Historical Park** (☎ 328-2288, www.nps.gov/puho). Known locally as "Place of Refuge," Pu`uhonua o Honaunau is a multi-faceted National Historical Park that you don't want to miss. Part of the park consists of the royal residence grounds of Hawaiian *ali`i* (royal chiefs), with a reconstructed *heiau* (temple) and *ki`i* (carved wooden images, like the Polynesian *tiki*) nestled in palm groves along a sheltered bay. The grounds are remarkably photogenic; you'll want to bring your camera for this.

The other main aspect of the park is separated by a stone wall – the *pu`uhonua*, or place of refuge. A place of refuge was a sort of get-out-of-jail-free card for Hawaiians who broke the *kapu* and were therefore sentenced to death. Before the *kapu* system was abolished in 1819, it was a social code that dictated many behaviors of Hawaiian life. For instance, a common person could not let his shadow fall on palace grounds or walk in the chief's footsteps. Women were forbidden to eat with men. If a person broke the *kapu*, the penalty was death – unless they could escape to a place of refuge. There a priest could perform a ceremony of absolution to appease the gods, and the condemned person could safely reenter society. It's mind-boggling to think about the people who frantically swam to this place of refuge with warriors trying to kill them before they could reach the safe haven.

A k`i, or carved statue, watches over the Historical Park

A self-guided tour of the park takes about a half-hour. Be sure to look for green sea turtles basking on the lava, or swimming near the royal grounds (as always, remember to stay 15 feet away). There is a fabulous picnic area in the rear of the park, past a grove of noni trees, with clean tables and grills in a palm grove right on the ocean – a prime whale-watching spot. There are also public restrooms and recycling bins in the area, which is open later than the park – to 8 pm weekdays, and to 11 pm Friday and Saturday. There is also a hike in the park and phenomenal snorkeling (see below). The park is open daily 7 am to 8 pm. Park admission is $5 a vehicle.

Place of Refuge entry point for divers (*shorediving.com*)

PLACE OF REFUGE

Place of Refuge is also one of the best places to snorkel on the Big Island, with vast coral gardens, tropical fish, eels and plenty of mellow turtles. See page 130 for an aerial view. Its protected waters make for great visibility. Though snorkelers cannot enter the bay from the park, there is easy access at nearby "Two Step." Rangers suggest visitors to the park change in their restroom, then walk there from the parking lot (head back out the entrance gate and down to the ocean). Swim over to the area in front of the *heiau* for great coral and a high chance of turtle sightings. Please remember to let them decide how close they want to get to you!

Puuhonua Point / Place of Refuge (Hawaiian Images)

Adventures on Foot

1871 Trail

Distance: 2 miles
Rating and type: easy, up-and-back plus a loop
Time: 1 hour

This is an easy ramble with a mild elevation gain that takes in some beautiful coastal scenery along Kona's south coast.

There is a lava tube about halfway in that you used to be able to walk through and then have a 20-foot cliff jump into the ocean at the end. Unfortunately, the park has closed the lava tube due to some large cracks that have appeared, threatening its integrity. However, a sign indicates that they may open it again some time in the future.

For now, you'll have to be satisfied with the tall palms, flowers, dramatic sea cliffs and Hawaiian ruins. Be sure to pick up a trail guide from the rangers at the info booth. There are interpretive signs corresponding to some detailed explanations in the guide that make this an interesting hike. The trail starts near the picnic area in the rear of the park.

Where to Stay

Aloha Guest House (Honaunau, ☎ 328-8955, toll free ☎ 800-897-3188, www.alohaguesthouse.com, five rooms, $150-$280). With finely appointed guest quarters, a phenomenal view above Kealakekua Bay, and the uncommon conviviality of the hosts, the Aloha Guest House is one of our favorite B&Bs on the island. The guest rooms are on the lower floor, arranged around a screened-in lanai stuffed with luxurious day beds and comfy chairs. Two of the rooms are on the west side of the house and feature the aforementioned view, with their beds arranged so that the windows are at the foot of the bed.

Aloha Guest House bedroom

Aloha Guest House kitchen

So why get up in the morning? Greg and Johann prepare a gourmet breakfast that features fruit from trees on the property, fresh-baked breads and anything else they're inspired to prepare in their cutting-edge kitchen. The Honu Room is a spacious suite with a king-size bed, queen-size sleeper, kitchenette and private entrance. The hot tub is smartly placed to maximize the views while you melt out any remaining anxieties. For those who can't unplug, the entire house has Wi-Fi available, and there's even a communal computer for those who don't haul a laptop with them on vacation. Some of the rooms have a TV, and the hosts keep a large, flat-screen TV and surround-sound system in the common area, with an ever-growing library of DVDs. The road up to the guest house is a little bumpy, but can be easily managed with any 2WD rental car. $$$

See page 65 for an explanation of the hotel $ price codes shown here.

Dragonfly Ranch, "The Big House"

Dragonfly Ranch (☎ 328-9570, www.dragonflyranch.com, five rooms, $100-$250). A chorus of windchimes cascading through monkeypod trees serenades guests at Dragonfly Ranch, a retreat with distinctive New Age influences. There is a small infrared sauna (healthier than steam, they say) with stereo speakers inside; the first use is free, then $15 a session. A beautiful second-story lanai has an aqua floor, hammock, table and chairs, with views of green foliage and of the bay. Past the organic garden, there is an open-air structure with a rainbow labyrinth painted on the floor and a bench for enjoying sunsets. Many walls of rooms

Dragonfly Ranch, Lanai

and around the property are made of screens, allowing breezes to fill the rooms. Owner Barbara can perform *lomi lomi* massage for guests. Breakfast is entirely organic, even the coffee. There is a shared library, plus snorkel gear and a kayak available for rent. Still, the ranch would be a much nicer oasis if it were kept up better – the labyrinth that looks so cool on the website needs to be swept and repainted, and there tends to be some clutter. At these prices, that's a shame. The intentions and vibes are all good, though. $$-$$$$

Nearby Attractions & Adventures

"I finally figured out the only reason to be alive is to enjoy it."
– Rita Mae Brown

Ho`okena Beach Park

This is a very popular beach with the locals, and it doesn't take too much time here to figure out why. The beach sits below a craggy bluff where the surrounding vegetation abruptly ends, clearly where the shoreline sheared off years before. Campers enjoy pitching their tents under the shady trees that back the beach (permits available from the county, see p. 52-53) while day-trippers bask in the sun and soak in the water. The snorkeling in the rocky bay to the south often has excellent clarity even when the water is surging, and there is a fine population of fish and corals. During our last trip here, we were joined by a fun-loving pod of spinner dolphins that continually circled back to swim with us in one of the highlights of our lives. The park is equipped with restrooms, showers, potable water, and a picnic pavilion.

Turn *makai* off of Hwy 11 between mile markers 101 and 102. The park is 2¾ miles down the hill. The parking area is actually on the left near the end of the one-lane road. If you miss it, it's easy to circle back from the very end of the road.

SWIMMING WITH DOLPHINS

If you encounter a pod of dolphins while swimming, your best chance of having them frolic with you is to act like a dolphin. It sounds stupid, but it works! Keep your arms to your side and just use your fins to propel you. Don't swim at them, but rather turn and swim with them. Additionally, don't splash or act erratically, and for the love of Aloha don't attempt to touch or ride them.

"While some dolphins are reported to have learned English – up to 50 words used in correct context – no human being has been reported to have learned dolphinese." – Carl Sagan

Miloli`i

Miloli`i *(Hawaiian Images)*

Braking constantly on the drive down the narrow, winding road to the village of Miloli`i, a sense of how remote this area is begins to pervade the senses. Newer houses perched on stilts dot a landscape that is dominated by the 1926 Ho`opuloa lava flow, which still appears recent despite having occurred over 80 years ago. The village has a measure of renown for being one of the very last Hawaiian fishing villages. Some elders still practice an ancient form of *opelu* (Hawaiian mackerel) fishing where the fish are trained with chum and fattened up before being harvested with a large net from a canoe. While some strive to preserve this heritage, a less-welcome custom has arisen – Miloli`i is now infamous for its problems with "ice" (crystal meth).

Outsiders and tourists who venture down to Miloli`i are often put off by the negative vibes they feel from the locals. The hike to Honomalino Bay, the chief draw to the area, particularly embodies this as the hiker is confronted with an array of "Keep Out" and "No Trespassing" signs of every shape and color. Nevertheless, this village, which is caught somewhere between Old and New Hawaii, seems determined to meet the challenges it faces. Whether that translates into a determined lack of interest in outsiders or simply an absence of the Aloha spirit is for each visitor to decide for themselves.

Miloli`i Bay *(shorediving.com)*

Honomalino Beach

Far and away the chief attraction around Miloli`i, Honomalino Beach boasts a wide arc of salt-and-pepper sand nestled in a protected bay. The beach is backed by towering palms, and one has the sense of having made a significant "find" here, despite the fact that there will likely be other tourists hanging out with similarly satisfied looks on their faces. The swimming is good, as is the snorkeling along the rocks of the bay. There are no facilities.

The half-mile hike to Honomalino begins at Miloli`i Beach Park and takes about 20 minutes. Some of the walking is over lava and can be a little rough. Flip flops are not recommended. The road that extends between the yellow church and the basketball courts leads to the trail head. To your left is a private driveway, and to your right should be a black and white sign marking the access to Honomalino/Okoe Bay. Proceed along the path past a cove with a massive tide pool. The path may lead through a bit of water at high tide. A nice white cut of beach at the far end of the cove may look inviting, but the *kapu* signs will remind you (again and again) to keep moving. The trail continues at the far side of the sand a little bit inland. Again, look for the black and white access sign, and follow the trail up and away from the beach. The trail is easy to follow here, and in about 15 minutes you should arrive at the beach.

Camping

Miloli`i Beach Park

At the end of Miloli`i Road is this small county park that has restrooms, a picnic pavilion and some interesting tide pools. Camping is permitted here with a county permit (see p. 52-53), though considering the local drug scene and the proximity of a much more attractive camping option nearby (Ho`okena Beach Park) it's difficult to recommend staying here.

■ North Kona

North Kona is the area that stretches from the Kohala coast resort area south to the "city" of Kailua-Kona. The coastal area sits in one of the harshest environments on the island, surrounded by rough *a`a* (jagged lava) flows from Hualalai and Mauna Loa, but gives way to some of the finest beaches the island has to offer, and gorgeous gem-like oases like Kiholo Bay and Makalawena Beach. The upcountry area of North Kona receives much more rain, and is greener and significantly cooler. You'll find many upscale residences here, as well as the Big Island Country Club and Makalei Country Club, two of the Big Island's most unusual golf courses.

The main artery through lower North Kona is Hwy 19, also called Queen Ka`ahumanu Hwy or just Queen K. The upper slopes are reached mainly by Hwy 190, aka Mamalahoa Hwy, and the Hawaii Belt Road. Kalako Drive winds 5,000 feet up the slopes of Hualalai before dead-ending in the cloud forest high above the coast. The 8,271-foot summit of Hualalai is on private, Bishop Estate land and is only accessible to the public through a tour led by Hawaii Forest and Trail (see below).

Practicalities

Kona International Airport at Keahole (KOA, ☎ 327-9520, www.hawaii.gov/dot/airports/hawaii/koa/) is in a harsh lava desert seven miles north of Kailua-Kona on Hwy 19. Due to its location out of town, you'll want to top off your rental car before returning it, to avoid an extra fee.

Chevron (74-5035 Queen Ka`ahumanu Hwy, ☎ 327-4200) is the closest gas station to the airport. It's open from 5 am-9:30 pm Mon-Sat, closing at 8:30 pm on Sunday.

Costco (73-5600 Maiau St, ☎ 334-0770) is in a large commercial area about two miles south of the airport. They have the cheapest gas on the Kona side of the island, but you need to be a member to pump gas there, and they accept only debit and credit cards. They also offer cheap slices of pizza and other fast food along with their bargain prices on wholesale foodstuffs and the like. Their hours are 10 am-8:30 pm Mon-Fri, 9:30 am-6 pm Sat, and 10 am-6 pm Sun. To get there, turn *mauka* on Hina Lani St just south of mile marker 96 on Queen Ka`ahumanu Hwy, then turn right on Kanalani St and left on Maiau St.

North Kona

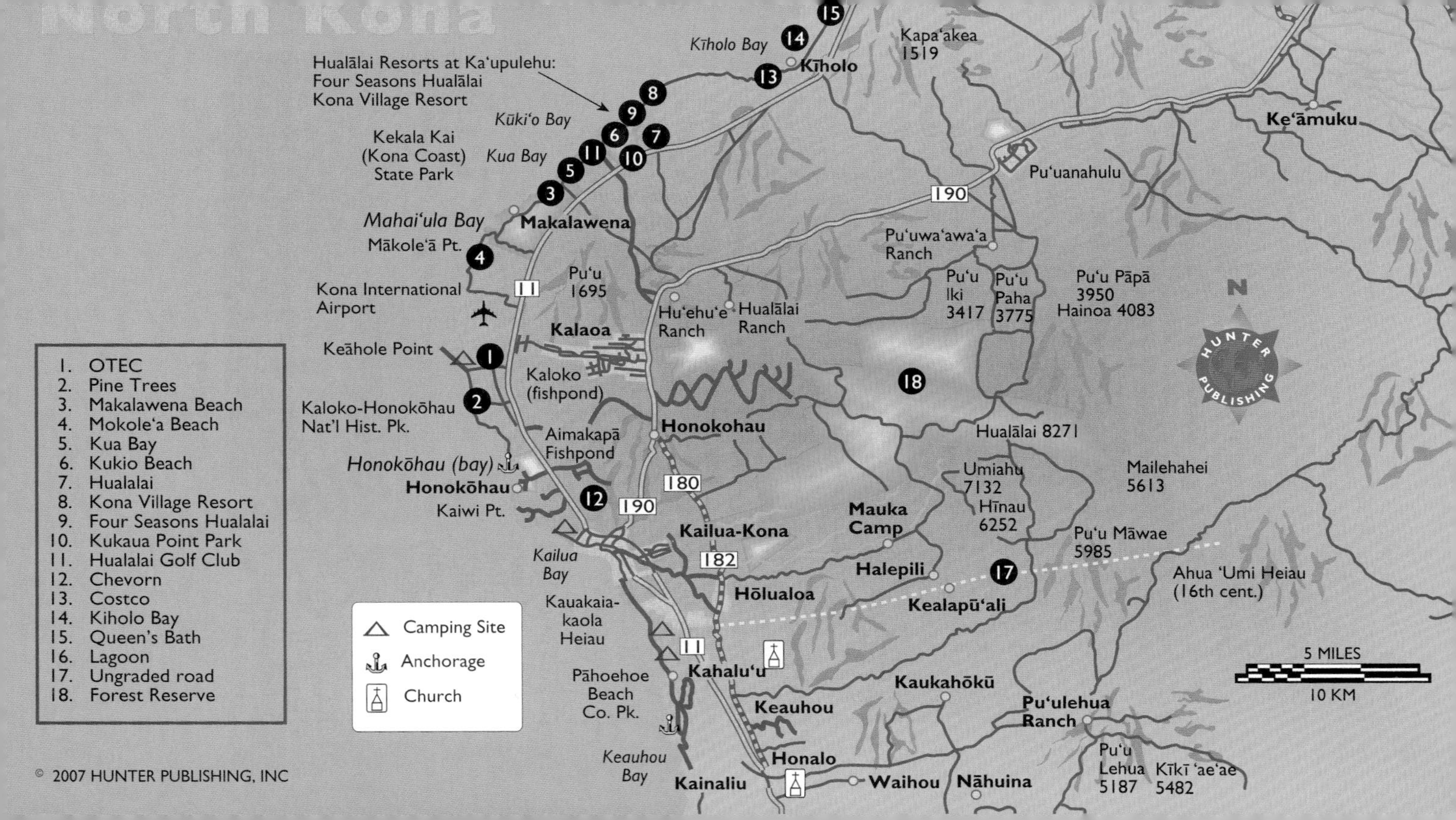

1. OTEC
2. Pine Trees
3. Makalawena Beach
4. Mokole'a Beach
5. Kua Bay
6. Kukio Beach
7. Hualalai
8. Kona Village Resort
9. Four Seasons Hualalai
10. Kukaua Point Park
11. Hualalai Golf Club
12. Chevorn
13. Costco
14. Kiholo Bay
15. Queen's Bath
16. Lagoon
17. Ungraded road
18. Forest Reserve

Honokohau Harbor

"Why do we love the sea? It is because it has some potent power to make us think things we like to think."
– Robert Henri

Honokohau Harbor

This is the center of activity for the sport fishing industry in Kona, and its bright boats and lively docks are fun and worth a stop. Fishing boats hoist flags that correspond to the types of fish that they have caught, making it easy to identify the vessels that have had good fortune as they motor back into the harbor. A number of dive, snorkel, sunset sail and whale-watching boats use the harbor as their base as well. One of the interesting things about the harbor is that it naturally flushes itself out with the tides on a daily basis, meaning you don't see the same kind of stagnant water and debris that is common in most harbors. This flushing process could explain the frequent presence of dolphins at the mouth of the harbor, who regularly greet boats, circling around to surf the wakes of the vessels coming in and out. This is the main harbor for Kailua-Kona, though it is actually north of town, about halfway on Queen Ka`ahumanu Highway between downtown and the airport.

Honokohau Harbor *(Hawaiian Images)*

Where to Shop

The **Kona Coffee and Tea Company** (74-5035 Queen Ka`ahumanu Hwy, ☎ 329-6577, toll free ☎ 888-873-2035, www.konacoffeeandtea.com). If you're on your way from Kona to the airport and you've forgotten gifts for the folks back home (or for yourself!), this is a great place to pick up last-minute souvenirs, like their wonderful coffee. Though their retail store is in dry North Kona, their beans are actually produced on their 100-acre Holualoa farm at 2,600 feet. Their "Private Reserve" is a mix of Extra Fancy and Fancy grade beans, and is available in medium, dark, and French roast. They also have a wide selection of flavored coffees, if you happen to swing that way. In addition to their coffees, they have a lot of gift-ready teas, variety packs, mugs and other Hawaiian-themed miscellanea. Located just behind the Chevron gas station on Hwy 19 between Kailua-Kona and the airport. Open 7 am-5 pm Mon-Fri and 9 am-5 pm Sat-Sun.

Hawaii Forest and Trail (74-5035 Queen Ka`ahumanu Hwy, ☎ 331-8505, toll free ☎ 800-464-1993, www.hawaii-forest.com). The outfitting store for this outstanding ecotourism company is the meeting place for many of Hawaii Forest and Trail's tours, and there's plenty to browse while you do so. It's also worth a stop even if you haven't booked a tour. The shop is on the small side, but carries a number of books and guides about Hawaii's natural environment, clothing, backcountry meal packets, water bottles, backpacks, daypacks, and other camping and hiking gear. Since the company offers two birdwatching tours, there's a great selection of books for birders, as well as cards, photographs and magnets representing Hawaii's avian population (we have one of the *`Io*, or Hawaiian hawk, on our fridge). This is another business tucked behind Chevron – just head toward the fleet of Hawaii Forest and Trail vans. Open 7 am-5:30 pm Mon-Sat and until 4:30 pm Sat and Sun.

Adventures on Water

AUTHOR'S CHOICE ★

Kamanu Charters (☎ 329-2021, toll free ☎ 800-348-3091, www.kamanu.com). If you like to sail – not just motor on a boat with a sail that doesn't get used – then take a trip with Kamanu. The company combines sailing on a catamaran with a snorkel trip to **Pawai Bay**, a gorgeous underwater gem that is essentially only accessible by boat, as the land it fronts is private (a land trust for Hawaiian children). Pawai (pronounced "Pah-VAI") is spectacular, with abundant coral heads growing on a lava flow that forms a dramatic wall to the ocean floor, where there is even more coral. You'll see all sorts of tropical fish and eels here, and a guide may even lead you to an underwater lava arch.

Kamanu Charters

As a bonus, the crew makes an effort to find spinner dolphins and in winter, humpback whales. Tours are small – four to 24 guests, usually closer to four except when there's a cruise ship in town – and include snorkel gear, inner tubes, snorkeling lessons, plus snacks and beverages (including beer and white wine). Trips are also fairly long, 3½ hours, so there's always time for a leisurely sail back to the harbor; as one captain said, "Then we do what we do best: eat and drink!" After 30 years, the company has realized what works, which is creating a relaxing cruise for their guests. This is a much more intimate experience than crowding onto a "cattle boat" with 100 other bodies. Tours leave at 9 am and 1:30 pm Monday through Saturday (Sunday by appointment for special groups, like weddings or ash scatterings). The price is $75 for adults, and $45 for kids 12 and under.

Captain Zodiac (☎ 329-3199, www.captainzodiac.com). This is a fun motorized raft trip that travels past 14 miles of Kona Coast to Kealakekua Bay, which is one of the top snorkeling spots in the state. It is similar to the Sea Quest rides that leave from the Keauhou Pier, but with the advantage of leaving farther north, which increases the chance of seeing dolphins and whales. Aside from the fabulous snorkeling at the bay (gear is included), Captain Zodiac tours include an added bonus of darting into shallow coves, sea caves and lava tubes (surge permitting). The 24-foot inflatable Zodiac rafts hold up to 16 passengers. There are two four-hour tours a day, leaving at 8:15 am and 1 pm, which cost $87 for adults and $72 for kids. There are usually discounts online. From December to April, the company also offers a three-hour whale-watch trip for $65, or $56 for kids.

Returning from a snorkel tour

SURF HOT SPOT: PINE TREES

If you're around OTEC (see below) on a weekend or a holiday, you might notice a steady stream of local trucks and SUVs headed down the dirt road at the big bend in OTEC Road. What are they doing there? Surf's up! The most famous and popular surf spot in Kona is about a mile down a 4WD road from Wawaloli Beach Park.

A long strip of land runs south from OTEC, fronted by reef and lava, which results in a consistent break that keeps locals and tourists coming. Those aren't pine trees along the beach, but tree heliotropes. It is said early surfers spotted mangroves on the beach that they mistook for pine trees, though neither mangroves nor pine trees exist there today. The road snakes through areas of beach where the trees provide enough shade to give a measure of privacy, so you can set up camp and spend the day eating, drinking and playing in the waves. Hand-painted signs are scattered through the area reminding people to "Surf the Earth," and "Surf with care." The road is really only rough near the beginning and, though it's better with 4WD, we've seen plenty of locals banging their 2WD cars down the road to get to some of that surf. Camping is available on-site during holidays, but it's mainly a local affair. There are several different breaks here, and the number and intensity depend on the direction and size of the swell. It won't be too hard to find a break; even on weekdays with low surf there will be plenty of dudes and *wahine* in various lineups.

To get here, turn *makai* onto OTEC Road just south of the airport, and follow the road until it turns abruptly north. Turn left onto the dirt road at the bend of the road.

Whale-Watching

Captain Dan McSweeney's Whale Watch (☎ 322-0028, www.ilovewhales.com). Though many whale-watch trips are incorporated with snorkel or dive tours (or time-share pitches), Captain Dan dedicates his three-hour boat cruises to

finding whales. He also is unique because he offers trips not just during humpback season; other times of the year he can find pilot, sperm, orca, beaked, melon headed and other whales that inhabit Hawaiian waters year-round. In fact, he has been gathering information about whales for the Wild Whale Research Foundation since the 70s – ask him how you can adopt a whale though the program! A nice touch to the tours is that Captain Dan guarantees a whale sighting or you can come again for free. He takes a hiatus in May and June. Tours are $70 per person, and $60 for kids.

Swimming with Dolphins

There are a number of outfits offering the chance to swim with dolphins (*nai`a*). Some are more sensitive to the dolphins and avoid harassing them while they are resting, while others are aggressive and detrimental to

their health and happiness. We've included some of the more eco-sensitive operators. Keep in mind that dolphins are wild animals, so there is no guarantee of an encounter.

Reverend Chris Reid (☎ 936-2653, www.dolphinskona.net) considers dolphins and whales a source of spirituality, and organizes private charters or shore excursions to lead you to spinner dolphins, where you can snorkel and watch them swim along the surface, or below you, their white bellies glowing through the aqua blue. Not only can she tell you ways to swim with them to avoid stressing them out (don't swim overhand with your arms, swim parallel with them), but she sends them positive energy and blows a sort of didgeridoo instrument to them to announce the boat's presence. The only bummer is that she is *so* sensitive to the needs of the dolphins, if another boat (say, one that arrived because her boat captain radioed to let them know where the dolphins are) sends its people into the water, she'll tell you to wait to let the dolphins adjust first to that group. (That's how you can lose opportunities to swim with them yourself.) Still, she's a lovely person who radiates love for dolphins and people. Prices range from $75 for a shore trip, to $650 for a private boat charter.

Sunlight on Water (☎ 328-8298, www.sunlightonwater.com). New Age couple Michael and Melainah have a beautiful mission statement: "to assist others in re-connecting to self, and thereby source, through the wondrous gifts of the dolphins and whales and all the elements of nature." They offer daily boat trips that leave the harbor each morning from 8 am-noon ($100/pp) that include snacks and snorkel gear. They sometimes offer longer retreats as well.

Adventures on the Links

Big Island Country Club (71-1420 Mamalahoa Hwy, ☎ 325-5044, $85). Designed by Perry Dye, the Big Island Country Club opened in 1997 on the cool, wet slopes of Hualalai. It has a drastically different topogra-

phy and climate than the coastal courses, so if you're coming from the coast it might be a good idea to phone ahead to see what the weather is like. It's a truly beautiful course with lots of untouched Hawaiian flora and fauna all around to distract you. The design is fascinating and offers lots of variety. Some holes are relatively easy (though never dull), especially in the beginning. Others give you all you can handle. There's water on nine holes, and it's not just for decoration. Two of the most memorable holes are the 17th and 18th, the first a downhill par 3 with an island green, the second a par 4 with a lake along the right side of the fairway that also runs in front of and protects the green. Careful strategy on every shot is essential on that hole.

The Big Island Country Club has not yet finished the clubhouse that was part of the original plan. They use a temporary building in the parking lot (though one wonders how many years something can go on being called "temporary"). And the course sometimes seems to need a little better maintenance. But, even with those drawbacks, it's consistently one of the highest-ranked courses on the island.

The Big Island Country Club is between mile markers 19 and 20 on Hwy 190. The quickest way to get there from the Kohala resorts is to take Waikoloa Road up the slope, then turn right on Hwy 190.

"The reason the pro tells you to keep your head down is so you can't see him laughing." – Phyllis Diller

Makalei Hawaii Country Club (72-3890 Hawaii Belt Rd, ☎ 325-6625, www.makalei.com, $99, $49 after 12:30 pm). Another wonderful golf course that's a bit out of the way is Makalei, 15 minutes from Kona high on the slopes of Hualalai. It's a fun and funky course with lots of elevation changes and unusual hole designs calling for some creative shots. It's nestled into the natural habitat and surrounded by great natural beauty, with bougainvillea growing everywhere. At its highest point it reaches nearly 3,000 feet above

sea level. Playing here when the fog is drifting across the fairways, hiding then suddenly exposing the wild fowl, the rock formations, and the panoramic views of the coastline below, is an unforgettable experience. The shop and services at Makalei are not elaborate but they're friendly. Makalei is between mile markers 32 and 33 on Hwy 190, about seven miles northwest of Kailua-Kona.

Where to Eat

Harbor House Restaurant (Honokohau Harbor, ☎ 326-4166). With great sunset views over the boats in the marina and $2.25 "frozen schooners" (frosty 18-ounce goblets) of beer, this is one of the top happy hour spots in Kona. The casual, open-air atmosphere of the large and often packed Harbor House makes for a pleasant place to put on a buzz. They have lots of fried food, like fish and chips, calamari, spring rolls with a sweet chili sauce, as well as stirfries, burgers and sandwiches. Happy hour 4-6 pm daily, except Sun till 5:30 pm; open 11 am-7 pm Mon-Sat and till 5:30 pm Sun. $-$$

Nearby Attractions & Adventures

He punawai kahe wale ke aloha. "Love is a spring that flows freely." – Hawaiian proverb

Kaloko-Honokohau National Historical Park (☎ 329-6881, www.nps.gov/kaho) protects two ancient Hawaiian settlements from the encroaching development nearby (Costco and an industrial park are across the street). This is an area where hundreds of Hawaiians fished and farmed in their *ahupua`a* (traditional land divisions) at Kaloko and Honokohau. Though no one knows for sure, it is rumored that the bones of King Kamehameha the Great were buried somewhere in this area.

The park is popular with beach-goers and with *honu* (green sea turtles), who swim and bask in the sun. Some of them are really big! People must stay 20 feet away from the federally protected turtles in the park. From the visitor center parking lot, a network of trails along *a`a* (jagged lava) connect the two areas. Though many people simply park next to the beach they like, they miss some primo turtle viewing that way.

Insider Tip: Locals know that the quickest way to access the sandy beaches of Kaloko-Honokohau N.H.P. is through Honokahau Harbor. Just turn into the harbor entrance off of Queen K Hwy between mile markers 97 and 98, then make your first right turn and follow it to the end. Walk north up the coast and pick your sandy spot!

The trail to **`Ai`opio Fishtrap** and its beach is only about a half-mile long. This is where you'll find a beach frequented by families, as the lava rock walls of the fishtrap create protected swimming (for humans and *honu*). Fish would enter the bay at high tide and then become trapped inside the walls once the tide dropped. There is a *heiau* (religious structure) here, and a canoe house that some people use for shade.

Continuing from this beach toward the Kaloko fishpond, you will pass the sandy beach of **Honokohau** (and some large basking turtles) and the bird-watcher hotspot along **`Aimakapa fishpond**. The black and white birds with long beaks and long legs are **Hawaiian black-necked stilts**; their squat neighbors that look like ducks with white faces are **Hawaiian coots**. These endemic birds, found nowhere else on earth, are endangered (so please scold anyone you see feeding them potato chips!).

Hawaiian coot (Bryan Harry, NPS)

To reach a special spot, when the beach trail turns inland and is met by a rock wall, turn *mauka* and follow the trail along the border of the *a`a* (jagged lava) and *pahoehoe* (smooth lava) toward the rock piles. Turn left between the second and third rock piles and walk about 30 yards to the **Queen's Bath**. This is a beautiful swimming hole in the middle of a lava desert.

Queen's Bath

It's fed by an underground spring, and is brackish – some salt, some freshwater. The golden algae glitters beneath the crystal clear water, where you can see small fish and a few larger ones like convict tangs (you'll understand the name when you see the stripes). There are no signs pointing you to Queen's Bath because park officials felt the area was being "abused." There also aren't any signs prohibiting you from walking on the well-worn trail. We used to like to take a dip in the bath until we were joined by a man who encouraged his two dogs to swim in the sacred waters. The magic was shattered, and we realized that the park rangers had a point. Remember that the park area is considered sacred, and treat it with respect.

Back on the trail, continue to **Kaloko Fishpond**, where a 6½-foot *kuapa* (seawall) stretches for 250 yards. This is a reconstruction (a work in progress) of the original wall, which stood for hundreds of years until it was abandoned, filled with cement to reduce maintenance costs, and subsequently destroyed by storms in the 1950s. They don't build 'em like they used to, except here. Cement is a detriment to the sea wall – the porous rock allows water to flow into the pond. The wall is also built at an angle to deflect waves, right where they tend to break. Though it may not appear so on first look, the *kuapa* is a feat of engineering.

From the Kaloka Fishpond, you can complete a loop back to the visitor's center by following the road out toward the highway, then turning south along the King's Highway, an old Hawaiian footpath built at the behest of King Kamehameha the Great.

The visitor center is open 8:30 am-4 pm daily. There are public restrooms here, but only the occasional portable restroom elsewhere. You'll want sunscreen, water and hiking sandals. Admission is free.

Keahole

NELHA aerial view

The tip of Keahole is the westernmost point of the Big Island, and the area is home to the Kona International Airport and NELHA, the Natural Energy Lab. It is a stark area, wasted by lava flows, and dry, receiving only 14 inches of rain per year. It is also the location of the steepest ocean drop-off in the state, making for excellent fishing, scuba diving and allowing the feasibility of OTEC.

What's in a name? While the name of this area was NELHA (Natural Energy Lab of Hawaii Authority), and is now really more HOST (Hawaii Ocean Science and Technology Park), most locals still refer to it as "OTEC" (Ocean Thermal Energy Conversion).

Sights

Keahole Point (Hawaiian Images)

Many visitors to Kona pass the strange, space-age buildings and solar panels stuck in the middle of a lava field a mile or so south of the airport and wonder what could have inspired someone to put them there. Well, the answer is renewable energy... and deep ocean water.

These buildings are NELHA Gateway, the visitor's center for the Natural Energy Lab. This is where they give talks about what goes on in the area and how it works.

So, what are they up to? Spread over 870 acres, they are in the business of pumping cold, nutrient-rich ocean water from 3,000 feet below the surface 24 hours a day. This water drives a thriving aquaculture industry that raises New England cold water lobster, abalones, sea horses, aquarium fishes, and spirulina. Most recently, Japanese companies have had success using reverse osmosis to desalinate the water, which they can market as high-end health water, because it contains over 80 of the 105 minerals in existence. It sells in Japan for a serious premium. And due to OTEC's proximity to an international airport and a deep water port, a thriving industry has sprung up that actually has very little to do with its original purpose.

"If you can dream it, you can do it." – Walt Disney

HOW DOES OTEC WORK?

OTEC (Ocean Thermal Energy Conversion) operates on the premise that a temperature differential of at least 36°F can create endlessly renewable energy. These temperature differences only exist within 20 degrees of the equator, and the process involves combining sun-warmed surface water with cold water pumped from the ocean's depths. The simplest version is referred to as an "open-cycle" system, and works by introducing the warm water into a low-pressure system where it boils, creating steam that drives an electricity-producing turbine. It's then condensed back into liquid by the cold water. This system has the beneficial byproducts of desalinated water and salt.

While no OTEC system presently exists at NELHA, the cold water benefits discovered during the process are still being used, such as using the cold water to cool buildings, and something called "chilled-soil agriculture." This process works by running cold water through underground pipes, which chills the soil and creates condensation that keeps the plants watered. Several plants that normally could not grow in the tropics end up thriving on the temperature differential.

In the spring of 2006, a Honolulu company inked a deal with NELHA to build a new 1.2-megawatt OTEC plant. This would be the third, and hopefully most successful, OTEC plant built at Keahole Point.

Mustang seahorse (Ocean Rider)

Ocean Rider (☎ 329-6840, www.seahorse.com). One of the unique businesses in OTEC using the cold water is Ocean Rider, a seahorse farm that raises the little beauties for aquarists. This is a terrific idea not only from a financial standpoint – the cheapest seahorse sells for $65 – but because all seahorses are endangered. A tour of the farm is pretty interesting if you like to look at the strange fish with faces like little horses. After washing their hands with iodine, guests feed seahorses that are only a few days old, and are so tiny you could probably thread them through a needle. Then you feed small red shrimp to larger ones, about six inches long, including the amazing prehensile tail. They suck the shrimp into their snouts like a vacuum.

Around this time, the guide points out some pregnant males – yup, males. After a graceful courtship dance, the female (two X chromosomes and all the "parts") squirts her eggs into the male's pouch, where he fertilizes the eggs and carries them for about 30 days. This is the part of the tour when the women cheer and the men shift their weight uncomfortably.

Sunburst seahorse (Ocean Rider)

Outside, there are large blue tubs with seahorses of various species – Ocean Rider has 15 – and ages. Guests pull back tarps to watch them swimming toward food, or wrapping their tails around each other. A mother in our group saw a seahorse that had wrapped its tail around the neck of another and declared, "They must be siblings!" (Her kids were not amused.) The highlight of the tour is a chance to put your hands in a tank and let a seahorse grab onto your pinkie finger. This is the moment that makes the high cost of admission seem worthwhile (though they really should make it more affordable). Tours take place at 1 pm Mon-Sat and cost $20. Reservations are required.

Nearby Attractions & Adventures

"Make your life count – and the world will be a better place because you tried." – Ellison S. Onizuka

Ellison S. Onizuka Space Center (☎ 329-3441, www.onizukaspacecenter.org). Everyone remembers where they were when they heard that the Challenger space shuttle exploded on January 28, 1986. The tragedy united our country in a grief that felt intensely personal, even though many of us never knew the astronauts who perished. The people of Hawai`i did. Astronaut Ellison S. Onizuka, a "down-to-earth Kona boy" and Hawaii's first astronaut, was one of the seven astronauts who died. The eponymous space center is a tribute not only to Ellison and his legacy, but to the other astronauts on the flight. It's also a source of inspiration, with interactive games and displays – many are for kids – about NASA and the space program. There are a number of videos in the screening room that are tailor-made for school field trips.

The Ellison S. Onizuka Space Center is right in Kona International Airport, adjacent to the departure terminals and across from the rental car booths (but not where you pick up the cars), so if you have some time before your flight, swing by! Open 8:30 am-4:30 pm daily. Adults $3, children 12 and under $1.

On the Beach

Kekaha Kai State Park

What appears from the road to be a devastated lava wasteland hides some of the finest beaches on the island. Unfortunately, only one of these gems is accessible by a paved road (see *Kua Bay*, below), but if you have a four-wheel-drive vehicle and aren't afraid to hike a little, or go without things like public restrooms, you are in for a treat. This is what Adventure Guide beach hunting is all about.

Important Note: The beaches of Kekaha Kai State Park are closed on Wednesdays.

Kekaha Kai State Park (*Hawaiian Images*)

The road down to most of the beaches in Kekaha Kai State Park is *makai* between mile markers 90 and 91 on Queen K. We recommend 4WD here. There was once a paved road, but it has deteriorated over the years, and now is primarily rough *a`a* and *pahoehoe* lava, with the pot-holed vestiges of the old road making up some of the toughest stretches. After 0.8 miles, most two-wheel-drive vehicles will be stopping if their driver has any sense (you can always park and hike in!). It's about a mile and a half to the first parking area, which is the crossroads to all of the beaches.

A short distance toward the water is a large parking area with a few pit toilets and port-a-potties, the only place to "go" in this part of the park. Fronting the lot is Kaelehuluhulu Beach, which has picnic tables and some coarse salt-and-pepper sand and lava outcroppings that make it an unappealing beach for swimming. A short walk around the point to the north over smooth *pahoehoe* lava leads to Mahaiula Beach, which has finer sand, and is better protected for swimming and snorkeling. There are still plenty of lava fingers offshore, so be sure to watch your toes! *Honu* (green sea turtles) seem to enjoy this area immensely. This beach can be reached directly from the first parking area along the trail that heads north.

While these beaches are reasonably accessible, locals know that one of the best beaches on the island is nearby, and is worth hiking past these beaches, either by taking the trail to the right from the parking lot, or by continuing along the beach and joining up with the trail past the water tower.

Makalawena Beach

After about 25 minutes of rough walking over jagged *a`a* lava (wear close-toed shoes for the hike and be on the lookout for wild goats), the trail reaches the verdant, sandy oasis of Makalawena. High white sand dunes covered with green vines hide what you've trekked this far to see: soft ivory sand, turquoise water and, depending on the day, placid snorkel coves or perfect bodyboarding waves. Either walk along the beach or follow the trail behind the dunes north to several parcels of sand, each labeled with a different Hawaiian name by the landholder, Kamehameha Schools (Bishop Estate). There is a small freshwater pool at the southern end that people dip in to wash off the salt, but it just doesn't look very attractive.

Makalawena is also accessible via an incredibly rough 4WD road between mile markers 88 and 89 on Queen Ka`ahumanu, which leads to the north end of the beach. It's a brutal drive. It's easier (and potentially less costly) to simply walk in from the south.

Another interesting beach in the park is **Mokole`a**, a small black sand beach, which is a rarity on the Kona coast. It's far from an idyllic swimming beach, but it's picturesque and worth the effort to get there. From the first parking area, follow the primitive, lava 4WD road south for 0.7 miles until you reach a right-hand turn marked by white coral. Some folks do get their trucks or SUVs down to the beach from here, but it makes more sense to park and walk in the quarter-mile to the water. The remains of wrecked cars along the way will lead you to believe you've made the right decision.

Kua Bay

AUTHOR'S CHOICE ★ Kua Bay, the Manini `Owali section of Kekaha Kai State Park, is an all-around great beach area, with powdery white sand, aquamarine water, plenty of room to swim, picnic tables perched above the beach, and amenities like restrooms, showers, drinking fountains and a most unusual feature: a security guard! The paved road

Kona

opened in late 2005, so it's easy to access, except for a short climb down boulders to the beach. There's also a rough concrete ramp near the picnic tables that's easier for older folks. On weekends, there are lots of families playing in the waves, building sandcastles, digging holes, snorkeling and generally enjoying themselves. Other days it might be filled with couples cuddling in the surf. There are some rock walls that are sacred, archeological ruins at the far end of the beach. There isn't any shade here, so bring a beach umbrella if sunburn is a concern.

To get here, drive north from Kona until you almost reach the 88 mile marker (the turnoff is 4/10 of a mile shy of it). You'll see a sign on the mountain side for the West Hawaii Veterans Cemetery; you want to turn the other way, *makai*, to drive the quarter-mile of paved road (a luxury!) to this beautiful beach.

Note: Kua Bay is open 9 am-7 pm every day except Wednesday, when it is closed.

Wawaloli Beach Park

Also known as "OTEC Beach" due to its location at the Natural Energy Lab, this is a fun little beach with a protected tide pool that serves as a natural swimming pool. An arch of white sand surrounds the pool like an amphitheater, providing elevated views of the lava boulders behind the pool that cause explosive splashes of waves when the surf is up. This is a great spot for families with little ones, when the tide is up. When it's low tide, the water drains from the pool and it looks much less attractive and will probably be deserted. In fact, we suggested this beach to visiting friends, who evidently went at low tide because they told us it was "gross."

A sign here warns you not to fly a kite due to low-flying aircraft. If they're flying that low, you might want to run for cover. The proximity to the airport runway is another drawback, making it hard to achieve that "away from it all" feeling most people crave in a Hawaiian vacation. On the plus side, kids love airplanes.

The park has restrooms, showers and picnic tables. Turn *makai* just south of the airport on OTEC Rd and follow it straight down to the ocean. Wawaloli is right at the bend of the road. The beach is a hundred yards south of the restrooms.

Hualalai

"I'd rather wake up in the middle of nowhere than in any city on earth." – Steve McQueen

Hualalai is a resort and residential area on the North Kona coast about six miles north of the Kona International Airport. Beginning with the opening of the ultra high-end Kona Village Resort in 1967, Hualalai has maintained a reputation for premium, luxury accommodation and services. The area is made up of the Kona Village Resort, the Four Seasons Hualalai and a sprawling, deluxe residential community called, simply, Hualalai. Aside from a few beaches, there is very little here to attract visitors on a budget. Any resort-related activity at Hualalai, be it golfing, dining or indulging yourself at a spa, will take a serious bite out of your wallet, which is precisely how some folks like it.

Adventures on the Beach

For the Littlest Adventurers: Kikaua Point Park

This is a perfect beach park for little kids because it has a large protected cove. It's a mellow area with tree heliotrope and palm trees for some shade. There are also tide pools here, and continuing on to the right there is a small lava tube, as well as a grassy area with views of Kukio Bay. (You can keep walking to Kukio Bay via the path over the lava). Amenities include restrooms, showers and a drinking fountain. The park is open from sunrise to a half-hour after sunset. To get here, turn *makai* on Kukio Nui Drive, the first entrance for the Four Seasons Hualalai that is just south of mile marker 87. Tell the guard you want to go to the beach and they'll tell you to veer left and then follow the beach access signs.

Kukio Beach

Kukio Bay *(shorediving.com)*

This isn't a great swim beach because of all the lava outcroppings, but the *honu* (turtles) love it. There's a nice stretch of sand made for a stroll. To get here, turn into the second entrance for the Four Seasons and ask the guard for a beach pass.

Adventures on Links

Hualalai Golf Club

Hualalai Golf Club (Queen Ka`ahumanu Hwy, ☎ 325-8480, www.fourseasons.com/hualalai/golf.html, $195). If you stay at the Four Seasons Resort at Hualalai, or you're the guest of someone staying there, then you'll have access to one of the finest courses on the island. The Jack Nicklaus-designed Hualalai course has a user-friendly layout with wide fairways and excellent, true greens. It tends to be a flat course but the design is imaginative and the scenery is beautiful, especially toward the end of the round. The No. 17, a par 3, plays right alongside the ocean and is as tough as it is pretty. Eighteen is a sweeping dogleg left with a carry over water and with deep pockets of sand along the left side to test your courage. The facilities and services here are unbeatable, and they have a fabulous pro shop.

Where to Stay

Four Seasons Hualalai (100 Ka`upulehu Dr, ☎ 325-8000, ☎ 800-819-5033, www.fourseasons.com/hualalai, 243 rooms incl. 31 suites, $625-$925, suites $1,050-$1,775). In 2005, *Travel and Leisure* magazine named the Four Seasons Hualalai the top hotel/spa in the United States and Canada, and the 20th best hotel in the world. That's right – the world. That's a lot to live up to, but it is a phenomenal resort. The Four Seasons has no high-rises – rooms and suites are no higher than two stories, and blend in with their environment. When you drive up to the lobby, you are greeted with a view of palm trees lining an "infinity" swimming pool that fronts the ocean – this is the Hawaii that glossy brochures are made of. The resort has an impressive attention to detail – there are a range of pools and Jacuzzis, from family to adults only, and simple but appreci-

Four Seasons Hualalai bedroom

Four Seasons Hualalai pool area

ated amenities, like CDs in the rooms, coffee beans that you can grind for your cuppa, gourmet room service and, always, attentive service. There are a host of activities such as fitness classes, canoeing (for kids, too), and surf and fishing lessons, golfing on their famous course – there's even an artificial snorkel pond with a daily 2 pm eagle ray feeding. Know what we mean? The only minus is that there isn't really a good swimming beach, but maybe that's a good thing – you might not leave the resort otherwise. $$$$

See page 65 for an explanation of the $ price codes given for each hotel.

Kona Village Resort *(Hawaiian Images)*

Kona Village Resort (☎ 325-5555, toll free ☎ 800-367-5290, www.konavillage.com, 125 *hales*, $580-$1050). "Welcome to Fantasy Island" may ring through your head as you enter Kona Village, an unusual Hawaiian resort that consists of thatched roof cottages (called *hale,* Hawaiian for "houses") devoid of televisions, radios, clocks and phones. The point is to unplug and unwind and not need to leave the resort – rates include breakfast, lunch and dinner as well as glassbottom boat tours, snorkels, boogie boards, canoes and kayaks, a kids' program, laundry machines, tennis courts and a fitness center. Upon arrival, guests are given a flower *lei* and rum punch or pineapple juice. There is a boardwalk through 450 petroglyphs, and an enclosure with donkeys. The salt-and-pepper beach is small, but the snorkeling in the area is excellent because it is a marine preserve. Massage, snorkel excursions, luaus and alcohol cost more, but the resort is essentially all-inclusive.

The *hales* are breezy, and some have Jacuzzis built into the front decks. Rooms have 100% Kona coffee beans and grinders, and a more modern feel than their exteriors would suggest – though guests who do not wish to be disturbed place a coconut on the doorstop. Turtles bask on the shores around the property. This is a peaceful place. Though normally full of families, couples flock to Kona Village in May and September when there aren't children rates or *keiki* programs. Renovations planned by new owner Ty Warner of Beanie Babies fame will take place in 2007 and 2008, and will close half the resort while the deluxe upgrades are made to the resort. $$$$

Kona Village poolside

Did you know? Kona Village Resort was the second luxury resort on the Big Island, opening in 1965 just months after the Mauna Kea in South Kohala. At the time, Kona Village was so remote that it had its own airstrip for visitors.

Where to Eat

**Pahu i`a** (Four Seasons Hualalai, ☎ 325-8000). Pahu i`a is home to our favorite lavish breakfast buffet on the island, with eggs, yogurt and fresh fruit, miso soup, a cereal bar with a milk selection that includes soy, pastries, breakfast potatoes and other temptations in a waterfront setting. We've seen whales breaching from our table! The omelette station has eggs, egg whites or egg substitute. You can also order à la carte options like gourmet *loco moco* (a bowl of rice, topped with a hamburger or other meat smothered in gravy and topped with a fried egg). Dinner is similarly bountiful, with plenty of fresh seafood options like

Pahu i`a

the guava-glazed scallops with white corn and clam froth. The restaurant name is Hawaiian for "aquarium" (we can only assume it's an approximation), and an impressive aquarium is the centerpiece of the restaurant. There's an ongoing debate among return guests about which restaurant is better, Pahu i`a or Alan Wong's restaurant (see below). Open for breakfast buffet 7 am-11:30 am (breakfast at 6:30 am), dinner 5:30-9:30 pm. $$$$

For an explanation of the restaurant $ price codes, see page 66.

Hualalai Grille

The Hualalai Grille by Alan Wong (Four Seasons, Hualalai, ☎ 325-8000). When the chef's name is incorporated into the restaurant's name, you have to figure they know what they're doing in the kitchen. Alan Wong is one of the award-winning chefs who helped make Hawaiian regional cuisine the recognized culinary art that it is today. You'll understand why if you try the red and yellow tomato soup – the server pours the two soups together for a yin and yang effect in your bowl, which is garnished with tomato sorbet and avocado salsa. Entrées include macadamia nut- and coconut-crusted lamb chops, and a sautéed catch of the day with stir-fried vegetables, red Thai lobster, butter shrimp and dried scallop risotto. Save room for desserts like the one that has five scoops of different flavors of crême brulée. Incidentally, the lychee martinis here are stupendous. Much of the seating overlooks the 18th hole of the Jack Nicklaus-designed golf course. Open daily for lunch 11:30 am-2:30 pm, dinner 5:30-9 pm, cocktails all day. $$$$

FOOLED US ONCE

Aside from the luau, non-guests should avoid eating at Kona Village Resort, as we learned the hard way. Because dinner rates are included in the price of accommodation, menus do not list prices. Our meal at Hale Moana was one of the most expensive of our lives and not even in the running for best.

Kiholo Bay

Even from the highway this looks like an idyllic beach oasis in the lava desert. Upon closer inspection, that impression deepens. Add turtles, surf and a laid-back party atmosphere and you've got Kiholo Bay. With one of the loveliest lagoons you'll find anywhere, the northern section of the area is the most frequented by tourists. They're drawn by the brackish lagoon that's created by the small lava and sand island a short distance offshore. The snorkeling is chilly, as cold, spring-fed water sits on top of the warmer salt water, but it can be incredibly rewarding when one of the many *honu* (turtles) who inhabit this water emerge from the cloudy, salty depths.

This area once held one of the largest man-made fish ponds on the island. After King Kamehmeha's favorite fish pond was destroyed by lava from the 1801 eruption of Hualalai, he ordered the construction of a new pond at the north end of Kiholo Bay. With a massive labor pool from at least three districts, Wainanali`i was completed in 1812. It was over two miles in circumference, and was a deep-water pond capable of holding large ocean fish such as *ahi*. The walls of this pond turned to liquid when lava poured from Mauna Loa and traveled 31 miles to the Kona coast in 1859. The remnants of the pond are on private property, but it's possible to peek in at it. It is a favorite nighttime resting spot for the local *honu*.

The northern part of the bay is most easily accessed from a trail off of the highway. Park at the vague turnout just south

Kiholo Bay

Kiholo Bay *(Hawaiian Images)*

of mile marker 81 on Hwy 19. From there, an old 4WD road serves as a trail to the beach. It's less than a mile along the old road. Turn right when you reach the beach. It will then take another 20 minutes to reach the lagoon, which is at the far northern end of the area.

The south side of Kiholo is mainly gravel and coarse sand beaches, tide pools, and shallow reefs. You'll find a lot of locals skirting the no-camping laws and setting up extensive bivouacs jammed with seemingly everything that might be needed, perhaps even a kitchen sink. The jewel down here is the **Queen's Bath**, a blown-out lava tube filled with crystal clear spring water. This is a splendid place to rejuvenate with a cool dip in an ancient bathing spot. The temperature isn't too chilly, just enough to refresh you. There is a ladder to facilitate your entrance and exit, and a short swim-through to another area with a hole in the ceiling. This place is fabulous.

The Queen's Bath is about 300 yards north along the beach from the parking area. You're getting close when you see the **Bali House**. The owner of Paul Mitchell salons had it built in this remote location. The beach in front of the house is public property, so it's fine to approach the compound, gaze upon its opulence, and wonder why no one is there.

The southern portion of Kiholo Bay is most easily reached by road. Isn't *that* convenient? Turn *makai* between mile markers 82 and 83 onto the primitive dirt road. The gate is generally open from 8 am to 4 pm every day. The road heads toward the water for less than a mile before jogging south. Park at the strange-looking abandoned building.

Nearby Attractions & Adventures

Adventures on Foot

Pueo Bay – Keawaiki Beach – Golden Pools

Difficulty: Moderate
Length and type: 2+ miles, combo
Time: 1-2 hours

Close to the South Kohala resorts, this is an interesting hike where few people ever go. It takes in exquisite coastline – areas where harsh lava flows meet the ocean with beautiful results – and includes a bizarre freshwater pool with golden algae thriving in it. There are ample snorkeling opportunities when the ocean is calm, as well as some pleasant swimming.

Begin the hike at the turnout just north of the 79 mile marker on Highway 19, about two miles south of the turnoff to Waikoloa. Follow the rough lava road that heads toward the water, go around some large boulders and then around a gate. When the road meets the fence line, follow the smaller trail to the right. The trail continues closely along the barbed wire fence all the way to the beach. It's a bit jarring to be subject to such crude security in this remote place, but authorities apparently felt it was necessary to prevent trespassing. This was the estate of Francis I`i Brown, an eccentric Big Island millionaire, whose generosity, love of sport and royal heritage made him a beloved personality during the early- and mid-20th century. Today his estate seems unnaturally well-protected.

When this trail meets the coast, you have arrived at **Keawaiki Bay**, a wide, steep beach of salt-and-pepper sand that is rarely visited. Turn to the north and continue until reaching the inlet of **Pueo Bay**, a big bite out of a rough slice of land with large black and white pebbles and generally calm swimming conditions. The northern tip of land is called **Weli Weli Point**, which is an area worth poking around. There is a house on the other side of the point, and a trail that picks up on the other side of the house and that can be followed back out to the highway. About three-quarters of the way around the back of the Pueo Bay, look for a large pile of white coral. This marks the trail to the **golden pools**, which are visible a short distance away due to the fact that they have the only vegetation in the otherwise barren area. The trail continues on from the pools. Turn

The Golden Pools feature glittering algae

right in a short distance onto the King's Highway, which intersects your previous trail at the fence line of the Brown estate. Turn away from the water and return to your car.

You can also reach this area by simply hiking south along the beach from A Bay. It's about two miles to Weli Weli Point from there, and there are many hidden snorkel spots and remote beach gems along the way. Have fun exploring!

"And in the end, it's not the years in your life that count. It's the life in your years." – Abraham Lincoln

South Kohala

Olai i kea he lau makani. "Life is in a gentle breath of wind."
– Hawaiian proverb

One word epitomizes South Kohala: beaches. This is where you'll find white sand, turquoise waters, sunny skies, palm trees, sunsets – and the resorts that follow.

IN THIS CHAPTER

Tourist accommodation and amenities abound in South Kohala, with high-end resort restaurants, luaus, spas and deluxe golf courses like the one at the Mauna Kea, reputedly the best course on the Big Island. There are numerous outfits offering adventure on and in the water, such as snorkeling, diving, windsurfing, boogie boarding, whale-watching, glass bottom boat rides and sunset sails. You can even touch and swim with dolphins as part of the Dolphin Quest program in the lagoon at the Hilton.

But there is more to South Kohala than the Hawaii of brochures. It's just a short hike to see the **Puako Petroglyphs**, mysterious figures chiseled into lava by ancient Hawaiians. The rock walls of several *heiau* (temples) surround the National Historic Site at **Pu`ukohola Heiau**, which King Kamehameha the Great built in 1790 to fulfill a prophecy that came true – if he built the *heiau*, he would rule all the Hawaiian Islands. The small harbor town of **Kawaihae** provides a glimpse of a more authentic Hawaii, where locals come to "grind" (eat), paddle, camp and fish. Nearby, the botanical garden **Pua Mau Place** provides the chance to wander among flowers, trees and sculptures, and hand feed peacocks.

If you don't mind leaving the pool bar, you can explore beaches that are still devoid of resort development. You don't

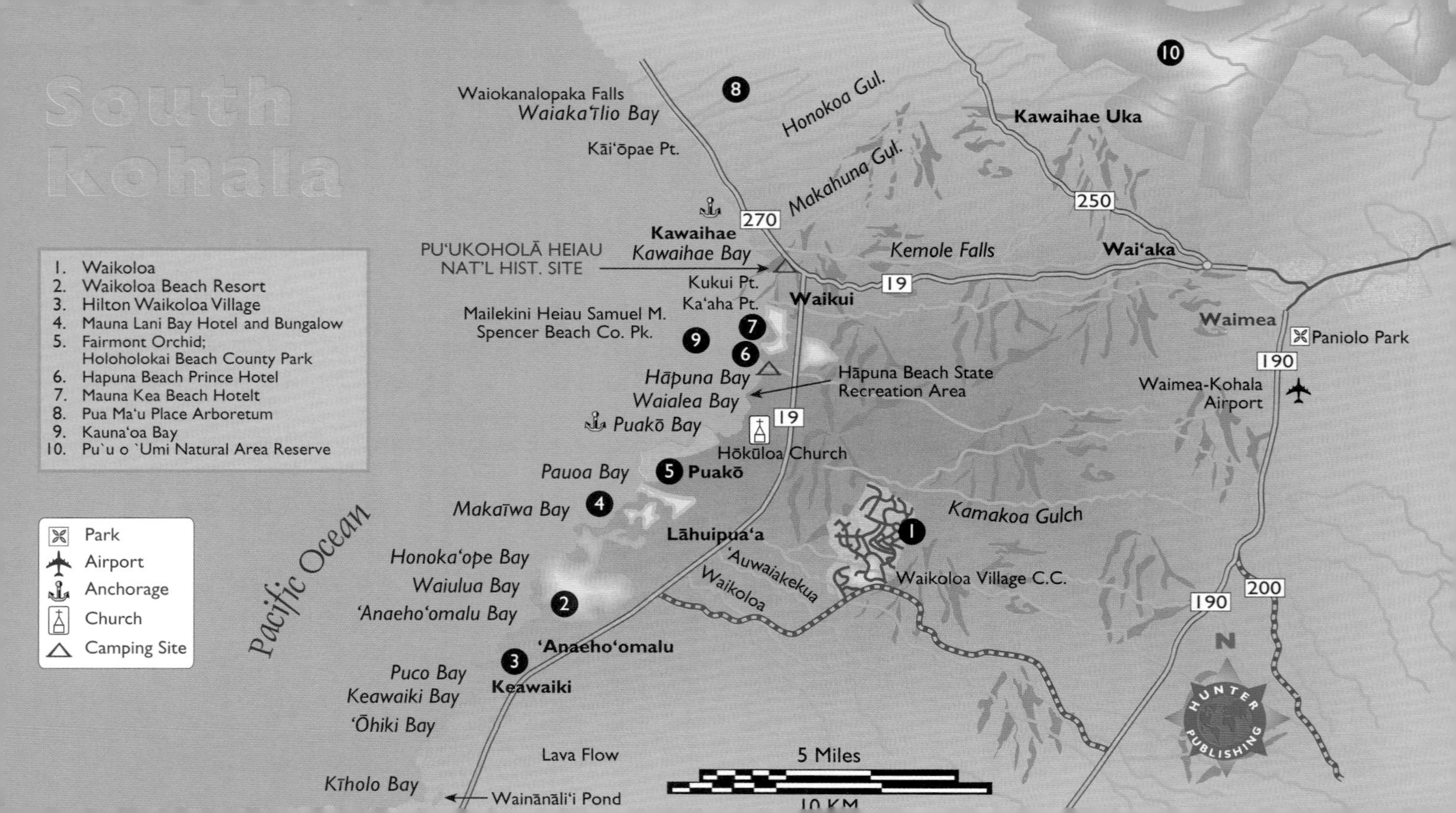

South Kohala
1. Waikoloa
2. Waikoloa Beach Resort
3. Hilton Waikoloa Village
4. Mauna Lani Bay Hotel and Bungalow
5. Fairmont Orchid; Holoholokai Beach County Park
6. Hapuna Beach Prince Hotel
7. Mauna Kea Beach Hotelt
8. Pua Ma'u Place Arboretum
9. Kauna'oa Bay
10. Pu`u o `Umi Natural Area Reserve
Park
Airport
Anchorage
Church
Camping Site
Pacific Ocean
Waiokanalopaka Falls
Waiaka'ilio Bay
Kāi'ōpae Pt.
Honokoa Gul.
Makahuna Gul.
Kawaihae Uka
Kawaihae
Kawaihae Bay
PU'UKOHOLĀ HEIAU NAT'L HIST. SITE
Kemole Falls
Wai'aka
Kukui Pt.
Ka'aha Pt.
Waikui
Waimea
Paniolo Park
Mailekini Heiau Samuel M. Spencer Beach Co. Pk.
Hāpuna Bay
Waialea Bay
Hāpuna Beach State Recreation Area
Waimea-Kohala Airport
Puakō Bay
Hōkūloa Church
Pauoa Bay
Puakō
Makaīwa Bay
Kamakoa Gulch
Lāhuipua'a
'Auwaiakekua
Waikoloa
Waikoloa Village C.C.
Honoka'ope Bay
Waiulua Bay
'Anaeho'omalu Bay
'Anaeho'omalu
Puco Bay
Keawaiki
Keawaiki Bay
'Ōhiki Bay
Lava Flow
Kīholo Bay
Wainānāli'i Pond
5 Miles
10 KM
270
250
19
190
200
N
HUNTER PUBLISHING

South Kohala Coast *(Hawaiian Images)*

have to venture far to find some seclusion, where you can stroll hand in hand with your special someone, looking for green sea turtles swimming or basking on shore. Afterward, you may be inspired to proclaim your love as locals do with environmentally friendly "graffiti" in the lava desert along the highway – white coral letters against the dark lava rock. Or you can toast with a cold mai tai at that evening's sunset, while native Hawaiians play the `ukulele and dance the hula. One way or another, you'll feel like celebrating – it's hard to be stressed in a vacation wonderland like South Kohala.

■ Orientation

Navigating around South Kohala is a simple affair, as Hwy 19 (Queen Ka`ahumanu Hwy) provides the only north/south access to the area. Waikoloa Road snakes *mauka* up to the suburban hamlet of Waikoloa Village, while Hwy19 jogs east just before Kawaihae on its way to Waimea.

The district lies firmly in the rain shadow of Mauna Kea, resulting in an arid region that, coupled with rough lava flows, produces a hot, barren wasteland that seems an unlikely place for some of the world's finest resorts. This topography is often shocking to first-time visitors who expect a lush, green Hawaii. However, the combination of perpetually sunny weather and billions of dollars in investment have transformed it into an ideal resort paradise.

Did you know? According to state law, all beaches in Hawaii are public. Resorts must provide shoreline access and parking for non-guests. So you can visit the beaches in front of resorts even if you aren't staying there. Yeah, brah!

MONEY-SAVING TIP: ONLINE DEALS

As one hotel employee said, "If you pay rack rate at a resort, you're not doing your homework." There are deals offered by virtually all of the resorts at their websites (which we've included) – such as package deals for families booking more than one room, or $100 toward services on the premises each day. Of course, there are also deals offered by online travel websites like Expedia.com (we prefer their customer service to Travelocity.com). A little time on the computer could save you money to spend on something other than accommodation, so get cyber-surfing!

Directional info: We've written the directions the way they're given on the Big Island: *mauka* and makai. Turn *mauka* means "toward the mountain," *makai* means "toward the ocean." This way you'll make sure to turn the correct way no matter which direction you're headed.

Waikoloa

Waikoloa (*Hawaiian Images*)

Waikoloa is the main resort area (actually, Waikoloa Beach Resort, though it's comprised of independently owned hotels, condominiums, stores and restaurants) that fronts some terrific beaches and a range of activities like water sports, golf, dining and shopping. It is closer to Kona, and more affordable than some of the upscale resort areas farther up the coast. There is a **gas station** adjacent to the Kings' Shops, open 6:30 am-10:30 pm daily.

Kings' Shops and all of the resorts have **ATM** machines. There's a plethora of shops at the resorts, as well as at Kings' Shops and Queens' Marketplace, both near the entrance to the Waikoloa resort area. For profiles, visit www.bigislandadventureguide.com.

Don't forget: There is only one area code for the entire island – 808.

KINGS' SHOPS' PETROGLYPHS

There is a short petroglyph walk adjacent to the Kings' Shops, accessed next to the restaurant Roy's. There are a few small areas where Hawaiians chiseled figures and names into the lava long ago. The path runs along one of the golf courses, and at some point access is denied due to the danger of being struck by an errant golf ball. This is a decent introduction to petroglyphs, but if you want to see a truly impressive display of them, head to the Puako Petroglyph Trail (p. 236).

Adventures

On the Beach

`Anaeho`omalu Bay

`Anaeho`omalu Bay aerial view (Hawaiian Images)

A beautiful crescent of sand facing a placid bay. "A Bay," as it's widely referred to, is a wonderful beach, popular with both visitors and locals. Ancient fish ponds provide a pleasant buffer between the shoreline and the Marriott, keeping the beach from being dominated by the resort and its guests. The bay is windy, but protected, making it an attractive destination for kitesurfers and windsurfers. In winter, the beach is lined by a high sand berm to protect against damaging surf, which results in a limited area to spread out towels and chairs. Most people throw a towel at the top of the berm and enjoy a splendid view of the day's activities.

There are good facilities here, including showers, restrooms and fresh water. Ocean Sports (see below) runs an activity

`Anaeho`omalu Bay (*beachweddingshawaii.com*)

booth at the north end of the beach, renting equipment for water sports, and booking boat trips. If you want more seclusion, consider a short wander down to Kapalaoa Beach (see below). To get to A Bay, turn *makai* directly across from the Kings' Shops.

HAWAIIAN MYTHOLOGY: BEACH NAUPAKA

Around the fishponds behind A Bay, as well as at many other beaches and resort areas in South Kohala, you'll find a plant with green shoehorn-shaped leaves, white berries and small white blossoms whose petals seem to form only half a flower. This is beach *naupaka*. Hawaii is also home to mountain *naupaka*, similarly composed of the other "half" of the flower.

According to Hawaiian mythology, the two *naupaka* blossoms are separated lovers. Pele, goddess of the volcano, was attracted to a young man who refused her advances because of his love for his girlfriend. Pele tried to isolate him in the mountains by surrounding him with lava, but her sisters compassionately turned him into mountain *naupaka*. When Pele's rage turned on the girlfriend, the sisters intervened by turning the girl into beach *naupaka*. The two half-flowers remain apart, but forever display that they are incomplete without their lover.

Kapalaoa Beach

To escape the Waikoloa crowds and feel like you're a million miles from civilization (though still in sight of it), walk south for 10-15 minutes along the sand from `Anaeho`omalu Bay. There are numerous private inlets of sand tucked into the *kiawe* and *milo*, as well as some excellent snorkeling in the shallow reefs that front the beach. These reefs are also a favorite hangout for *honu* (sea turtles) who congregate in the shallow tidepools and venture onto the rocks and sand to bask in the sun. Please remember to stay at least 15 feet from them.

On Water

There are tons of water sports activities at A Bay, from legitimate ones like snorkeling, to goofy inventions like "hydrobikes" – a bicycle suspended on a float that you can pedal around A Bay. **Ocean Sports** (☎ 886-6666, www.hawaiioceansports.com) has a booth labeled "Ocean Activity Center" at A Bay that rents everything you need for a beach adventure, with windsurfing lessons for $60/hour (or rental for $30/hour), snorkel gear for $6/hour or $20/day, boogie boards for $5/hour, kayaks $12 for 30 minutes, and hydrobikes for $25/hour. They also offer boat trips like sunset sails, glass bottom boat tours in the mornings, and whale-watching trips in the winter.

Similar trips and rentals can be arranged at the Hilton (and the Hapuna Beach Prince Hotel) through **Red Sail Sports** (☎ 886-2876, www.redsailhawaii.com). Red Sail Sports also has a kayak tour along the Kohala Coast to snorkeling spots ($45), and a bicycle tour to achieve views of the coast ($80 per person).

Note: The snorkeling at A Bay is on the murky side, with the best visibility on the right side of the beach farther away from the shore.

GLASS-BOTTOM BOAT TOURS

Several times each morning, Ocean Sports has 45-minute glass-bottom boat rides. There is a thick piece of glass on the bottom of the boat, through which you can see the reef and its inhabitants below. Snorkelers and divers won't be impressed because nothing beats actually being in the water, but there's something about glass-bottom boats that captures the imagination of children. Our niece and nephew are still talking about it a year later. Tours are $21, kids $11, children under three free.

"It is an important and popular fact that things are not always what they seem. For instance, on the planet Earth, man had always assumed that he was more intelligent than dolphins because he had achieved so much – the wheel, New York, wars and so on – whilst all the dolphins had ever done was muck about in the water having a good time. But conversely, the dolphins had always believed that they were far more intelligent than man – for precisely the same reasons."
– Douglas Adams

Mother and baby cavort in the Dolphin Quest pool at the Hilton

Dolphin Quest (☎ 886-2875, www.dolphinquest.org). Have you ever met anyone who didn't adore dolphins? They frolic, they do flips, and they always seem to be smiling. The Hilton Waikoloa offers a chance to get up close and personal with Atlantic bottlenose dolphins in their lagoon through a unique program called Dolphin Quest.

There are a range of "encounters," from a four-hour kids' camp (with 10 minutes of dolphin time), to a 1½-hour adult program including 40 full minutes with the dolphins. There are "interactive" times when you ostensibly "train" but basically kiss and cuddle the loveable porpoises, and then buy photos of the experience – the Dolphin Quest website is full of snapshots of celebrities doing just that. It's a pricey proposition, ranging from $150 to $330, or $1,025 for up to five people in your group, but as commercials remind us, the cost of snuggling everybody's favorite sea animal is priceless. Reserve early; they are often booked two months in advance.

Sunset Sails

People noticeably relax on sailboats when the captain cuts the engine and lets the wind take over. So if you want to really relax and enjoy a sunset, a ride on a sunset sail, coupled with *pupus* and an open bar – and breaching whales in winter – is about as good as it gets.

Hawaii sunset sail (viator.com)

There are several operators with sunset sails. We had a fantastic time with **Ocean Sports** (☎ 886-6666, www.hawaiioceansports.com), which shuttles people from the booth near the tennis courts at the Marriott to the harbor in Kawaihae. Our shuttle held about 20 women in a local chapter of the Red Hat Society, so it was a boisterous ride. The subsequent sail on a 63-foot catamaran was lovely; few things lower blood pressure like the gentle roll of the ocean. The crew brings you drinks that aren't watered down, as well as brownies and a glass of champagne at sunset for a toast. The captain is good about seeking out whales and then letting the boat drift in their vicinity – we had whales breaching 50 yards from the boat. Sweet! Ocean Sports sails Monday, Wednesday and Friday ($76, children $55).

There are also sunset sails offered by **Red Sail Sports** (☎ 886-2876, www.redsailsports.com) on Wednesday, Friday and Sunday from A Bay ($62, half-price for kids).

See the Mauna Lani section for sails leaving from that resort.

On the Links

Kings' Course (☎ 886-7888, www.waikoloabeachresort.com/kings_course.php, $195 non-resort guest, $130 resort guest). The Waikoloa Kings' Course is a challenging, links-style layout designed by Tom Weiskopf and Jay Morrish, which features several lakes and many Scottish-style pot bunkers. It's a flat course with tough, undulating greens and plenty of lava outcroppings to contend with. The juxtaposition of a Scottish links layout in a tropical seaside setting is very appealing. The signature hole is No. 5, a drivable par 4 with a deep, lava-accented bunker just short of the green that swallows the balls of those who don't make the shot. The course is very well maintained, and has some spectacular views.

"I have a tip that can take five strokes off anyone's game: it's called an eraser." – Arnold Palmer

On the Kings' Course

Beach Course (☎ 886-6060, www.waikoloabeachresort.com/beach_course.php, $195 non-resort guest, $130 resort guest). Waikoloa's Beach Course is a typical resort course, not as imposing as the Kings', but with greens that can bewilder the best of them. The fairways are a bit wider than the Kings' and the bunkers aren't quite as deep, but the lava is just as unforgiving when it sucks balls in (and sometimes spit them out with fantastic results). The Robert Trent Jones, Jr. design has some great ocean views, epitomized by No. 12, the signature hole, that's as beautiful as any ocean hole on the island. The

On the Beach Course

short par 5 with a sharp dog-leg left requires a conservative tee shot or the risk of hitting straight through the fairway and onto the rocks below. The allure of a long second shot into the green is even riskier, as the green is perched tightly against a precipitous drop to the sea. The Beach Course gets a little more crowded than the Kings', but it does provide a forgiving golf experience and a satisfying day of Hawaiian golf.

Wondering what that tan bird is that you keep seeing around golf courses? It's not a duck, it's not a chicken, but it's pretty goofy? It's a **gray francolin**, a partridge drawn to irrigated places in dry habitats – like a golf course in the middle of a lava desert.

In the Spa

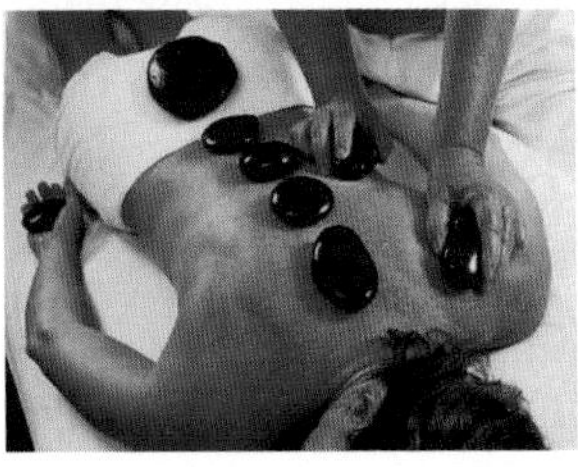

Located in the Hilton, the **Kohala Sports Club and Spa** has a weight room and cardio room where every machine has a flat screen TV – but how is working out on your vacation relaxing? The Spa is where it's at, with a steam room, rock Jacuzzi, and a range of treatments such as *lomi lomi* massage.

Where to Stay

In addition to the resorts, there are a number of condominiums (popular with time share operators) in Waikoloa. This is a good option if you want a kitchen. See the Waikoloa Beach Resort website at www.waikoloabeachresort.com for more information.

See page 65 for an explanation of the hotel $ price codes given below.

Hilton aerial view

The Hilton Waikoloa Village (425 Waikoloa Beach Dr, ☎ 886-1234, www.hiltonwaikoloavillage.com, 1,242 rooms incl. 57 suites, rooms $199-$639, suites $1,060-$6,150). This is the "Disneyland" resort, with all kinds of gaudy (and fun) bells and whistles: a waterslide, waterfalls in the swimming pool (one of them), a fake beach, flamingoes, and even a dolphin lagoon, where you can watch trainers working with them – or pay for the privilege to work with them yourself. There are more subtle touches like well-placed hammocks and Asian sculpture around the property. You can travel about the resort on foot of course, but why not take the boat or the tram? As we overheard one repeat guest enthuse, "I love it here. I grew up in a small town in southern Vir-

The pool area

Ocean-view double room

ginia so I like having everything at my fingertips."

For romantics, there is a wedding chapel and wedding planner on the grounds. For parents, there is Camp Menehune, a place where your kids can play while you pursue your own vacation, possibly on one of the eight tennis courts, or in the spa. **Red Sail Sports** (www.redsailhawaii.com) offers water sports gear rental, sunset sails, and scuba trips, or you can peruse $7 million worth of art on the mile-long Museum Walkway. And there is plenty of upscale shopping. Like most resorts on the Big Island, the Hilton is designed to prevent you from wanting or needing to leave the premises, and spending money elsewhere.

The major drawback – there is a fairly serious lack of professionalism in much of the hotel staff (just try to get a call through to the front desk!), and many former guests have complained of nickel-and-diming. Fortunately, management has caught on, and has instituted more freebies; the in-room coffee is now complimentary instead of $3.50 a day, for instance. If you're hoping to be pampered, you'll probably want to look elsewhere. But, if you're on a family vacation or want to stay in a resort full of "eye candy," this might be an ideal place for you.

This is a huge complex with rooms in three "towers." The lagoon tower is popular because rooms have views of the dolphins in the lagoon, though couples tend to prefer the ocean tower and its adults-only swimming pool. Standard rooms are reasonably spacious and have a modern design. One nice touch: small stuffed dolphins sit on the beds and are available for purchase. $$$-$$$$

"The great advantage of a hotel is that it's a refuge from home life." – George Bernard Shaw

Waikoloa Beach Marriott (69-275 Waikoloa Beach Drive, ☎ 886-6789, toll free ☎ 888-924-5656, www.waikoloabeachmarriott.com, 545 rooms, $269-$389 after construction). The Marriott is undergoing a huge renovation, so it's hard to know what the new-and-improved version will be like, though the

Waikoloa Beach Marriott

specs are intriguing. They're going for a more contemporary look, replacing steel-rod balcony bars with glass plates, for example. They are also building a new two-story spa, adding an adult swimming pool, extensively remodeling the lobby and poolside restaurant, and giving rooms a face lift.

We hope they will keep the Herb Kane mural and 1890 *koa* fishing canoe in the lobby, a nod to the rich culture here, though it sounds like those will be replaced by a doorway to the new 12,000-square-foot ballroom. The renovation should be finished by the time you read this.

The new, stylish rooms have all the basic amenities and a "Poly-Asian" flair, with Japanese touches and underwater photos on the walls. Rooms have two double beds or a king. The resort fee ($15 a day at the moment) includes self-parking, snorkel equipment, wireless Internet access, use of the tennis courts, and two *mai tais* daily. $$$$

Garden-view room

Where to Eat

Waikoloa Beach Grill (69-1022 Keana Pl., ☎ 886-6131, www.wbgrill.com). On the golf course (the Waikoloa Beach Course) rather than the beach, the Waikoloa Beach Grill has views of Mauna Kea and mai tais made they way they should be – light on juice, devoid of sour mix, and heavy on the rum. They don't even bother with the usual umbrella-in-a-pineapple garnish. Their recipe comes from Trader Vic's, the ultimate *tiki* restaurant in the '70s (and still great, if you're ever in California). Best of all, they're cheap by South Kohala standards – only $7.50. You'll need a *pupu* to absorb some of that rum – maybe a gourmet grilled cheese sandwich with fontina cheese, grilled onions and country olives on sourdough ($9.50). Or head straight to dessert; they have a rotating menu of fresh pies. Open 11 am-9 pm. $$-$$$

For an explanation of the restaurant $ price codes, see page 66.

Kings' Shops

There is a food court with public restrooms at Kings' Shops, offering scary pizza, nachos, $8 bagel sandwiches and a Subway. There are outdoor tables on a lanai overlooking the koi pond.

GOOD VALUE ★ **Merriman's Market Café** (Kings' Shops, ☎ 886-1700). This Mediterranean café with a dash of Hawaiiana is the less expensive cousin to famed chef Peter Merriman's Waimea venue, Merriman's Restaurant. You won't be able to eat store-bought hummus after you sample it at Merriman's Market Café; we like to pair it with marinated olives with thyme and garlic. There are daily fish specials, as well as classics like lamb pita with tsatziki and marinated tomatoes, kalamata olives and roasted peppers. This is a place where you won't be the only person sneaking a glass of wine with lunch. Open 11 am-9:30 pm daily. $$

Merriman's

Big Island Steakhouse (Kings' Shops, ☎ 886-8805) has a casual atmosphere with a nautical theme set on the lake. Want to see what a six-egg omelette looks like? Then stop on in for breakfast and try the seafood special with crab, lobster, tomatoes and cheese. Or opt for something slightly less artery-clogging like macadamia nut pancakes. Lunch is a reasonably-priced option for the area, with selections ranging from steak burgers and crab cake sandwiches with red pepper aioli to club sandwiches or fish and chips. The steak fries that come with the sandwiches are pretty good, but they're stingy with them. Dinner is the most popular meal served here, with folks choosing from three different sized cuts of prime rib, as well as filet mignon, New York strips, and nice fresh fish. There's not much for the veg head in your group, but there is a fully-stocked bar. Open 7 am-2:30 pm (breakfast till 11 am) and 5:30-9 pm daily. $$-$$$

AUTHOR'S CHOICE ★ **Roy's Waikoloa Bar & Grill** (Kings' Shops, ☎ 886-4321). Food and service may dip at other restaurants, but for over a decade we've been completely satisfied at Roy's. Roy Yamaguchi was one of the innovators of Hawaiian fusion cuisine, and we love him for it. In fact, he was Hawaii's first winner of the James Beard Award, a culinary Oscar, so to speak. At Roy's, you'll find innovative dishes with great flavor combinations and fresh, local food served with an artful flourish. The menu changes often here, but a few favorites are always available, like the macadamia nut crusted *mahi mahi* in Kona lobster essence. The chocolate soufflé is legendary. The atmosphere is contemporary, with modern art adorning the walls, track lighting and a huge open kitchen. Be sure to make reservations, since they often sell out for the night. Open 5-9:15 pm (last seating). $$$$

"A gourmet who thinks of calories is like a tart who looks at her watch." – James Beard

The Hilton Waikoloa

The Hilton Waikoloa has several pool-side eateries ($$) with the usual sandwiches and salads – and at the **Orchid Café**, a "soda shop" with sweets like waffle cones and banana splits. The **Lagoon Grill**, next to the dolphin lagoon, has draft beer and sinful curly fries. The nachos are gross

The Orchid Café

(unless you like the goopy "cheez" used on ballpark nachos), but the sandwiches are pretty good.

The free boat ride to the restaurants from the lobby area (and around the resort) runs every 15 minutes from 7 am to 11 pm The tram runs every 10 minutes from 6 to 1 am.

Kirin Chinese Restaurant

Kirin Chinese Restaurant (☎ 886-1288) has great Chinese food in a relaxed atmosphere. Their drinks pack a punch, too. We toasted repeatedly with several family members here when we learned our brother-in-law had never had a mai tai. Later, we realized that inebriation makes the silly boat ride especially fun. Open 11 am-11 pm. $$$

AUTHOR'S CHOICE ★ **Donatoni's Restaurant** (☎ 886-1234). We can't resist fine-dining Italian food, which is remarkably hard to find on the Big Island. Luckily, there's Donatoni's for anniversaries and Valentine's Day. This is one restaurant that the Hilton can be proud of. The food, service and atmosphere are fabulous. The menu will have you drooling (once you read the translations, or use the glossary to help explain some Italian ingredients) with dishes such as the wide ribbon pasta with artichokes, mushrooms, olives, sun-dried tomatoes and pesto in the Primi section, or try a meat or seafood dish from the Secondi section – the grilled swordfish with spicy caponata, for example. Starters are great, such as the antipasto of cheese and cured meat from Northern Italy, or the Padua soup of potatoes, leeks and spinach. In the ultimate touch of decadence, Donatoni's offers both a risotto and a gnocchi of the day. Open 6-10 pm nightly. $$$$

"The trouble with resisting temptation is that you may not get another chance." – Edwin Chapin

The Marriott has ***Nalu's Bar & Grill*** *by the pool, which is open for lunch. There is no fine dining restaurant on the property. Nalu (pronounced "NAH-loo") is the Hawaiian word for "wave."*

Entertainment

The Hilton's **Malolo Lounge** feels like an airport lounge, with faded carpets and $11 martinis. A glass of Kendall Jackson Chardonnay for $12? A glass of Maker's Mark for $14? Wow. But there is a pianist there every night, which improves the ambiance considerably.

Royal Marriott Luau (☎ 886-6789). The Marriott's luau has a reputation as one of the best on the island, a Hawaiian feast with a Polynesian show. The table of kids next to us was enthralled by the dancing and fire twirling. Shows are Sundays and Wednesdays for $75, $36.46 for kids six-12.

The centerpiece of Hawaiian luaus is usually the *imu* ceremony, in which a pig is removed from the *imu*, an underground oven, after cooking there all day.

Legends of the Pacific (☎ 886-1234, ext. 54). This is the Hilton's luau, held every Tuesday and Friday. It also has a Polynesian show and a buffet dinner. Tickets are $78 for adults, $39 for children five-12.

■ Waikoloa Village

This residential area has grown immensely since the golf course was built in the early 70s. Its commercial hub is the Waikoloa Village Shopping Center, detailed below. With an elevation around 1,000 feet, it's cooler up here than on the coast. The area is known to get quite windy in the afternoon. It's up Waikoloa Road, just a few miles upcountry from Waikoloa Resort.

Practicalities

Waikoloa Village Market is a grocery store open 6:30 am-9 pm daily.

B Natural (☎ 883-3986) is a health food store tucked in the back of the Waikoloa Village Shopping Center. Billie (the "B" in the store's name) sells organic food, groceries and supplements, as well as fresh soups and sandwiches in her deli. Open 9 am-6 pm daily.

There is an **ATM** outside of the First Hawaiian Bank.

The **76 gas station** is open 4:15 am-11:30 pm Mon-Sat, 5 am-10 pm Sun.

Adventures on the Links

Waikoloa Village Golf Club (☎ 883-9621, www.waikoloa.org/golf, $75). This Robert Trent Jones, Jr. course is just enough off the beaten track to be a great option for those who want to squeeze in a quick round. The course has a fun, forgiving layout, but the frequent winds can transform it from a lamb to a lion. The greens are also infamously beguiling. Water only comes into play on three holes, but when it does, such as on #18, it can be challenging. The sand in the bunker is especially coarse, but it needs to be or the wind would rob the course of its sand in a single afternoon. The views are astounding on clear days, especially on the front nine. The low greens fees make this course a tremendous value, and if you catch it on a day when the wind is down you can score extremely well.

Waikoloa Village Golf Club

Where to Eat

Anthony's Italian & Irish Restaurant & Pizzeria (☎ 883-9609). This understaffed restaurant has menu issues, serving dishes like bangers and mash (Scottish sausages with mashed potatoes, sautéed onions, peas and brown gravy), shepherd's pie, pastas and taco salad. We tend to stick to pizza (the 12-inch pies start at $12) with a pint of Guinness. Even weirder than the food selection, the menu notes, "Due to limited seating, we require $10 minimum food order per person." Wacky. Still, the atmosphere is amenable, with red sponge-painted walls and jazzy art. Open 11 am-10 pm daily. $$

For an explanation of the restaurant $ price codes, see page 66.

Mauna Lani Resort Area

"Money is better than poverty, if only for financial reasons." – Woody Allen

Mauna Lani

Mauna Lani Bay Hotel (*Westrav International*)

Not only is the Mauna Lani one of the finest resorts on the Big Island, but they have made serious and successful efforts to be a low-impact resort that walks the fine line between offering their guests the ultimate in luxury while remaining steadfastly "green." They have also done an excellent job of preserving the rich cultural history of the area, presenting it in such a way that it actually augments the resort experience without compromising the integrity of the culture. The Mauna Lani has successfully woven together such seemingly disparate elements as ancient Hawaiian fish ponds with a modern hotel design, nature trails with top-end golf courses, and cultural respect with luxuriously indulgent resort services.

Mauna Lani operates with an understated elegance, which is not to say that it lacks opulence. The centerpiece of the lobby is a glimmering, modern waterfall, and the hotel atrium boasts saltwater pools inhabited by tropical fish, rays and baby sea turtles. There is upscale shopping, high-end dining, two fantastic golf courses and a cutting-edge spa. This is a resort that caters to those who expect impeccable service in order to completely relax. You won't find a raucous *luau* at the Mauna Lani, but rather quiet music and the sound of the ocean. Guests calmly wander among the palm trees, seeking the perfect hammock or a well-positioned cabana, luxuriating in the serenity of the surroundings.

Mauna Lani has the most solar electric generating capacity of any resort in the world, with a three-acre installation of solar panels and a fleet of solar-powered golf carts.

The Fairmont Orchid

Built in 1990 and opened as a Ritz-Carlton, the Fairmont Orchid already feels like an old, established hotel. Elegant, and almost a bit stuffy, there are many extra touches here that make the hotel feel especially genteel. Look for chandeliers hanging from any potential open space, such as the elevators or the fitness center. The Fairmont is just now completing renovation of all of its guest rooms and hallways. Yellows pervade the design scheme, with an emphasis on floral prints and pastels in the wallpaper, carpets and drapes. Guests look a little out of place strolling the formal halls in their bikinis and sarong wraps, but they don't seem to mind. Elegance and luxury can have that kind of effect.

The Fairmont Orchid (Westrav International)

The Fairmont Orchid at left (*Hawaiian Images*)

The main beach area consists of a man-made lagoon and imported sand, but that doesn't diminish the effect of a very user-friendly experience. The waves lose their energy over the breakwall, which makes the area calm for swimming, kayaking or snorkeling. The more adventurous will want to venture outside of this beach to the reefs that front the hotel. *Honu* (sea turtles) abound here, and visitors (as well as locals!) can't get enough of them. It is not uncommon to see 10 or 15 turtles basking in the sun on the rocks while snorkelers circle around others in the bay. The pools are also very attractive, and there is a seemingly endless maze of waterfalls, a new braid of water around every corner.

Adventures on the Beach

While there are several beaches within the Mauna Lani complex, most of them are small, man-made resort beaches, strewn with cabanas and dominated by hotel guests. While technically all of Hawaii's beaches are public, it may be awkward to carry in a cooler and radio and throw down your towel. However, we've visited the beach at **Makaiwa Bay**, a well-protected swimming beach with decent snorkeling around the southern point. There are restroom facilities and a casual, overpriced restaurant. Access to the beach is through the Mauna Lani trail network. Park at the public access lot across from the Mauna Lani spa and follow the path through the fish ponds, then south to the beach.

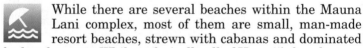

Honoka`ope Beach is another reasonably attractive public beach. It's a small strip of salt-and-pepper sand wedged between rough lava outcroppings at the extreme southern end of the Mauna Lani complex. The swimming and snorkeling is okay here when it's calm, but it's nothing to go out of your way for, unless you have exhausted your other options. While the Mauna Lani Hotel has done a wonderful job of blending into its surroundings, sprawl has taken over the outskirts of the resort, which is now packed with condo complexes and upscale private residences. This beach is sort of lost in the maze of development. From Hwy 19, turn into the Mauna Lani, then take your first left, following signs to the golf courses. Proceed past the golf clubhouse, and take a left at 49 Black Sand Beach. You'll have to pass through one of the ubiquitous checkpoints. Simply tell the guard you're headed for the beach and you'll receive a pass. There is a restroom and potable water at the parking lot.

Adventures on Water

HAWAIIAN FISH PONDS

A centerpiece of the Mauna Lani resort complex is the incorporation of anchialine ponds into its design. Anchialine ponds are brackish pools of water adjacent to the ocean that were used by Hawaiians for aquaculture for at least the last several hundred years. Most were built by hand around natural tide pools that filled the pool with water and fish at high tide, then stranded the fish as the tide receded. A *makaha* (sluice) was also used as a gate that allowed smaller fish to enter but kept larger fish from getting out. The small fish would fatten up on abundant algae and fresh-water shrimp, growing too big to leave again. Fish ponds were kept for the *ali`i* (royalty), and serviced by the commoners. The Big Island has the largest concentration of anchialine ponds in the world. Some of the finest ponds still exist, including those at `Anaeho`omalu and the Kalahuipua`a fish ponds that run throughout the Mauna Lani resort.

The Mauna Lani has its own water sports center, **Mauna Lani Sea Adventures** (☎ 885-7883, www.

hawaiianseaadventures.com). This outfit has a booth on the beach at Maka`iwa Bay, and offers a variety of boat trips, such as snorkel sails ($59) on Tuesday, Thursday and Friday; Sunset Sails ($55) on Sunday, Tuesday, Wednesday and Friday; whale-watching in winter ($50) on Sunday, Tuesday-Friday, as well as daily scuba diving trips ($144 incl. gear and two tanks), intro classes and certification. One-stop shopping!

Adventures on Foot

Mauna Lani scrupulously maintains a network of trails that includes a self-guided tour to the fish ponds, petroglyphs, an ancient habitation cave, the Eva Parker Woods Cottage, and more. Ask the front desk or concierge for a map and guide.

Malama Trail to Puako Petroglyphs

Difficulty: Easy

Distance and type: 0.75 miles total, out-and-back

Time: 30 minutes

Puako petroglyph (HVCB)

This short hike leads to the Puako Petroglyph Archaeological Preserve, a lava slab with an astonishing concentration of an estimated 3,000 ancient petroglyphs. The meaning of the symbols is a mystery, as well as why ancient Hawaiians traveled to this area to chisel them – it seems to be in the middle of nowhere. The common conclusion is that it must have had a spiritual significance, perhaps as a center of *mana* (power).

The trail is unpaved and passes through dense *kiawe* (you'll want to wear thick-soled shoes, since *kiawe* thorns can easily puncture a slippah and poke your foot). A trail circumnavigates the collection. Please don't touch the petroglyphs, no matter how much you'd like to make a rubbing. (If you really can't resist the urge, make a rubbing of the petroglyph replicas near the trailhead.)

The trailhead is at the parking area of Holoholokai Beach Park. Turn into the Mauna Lani complex from Hwy 19, then turn right toward the Fairmont Orchid, taking another right at the sign for the beach park.

Photography Tip: The best time to visit the petroglyphs is early in the morning or late in the afternoon, when the sunlight isn't directly overhead.

Adventures on the Links

Francis I'i Brown Golf Courses (☎ 885-6655, www.maunalani.com, $205 non-resort guest, $140 resort guest). Both of the Mauna Lani's two courses are excellent, with the stark beauty of emerald grass cut by black lava rock, which, incidentally, can completely destroy a golf ball and can also be very dangerous if you fall down in it. So do not go into the lava after wayward balls. Mauna Lani has a terrific golf shop and excellent service. Play either course or both for Hawaiian golf at its best.

Mauna Lani South, 15th hole

- **Mauna Lani South** is a bit more forgiving than the North and has some of the most beautiful scenery on the island. The 7th is a long par 3 that borders the ocean, allowing players to take in the views while they desperately try to keep from hacking their balls into the big blue. The signature hole is the 15th, a par 3 that features a tee shot over a bit of the Pacific Ocean, and is an exhilarating experience, especially if you make it over the crashing waves. The South isn't a long course, but requires relatively straight shots to score well on its narrow holes.
- **Mauna Lani North** is, arguably, slightly superior to the South, though it's a close call. The North plays a bit

tougher, with more trees and elevation changes, and has a better mix of holes, though it might not offer quite as many photo opportunities. The par 4 6th would be quite a simple hole if there weren't a tree in the middle of the fairway, forcing you to hit your tee shot right and very long, or to the left over (one hopes) a line of traps, or short with the hope of hitting an approach shot high enough to clear the tree, and long enough to carry the lake in front of the green. The par 4 at the 9th hole would be a par 5 if there were any justice in golf – it's 437 yards dead into the onshore wind, and that wind sometimes stops the ball in mid-air. And, if that's not enough, the green is guarded by big bunkers and a lake.

Heads Up: Whales

If you're on the 15th or 16th hole of Mauna Lani's South Course between January and March, don't forget to look for whales. We've seen them leaping out of the water like popcorn from here. In fact, as one launched out of the water near the shore, we screamed in delight and started cheering like lunatics. Then we remembered where we were, and apologized to the group that was teeing off behind us. For the record, one of the women was very gracious about our faux pas, saying, "That's alright – we should've been watching!" The Mauna Lani trail network passes through here so, come to think of it, you should also watch for hikers screaming during your backswing.

Spa Adventures

The Spa

The Spa at Mauna Lani (☎ 881-7922, www.maunalani.com) is constantly garnering accolades. Here's one more: it is certainly one of the best on the island, with a range of luxurious "treatments." In addition to classics like massage (in outdoor *hales*, or houses) and mud wraps, there are more unusual treatments like body exfoliation with Kona coffee and raw Hawaiian sugar. The centerpiece of the spa is something called Aquatic Body Therapy, which seeks to recreate the womb experience as you float in a pool heated to body temperature, inside a lava tube. You are massaged and stretched in the pool while listening to soothing music broadcast under the water and the cascade of a waterfall. We know someone who tried this treatment and then had to cancel all of his plans for the rest of the day because he was too much of a relaxed "noodle" to do anything.

Spa Without Walls (☎ 885-2000, www.fairmont.com/orchid).The spa at the Fairmont Orchid is another lovely place to pamper yourself. Spa Without Walls offers 15 massage *hales*, small huts scattered around the gardens, with nothing but the sound of waterfalls and birds to serenade you. Ask for the special one with the *puka* (hole) in the floor that allows you to watch the fish swim in the pond beneath you. The spa also offers an array of skin treatments, wraps and Ayurvedic experiences.

At the Spa Without Walls

Where to Stay

The Mauna Lani (68-1400 Mauna Lani Dr, ☎ 885-6622, toll free ☎ 866-877-6982, www.maunalani.com, 343 rooms, $430-$1,860, bungalows $4,800-$5,900). The rooms at the Mauna Lani are luxurious, with large lanais and screen doors – flick off the A/C, slide the louvered wooden doors closed and allow the sea breezes and the sound of the ocean to lull you to sleep. The beds are addictively comfortable. If you want to live in the lap of luxury, consider a stay in one of the oceanfront bungalows

with private pools, fishponds and even 24-hour butlers adept at mixing mai tais. $$$$

The Fairmont Orchid (☎ 885-2000, toll free ☎ 800-845-9905, www.fairmont.com/orchid, 540 rooms incl. 54 suites, $329-$759, suites $959-$3,000). The guest accommodations at the Orchid are split into two towers, one for families and the other for adults – a superb idea. The latter includes a "Gold" level floor, accessible with a special elevator key, which has a lounge serving complimentary breakfast, happy hour, a large screen TV and a private concierge. All guest rooms boast marble-tiled baths, large closets, fine furnishings and spacious lanais. Ocean-view rooms offer tremendous views of the crashing waves, but the garden-view rooms aren't bad either, with lush greenery and waterfalls. $$$$

Bedroom in the Fairmont Orchid

See page 65 for an explanation of the hotel $ price codes given above.

Where to Eat

Mauna Lani

The Bay Terrace Restaurant (toll free ☎ 866-877-6982 ext. 36) serves a glorious breakfast buffet, with fresh island fruit, an omelette station, breads, fresh juices, miso soup, meat – a great way to start the day, though you may need a nap on the beach afterward. The Bay Terrace is also open for dinner, with an Italian theme, serving pastas like seared prawns with farfalle pesto and cannelloni beans, fresh catch with lemon risotto, and even a grilled New York steak. Open daily for breakfast 6:30-10:30 am, dinner 6-9 pm except Tues and Wed. $$$$

AUTHOR'S CHOICE ★ **The Canoe House** (☎ 881-7911), the Mauna Lani's "signature restaurant," offers fine dining on a large lanai next to the ocean, making it a tremendous sunset spot (the subsequent starlit night sky is equally fabulous). The food, by Chef Jon Natsubara of Honolulu, is fantastic. The Hamakua mushroom soup with truffle oil dissolves on the tongue, readying you for other delectable dishes like the goat cheese and potato ravioli, the grilled rack of lamb, the seared fresh fish served with crab and asparagus fondue, the bananas foster with cinnamon balsamic ice cream and a hazelnut crisp... you'll know you're on vacation in paradise if you eat here. Open 5:30-9 pm daily. $$$$

The Canoe House

For an explanation of the restaurant $ price codes, see page 66.

The Gallery Restaurant (☎ 885-7777). Even the golf course restaurant is great at the Mauna Lani. With appetizers like *ahi* tuna tartare, entrées like roasted *mahi mahi* with a rock shrimp, asparagus and pearl pasta, plus desserts like white and dark chocolate swirl cheesecake, the Gallery Restaurant is a sweet reward for a "rough" day on the links. Also open for lunch 11 am-2 pm, dinner 6-9 pm daily. $$$$

The Fairmont Orchid

"Gathering of the Kings" Polynesian Feast (☎ 885-2000). This is essentially the Fairmont's luau, though it is called a "Polynesian Feast" because there is no *imu* (underground oven for cooking a pig). All the other bells and whistles are here, though – dancers, fire-twirlers, all-you-can-eat buffet and open bar. Saturday nights, adults $99 (half-price for children).

South Kohala

The Grill

The Grill (☎ 887-7320). *Koa* wood panels, elegant furnishings, white linens and a grand piano create an atmosphere of classic elegance at the Fairmont Orchid's signature restaurant. The menu follows tradition, but with an updated, contemporary twist. Choose from an array of steaks, lamb and fresh fish, all deliciously prepared. Try the Kona Coffee-Brined Duck Breast with Ohelo Berry Chambord Coulis or other à la carte offerings, or choose the Hôte Menu, which includes a soup, appetizer, choice of entrée, and dessert for $72. The Grill is pricey but delicious. Reservations are required. $$$$

AUTHOR'S CHOICE ★ **Brown's Beach House** (☎ 885-2000) is a place everyone seems to love, and how can you not? Located on an outdoor lanai overlooking the Orchid's beach, Brown's has some outstanding offerings even at lunch, like the lobster fried rice with shitake mushrooms, vegetables and egg. Even the burger is elevated to an art form (it *should* for $16), combining Black Angus sirloin and Kobe beef with a balsamic glaze, Maui onions, local heirloom tomatoes and melted brie. Dinner entrées are similarly upscale, with meat and seafood selections, such as the *ahi* tataki and local exotic mushrooms, as well as several vegetarian options, including fresh linguine with Hamakua mushrooms, asparagus and grape tomatoes. $$$$

Puako

"The Constitution only gives people the right to pursue happiness. You have to catch it yourself." – Benjamin Franklin

The relaxed beach neighborhood of Puako is a strip of middle- and upper-end homes arranged around Puako Bay. The reef here is extensive, pristine, and it drops off steeply, making for some excellent scuba diving. There are lots of *honu* (sea turtles) around here, drifting lazily in the light surf that breaks over the reef. There isn't much in the way of a sandy beach, just several public access points along the rocky shoreline, and a municipal boat launch.

Practicalities

M's Puako General Store (☎ 882-7500, 07 Puako Beach Dr, www.puakogeneralstore.com). Groceries, beer and general sundries are on sale here, a place frequented by locals and the many visitors staying in vacation rentals around here. They also serve take-out pizza. Open 5:30 am-7:30 pm daily.

Adventures in Water

Puako can't boast any good swimming beaches, but its fame for scuba diving is well-deserved. Snorkeling can also be fantastic here, though it should be limited to intermediate and advanced snorkelers, since the reef is shallow and afternoon wind conditions can quickly turn the area from balmy to treacherous. Scuba divers and intrepid snorkelers will find a dazzling array of lava tubes, pinnacles and walls, as well as healthy reef life, along the outer reef.

To reach Puako from Queen Kaahumanu Highway (Hwy. 19) turn makai onto Puako Beach Drive between mile markers 70 and 71. The reef spans the entire length of the Puako area, but there are two main entrance areas. The most popular access is from the rocky parking lot just before Puako Beach Drive ends at a gated community, about three miles from the highway. There are several possible entries here, but the easiest one is south of the parking lot along a good path, just past the Na Ala Hele trailhead sign for the Ala Kahakai. A few yards past the sign is a small sandy beach that affords a good entry point for snorkeling or shore diving. Be careful only to snorkel here when it is calm, and, if you notice the wind picking up, head in quickly. The afternoon trades can make it difficult to come back over the reef to exit.

Another popular access area is at pole No. 120, across from a church just over two miles from the highway. What used to be a nice parking area now has several boulders blocking the way, but one or two cars can still park in front of them. Walk past the boulders down to the water for a relatively easy access. However, keep your eyes open for black sea urchins, which will leave a painful reminder of your day on the water.

■ Mauna Kea Resort Area

"Rest: the sweet sauce of labor." – Plutarch

Adventures on the Beach

Kauna`oa Bay (Mauna Kea Beach)

Mauna Kea Beach

The white sand, crescent beach in front of the Mauna Kea, on Kauna`oa Bay, is one of the most beautiful on the island – Rockefeller knew what he was doing. There are a number of lounge chairs with distinctive orange towels here, so you won't forget where you are. One employee told us that when the resort was renovated in 1994, the hotel introduced aqua towels. Return guests were outraged, and the orange towels came right back.

> **Tip:** *By law, all beaches in Hawaii are open to the public. The Mauna Kea tries to minimize the number of non-guest beach users by issuing just 30 parking permits for the beach each day – arrive at the security gate at noon and you'll be told it's full. (But if you're, say, coming to the hotel to eat or shop, you're allowed to park in the already crowded lot.) Follow the "shoreline access" signs to the beach.*

Hapuna Beach

This is *the* beach on the island. A quarter-mile of the white sandy stuff, endless boogie-boarding waves in winter, a luxury hotel anchoring the north side, coral reefs around the southern flank, camping A-frames, gear rentals, snack shop, picnic pavilions... it's all here. And, well, so are a lot of the

Hapuna Beach (BIVB)

island's residents and most of its visitors, it seems. Finding parking in the ample lot can be a challenge, especially on weekends, but staking out a square of sand usually isn't as competitive. This is just a great place to come for a big day at the beach. Snorkeling is really only a summer thing, as the bay is wide open to the ocean and unprotected from the waves rolling around from the north side, or from the winds that generate a lot of choppy surf in the channel. Bring a boogie board!

Hapuna and Mauna Kea Beaches (Hawaiian Images)

Hapuna Beach is around mile

marker 69 on the Mamalahoa Hwy, about three miles south of Kawaihae. Just follow the signs.

69s

Actually called Waialea, this sleepy beach is usually occupied by friendly locals. Shady ironwood trees back the beach, providing ample protection from the sun, which makes this a great place to come if you haven't had your fill of the beach but your skin can't tolerate any more sun. The beach got its "street" name due to its location at telephone pole No. 69, which has confusingly been re-labeled No. 71.

There's good swimming here when it's calm, and the snorkeling can be decent around the northern point or at the extreme southern end. Facilities include uninviting restrooms, drinking water and some picnic tables. A paved parking lot and driveway have recently been completed, virtually ensuring that the popularity of this beach is going to skyrocket. No matter, it's a wonderful beach. To get here, turn off Hwy 19 at the Hapuna Beach turnoff, then drive past the Hapuna lot for about a mile. Look for the driveway around pole No. 71.

Adventures on the Links

Mauna Kea (☎ 882-5400, www.princeresortshawaii.com/big-island-golf.php, $210 non-resort guest, $150 resort guest). This is one of the best, if not *the* best, golf course on the Big Island, and one of the very best in the state. It was the first golf course on the Kona Coast, built in 1964 by Robert Trent Jones, Sr. for Laurance Rockefeller as part of the Mauna Kea resort. It is, like most of the coastal courses here, built on the black lava of which the island is formed, which creates a beautiful contrast with the green grass, the white sand bunkers, and the blue waters of the Pacific.

Mauna Kea Golf Course (teetimesworld.com)

Mauna Kea is a delight. Every hole is interesting and presents a unique challenge. And virtually every hole is on the water or has sweeping views of the coastline. The most famous is No. 3, a heart-thumping par 3 over an inlet of crashing ocean waves (and a billion submerged golf balls). It's one of the most beautiful and terrifying shots in golf, especially since it's so early in the round and more especially with a strong wind. Another favorite is the 6th hole, a par 4, which begins with a shot from an elevated tee to a gently curving fairway far below, and then requires a precise approach to an elevated and well-bunkered green. The par 3 at the 11th is another palm-dampener, downhill straight toward the ocean to a green surrounded by sand traps, a combination of beauty and intimidation.

But it's a shame to single out particular holes when almost all of them are fascinating.

Mauna Kea is expensive and can get crowded at times, but it's well maintained and has a very nice shop. And it is the classic Big Island golf experience.

Hapuna (*teetimesworld.com*)

Hapuna (☎ 880-3000, www.princeresortshawaii.com/hapuna-golf.php, $150 non-resort guest, $120 resort guest). The sister course to Mauna Kea is Hapuna at the Hapuna Beach Prince Hotel, a much newer course designed by Arnold Palmer. It's a links-style course and was meant to be ecologically friendly and harmoniously situated within the natural vegetation, which means, to the golfer on the course, there's lots of native grass to eat lots of golf balls. It's a very good course with many interesting holes, but sight lines it can be confusing the first few times you play it. Get a yardage booklet with maps of the holes, and even then you'll be guessing where to aim certain shots. It's target golf, with lots of sand, many elevation changes and three lakes. And the wind, which is a factor on all Hawaiian courses, can be very strong here.

Where to Stay

Mauna Kea Resort was the original luxury hotel on the Big Island, and it exudes an old school elegance that defines it as a classic. Built in 1965 by Laurance Rockefeller, this resort is on one of the island's best beaches – and its sister resort, the Hapuna Beach Prince, fronts the popular Hapuna Beach. As the adage goes, it's all about location, location, location.

As we all know, the Rockefellers were rich, thanks to oil industrialist John D. Rockefeller, who was at one time the richest man in the world. Laurance Rockefeller (his grandson) used some of his inheritance to collect art. He then scattered over 1,600 pieces of unmarked art around the Mauna Kea property – no identifying plaques – because he wanted it to feel like a home, rather than a museum. Turn a corner and you may see a rare pink granite Buddha smiling down at you, or a glittery Thai deity dancing on a dragon.

The Mauna Kea Resort shows over 1,600 artworks from Laurance Rockefeller's collection

This careless opulence is incredible, and offers plenty to see as you explore the resort grounds. In the course of your investigation, you'll most likely stumble upon the fitness room, with $60,000 of equipment, or the light that shines down into the ocean each night to attract manta rays, or any number of mature trees. This is a beloved resort for some long-time Big Island visitors – we met a man who has stayed here every year since 1972. Coincidentally, the same lifeguard has worked here since 1972 – employee turnover is low at the Mauna Kea.

Oysters Rockefeller, invented in 1899 at Antoine's Restaurant in New Orleans, were so named because of the richness of their sauce – as rich as a Rockefeller.

Mauna Kea Resort (62-100 Mauna Kea Beach Dr, ☎ 882-7222, toll free ☎ 800-882-6060, www.maunakearesort.com, 310 rooms and 10 suites, rooms $390-$615, suites $975-

$1,650). The rooms at the Mauna Kea still use a traditional key instead of one of those newfangled plastic cards. Inside, rooms are on the small side because Rockefeller wanted guests to spend less time in their rooms and more time on the beach (the pool is on the small side for this reason as well – enjoy the beautiful beach!) The TV is small, too. High-speed Internet access was recently added because of guest demand.

The Mauna Kea Resort

What sets the rooms apart are the large lanais that are completely private – your neighbors can't see you. There are other nuances as well. Each room has an original piece of art on the wall, and you get a free postcard of your room's art. There is also a book about the resort's art collection. Then there are the trademark orange Mauna Kea touches – orange slippers, orange bathmat, orange shower cap. This is no cookie-cutter hotel chain – this is the real deal. $$$$

See page 65 for an explanation of the hotel $ price codes.

The Hapuna Beach Prince Hotel is the sister resort to the Mauna Kea; a free shuttle transports guests between the two every 20 minutes. Built in 1994, Rockefeller had originally envisioned it as the resort for business gatherings. Such delineation hasn't really taken hold – families love the beach at Hapuna – though the Hapuna Prince has conference facilities and is the only hotel on the island with its own business center for making copies, shipping, or using the Internet.

The Prince has a more contemporary feel than the Mauna Kea, with mood lighting in the elevators and suites shaped like "bubbles" coming out of the hotel's façade. The pool is designed (sort of) in the shape of a whale, with an "infinity edge" – when the water is filled to the rim of the pool. It doesn't have the classic vibe of the Mauna Kea, but there can only be one classic. One tremendous advantage the Prince does have is that all the rooms have ocean views.

Hapuna Beach Prince Hotel

Hapuna Beach Prince Hotel (62-100 Kauna`oa Dr, ☎ 880-1111, toll free ☎ 800-882-6060, www.priceresorts-hawaii.com, 351 rooms incl. 36 suites, rooms $370-$650, suites $1,250). As mentioned before, all rooms at the Prince face the ocean, and have lanais from which to gaze at the water or watch the sunset. They have all the usual resort amenities, such as a safe, refrigerator you can stock, ironing board and wireless Internet service. Unlike other resorts, there is no "resort fee" built into the price for amenities like using the fitness center. There are also special 8,000-square-foot suites, with a 24-hour chef. $$$$

Guests at the Mauna Kea or Hapuna Beach Prince Hotel who are between the ages of five and 12 can spend time at the **Prince Keiki Club**, a day camp for kids. Keiki activities include building sandcastles, arts and crafts like making *leis*, swimming at the pool and learning to hula. A full day (9 am-4 pm) is $50, though it is half-price in summer from May 1 to Sept. 30.

Where to Eat

Mauna Kea

The Pavillion at Manta Ray Point (☎ 882-5810). This is the Mauna Kea's main restaurant, with a wide lanai overlooking the ocean. There's the usual lavish breakfast buffet here in the mornings. Dinner is Hawaiian regional cuisine (that delectable fusion of fresh fish, produce and other local ingredients for fine dining selections), with dishes such as fresh fish sautéed with macadamia nut basil pesto, or grilled with a fresh pineapple and tomato salsa. There's live jazz Thurs-Sat. Open for breakfast 6:30-11 am, dinner 6-9 pm daily. $$$$

For an explanation of the $ price codes, see page 55.

The Copper Bar (☎ 882-5810), "seven pillars down" from The Pavillion, is one of our favorite swanky places to enjoy a sunset. Set in a high-ceilinged, open-air hallway, a bar made of copper (hence the name) provides excellent mai tais ($10. 75) for the tables set around a stage, where Hawaiian trios harmonize, graceful dancers move to the *hula*, and the sun sets behind them. The sunsets in summer aren't as ideal as the rest of the year, as it sets more to the north – still, it's a great setting. Your drink price includes complimentary *pupus* like macadamia nuts and potstickers. Look at the ceiling over the bar, which has a hole built for a palm tree several stories high. Music from 6:15-7 pm. Open 5-9 pm daily.

"Too much of a good thing can be wonderful." – Mae West

Batik (☎ 882-5810). This posh Indonesian restaurant features a dreamy salad of artichoke petals with artichoke hearts, tomato, avocado and asparagus with fresh herb dressing and specialty curries presented in a silver tureen with shrimp, lobster, or chicken, and side cups with coconut, raisins and other accents. Other dishes include blackened *ahi* steak with mango relish and *liliko`i* (passion fruit) sauce, stir-fried vegetables and crispy truffle potato raviolis. Most of the waiters have worked here for over 15 years, so the service is outstanding. Note that they are only open twice a week, so reservations are extremely important. Open 6:30-9 pm Wed-Thurs. $$$$

Some options at Batik

There is a Tuesday night luau at the Mauna Kea with fantastic hula dancers. $79 adults, $38 kids.

Hapuna Beach Prince

Ocean Terrace (☎ 880-3192). This is the place for the lavish breakfast buffet at the Prince, and what a location: overlooking Hapuna Beach. Open 6:30 am-11 am. $$$$

Hakone Steak House & Sushi Bar (☎ 880-3192). The food is good here; we once sat at the sushi bar next to a couple that was determined to try everything on the menu. While we would've liked to do the same, our wallet limited us to a few rolls, like the dynamite Extra Spicy Tuna Roll. We also indulged in a sake flight: three premium sakes arranged for a taste test. There is a popular Japanese buffet here Friday through Sunday with sushi, soup, fish and meat dishes. $$$-$$$$

Coast Grille and Oyster Bar (☎ 880-3192) is the signature restaurant of the Hapuna Prince. The dining room sits below a white rotunda, while one arc of the circle is tables on a lanai looking out over the beach and, in winter, the sunset. The food here is standard resort dining room fare, with lots of expensive fresh fish and steaks. They have some delicious appetizers, including a Puna goat cheese torte and an Asian guacamole with taro chips. As the name makes clear, they also have an oyster bar, and a list of very fine, very expensive champagnes. There's live music here every night, with a dance floor for a slow, romantic spin. Open 5:30-9 pm nightly. $$$$

■ Kawaihae

"Success is getting what you want. Happiness is wanting what you get." – Dave Gardner

Locals cool off at Kawaihae Harbor

This harbor town may be small, but it has plenty to offer people looking for a break from the resort areas. The majority of the businesses listed are in the Kawaihae Shopping Center, which houses a few jewelry stores and one of the two Harbor Galleries. Across from the center is a small boat harbor with public restrooms. Several local canoe clubs put in here.

Practicalities

The 76 **gas station**, adjacent to the Kawaihae Shopping Center, is open 5 am-9 pm daily.

Kawaihae Market & Deli is a convenience store that also sells burgers, bentos, a few sandwiches made to order, fresh salads and fishing supplies. Open 4:30 am-9 pm Mon-Fri, 6 am-8 pm Sat-Sun.

Adventures

"Rich and various gems inlay
The unadorned bosom of the deep." – John Milton

Under Water

Kohala Divers (Kawaihae Shopping Center, ☎ 882-7774, www.kohaladivers.com) offers boat dive trips to North Kohala dive sites, certification courses and gear rentals, as well as kayaks and boogie boards. In winter, they also combine dive trips with whale-watching tours ($59) by dropping off the divers and then cruising around while they're at depth. Even if you're diving, you'll most likely see tons of whales (literally "tons"!) and spinner dolphins on your way to the dive sites, a huge bonus. This is a laid-back crew that has great respect for the ocean's inhabitants. Our only complaint is that if there are snorkelers on the tour, you end up at shallow dive sites you could access on a shore dive.

Kawaihae Harbor (Hawaiian Images)

On Foot

**Pu`ukohola Heiau** (☎ 882-7218, www.nps.gov/puhe). It isn't difficult to sense the *mana* (spiritual power) emanating from Pu`ukohola Heiau, a sacred Hawaiian temple and National Historic Site. Kamehameha I, the Big Island king who united the Hawaiian Islands under his rule, had it constructed in 1790 after a prophet told him that if he built the temple in honor of the war god Ku on "Whale Hill," he would conquer all of the islands. (For the record, he annexed Kaua`i through treaties rather than conquest, a source of pride for the people of that island – "We were never conquered!")

The *heiau* is large – 224 by 100 feet, with 16- to 20-foot lava rock walls constructed without the use of mortar. You may be tempted to go inside, but you must go no farther than the mouth – only Hawaiians may enter it for religious purposes.

PU`UKOHOLA HEIAU

King Kamehameha I wasted no time fulfilling the prophecy for which he built the *heiau*. He invited his chief rival – and cousin – Keoua Kuahu`ula to the temple's dedication ceremonies in 1791. Upon arrival, Keoua and most of his entourage were killed, and Kamehameha offered Keoua as a sacrifice to Ku. With Keoua removed from power, Kamehameha I could focus on conquering the other islands, becoming the sole ruler of them all by 1810, and securing his legacy as King Kamehameha the Great.

A short walk down the park's path leads to another temple, **Mailekini Heiau**. This is an older, less well-constructed *heiau* shrouded in mystery, as its purpose was kept a secret by Hawaiian priests. Kamehameha I later converted it into a fort with 21 cannons on the front walls to ward off invaders.

This small bay is the site of Hale o Kapuni Heiau

Continue to a lookout for the submerged **Hale o Kapuni Heiau**, a temple to the shark gods. You can see the leaning stone where Chief Alapa`i kupalupalu mano is believed to have watched sharks devour his offerings. What is remarkable about this spot is that, though sharks don't usually frequent shallow, sunny areas like this one, black-tipped reef sharks swim here year-round. Look for their dorsal fins circling, and remember that this isn't the best place to swim. You won't even want to stick your toe in – standing at the water's edge for a closer look, we were startled by a school of fish flying out of the water nearby, desperately fleeing a shark. There's something really cool about this area. Admission is free. The air-conditioned Visitors Center is open 7:30 am-4 pm daily, closed noon-12:30 pm for lunch.

Mano (pronounced "MAH-no") is the Hawaiian word for "shark."

Ala Kahakai

The Ala Kahakai (Trail by the Sea) provides an interesting amble through old and new Hawaii. The trail leads to secluded beaches and pristine snorkeling spots, but also through the heart of several luxury Kohala resorts. Trail runners are acceptable for this hike, though hiking sandals are ideal. It's nice to be able to flip off your sandals and dig your toes in the sand during the beach portions of the hike without having to worry about wet, sandy socks.

Ahu (stone cairns) mark the Ala Kahakai

In 2000, President Bill Clinton signed into law the "Ala Kahakai National Historic Trail Act," which will eventually be a 175-mile trail from North Kohala to Hawai`i Volcanoes National Park. Presently, the only maintained and signed part of this trail is from Spencer Beach Park to 69s beach, then from Holoholokai Beach to the southern section of the Mauna Lani complex.

Ala Kahakai - Spencer Beach Park to Waialea Bay (69s)

Difficulty: Moderate

Distance and type: 6.5 miles total, out-and-back

Time: 4-6 hours

This is a bizarre hike, as it passes through areas of raw Kohala coast as well as two of the most luxurious resorts on the island. It should take two to three hours each way, but that will depend on how many pictures you take, or how many beaches you stop at for a swim. The trailhead can be found at the south end of Spencer Beach Park, right by the pavilion. The trail starts off through a particularly dense *kiawe* thicket. Shortly, you'll arrive at the secluded Mau`umae Beach, which is a beautiful slice of paradise. You'll wind through some private property before coming to the Mauna Kea resort complex.

Number 3 hole, Mauna Kea Golf Course, where the trail passes

The trail cuts right past the No. 3 hole of the Mauna Kea Golf Course – the signature hole, a par 3 over the ocean. Take a few minutes and watch some groups go through here; it's amazing how many people's knees buckle with the sea battering on the rocks between them and the green. From here, the trail stays within the complex until reaching the Hapuna Beach Prince Hotel at Hapuna. Just before this point, there are some interpretive plaques explaining that this area was a housing site for the rich and elite of ancient Hawaiian civilization. As your eyes focus from the sign to the massive luxury bungalows that back it, you'll realize how little some things change.

The trail picks up at the southern end of Hapuna Beach, crossing several 4WD roads on its way to 69s. This part of the trail is dusty and hot, and following the trail can be confusing. Look for *ahu* (rock cairns) to help guide your way.

On the Beach

Spencer Beach Park

Spencer Beach Park

The beach here is soft and sandy. The swimming is okay, but there are coral heads scattered just off of the beach that can cut an unwary foot. The snorkeling is marginal due to the usual lack of clarity here, probably from the beach's proximity to Kawaihae Harbor. There are several picnic tables, some with shade, right on the beach, making this a nice picnic spot. The sunsets here are wonderful.

Camping

The camping at Spencer Beach Park is crowded even when it's half-full. With space for 68 people, there isn't much privacy here, unless you camp on the sloped sites to the north of the main camping area. There is a strict checking of permits, and you cannot enter the site after 11 pm (they will close the access gate on you). You can only imagine the amount of partying that used to go on here that led to such diligent enforcement of regulations. Alcohol and drugs are forbidden and an infraction invalidates your permit. A county permit is required (see Camping, p. 52-53). There are showers, restrooms, potable water and a pavilion with electricity.

Where to Eat

"Seize the moment. Remember all those women on the 'Titanic' who waved off the dessert cart." – Erma Bombeck

Tres Hombres Beach Grill (Kawaihae Shopping Center, ☎ 882-1031) serves good Mexican fare in a festive atmosphere. Combination plates are the way to go, especially if they include a delicious chile relleno. The

South Kohala

refreshing margaritas have a tendency to slide down a little too easily. We ate here one time with 12 family members, including six small kids, and the waitress managed to keep smiling, which we found miraculous. Open noon-9 pm Sun-Thurs, until 9:30 pm Fri-Sat. $$

For an explanation of the $ price codes, see page 55.

Something's Cookin' in Paradise (Kawaihae Shopping Center, ☎ 880-9700). This is a small place – only tables for two – with surprisingly great food. Breakfast (served till 10:30 am) includes standards like French toast, as well as more unusual fare, such as the fried rice omelette with bacon, Portuguese sausage, spam and green onions. Lunch includes plate lunches, wraps, salads and sandwiches – the panini with Swiss cheese, turkey, avocado and sun-dried tomatoes is outta sight (especially if you substitute fries for chips). Open 7:30 am-2 pm Tues-Fri, 9 am-2 pm Sat. $-$$

AUTHOR'S CHOICE ★ **Kawaihae Harbor Grill** (☎ 882-1368, www.theseafoodbar.com) is a well-loved restaurant for breakfast, lunch and dinner. It combines a nautical theme – fishing nets, glass floats, and canoe paddles adorn the walls – with Hawaiiana, like old photos from the area, or the old grass skirts and coconut tops in the ladies' room (marked "Gulls"). It's a very pleasant place to enjoy homemade biscuits with pepper gravy, or Seafood Eggs Benedict (with crab cakes or the fresh catch) for breakfast, and fresh fish or mac-nut crusted pork chops for dinner. This is not a place for people on a diet; order a single biscuit and it will not only be topped with melted cheese, but sliced in half, grilled and buttered. You'll be licking your fingers.

Kawaihae Harbor Grill

Cocktails and pupus are served upstairs at the restaurant's **Seafood Bar**, with "lite dining" treats like ginger steamed mussels ($16), Oysters Rockefeller ($10), or crab-stuffed pasilla pepper ($14). As in the Kawaihae Harbor Grill, the food here is great. Plus, it's open late – till 11:30 pm. The

Kawaihae Harbor Grill is open daily for breakfast 6:30 am-11 am, lunch 11:30 am-2:30 pm and dinner 5:30-9:30 pm. $$$-$$$$

Na po`o po`o Sunset, by Jurgen Wilms

If you have to wait for a table at a Kawaihae restaurant, you can kill some time by admiring the art at **Harbor Gallery**. A painting by one of their artists in shown above. It is open until 8:30 pm daily in both of its locations, in the Kawaihae Shopping Center as well as next to the nearby Harbor Grill. More info at www.harborgallery.biz.

Café Pesto (Kawaihae Shopping Center, ☎ 882-1071). We love Italian food, so we love Café Pesto, which manages to be lively and romantic at the same time. (We wish they'd open a restaurant in Kona!) We know we should try a different salad than the Volcano Mist, but we can't seem to do it. The mixed greens drizzled with gorgonzola cheese and balsamic vinaigrette are shaped into a "volcano" by ripe tomato slices and topped with crispy fried onion strings. Yeah baby, yeah! They have gourmet pizzas, huge portions of salads and, of course, wine. Best of all, it's an affordable indulgence. Open for lunch 11 am-4:30 pm, dinner 4:30-9 pm daily. $$-$$$

Café Pesto

Nearby Attractions & Adventures

Pua Mau

Pua Mau Place (10 Ala Kahua, ☎ 882-0888, www.puamau.org). Pua Mau ("Continuously Flowering") is a charming botanical garden that is still uncrowded. You won't find orchids here in the arid climate, but there are plenty of other beautiful flowers and vistas in a network of walking trails. Kids will love the chance to ring the sonorous bells, or hand-feed peacocks and other fowl in the aviary. Be warned: the peacocks peck kind of hard. It's startling! There are large bronze sculptures throughout the grounds – butterflies, scorpions and giraffes.

There are over 200 species of hibiscus in the "**Hibiscus Maze**." Wander up to the Visitors Center, with restrooms and a deck for whale-watching in wintertime.

The 15-acre park – a nonprofit undertaking – is still being developed, but it's already well worth the admission price (roughly the cost of a tropical drink). Keep in mind that no pesticides are used on the grounds, so slather on the insect repellent: either your own, or the organic one the gal at the admission desk can provide free of charge. There is also a gift shop with mugs, books, cards, clothing and plant starts that you can take back to the mainland.

To get here, drive north of Kawaihae to the *mauka* turn between mile markers 6 and 7 – there is a historical marker on the *makai* side that is easy to drive past, for some reason. Pua Mau is open from 9 am-4 pm daily. Admission is $10, seniors and kids 10-17 are $8, children under 10 free.

"A day without laughter is a day wasted." – Charlie Chaplin

Spencer Beach Park *(Hawaiian Images)*

North Kohala
Kohala Historical Sites State Monument
Pacific Ocean
Alenuihaha Channel
'Upolu Airport
'Upolu Pt.
Mo'okini Heiau
Kamehameha I Birthplace
Honoipu Landing
Hikapoloa
Hiana'ula Pt.
Hā'ena Pt.
Hā'ena
Kapa'a Beach Co. Pk.
Māhukona Harbor
Māhukona Beach Co. Pk.
Māhukona
Koa'ie
Lapakahi State Historical Park
Camping Site
Airport
Anchorage
Kamehameha I Statue
Kamehameha Co. Pk.
Keawa'eli Bay
Honomaka'u
270
Hāwī
Pu'u'Ula
Pu'u Mamo
Kapa'au (Kohala)
Hala'ula
Hālawa
Makapala
Niuli'i
Lookout
Pololū Valley
Kēōkea Beach Co. Pk
St. Paul's Episc. Church
Kēōkea Bay
Kauhole Pt.
Kapa'aiki Pt.
Kalalae (Pt.)
Paoakalani I.
Kā'ilikaula
Kamehameha Rock
Pu'u o Nale
250
Kapa'au Gul.
Wainaia Gul.
Wala'ohi'a Gul.
Niuli'i Str.
Wai'āpuka Gul.
Ohiahuea Str.
Waikaloa Str.
Pu'u Hue Ranch
Pu'u Kehena
Pu'u o Lani
Pu'u Lepo
KAWAIHAE
KOHALA
MOUNTAIN
Kahuā Ranch
Von Holt Mem. Pk
Pu'u o 'Umi Natural Area Reserve
Kaunu o Kaleiho'ohie 5480
Keawe'ula Bay
Māla'e Pt.
Kohala Ranch
Hō'epa
Waipahoehoe Gul.
Kawaihae Uka
Kohākōhau St
Waiokanalopaka Falls
Kohala Estates
N
HUNTER PUBLISHING
HAWI-KĀWĀIHAE
19 Miles
5 MILES
10 KM

North Kohala

IN THIS CHAPTER

North Kohala is less than a half an hour from the resorts of South Kohala, but it feels like a world away. Less visited and densely populated than many other parts of the Big Island, residents proudly consider it a last bastion of Old Hawaii.

North Kohala has a rich cultural heritage, symbolized by its statue of King Kamehameha the Great, the monarch who united the Hawaiian Islands under his rule. Kamehameha was born in North Kohala, near Mo`okini Luakini Heiau, whose rock walls once witnessed thousands of human sacrifices. Nearby Lapakahi State Historical Park holds the remains of an ancient fishing village; with turquoise waters and views of neighboring Maui, it's not hard to see why early Hawaiians wanted to live here.

The North Kohala countryside (BIVB)

The North Kohala Coast (Hawaiian Images)

The natural surroundings contribute not only to the palpable *mana* (spiritual power) of North Kohala, but also to the tremendous adventure possibilities. Gallop on horseback across private ranches in the rolling Kohala Mountains, the oldest on the Big Island, or snorkel above lava and coral, diving down to hear the conversations of humpback whales in winter – North Kohala is one of the best spots for whale-watching on the island. And the incredible views at the Pololu Valley Lookout might inspire you to strap on your boots for one of the most spectacular hikes on the Big Island.

Throw into the mix some exceptional dining and shopping in North Kohala's two towns, Hawi and Kapa`au, and you'll begin to understand why visitors to North Kohala feel as though they've been let in on a fantastic secret.

■ Orientation

North Kohala is an area of stark, beautiful contrast. The main artery is the **Akoni Pule Hwy** (Hwy 270), which enters the area just north of Kawaihae in a rough, arid grassland hiding ankle-busting lava and covered with thorny *kiawe* trees. As the highway arcs from north to east, you will quite suddenly notice a change in vegetation, and often, weather – the transition from the dry leeward side of the island to the wet windward side. In the afternoon, this can make for awesome rainbows as the late-day western sun strikes the inevitable afternoon rain clouds. The Akoni Pule Hwy is packed with cultural sites and beach parks, travels through Hawi and Kapa`au, and terminates at the Pololu Valley Lookout.

Kohala Mountain Rd (Hwy 250) is the upland road, which runs from the south side of Waimea all the way to Hawi. The views above the coast are wonderful as the road roller coasters over the incandescent green hills of upcountry Kohala.

A SCENIC LOOP

Consider making a loop of your trip to North Kohala by taking the *mauka* road in the morning before the afternoon rains, and the *makai* road in the afternoon to catch the rainbows. It won't add more than a half-hour to your travel time.

Directional info: When giving directions, we will refer to *mauka* (toward the mountains) and *makai* (toward the ocean) so that you will know which way to turn whatever direction you are heading.

Along Akoni Pule Highway

Lapakahi State Historical Park

Lapakahi State Historical Park

This cultural park allows a glimpse into the life of an ancient Hawaiian fishing village. Be sure to grab a handout from the friendly volunteer in the info house at the parking lot. It's jammed with information on the structures and the history of the site, as well as information on how to play the ancient games that you'll encounter on the hike, and a map that corresponds to the plaques around the site.

From the park you can see Maui looming in the distance

What really makes this an enjoyable place is how gorgeous it is. It's not difficult to see why the Hawaiians of yesteryear would have chosen this spot to homestead. Additionally, there's some great snorkeling here, though if you decide to snorkel there are strict rules since it's in the park. You have to check in at the info house, where you'll get some guidelines for use (such as no towels or radios), as well as an update on the water conditions, where to access the water, and what you might see. Please be respectful. Admission is free.

To get here, turn *makai* between mile markers 13 and 14 on Akoni Pule Hwy.

Mahukona Beach Park

Aerial view of the Mahukona diving area
(shorediving.com)

Mahukona is a simple county park with a boulder beach that's good for enjoying sunsets, and whale-watching in winter. There is an expanse of lawn for camping, though the sites are better up in the trees (see *Camping*, p. 52-53). Locals and tourists gather in the parking lot by the old pier to hang out, fish and snorkel. There is a serious overpopulation of feral cats here, and they can sometimes wake you up at night doing what cats do. Oddly enough, there is a

"No Dogs Allowed" sign prominently displayed here, which may explain this infestation of wild felines. There are restrooms with showers, a pavilion with electricity and picnic tables, but no potable water. Turn *makai* between mile markers 14 and 15 on Akoni Pule Highway.

MAHUKONA

In ancient times Mahukona was the site of a fishing village named for a volcano that has since sunk into the Pacific Ocean, but any evidence of the community was largely destroyed by the docks, warehouses and machinery that sprang up here when Mahukona served as the main port for Kohala around the turn of the 20th century. The first railroad on the Big Island ran from the port of Mahukona to Hawi, and was the central artery for exporting sugar and pineapples, and importing everything for the area. There is quite a bit left over from this period, including the landing, docks, and some buildings, which makes for an interesting post-industrial study.

Adventures under Water

The snorkeling is good at Mahukona when it's calm. There is a substantial fish population, but coral is somewhat sparse. The visibility can be limited when the swell is up or there's a sharp onshore breeze, but is excellent when it's balmy. There's an interesting shipwreck about 100 yards offshore. Although opinions differ about the identity of the wreck, most seem to believe that it's the remains of the Inter-Island Steam Navigation Company ship *Kaua`i*, which ran aground here on Christmas Eve, 1913. To explore it, just follow the huge anchor chain which runs out from the old dock opposite the ladder. The engine, drive shaft

Bullethead parrotfish

and propeller can still be seen. Enter the water at the end of the parking lot by the old docks. You can probably drop right over the side of the pier if the tide is high enough, but it is a little shallow. Use the ladder to exit, or to ensure a safe entrance.

When the water is calm, the diving and snorkeling can be excellent at Kapa`a. The small beach is rocky, but provides a reasonable entry to the cove. Dive booties make this much easier. There is good visibility, as the bottom drops off quickly, which makes this a popular shore dive site, and increases the likelihood of viewing some larger fish, manta rays, and a small population of turtles. During the winter, the presence of loquacious whales can be heard while snorkeling. Be sure to dive down a ways to catch the sound – like the creaking of giant doors.

> **Did you know?** *Female humpback whales are longer than males – females reach 40 feet, while males are around 35 feet long. Calves are 10 to 15 feet long at birth, and weigh up to a ton!*

Adventures on Foot

Mahukona Beach Park to Kapa`a Beach Park

Difficulty: Easy
Distance and type: 3 miles, out-and-back
Time: 60-90 minutes

An old road along the former path of the railway that once ran from Mahukona to Hawi provides a great way to beat the crowds. The trail climbs very gradually as it meanders toward its junction with the road at Kapa`a Beach Park, a mile and a half away. There are some great, unspoiled reefs here that make excellent snorkeling opportunities for advanced snorkelers, but access is a big challenge. Only consider this when the sea is glassy calm. This trail also makes for a good mountain bike ride, but there are a few gates that necessitate heaving your bike over them, so a light-weight aluminum frame is an advantage. Also, the huge *kiawe* thorns result in a lot of flat tires.

A spur trail a half-mile from the trailhead leads to an ancient navigational *heiau*. The pattern of stones once pointed the way to important destinations for the early residents of the island. It is said that in ancient times this *heiau* was so important it ranked only a single class below important sites like Mo`okini, where human sacrifices were regularly performed. The *heiau* was badly damaged by the installation of a World War Two-era machine gun nest, but it has been restored. The view above the sea, across the channel to Maui, and to points beyond is a wonderful place to contemplate the bygone world. This is also a great vantage point for wintertime whale-watching.

The trailhead is just past the big warehouse when entering the park. Park at the closed gate.

"Nature is not a place to visit, it is home." – Gary Snyder

Camping

Kapa`a Beach Park

This laid-back little beach park is another terrific place to watch a sunset, look for whales, or simply kick back and ponder the panorama of Maui across the channel. Camping is permitted here (see *Camping*, p. 52-53) and there are some great campsites tucked up in the *kiawe* trees with wonderful views of the water. However, these sites can fill up quickly. Additionally, there is an unofficial group campsite just to the north of these sites that *can* get a little boisterous. However, we have enjoyed some very peaceful nights of sleep at Kapa`a – even on weekends. Amenities include restrooms, a picnic pavilion, BBQ pits and a shower down on the beach. There is no potable water.

Turn *makai* around mile marker 16 on Akoni Pule Highway.

Mo`okini Luakini Heiau

(☎ 591-1170). This very sacred *heiau*, or temple, is so significant that it was named as the state's first National Historic Landmark in 1963. Roughly spanning the length of a football field, Mo`okini Luakini Heiau was built in 480 AD for the Hawaiian war god Ku, according to Hawaiian chants. Legend is that Kuamo`o Mo`okini enlisted the help of 18,000 "little people," who passed the stones for the structure hand-over-hand in a human chain stretching 14 miles from the Pololu Valley – and completed the construction in one night. This legend is recounted in a children's book written by a Mo`okini descendant, Leimomi Mo`okini Lum, the current Kahuna Nui of the *heiau*, called *The Legend of Kuamo`o Mo`okini and Hamumu the Great Whale.*

The site's subsequent history, after Samoan priest Pa`au restructured Mo`okini Heiau sometime after his arrival in 1000 AD – and most likely instituted the practice of human sacrifice – is less suitable as a bedtime story. Thousands of people were sacrificed at the *heiau*, stripped of their skin on the sacrificial stone that still stands today.

Mo`okini Heiau, situated next to the ocean with views of Maui on clear days, instills a sense of holiness in the visitor. Indeed, it is not just a historical point of interest but a temple where people still leave offerings of *leis* to a carved statue (*ki`i*) of Ku inside the walls. Consider yourself in a church, and please be respectful of the site. Be sure not to remove anything.

Perhaps because of the relative inaccessibility of the site and its lack of facilities like interpretive signs or restrooms, it is easy to grasp the *mana* (spiritual power) of the *heiau* because you will probably find yourself alone. There are no hordes of tour bus groups jostling for photo ops, just a chance to pay respect to one of the most sacred places in Hawaii.

Leaving the site, you can turn left and walk a short way to another revered *heiau* that marks the place of King Kamehameha the Great's birth, **Kamehameha Akahi Aina Hanau Heiau**. Also known as Kamehameha I, he is believed to have been born here in 1758 as Halley's Comet passed overhead. He became a mighty monarch empowered by Ku, conquering the Hawaiian Islands (except Kaua`i) and then uniting them all under his rule. He later abolished the practice of human sacrifice.

To access these *heiaus*, you should turn *makai* at the sign for Upolu Airport (a seldom-used tarmac) between mile markers 19 and 20, then left when the road hits a T at the airport. You will need a 4WD vehicle for the dirt road (about two miles) – or drive until the puddles are impassable and then walk in. The walk is a good way to get yourself into the proper mindset.

An alternative access that doesn't require 4WD is from Old Coast Guard Station Rd, *makai* on Akoni Pule Hwy between mile markers 18 and 19. Follow the road for about a mile and turn right on an unmarked road where you'll encounter a cattle gate. You must call ahead for the gate to be left open for you (☎ 373-8000). It can be hard to reach someone, and they might not return a message left by a cell phone with a mainland area code.

Hawi & the Kohala Coast (Kanoa Withington)

Hawi

Hawi (pronounced "Hah-VEE") is a mix of Old Hawaii and hip newcomers looking for a slice of paradise. The town has just under 1,000 inhabitants, but a lot of amenities you'd expect to find in larger towns – excellent restaurants, art galleries and shops. Hawi foundered a bit when Big Sugar collapsed in the '70s, but the opening of Bamboo Restaurant in 1993 helped spur an economic recovery based on tourism.

Practicalities

Don't forget: There is only one area code for the entire island: 808.

The **post office**, just off Akoni Pule Hwy near the intersection with Hawi Road, is open 8:30 am-noon and 12:30-4 pm Mon-Fri, 9 am-10 am Sat.

Takata's (54-3627 Akoni Pule Hwy, ☎ 889-5261) is the main area **grocery store**. Open 8 am-7 pm Mon-Sat, 8 am-1 pm Sun.

> **Note:** *There is no door-to-door mail service in the towns of North Kohala, so most businesses use their post office box for their address. Fortunately, the majority of businesses in Hawi and Kapa`au are clustered on "main drags" along Akoni Pule Highway, making them easy to find.*

Where to Shop

Hawi is home to a number of stores along Akoni Pule Highway with unique shopping opportunities for the shopaholic in your group.

As Hawi Turns (Akoni Pule Hwy, ☎ 889-5023) is a small, hip store across from Bamboo that sells bathing suits, toe rings, shell hair clips, clothing, jewelry, candles in coconuts and other gifts. Open 10 am-6 pm Tues-Sat, 10 am-5 pm Sun-Mon.

"I always say shopping is cheaper than a psychiatrist."
– Tammy Faye Bakker

Persimmon (55-3435 Akoni Pule Hwy, ☎ 889-1050, www.persimmon-shop.com). This boutique store has cool clothing, cards and a children's table with journals. Open 11 am-6 pm Mon-Sat.

Treasures of Lemuria (Akoni Pule Hwy, ☎ 889-0913) is another lovely store, offering window ornaments, art, quilted pot holders, jewelry, incense and other souvenirs. Generally open 11 am-5:30 pm Mon-Sat.

Daanykinegifstoa/Krazy 8'z/Aunty Helen's (Akoni Pule Hwy, ☎ 884-5626). "Zero" Samuels and his family members own and operate three businesses in one building: Daanykinegifstoa (roughly translated from Pidgin: "the any kind gift store"), Krazy 8'z Pool Room and Aunty Helen's Take Out and Catering. Basically, there's a reggae store with red, yellow and green goods, like Bob Marley shirts, as well as hemp purses, stickers, incense burners and serious-looking knives. Mellow reggae plays while you browse, or head to the adjoining pool house – Krazy 8'z. There are puzzles affixed to the walls of this spacious room that has two pool tables. It's $1 a game – the loser pays. A sign outside proclaims, "We are not a head shop" – and indeed, there is no smoking, drinking or drugs allowed in the establishment. It's a great place for locals and local kids (and tourists – "we no bite") to hone their skills in a healthy environment. They recently added food with Aunty Helen's; menu items include local dishes and delicacies like sweet and sour pigs feet. Posted hours: "M-F 10 2 7, Sat 10-ty-erd, Sun-dee-penz."

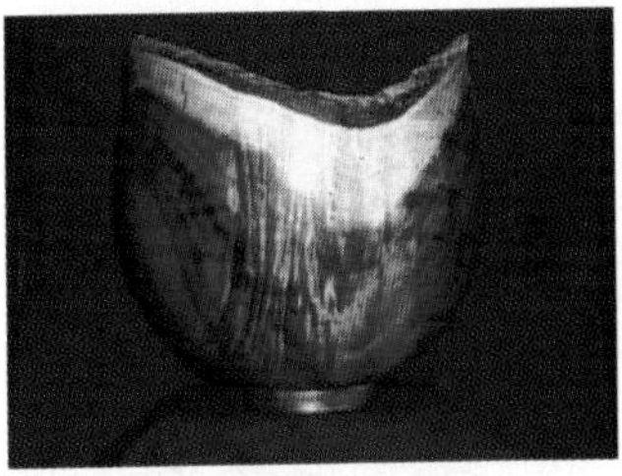

L. Zeidman Gallery (Akoni Pule Hwy, ☎ 889-1400, www.lzeidman.com). Looking for gorgeous, artistic woodwork? Larry's artistic Hawaiian wood bowls at L. Zeidman Gallery will have you reaching for your wallet. He often leaves a part of the bowl unshaped, so that the natural beauty of the wood can speak for itself. Open 10 am-6 pm daily.

HAWI FARMERS MARKET

The Hawi Farmers Market takes place Saturday mornings until about 1 pm. It's held among the banyan trees across from the Kohala Village Inn, with produce, crafts, Thai food (also here on Wednesdays from 3:30-5:30 pm) and anything else locals feel like selling while they socialize in the relaxed, shady setting. It's a chance to experience the mellow vibe of Hawi.

Where to Stay

Kohala Village Inn (55-514 Hawi Road, ☎ 889-0404, www.kohalavillageinn.com, 19 rooms, $65-$120). An "Aloha" sign welcomes you to the Kohala Village Inn, a motel-style accommodation in the heart of Hawi, just off Akoni Pule Hwy. Most of the simple, tidy rooms with hardwood floors surround a small courtyard. Continental breakfast is served from 5:30-9:30 am, and a computer room with Internet service is open from 9 am-8 pm. The loca-

Kohala Village Inn bedroom

tion can't be beat. There's an attached restaurant that recently underwent renovations. $-$$

Where to Eat

Sushi Rock (55-3435 Akoni Pule Hwy, ☎ 889-5900). Fusion sushi – need we say more? Foodies around the island get excited about the food at Sushi Rock – it is fabulous. Their edamame is infused with green tea and sesame oil. In addition to classic sushi rolls, chef Rio Miceli has a menu with inventive dishes like Broken Mouth (seasonal fish *poke*, cucumber, and macadamia nuts, wrapped in *unagi* and avocado), and appetizers like Shitake Poppers (mushrooms stuffed with rice, topped with melted parmesan and drizzled with scallion cream). Complement your meal with one of the fine sakes and your mouth will thank you. Only a few minor drawbacks: the miso soup isn't very salty, and the venue, though chic, is tiny. If singer/songwriters aren't your cup of tea, request a seat outside if one is performing during dinner. With so many temptations on the menu, it's easy to reach the $25 credit card minimum here. Open daily except Wed from noon to 3 pm and 5:30 to 8 pm (till 9 pm Fri and Sat). $$-$$$

AUTHOR'S CHOICE ★ **Bamboo Restaurant and Gallery** (Akoni Pule Hwy, ☎ 889-5555, www.bamboorestaurant.info). Bamboo is a restaurant that locals point to with pride, and rightfully so – people drive up from Kona to dine at this fine-dining award-winner. It's partially responsible for the revival of North Kohala in the 1990s, not only by attracting tourist dollars to the area, but by supporting local farmers and fishermen.

The ambiance is splendid, with tropical tablecloths, fairy lights, and an art gallery upstairs. There's also a gift shop with high-end items like *koa* lazy susans, silk kimonos and the $250 Australian-made toilet seats filled with sand and shells that are in the bathrooms. There is live music at dinner on Friday and Saturday nights – try to catch traditional Hawaiian duo Pahoa, or renowned slack key guitarist John Keawe, if possible.

The "Fresh Island Style" cuisine is the star of the show, however. Perhaps start with a Caesar Mac-nut Salad, and move on to a fresh fish selection from the "Makai" side of the menu, or a maybe a rack of BBQ pork baby back ribs with roasted pineapple barbecue or spicy *liliko`i* sauce from the "Mauka" selection, which includes vegetables and a choice of rice or their delicious ginger scallion mashed potatoes. Vegetarians will be pleased to have an option other than the pasta primavera found elsewhere – Pacific Stir Fried Noodles (with vegetables and fried tofu) in teriyaki or a rich Thai coconut sauce are prepared in "Da Local Style." Save room for dessert: Bamboo's Mocha Cappuccino Cheesecake won first prize at the Kona Coffee Festival. Open for lunch 11:30 am-2:30 pm and dinner 6-9 pm Tues-Sat, Sunday brunch 11 am-2 pm. $$$$

North Kohala

■ Kapa`au

Kapa`au is just slightly larger than the neighboring town of Hawi and only about two miles away. Kapa`au was another town hit hard by the demise of the area sugar industry in the '70s, but has weathered the storm because of its historical interest, the grand statue of King Kamehameha I in the center of town, and its proximity to the Pololu Valley – a number of North Kohala tours leave from here.

Practicalities

There is an **ATM** machine at the Bank of Hawaii on Akoni Pule Hwy, next to the King Kamehameha statue.

A **post office** and Aloha **gas station** are on the Akoni Pule Highway, on the way from Hawi.

A. Arakaki Store (53-4142 Akoni Pule Hwy, ☎ 889-5262) is a small **grocery store** that also sells Hawaiian books, beer and liquor, flowers and fishing supplies. Open Mon-Sat 9 am-7 pm, 9 am-5 pm Sun.

The Bond Memorial Public Library is named after Dr Benjamin Davis Bond, the son of missionaries Elias and Ellen Bond, who was the region's physician from 1883 to 1923.

Sights

The **Statue of King Kamehameha the Great**, the Hawaiian monarch who conquered and united the Hawaiian Islands, stands over eight feet tall on the lawn of the North Kohala Civic Center in Kapa`au on Akoni Pule Hwy. Though it looks like a replica of the one in Honolulu, it is actually the original statue, commissioned in 1878 by the Hawaiian legislature. Designed by American sculptor Thomas Gould, then cast and shipped from France, the statue went missing when the boat it was on caught fire off the Falkland Islands. A second statue was commissioned before the original was recovered and sent – in poor condition – to North Kohala, the king's birthplace. The statue was repaired and is currently on its 23rd layer of paint.

Kamehameha I became the first king to unite all of the Hawaiian islands under one rule. For nearly 30 years he fought to conquer each island one by one, and in 1810 his goal was achieved when the leader of Kaua`i ceded the island to him.

KING KAMEHAMEHA DAY

June 11 is celebrated as King Kamehameha Day throughout the state, but it has special meaning in the region of his birth. Kapa`au erupts in celebration, with a parade, ceremonies and a big party in the park with lots of food. The statue of King Kamehameha is covered with *leis*. If June 11 happens to fall on a Sunday, the parade and most festivities are held the day before so that people can go to church.

Kalahikiola Congregational Church was completed in 1855 (the fifth attempt) by renowned missionary Elias Bond (see box below). To reach this historic church, turn *mauka* onto `Iole Road from Akoni Pule Highway, then drive about a half-mile past banyan trees and an organic orchard to see New England architecture on the Big Island of Hawaii – an unusual sight. There are Sunday services at the church, where Bond's great-great-grandson (local legend Boyd Bond) sings in the choir.

THE BOND ESTATE

Maine minister Elias Bond and his wife Ellen moved to North Kohala as missionaries in 1841, and demonstrated a remarkable interest in the welfare of the community in which they served. The Bonds built a teachers' school and over 30 other schools in the area, including a girls' school. However, while helping locals learn to read and write in English, Father Bond also became fluent in Hawaiian, and led church services at Kalahikiola Church in the local language. He established other churches for immigrants in their languages, such as Japanese and Korean; the English-speaking church was called the "Foreign Church." Later, Bond helped spur the local economy in the 1860s by establishing the Kohala Sugar Plantation to create jobs and keep local people of faith in the area. An earthquake in 1973 badly damaged the buildings, and the sugar operation shut down in 1975 after being a major area employer for over a century. A private owner purchased the historic estate a few years ago, so it is currently off-limits to the public.

Where to Shop

AUTHOR'S CHOICE ★ **Kohala Book Shop** (54-3885 Akoni Pule Hwy, ☎ 889-6400, www.kohalabooks.com). If you have a thing for bookstores, you have to visit this, the biggest used book shop in the state. Owners Frank and Jan Morgan also carry a terrific selection of new books on Hawaiiana (reputed to be the largest in the US), and can help steer you toward the perfect book from over 25,000 in their inventory. The Morgans have a prized case of rare Hawaiian books, like a 1921 New Testament written in Hawaiian and English ($250), a first edition *Journal of William Ellis* from 1826 ($650), and 14 books from the Great Hawaiian Books series that are signed by authors like Mark Twain and Herb Kane. Buy a book and read it next door while you sip coffee at the Nanbu Courtyard Café. Open 11 am-5 pm Mon-Sat.

Victoria's Fine Art Gallery (Akoni Pule Hwy, ☎ 889-1711, www.victoriafineart.com). Victoria presides over her gallery while strumming a guitar and greeting visitors with a warm smile, encouraging them to browse through her watercolor paintings and prints that "tell a story of the eternal feminine." One of her prints of koi swimming though purple orchids graces the wall of our home. Open 10 am-5 pm.

Elements (54-3885 Akoni Pule Hwy, ☎ 889-0760, toll free ☎ 800-686-0760). Also in the Nanbu Building, Elements features unique gifts by local artists, such as ceramics, textiles and blown glass. The owners are jewelry artists – John Flynn is a metalsmith who works with niobium (ask for a fascinatingly mind-boggling explanation of how the colors are created by changing light reflections), and his wife Prakash works with gemstones. Open 10 am-6 pm Mon-Fri, 10 am-5 pm Sat.

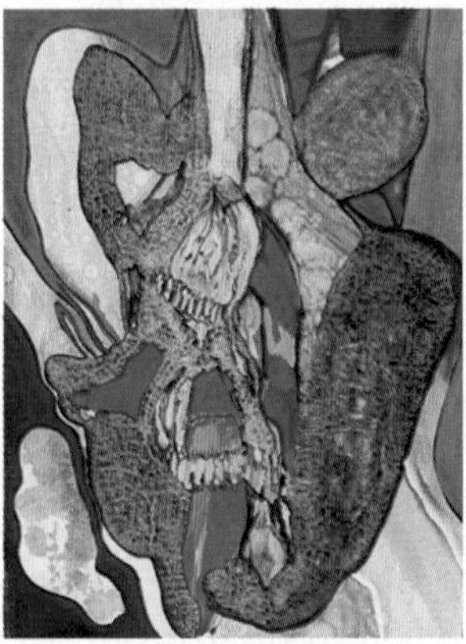

Ackerman Galleries (Akoni Pule Hwy, ☎ 889-5137, www.ackermangalleries.com) has continued to expand in size over the past 20 years, and serves as the gift shop for artist Gary Ackerman, whose studio is only about a block away. This space has some incredible glass artwork – vases, paperweights, plates, ornaments – and other gifts like jewelry boxes, custom frames, paintings, clothing, lotions and even Samoan war clubs. Open daily – even on Kamehameha Day, when the aroma of *leis* draped over the king's statue across the street wafts inside. Open 9:30 am-6 pm daily.

Adventures

On Wheels

ATV Outfitters Hawaii (☎ 889-6000, toll free ☎ 888-ATV-7288, www.atvoutfittershawaii.com) offers three guided all-terrain vehicle tours of North Kohala, childhood home of Bill Wong, a fourth-generation native Hawaiian, who owns the company with his wife, Sandie. Two tours run twice a day: the 1½-hour Ocean Cliff Trail ($109/pp), and the 2½-hour, 15-mile waterfall tour ($169). There is also a special three-hour, 22-mile rainforest and waterfall tour ($249). Call ahead for reservations. Adults must be at least 16 and weigh 90 to 300 pounds; kids ages seven-15 must weigh 45 to 120 pounds and ride with the guide (there is a lower children's rate). They recently added a Buggy Tour – two-seaters and single-seat buggies with something called a roll cage. ($114/single, $78/pp two-seater).

Kohala Carriages (☎ 889-5955). Belgian draft horses pull a cedar wagon through pastureland to views of the coast for lunch. The "Puka Hale" tour lasts 2½ hours and costs $47.50/pp.

On Horseback

Paniolo Adventures (☎ 889-5354, www.panioloadventures.com) is distinguished by the fact that they not only offer "open range" tours for novices ($96), but "wrangler" trips for experienced riders "who need a ride fix" ($149). We're novices (under 50 rides), but can imagine what a treat it would be for horse owners to have the chance to race around an 11,100-acre private ranch with stunning mountain and coastal views of Hawaii. There is also a new 5½-hour class called the Upcountry Horsemanship Program ($300), a picnic tour ($124), and sunset ride ($79).

**Na`alapa Stables** (☎ 889-0022, www.naalapastables.com). This company, which also conducts fun tours in the Waipi`o Valley, offers 2½-hour rides each morning ($88.54) and 1½-hour tours in the afternoons ($67.70) on Kahua Ranch, one of the oldest working ranches in Hawaii. They also have a horse-drawn wagon tour, which includes a narration about the history of ranching in Hawaii (adults $36.46, kids $17.71, children three and under free).

Note: Horseback riding in North Kohala is a thrill because riders can canter and gallop on private ranches, rather than walking "nose to tail" to their destination. These trips leave from stables on Highway 250, and prices include tax.

Where to Stay

Kohala Country Adventures Guesthouse (off Hwy 270, ☎ 889-5663, www.kcadventures.com, three rooms, $85-$160). This bright, turquoise house has a welcoming, easy-going feel, mostly because owner Bobi Moreno is so friendly and gracious. She's a passionate artist who is eager to talk about all the activities the area has to offer – hence the "adventures" in the name of her lodging. Each of the guest rooms has a different ambiance, and range in price to fit different budgets. The Garden Bedroom is popular with honeymooners because of the big windows, Jacuzzi bathtub, and private deck, while the Sundeck

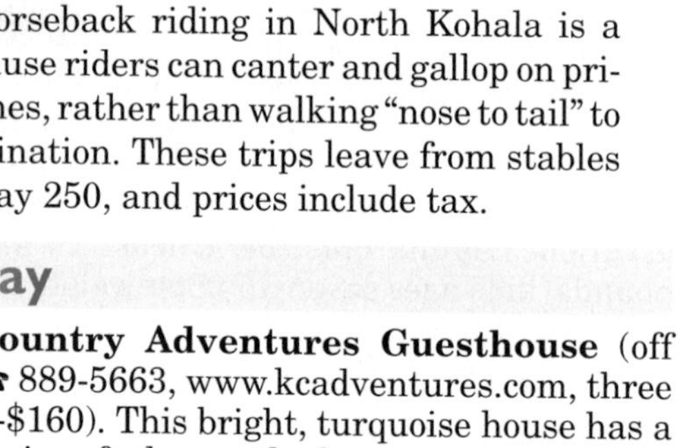

Sundeck Suite

Suite is bright and spacious with sweeping views, two beds, and a living and dining area. The Cozy Bedroom can adjoin with the suite for larger groups, or be rented by those on a budget. As the name suggests, the room is cozy and homey with two single beds and a full-size bed, with a private bath just outside the door. A path wanders through Bobi's garden and up to the sundeck, which offers a satisfying view of the local greenery as well as a distant glimpse of the ocean. $$

See page 65 for an explanation of the hotel $ price codes.

Where to Eat

Nanbu Courtyard Café (Akoni Pule Hwy, ☎ 889-5546). This popular café serves quality coffee drinks, soup, salads and deli sandwiches, like the BLT, Reuben and a veggie sandwich that comes with basil or black olive pesto. There are a few tables inside and in front, but the courtyard in back is a relaxing place to enjoy a meal – even in a drizzle. Often local committee meetings are held here. Plans for an open-mic night on Sundays are in the works. Open 6:30 am-2 pm Mon-Fri (not Wed). $-$$

For an explanation of the $ price codes, see page 55.

Kohala Rainbow Café (54-3897 Akoni Pule Hwy, ☎ 889-0099). Also known locally as "the ice cream place," Kohala Rainbow Café serves healthy treats like smoothies, and salads with organic greens and dressings such as Maui onion or *liliko`i*. They also offer wraps, including the local club with turkey, applewood bacon, greens, tomatoes and Kohala ranch dressing. Sandwich specialties include the Leimomi with Kalua pork, Asian BBQ sauce and two kinds of cheese, and burgers (chicken, lamb, grass-fed beef). Save a little room for ice cream, which is from the delicious Hilo Homemade. Located directly across from the King Kamehameha statue, and open 11 am-5 pm Mon-Fri, 11 am-4 pm Sat. $$

Pololu Valley Store (54-4659 Akoni Pule Hwy, ☎ 884-5686). A great stop for refreshment on your way to or from the Pololu Lookout, the brightly painted Pololu Valley Store serves delicious mango-banana-papaya-strawberry smoothies, shave ice, root beer floats, and ice cream sundaes. More substantial snacks include hot dogs, chili, sandwiches like tuna fish and PB&J, and macadamia nuts. Once a bar where *paniolos*

(Hawaiian cowboys) would tie up their horses and down a drink, the store now sells knick-knacks, magnets, stuffed animals, tiles and t-shirts. Open 9:30 am-5:30ish, generally closed Thursdays or, as owner Fred says, "if there's good surf." $

Nearby Attractions

Kamehameha Rock, between mile markers 26 and 27 on Akoni Pule Highway, is easily identified by the sign above it from the Hawaii Visitors and Convention Bureau. King Kamehameha the Great is said to have placed the stone there to exhibit his physical strength. It's hard to believe a human could lift it, but he is reputed to have stood over seven feet tall and weighed more than 300 pounds, so anything's possible.

The Kohala Tong Wo Society Building is a picturesque structure fronted by a cemetery in the small settlement of Halawa on the highway to the Pololu Lookout.Makapala

This is a tiny town on the way to the Pololu Lookout with a few worthwhile stops of its own.

Rankin Fine Art Gallery (☎ 889-6849). Located at the former site of the Wo On Store, Rankin Fine Art Gallery is another excellent Hawaiian gallery with paintings of local scenes – and also cowboys. Owner/artist Patrick Louis Rankin used to live in a town we're partial to: Durango, Colorado. Open 11 am-5 pm Tues-Sat, noon-4 pm Sun.

Keokea Beach Park

Have you noticed that we like to picnic? Here's another beautiful picnic spot, a rocky beach with views of reddish cliffs, pounding surf and, sometimes, endangered Hawaiian monk seals (signs remind you not to approach them). There is no longer camping here – the yellow gate opens at 7 am and closes at 11 pm. It's also a little too far north to see the actual sunset, though the sky will glow with pink or orange hues. Turn *makai* at the sign for Keokea Beach Park by the 27 mile marker on Akoni Pule Highway.

■ Pololu Valley

At the end of Hwy 270 you'll arrive at the Pololu Valley Lookout. The lush windward valleys of the Big Island are bookended in the east by Waipi`o Valley, and in the west by the lovely Pololu Valley. The view from the lookout is staggering. The walls of the valleys to the east drop precipitously into the windward sea and the islands of Paokalani and Mokupuku lie just off shore like leftover clumps of paint on an artist's palette, while long white breakers roll into the black sand beach below. There will likely be many cars vying for a few awkwardly angled spaces that make leaving a bit of a challenge in the narrow strip of asphalt. Consider parking up the road slightly if there are other cars parked up there.

The Pololu Valley Lookout

Take lots of pictures here, but don't waste too much energy, as you're going to want to go down and check out the valley on foot. The walk down takes 15-20 minutes, and can be slippery and difficult in places. The valley floor lies about 400 feet below the lookout, so expect a more strenuous hike coming back up. That said, this is a hike that most able-bodied people should be able to handle, and the reward is immense. The beach that fronts Pololu Valley is comprised of fine, gold-flecked black sand, the result of an eruption of basalt from the Big Island's first volcano; the last eruption occurred about 60,000 years ago

The Big Island is the youngest of the Hawaiian Islands, and the Kohala Mountains were the first land mass to rise from the ocean on the island, the result of volcanic eruptions dating back over 500,000 years. The deep-cut windward valleys of northwest Hawai'i make up the only area on the island that has had time to erode in such a dramatic way.

The windswept beach is backed by towering ironwood trees that offer a refreshing respite from the sun. Over time, folks have strung hammocks, swings and ropes in a haphazard, playful fashion that make the woods fun to explore. The floor of this forested dune is covered in bright green vegetation that gives the area a luminous glow. Check it out. Keep in mind, you'll want to resist a full swim in the water here, since the currents are stronger than you are. The valley was once home to a significant population that thrived on its tarot patches, fresh water and fish ponds. Today, the valley is uninhabited.

Adventures on Foot

Hiking Pololu to Honokane Iki

If you are intrigued by the views in and above Pololu Valley, you will likely feel the distant valleys beckoning you to explore them. If you've got the time and the energy, go for it.

The peaceful Pololu Valley (BIVB)

Honokane Iki Hike

AUTHOR'S CHOICE

Difficulty: Difficult

Distance and type: Seven miles, out-and-back

Time: six-eight hours

The hike from Pololu Valley to Honokane Iki is one of the very best hikes on the island, but be sure to properly prepare.

The beach in Pololu (BIVB)

Bring enough food to keep yourself energized. Bring enough water to remain hydrated, or be prepared to treat the water you collect from the stream. Do not drink any water you find without treating it. Be sure to wear proper footwear; your new white sneakers need not apply. Even hiking sandals are not recommended. Wear hiking boots or cross trainers. Be prepared for rain. Consider using a hiking pole, as this will help you avoid some potentially painful slips.

Along the seven-mile round-trip you'll wind your way up and down nearly 5,000 feet of vertical. From the Pololu Valley Lookout all the way to the beach at Honokane Iki and back should take you six-eight hours, including time for lunch, well-deserved rests, and time to gawk and snap photos of the awesome views. Of course, it could take more or less time depending upon your fitness level and the weather. It's wise to start early, since it tends to rain in the afternoon in this area, and wet weather makes this already difficult hike even more so. However, if you get lucky and experience a clear late afternoon on this hike, the golden "magic hour" light is glorious.

From the beach in Pololu, the trail to the other valleys is under the tall ironweed trees that back the beach. The trail is cleanly cut and easy to follow as it climbs out of the east side of the valley beneath the trees. The initial climb is often muddy, but should dry up a bit as you reach the top after about 30 minutes. You are rewarded for this first climb with a wonderful view of the Honokane Nui Valley and the islands and cliffs below. Some may wish to stop here. For those who are going on, the trail drops down along some switchbacks into Honokane Nui. As soon as you hit the valley floor, you'll find yourself surrounded by tall bamboo. A barely visible spur trail leads to the boulder-strewn beach. Continue along the main trail until it intersects the stream bed. You may also pick your way along the rocks of the streambed to get to the beach.

The trail to the next valley picks up about 10 yards downstream on the other side of the streambed. You'll encounter a fork in the trail a short distance in. You want to go right, which should be obvious since it's the one that goes *up*. The climb to the ridge isn't a long distance, but the grade is high. The trail is a wide cut, which allows plenty of room and comfort, but if it's been raining recently the steepness can be challenging going up or down. A climb of 400 feet leads to awesome views of both valleys on the narrow sliver of land that divides them. Pause for breath, pictures and self-congratulations, then enjoy the last descent (of this leg) into the narrow valley of Honokane Iki.

The valley floor contains ruins, huge banyan trees, an idyllic stream, a narrow rocky beach, and an old Kohala Ditch Company cabin. Take the time to enjoy the soul-stirring surroundings that so few people will endeavor to see, before facing the return journey. Feel free to chuckle at the tourists in white sneakers on your way back. You've earned it.

"The most beautiful thing we can experience is the mysterious. It is the source of all true art and all science. He to whom this emotion is a stranger, who can no longer pause to wonder and stand rapt in awe, is as good as dead: his eyes are closed." – Albert Einstein

Waimea & Mauna Kea

O na hoku no na kiu o ka lani.
"The stars are the eyes of heaven." – Hawaiian proverb

IN THIS CHAPTER

The upcountry town of Waimea, the towering peak of Mauna Kea, and the high-elevation Saddle Road are irrevocably linked. Rich in natural beauty, history, culture and adventure, they compose a special region well worth exploring.

Mauna Kea, the tallest mountain in the Hawaiian Islands, looms above Waimea. To people familiar with the town, the name conjures images of the unnatural hue of the surrounding pastures, which glow fluorescent green in the sunlight while majestic horses graze. This is "Paniolo Country," home to the Hawaiian cowboys who have been wrangling cattle here since the early 1800s. King Kamehameha I gifted a parcel of land here to John Palmer Parker, a New Englander whose ranch continued to grow over the generations – at 175,000 acres, it is now one of the largest privately owned ranches in the United States.

Many of Waimea's attractions revolve around Parker Ranch, such the Parker Museum and Parker residences. One of them, Puuopelu, boasts an Impressionist art collection and lovely gardens; *Mana* is made entirely of *koa* wood. Exploring the ranch itself is the biggest adventure, preferably while galloping on horseback across its luminous fields.

Waimea is also renowned for its outstanding art galleries, shops and restaurants, many of which serve organic greens grown by local farmers – tours of these farms grow increasingly popular with tourists. Despite the diversity of its community, Waimea remains a tranquil town shared by organic farmers and paniolos (Hawaiian cowboys), restaura-

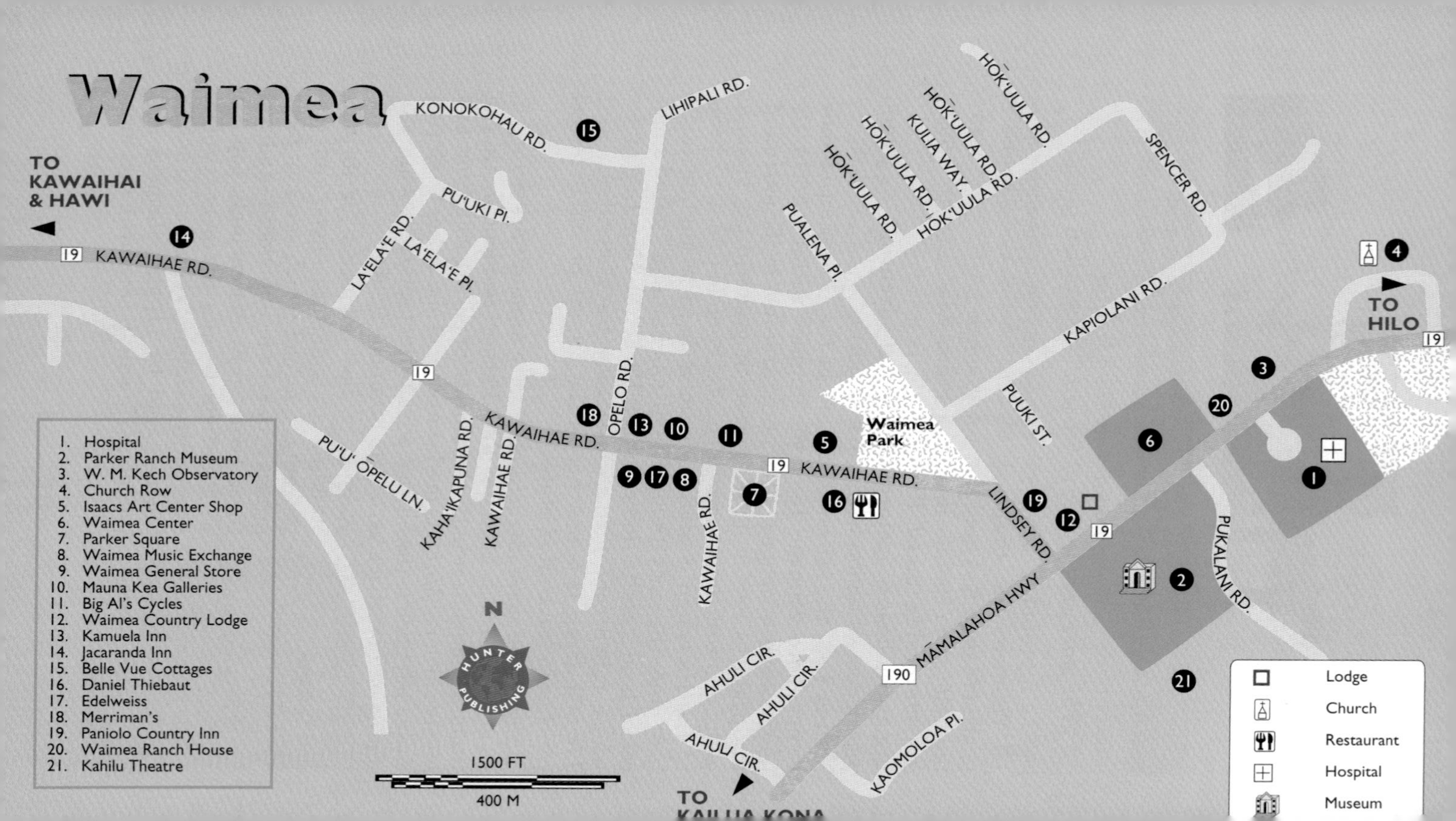
Waimea
TO KAWAIHAI & HAWI
TO HILO
TO KAILUA KONA
KAWAIHAE RD.
KONOKOHAU RD.
LIHIPALI RD.
PU'UKI PI.
LA'ELA'E RD.
LA'ELA'E PI.
PU'U'ŌPELU LN.
KAHA'IKAPUNA RD.
KAWAIHAE RD.
OPELO RD.
PUALENA PI.
HŌK'UULA RD.
HŌK'UULA RD.
KULIA WAY.
HŌK'UULA RD.
HŌK'UULA RD.
HŌK'UULA RD.
SPENCER RD.
KAPIOLANI RD.
PUUKI ST.
Waimea Park
LINDSEY RD.
PUKALANI RD.
MĀMALAHOA HWY
AHULI CIR.
AHULI CIR.
AHULI CIR.
KAOMOLOA PI.
19
190
N
HUNTER PUBLISHING
1500 FT
400 M
Lodge
Church
Restaurant
Hospital
Museum
1. Hospital
2. Parker Ranch Museum
3. W. M. Kech Observatory
4. Church Row
5. Isaacs Art Center Shop
6. Waimea Center
7. Parker Square
8. Waimea Music Exchange
9. Waimea General Store
10. Mauna Kea Galleries
11. Big Al's Cycles
12. Waimea Country Lodge
13. Kamuela Inn
14. Jacaranda Inn
15. Belle Vue Cottages
16. Daniel Thiebaut
17. Edelweiss
18. Merriman's
19. Paniolo Country Inn
20. Waimea Ranch House
21. Kahilu Theatre

teurs and gallery owners, astronomers and artists. That these groups can coexist so peacefully is perhaps a testament to the soothing properties of the area's natural environment.

Additionally, Waimea is a great base from which to explore Mauna Kea. Rising 13,796 feet from sea level, "White Mountain" is actually the earth's tallest mountain when measured from its base 16,000 feet deeper on the ocean floor. The importance of the dormant volcano to Hawaiians as well as the scientific community cannot be overstated. Native Hawaiians revere Mauna Kea as an ancestor, home to the snow goddess Poli`ahu. Its Lake Wai`au is the third-highest lake in the United States, believed to be the umbilical cord that connects the Hawaiian archipelago with the heavens.

Mauna Kea *(Hawaiian Images)*

Mauna Kea is also one of the world's best sites for astronomy, with its isolated location in the middle of the Pacific Ocean and peak that rises above the clouds. The summit is crowded with 13 telescopes, representing nine countries, which spring to life at sunset. Astronomers have discovered hundreds of planets based on observations made here. Amateurs can make their own observations while stargazing at the visitor center of Mauna Kea each night – you won't believe how many stars you can see.

Visitors to Mauna Kea usually drive there from Waimea via Saddle Road, named because it runs across the "saddle" between the peaks of Mauna

Summit observatories *(Hawaii Forest & Trail)*

Birding in Hakalau Forest (*Hawaii Forest & Trail*)

Kea and Mauna Loa. Saddle Road winds past cinder cones and lava flows, and has trailheads that lead through lava fields to old growth forests filled with native songbirds, and lava tubes for caving adventures. Hakalau Forest National Wildlife Refuge is a birder's paradise, with eight species of endangered native birds, 13 species of migratory birds, and 20 introduced birds – watch for wild turkeys!

Whether you want to enjoy the amenities of Waimea, ride horses through Paniolo Country, tour an organic farm, hike to geological wonders, marvel at the universe or watch a blazing sunset from the highest point in Hawaii, this region of the Big Island beckons.

Waimea

Waimea ("why-MAY-uh") is a welcoming mountain town of around 7,000 people. Its elevation at 3,000 feet means chillier temperatures, but it's only a 10-minute drive from the beach at Spencer Park. This is a great art and restaurant town; many businesses here could be singled out for excellence in special boxes, but we can't put a box around the entire town! Waimea is sleepy at night – go for a stroll at 10 pm and you might find yourself the only person on the streets.

WAIMEA VS. KAMUELA

On maps, in advertisements and in addresses, you will hear Waimea also called Kamuela. Here's the scoop: Waimea ("Red Water") is a common name for towns (and bays and canyons) on different islands in Hawaii so, to avoid confusion at the post office, the town was renamed Kamuela (Hawaiian for "Samuel") to honor Samuel Parker of Parker Ranch, who helped make the town something of a center for high society. Most native Hawaiians still refer to the town as "Waimea" because it is the original Hawaiian name, but mail is addressed to Kamuela. As one resident explained, rolling her eyes, "If people accidentally address my mail to Waimea, it ends up in Kauai!"

Practicalities

There are several gas stations and banks with **ATM** machines on the Mamalahoa Highway in town, and at the Waimea Country Store across from Merriman's. This gas station's **mini-mart** (open 4 am-9:30 pm Mon-Sat, 5 am-8:30 pm Sun) sells beer and wine and has an ATM.

North Hawaii Community Hospital (67-1125 Mamalahoa Highway, ☎ 808-885-4444) is across from the W.M. Keck Observatory.

There are two **grocery stores** in the main malls, **KTA** (6 am-11 pm daily) in the Waimea Center, and **Foodland** (5 am-11 pm daily) in the Parker Center. The excellent health food store in the Parker Center, **Healthways II**, is expanding, "in size and consciousness," enthused one employee. Healthways has a great deli with sandwiches (like tofu pesto) that you can eat outside on a picnic table. Eat on the hour and watch the Parker Ranch horse-drawn wagon clip-clop by. Healthways is open 9 am-7 pm Mon-Sat, 9 am-5 pm Sun (deli closes at 5 pm daily except 3 pm Sun).

Rush Hour Traffic: Though it is a small town with only a few traffic lights, Waimea's traffic becomes stop-and-go around 5 pm.

There are public **restrooms** at the Waimea Center, behind the goofy statue of a paniolo (a cowboy, little kids love it) by Kamuela Coffee N Cones (which kids also love). Be sure to look up at the stained glass windows before you "hit the head." The public restrooms across the street at the Parker Center are in the food court.

Sights

Parker Ranch

In 1809, 19-year-old New Englander John Palmer Parker jumped ship on the Big Island of Hawaii, and soon became a

Horses graze at Parker Ranch

trusted friend of King Kamehameha the Great. When he later demonstrated an uncanny marksmanship, the king rewarded him with the job of hunting and containing the wild cattle that had decimated the vegetation of the island after Captain George Vancouver presented some to Kamehameha as a gift in 1793. Once private land ownership was legalized in Hawaii, Parker was given two acres of land by the king and a legendary ranch was born. Today, the Parker Ranch totals over 175,000 acres with between 30,000 and 35,000 head of cattle and produces some of the finest grass-fed beef in the world.

"You're here for only a little while. Don't hurry too fast, don't hurt anyone, and don't forget to stop and smell the flowers."
– credo of John Palmer Parker

Parker Ranch Museum (Parker Ranch Center, ☎ 885-7655, www.parkerranch.com). Located in the rear of the Parker Ranch Center, Parker Ranch Museum provides an absorbing look into the last 200 years of history around Waimea, which has been tied to the fortunes of the Parker Ranch. The museum traces the saga of the Parker family, as well as those of the world-famous *paniolos* (Hawaiian cowboys), whose prowess with horses and cattle has long been revered. There are displays of Victorian-era family heirlooms, including furniture, photos and Hawaiian quilts, as well as antique ranching tools, clothing and letters. The museum also shows a well-produced video that documents the history of the ranch from its beginnings with the young, soon-to-be rancher John Parker almost 200 years ago to the ranches' present incarnation as a charitable trust. Open 9 am-4:45 pm Mon-Sat. Admission: adults $7, seniors $6.50, children $5.50. There are discounts if you show your AAA card, or if you buy extra tickets for tours of the homes or the wagon ride (see *Adventures for Keiki* box below).

Historic Homes and Gardens (Mamalahoa Hwy, a half-mile west of town, ☎ 885-5433, www.parkerranch.com). The Historic Homes and Gardens of Parker Ranch comprise two homes and adjoining grounds. **Puuopelu** is the ranch estate most recently occupied by Richard Smart, the sixth-generation descendant of John Parker I. The home was built in 1862 and purchased by John Parker II in 1879. It was continually upgraded and renovated by Richard Smart, an accomplished stage actor and entertainer, to accommodate his growing needs and house his collection of fine art. Today, Richard Smart's art collection hangs on the walls of the living room, and includes many French Impressionist works, including paintings by Edgar Degas and Lucien Pissarro. There is also a considerable collection of Chinese art around the house, including Ming vases and Peking glass.

Puuopulu

Mana, the original home of John Parker, is a Cape Cod-style home built on land given to him by King Kamehameha III, in a style that he remembered from his native New England. What's amazing about the house is the interior, which is built entirely of native *koa*. Given the astoundingly high prices of small *koa* bowls for sale in stores around the island, this house can be likened to a gold brick palace. For this reason, Richard Smart had the interior removed plank by plank from its original location farther up the slopes of Mauna Kea, and rebuilt it in this exact replica that stands next door to Puuopelu. Open 10 am to 4 pm Mon-Sat. Admission: adults $9, seniors $8.50, children $7. Tickets can be purchased inside Puuopelu or at the museum, where a discounted admission is available for more than one tour.

Mexican cowboys (paniolo) at Parker Ranch (HTJ)

Church Row, along the lawn lined with cherry trees near the W.M. Keck Observatory Center, is a group of several picturesque and historic churches with Sunday services. **Imiola Congregational Church**, built 1855-57, is marked with a Hawaii Visitors Bureau marker because it was a base for missionary activities. **Ke Ola Mau Loa Church** was founded in 1931; a fruit and vegetable stand on the property matches its green paint with white trim. The **Kamuela Hongwanji Mission**, a Buddhist center, is also along the row.

The sculpture of a cowboy roping a bull in front of the Parker Ranch Center pays tribute to Ikua Purdy, a *paniolo* (Hawaiian cowboys) who went stateside to compete at rodeos and became the 1908 World Champion Roper. He was inducted into the National Cowboy Hall of Fame in 2000. The base of the sculpture has the names and brands of local ranches and farms.

AUTHOR'S CHOICE ★ **Isaacs Art Center** (65-1268 Kawaihae Road, ☎ 885-5884, http://isaacsartcenter.hpa.edu). In 2002, a local elementary school dating back to 1915 was restored and moved to the site of the Isaacs Art Center, a Hawaiian museum and art gallery with an outstanding collection. The building is now on the State Register of Historic Places, but that doesn't mean it has a stuffy atmosphere; ask one of the enthusiastic docents to pull out one of the sliding doors to reveal a chalkboard. They say that former students and teachers visit the center, point at rooms and exclaim, "I sat

Isaacs Art Center

over there! I taught over there!" As a former school, it is fitting that the proceeds from the center are used to create scholarships for students at Hawaii Preparatory Academy (www.hpa.edu).

The exhibiting artists are high-caliber, and displays from the permanent collection insure that every visit will intrigue collectors as well as people who just want to look at cool art. Behind the docents' desk is Herb Kane's painting of Captain Cook's arrival in 1778 during the Makahiki Festival, as Hawaiians greet the ship bearing – they believe – the god Lono. Each of the hundreds of faces is a unique "portrait." At the other end of the gallery, Madge Tennent has several paintings depicting full-figured Hawaiian women as graceful goddesses – you'll probably find yourself staring at them for a while. We could prattle on, but we'll leave it at this: if you have even the slightest interest in art, you cannot miss the Isaacs Art Center. Admission is free. Open Tues-Sat 10 am-5 pm.

"Every child is an artist. The problem is how to remain an artist once he grows up." – Pablo Picasso

Waimea Park has sporting fields and a large system of slides, swings, stairs and bars that constitute the **Anuenue Playground**. Let your kids burn off some energy here anytime during daylight hours.

Waimea

Where to Shop

Dan DeLuz's Woods (64-1013 Mamalahoa Highway, ☎ 885-5856). For over 40 years, Dan DeLuz has been "bowl turning," creating striking *koa* bowls and other wood sculpture, as well as teaching the next generation the skill. His showroom in Waimea includes a collection of 65 bowls worth $100,000, and a window into a storeroom of bowls waiting to be completed. There are smaller gift items like crosses and Christmas ornaments in the front room – don't make the mistake of leaving before you walk past the register into the room with his bowls and other higher-end items, including a $3,000-plus lotus blossom. Open 9 am-5 pm daily.

AUTHOR'S CHOICE **Mauna Kea Galleries** (65-1298 Kawaihae Road, ☎ 887-2244, toll free 877-969-HULA, www.maunakeagalleries.com) showcases historic Hawaiian and Polynesian art and artifacts, ranging from old books and *poi* pounders to Duke Kahanamoku's surfboard. The reproductions of vintage posters, such as for Elvis in "Blue Hawaii," or for airlines, are classic. There are *koa* dining sets and a rattan bar circa the 1940s that may leave you drooling. Owner Mark Blackburn is something of an expert on Hawaiiana, having authored a number of books such as *Hula Girls and Surfer Boys*, and *Tattoos from Paradise*. Open 11 am-6 pm Mon-Sat.

Crackseed, etc. (65-1290 Kawaihae Road, ☎ 885-6966, www.crackseedetc.com) sells its own Hawaiian snacks of seeds and preserves, including pineapple coconut balls, dried orange peel, pickle mango and crispy plum – which are also available at their online store – to Hawaiians who miss their childhood treats. They also sell handmade local crafts like table runners, *koa* gourds, *lauhala* pillow covers, as well as ice cream, cold drinks and packaged candy. Open 9:30 am-4:30 pm Mon-Fri, 10 am-4 pm Sat.

Crackseed is a popular Hawaiian snack that refers to a variety of dehydrated and preserved fruits, often salty or sweet, and sold in little packages. Crackseed was introduced to Hawaii by Chinese plantation workers, who used the preserved, vitamin-rich (and inexpensive) food to endure long sea voyages.

The Parker Ranch Center (67-1185 Mamalahoa Highway), a shopping mall that is home to the **Parker Ranch Store and Visitor's Center**, has plenty of shopping opportunities, with boutique stores, a surf shop, a quilt shop (finished quilts and pillow kits, but no fabric), a kids' store and **Reyn's**, which sells alohawear. Avoid the Parker Ranch store if there is a tour bus out front; it will be crammed with people buying cowboy duds. The Parker Center is across from the Waimea Center (65-1158 Mamalahoa Highway), another strip mall.

The smaller **Parker Square**, on Kawaihae Road, has public restrooms and several excellent shops. See www.bigislandadventureguide.com for details.

FARMERS MARKET

The Homestead Farmers Market takes place Saturday mornings from 7 am-noon on the lawn of the State of Hawaii Dept. of Hawaiian Homelands; a sign marks the spot on the Mamalahoa Highway. This is a great farmers market – it's on the small side, but quality is more important than quantity, right? There are flowers (only $2 for a giant protea!) and produce from area farms, as well as food stalls serving homemade goodies ranging from muffins and sandwiches to Indian curry and Mexican tamales. Yum! There are other local goods for sale, like baby blankets inscribed with Hawaiian words, or oils and sprays from the lavender farmer, who sprinkles lavender sprigs in front of his booth to enhance your browsing experience – just another reason to fall in love with Waimea.

Adventures

"Whoever said a horse was dumb, was dumb." – Will Rogers

As you might expect, Parker Ranch offers a slew of tours on the property. You almost wonder why they still bother with cattle ranching!

Kids love the Parker Ranch wagon rides

Parker Ranch Wagon Tours (☎ 885-7655, www.parkerranch.com). Every hour on the hour, there is a horse-drawn wagon ride into a small portion of Parker Ranch, which is a great way for kids to see grazing horses up-close, and for parents to see the rolling hills and old rock corrals of Parker Ranch. A driver in Western gear tells some of the history of the ranch while the little kids yell things like, "Was he a cowboy?" and "We're not going fast!" or conversely, "We're going fast!" Our cowboy eventually got the children on our tour to listen by explaining that in Hawaii, cows are called *pipi* ("pee pee"), eating is *kau kau* ("cow cow") and appetizers are called *pupu* ("poo poo") – so we eat *pipi* and *pupu*. That's humor anyone can enjoy, right? It's worth the $15 ($13 for seniors, $12 for kids) just to ride through a parking lot in a covered wagon (let alone all that glorious countryside). Tours run 10 am-2 pm Tues-Sat.

On Horseback

Parker Ranch (☎ 885-7655, www.parkerranch.com). Wanna play *paniolo* (cowboy)? Parker Ranch offers horseback rides on its 175,000-acre property three times a day. It's geared toward families, as the minimum age for riders is seven. The lush pasturelands are a great place to bond! The two-hour tours (the 4 pm tour is only 1½ hours) involve walking the horses on the open range, a stop so that the guide can tell you about the property and horses, and then at the end, guests can gallop if they like. Tours leave at 8:15 am, 12:15 pm and 4 pm, and cost $79.

On Wheels

Parker Ranch (☎ 885-7655, www.parkerranch.com). Though a ride on an ATV has little to do with being a cowboy wrangling cattle on the open range, Parker Ranch offers ATV rides on the property. There are two-hour tours in the morning and afternoon, and a 90-minute sunset tour. All include snacks and beverages. Riders must be at least 16 years old. The cost is $95.

Parker Ranch also offers a 4WD van tour of part of the Mana Road (see *Saddle Road* section, p. 317), and the two Parker residences, Puuopelo and Mana Hale. The tour concludes with a BBQ lunch at the ranch's Pukalani Stables, which includes BBQ beef, teriyaki chicken, corn on the cob, organic

Waimea green salad, baked beans and live music, a petting corral and lasso roping. The half-day tour is $120, or you can just pay $45 for the lunch.

On the Links

Waimea Country Club (47-5220 Mamalahoa Hwy, ☎ 885-8053, www.waimeagolf.com, $70, cart extra). This is a public course just over the wet, windward shoulder of Waimea. It's set in rolling pastureland, and boasts many majestic trees and fabulous greenery. It's off of the tourist track and is relatively inexpensive. The course has a terrific layout with some fine golf holes, and is up in a cooler climate that is sometimes calm when the courses on the coast are besieged by wind. It's not as well groomed as the resort courses and suffers from lots of play, but it may be worth a trip for a relaxed round in a different part of the island. There are a few ponds and some large bunkers to contend with, but the fairways are wide and the frequent moisture helps balls hold on the greens. The 7th is a par 5 that's reachable in two if you are willing to risk putting your second shot in the green-side water. It's best to call ahead to make sure it isn't pouring rain before you venture over from the sunny side of the island.

Agritourism

"To be the agent whose touch changes nature from a wild force to a work of art is inspiration of the highest order." – *Bob Rodale*

Hirabara Farms (☎ 887-2400, pam@hirabara.net). You will notice on menus in Waimea and along the coast (and even at the Parker Ranch BBQ lunch!) that certain produce will be described as "Waimea tomatoes" or "Waimea greens." This is because there are a number of farmers working on farms – often organic – in Waimea that grow flavorful vegetables and herbs in the cool, wet environment. Hirabara Farms is a leader in the industry, supplying organic, gourmet produce like baby lettuce to resorts such as the Mauna Lani and fine dining restaurants like Merriman's.

Kurt and Pam Hirabara give tours of their farm, nestled in the shadow of Mauna Kea on one acre of land that glows bright green and deep purple with rows of colorful crops. Nothing is mechanized – shoots are watered by hand because the couple feels strongly that it is important to give each plant the attention it needs. Tours can be arranged to coincide with a visiting chef preparing a meal in their outdoor kitchen. The wall of autographs from guest chefs includes Hawaiian household names like Peter Merriman and Alan Wong – and his mother, who claimed "I taught Alan Wong everything he knows" on the wall near his name – as well as international superstars like Iron Chef Mario Batali, who declared, "Lasagne is truth." Call or e-mail Pam Hirabara to arrange a customized tour.

Where to Stay

Aaah, the Views! (66-1773 Alaneo St, ☎ 885-3455, www.aaahtheviews.com, three rooms and a cottage, $80-$155), as the name implies, has beautiful views in each of its rooms, which are quirkily constructed. As co-owner Erika Stuart remarked, "It's like a ship-builder made it." Some rooms have loft beds (kids love them), or window nooks where you can gaze out at Mauna Kea, or up at the stars, or down at the gurgling stream that runs across the property (occasionally dry, depending on weather). There is a large and comfortable common area with couches and a porch swing on an outdoor lanai – with the same stunning views – and a kitchen area. Erika and her husband Derek (and their twin toddlers) serve their B&B's breakfast of "generous Hawaiian continental" (fruit and baked goods) here. Other amenities include a yoga room where lessons can be arranged, and in-house massage. This isn't a fancy place, just a relaxed getaway that may be just what you're looking for. $$-$$$

Aaah, the Views!

Waimea Country Lodge
(BookIt.com)

Waimea Country Lodge (65-1210 Lindsey Road/Rt. 19, ☎ 885-4100, toll free ☎ 800-367-5004, www.castleresorts.com, 21 rooms, $105-$125). A basic motel-style layout, with some recently renovated rooms. Nice touches include homey wood furniture and Hawaiian quilt-style comforters. The windows are small, but have good views of the rolling green hills above Waimea. Wireless Internet service is available for $10 a day. $$

The Jacaranda Inn

AUTHOR'S CHOICE ★ **The Jacaranda Inn** (65-1444 Kawaihae Rd, ☎ 885-8813, www.jacarandinn.com, eight rooms, $159-$225, one cottage for up to six people $450 with a five-night minimum). This is an intimate inn with eight ample guest rooms, sizeable grounds and a network of walkways leading over the property. There is a sun-lit dining room where breakfast is served each morning, and a dark billiard room that begs to be enjoyed with a fine scotch. Each guest room is well decorated with its own theme, from traditional to modern to whimsical, and most have their own Jacuzzi tub. There is also a three-bedroom guest cottage with full kitchen facilities and a hot tub on the lanai. The house was built over 100 years ago for the manager of Parker Ranch, and has since been owned by the Rockefellers, as well as several other entrepreneurs. The grounds boast excellent views of the verdant hills and a veranda where you can relax and enjoy the view of the lovely seasonal waterfall on the property. $$$

Where to Eat

Waimea is a fantastic restaurant town, whether you're looking for a budget meal or fine dining.

Paniolo Country Inn (65-1214 Lindsey Road, ☎ 885-4377) is a great homestyle breakfast place in a comfortable wood-paneled ranch house decorated with branding irons and cowboy-themed art. The prices can't be beat: one fresh ranch egg any style, two slices of bacon or link sausage, toast and hash browns is only $3.85; macadamia nut hotcakes are $3.75. There's also a bar, so you can have a Bloody Mary if you like. The dinner and lunch menu are the same, and include burgers, sandwiches, chili, soup and salads, a range of pizzas. With a cowboy theme, there are also south-of-the-border dishes like tacos and nachos, and steak platters. You won't leave hungry, especially if you order dessert like mud pie with Kona coffee ice cream. Open 7 am-8:45 pm daily. $$

Merriman's (65-1227 Opelo Road, ☎ 885-6822, www.merrimanshawaii.com). Peter Merriman is one of the pioneering chefs who launched the Hawaiian regional cuisine trend in restaurants throughout the state – essentially Hawaiian fine dining. He has a laudable preference for using local, organic food whenever possible. The restaurant's ambiance manages to be sophisticated yet homey, with a large dining room and an open kitchen. The complimentary, piping-hot taro wheat loaf is a promising sign of things to come, such as the goat cheese and mango tart appetizer with a strawberry vinaigrette, or kalua pig and sweet onion quesadilla. Entrées are "*mauka* and *makai*" – nice surf and turf dishes with resort prices; "smaller portion" steaks start at $36. The only vegetarian dish is a vegetable curry with pumpkin and peppers. Open for lunch 11:30 am-1:30 pm Mon-Fri, dinner nightly from 5:30-9 pm. $$$$

"Good wine is a necessity of life for me." – Thomas Jefferson

GOOD VALUE ★ **Solimene's** (Waimea Center, ☎ 887-1313) has delicious, oversized Italian fare at truly affordable prices. Share your salad! The spinach and artichoke dip will start you on the right foot, but try to save room for a pasta like the chicken parmesan or penne alla vodka, which includes garlic bread and the option to add a side salad for $2.50. We're fans of their pizzas, such as the Napa: artichoke hearts, olives, red peppers, red onion, mozzarella and herbs. This is a great place for carnivores and vegetarians. You can BYO wine, and there is no corkage fee. Also worth a stop at lunch for their paninis. Open Tues-Sat for lunch 10:30 am-3 pm and dinner 5:30-9 pm, lunch only on Sundays 10:30 am-3 pm. $$

Hawaiian Style Café (64-1290 Kawaihae Road, ☎ 885-4295). Vegetarians, people watching their cholesterol and picky eaters should avoid the Hawaiian Style Café – there are no substitutions or even egg whites, and the only vegetarian option is a grilled American cheese sandwich. But, if you're after a big greasy breakfast or lunch for cheap, look no further – this place's reputation is legendary. Meals include fried rice, two eggs and corned beef hash, pancakes, burgers and fries, and daily specials written on dry erase boards. There are also *keiki* (children's) specials and a bookshelf with books for kids. Open 7:30 am-12:30 pm Mon-Fri, 7:30 am-10:30 am Sun. Closed Sat as well as the last Sun and Mon of each month. "Come early – closed early when food is gone." $

AUTHOR'S CHOICE

Waimea Ranch House (65-1144 Mamalahoa Highway, ☎ 885-2088). It's not surprising that the Waimea Ranch House is in a ranch house, but it is rather surprising that it serves outstanding Italian-themed food. The décor is simple and warm, with rich wood paneling and a fireplace. The food is fabulous, from the pastas, such as the rotini with thin mushrooms in a zesty tomato sauce, or the filet mignon with gorgonzola and Merlot sauce ($31). Antipasti range from good-sized salads lightly dressed, such as the Caesar and the Waimea tomato, mozzarella and basil, to baked cheese concoctions. The moderately priced wine list will provide a nice complement for your meal. The chefs are flashy with their use of fresh herbs, which they grow in gardens alongside the restaurant, along with the greens for the salads. Walking in the fragrant garden is similar to the experience of walking through the Garden for the Blind in New Zealand – the aromas are strong and distinctive. There is also an adjoining bar with a less expensive menu, including great pizzas. Open for lunch 11:30 am-1:30 pm and dinner 5-9 pm daily except Tuesday. $$$

Tako Taco (64-1066 Mamalahoa Highway, ☎ 887-1717). Mexican-food addicts from Waimea to Hilo suffered withdrawal when Tako Taco closed to expand to a much larger space, which reopened in 2005. It was worth the wait – aside from the obvious advantage of having more than two parking spaces, the new Tako Taco serves fresh-squeezed lime margaritas and often has live music in the evening. The food is good and healthy – no lard in the black or pinto beans – and has the whole range of Mexican grinds, like quesadillas, tacos including tofu cooked in ranchero sauce, burrito logs, salads, tostadas and nachos. Yum! The only drawback is that they don't have a scorching hot sauce, just a mild pineapple tomatillo, medium tomato, and pico de gallo. Happy hour has drink and food specials 4-6 pm Mon-Sat. Open 11 am-8 pm Mon-Sat. $-$$

Kamuela Deli (Waimea Center, 65-1158 Mamalahoa Highway, ☎ 885-4147). Don't even think of going to the McDonald's in the Waimea Center when you are so close to the Kamuela Deli, which has cheap hamburgers ($1.50), as well as sandwiches, plate lunches, seven kinds of saimin (including vegetarian) noodle soup (and four fried versions) – plus breakfast all day, with 99¢ hash browns and fried egg sandwiches for $1.85. Eat local grinds, brah! Open 5:30 am-9 pm daily. $

Daniel Thiebaut Restaurant (65-1259 Kawaihae Road, ☎ 887-2200, www.danielthiebaut.com). Loyalists may disagree, but Daniel Thiebaut has displaced Merriman's as the reigning fine dining restaurant in Waimea. Innovative "French Asian cuisine," terrific ambiance in a former general store, attentive service – it's hard to imagine anyone leaving here disappointed. How could they, with appetizers like lobster bisque flavored with brandy and topped with a cilantro coconut cream? The catch of the day is prepared with a macadamia nut-vinaigrette, a lemon caper sauce, or crab-crusted with sweet chili butter sauce. Other temptations include duck, lamb, pork, seafood, beef and tofu dishes. Though it's a fabulous place for dinner, lunch is an affordable way to try dishes like *liliko`i* barbecue shortribs or miso-glazed salmon salad for $10.50.

There are five dining rooms, which is convenient if you are with a large group. Fourteen of us once occupied a separate room; since six of them were children under seven years of age, it was a great arrangement, as the kids could roam

around without tripping all of the waiters in the restaurant. Great mai tais, too – the bar area makes you feel thirsty. Some Sunday evenings there is a special live music show with a light dinner menu starting at 4 pm. Open 11:30 am-2 pm lunch, 5:30-9 pm daily, except Sunday brunch buffet 9 am-1:30 pm. $$$$

There are ethnic restaurants in the Parker Ranch Center's food court, and across the street in the Waimea Center at **Charley's Thai Cuisine**, **Great Wall Chop Sui**, and **Yong's Kal-Bi Korean Restaurant**.

■ Mauna Kea

Mauna Kea, kuahiwi ku ha`o i ka malie.
"Mauna Kea, astonishing mountain that stands in the calm."
– Hawaiian proverb

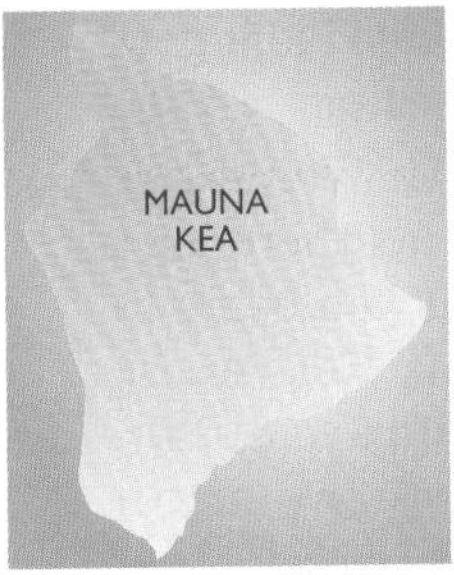

Few land use disputes have been as contentious as the battle over Mauna Kea, the tallest mountain in Hawaii. The summit of Mauna Kea is a sacred place to native Hawaiians because it is the *kinolau* (physical embodiment) of Hawaiian deities. This is where *Papa* (Earth Mother) and *Wakea* (Sky Father) met and began the race of Hawaiian people before separating into two realms. Not only is it home to gods, particularly Poli`ahu, the snow goddess, but is the burial ground for chiefs and priests. Mauna Kea figures prominently in the Hawaiian creation chant, Kumulipo, and genealogy chants, making it an ancestor to the Hawaiian people.

Mauna Kea is revered by astronomers because it provides a unique opportunity to study the stars. Because it is situated on the most isolated land mass on earth – about 2,500 miles from continents and their light pollution – and rises above 40% of the Earth's atmosphere and 90% of its water vapor,

Mauna Kea has the clearest views of space in the world. Because it is less than 20 degrees north of the Equator, Mauna Kea telescopes can see 90% of visible stars.

Since scientists erected the first observatory at the summit in 1967, finding common ground has been a challenge. In 2000, representatives from both sides worked in the spirit of compromise on a management plan to minimize future impact on Mauna Kea, restricting the amount of future observatory development. Today the summit is covered with 13 telescopes, though the highest point on the summit cindercone of Pu`u Wekiu is home to a traditional lele, or structure used for making offerings to gods.

Orientation

The visitor center is six miles up Mauna Kea Road, and the summit is about nine miles farther. To get here, take the Saddle Road and turn at the 28 mile marker. It takes about an hour to get to the top from Hilo, and about two hours from Kona. We urge you to allow plenty of time for the trip (see below).

IMPORTANT TIPS FOR VISITORS

■ Be sure to dress as warmly as possible, as it gets really cold here, from 50° to below freezing.

■ Be sure to fill your tank with gas in Waimea or Hilo before you drive to Mauna Kea, as there isn't any gas available at the mountain. As you begin to ascend to the visitor center on Mauna Kea Access Road, you should loosen your gas cap to avoid stalling or loss of power due to vapor lock (we met a woman who blamed two different rental cars for "dying" on the way to the visitor center – she hadn't heard of vapor lock).

■ Do not proceed to the summit without stopping for at least 40 minutes at the visitor center (at 9,300 feet elevation) in order to acclimate – driving from sea level to nearly 14,000 feet in a few hours is a surefire way to develop altitude sickness (which is not fun at all).

- You'll want a 4WD vehicle for the steep grades and rough road.
- Be sure to shift to low range during the descent to avoid burning your brakes (you don't want brake failure on this windy road). Snow, ice and sudden storms create additional dangers.
- Finally, drive slowly and be on the lookout on the access road for "invisible cows" – the white ones are invisible if its foggy; the black ones are invisible if its dark and clear. So many speeding cars and cows have collided that the visitor center even sells bumper stickers warning "Beware of Invisible Cows."
- Call ahead for road conditions and closures at ☎ 935-6268.

Sights

"The wise man's home is the universe." – Democritus

The **Onizuka Center for International Astronomy Visitor Information Station** (☎ 961-2180, recorded road condition hotline ☎ 935-6268, www.ifa.hawaii.edu/info/vis/). Situated at 9,300 feet, the visitor center is a necessary stop before you ascend to Mauna Kea's summit. It was constructed in 1982 as a place for astronomers and technicians to acclimatize, and is named for Big Island hero Ellison Onizuka, one of the astronauts who died in the *Challenger* explosion (for information about the space museum named after him in Kona, see p. 199). Inside, you'll find a few interactive displays, a movie and pamphlets about Mauna Kea, rangers who can answer questions and a small gift shop. There are public restrooms outside. The Onizuka Center is open from 9 am-10 pm daily.

There is a 10-minute lung-buster hike near the visitor center to a western-facing vantage point with some excellent sunset views for those who can't make it to the summit. Unlike the summit, however, this elevation isn't always above the inversion layer, so it can be cloudy at any time, including sunset. But if it's clear, cross the street from the visitor center parking lot and follow the clear-cut trail up the hill. There will likely be dozens of people on tours who are trudging up there, as well.

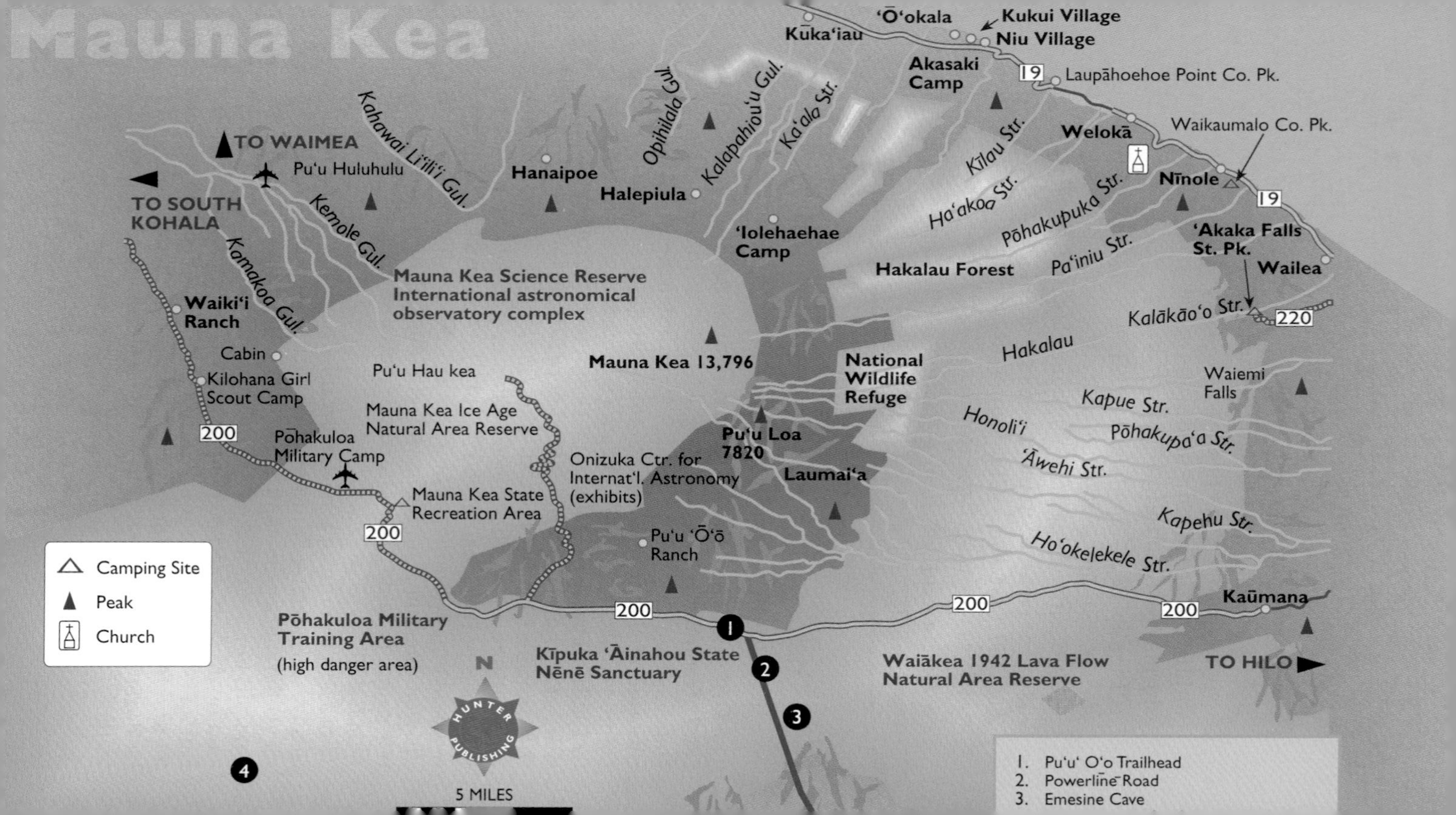

Mauna Kea
Kūka'iau
'Ō'okala
Kukui Village
Niu Village
Akasaki Camp
19
Laupāhoehoe Point Co. Pk.
Weloka
Waikaumalo Co. Pk.
Nīnole
'Akaka Falls St. Pk.
Wailea
TO WAIMEA
TO SOUTH KOHALA
Pu'u Huluhulu
Kahawai Li'ili'i Gul.
Kemole Gul.
Kamakoa Gul.
Hanaipoe
Halepiula
Opihilala Gul.
Kalapahio'u Gul.
Ka'ala Str.
'Iolehaehae Camp
Kīlau Str.
Ha'akoa Str.
Pōhakupuka Str.
Pa'iniu Str.
Hakalau Forest
Kalākāo'o Str.
220
Mauna Kea Science Reserve
International astronomical observatory complex
Waiki'i Ranch
Cabin
Kilohana Girl Scout Camp
Pu'u Hau kea
Mauna Kea 13,796
National Wildlife Refuge
Hakalau
Waiemi Falls
Mauna Kea Ice Age Natural Area Reserve
Pōhakuloa Military Camp
Kapue Str.
Honoli'i
Pōhakupa'a Str.
Pu'u Loa 7820
Laumai'a
'Āwehi Str.
Onizuka Ctr. for Internat'l. Astronomy (exhibits)
Mauna Kea State Recreation Area
200
Pu'u 'Ō'ō Ranch
Kapehu Str.
Ho'okelekele Str.
Kaūmana
Camping Site
Peak
Church
Pōhakuloa Military Training Area
(high danger area)
Kīpuka 'Āinahou State Nēnē Sanctuary
Waiākea 1942 Lava Flow Natural Area Reserve
TO HILO
N
HUNTER PUBLISHING
5 MILES
1. Pu'u' O'o Trailhead
2. Powerline Road
3. Emesine Cave

Astronomy Etiquette: Driving to the summit of Mauna Kea at night is more than frowned upon; we've heard of astronomers leaving observatories to holler at the people responsible for car headlights disrupting their observations.

Adventures at the Summit

Observatories at the summit

While it's true that the vast majority of visitors to the Big Island are content with remaining on the coast for the duration of their trip, many others are intrigued enough by the hulking mass of Mauna Kea to spend an afternoon finding out exactly what's up there. From the Kohala Coast, Mauna Kea doesn't appear nearly as high as its 13,796 feet, but for those who make the long, winding journey to the top, these doubts dissolve. The rewards for the trip are crystal-clear skies, 360-degree views, mind-blowing sunsets and, after dark, some of the best stargazing in the world. While the rarified air of Mauna Kea isn't for everyone, those who make it are secure in the knowledge that they are seeing a place where most tourists never go.

Though most observatories are closed to the public, the views are worth the effort. After stopping at the visitor center for at least 40 minutes to acclimate while using the interactive displays or watching a video about Mauna Kea, you can drive up the 4WD road. The road is unpaved initially, making for a dusty ascent. When you burst through the cloud layer, you are rewarded with rust-colored moonscapes, sometimes blanketed with snow. You may notice footprints in the snow on some of the nearby cinder cones, as well as tracks laid down by skis and boogie boards. The final ascent is paved, in deference to the astronomers.

A lele (offering platform) at the summit of Mauna Kea

A SLEEPING VOLCANO

Though Mauna Kea hasn't erupted in over 4,000 years, it is still classified as dormant, rather than extinct. Another eruption is unlikely, but there is still a slight possibility that it could blow its top – and blow an astronomical amount of money.

A safe way to visit the summit of Mauna Kea is with one of the free guided tours offered at 1 pm Saturdays and Sundays from the visitor center. Participants watch the one-hour movie about Mauna Kea's importance to native Hawaiians and astronomers and efforts to reach a compromise between the two groups. Then everyone caravans to the summit.

Students lead the tour and will take you into Keck 1, one of the twin Keck telescopes, to warm up and also to stand in the viewing area while they explain some of the more interesting features of the telescope. Then, it's off to the 88 mm University of Hawaii telescope, the second-oldest telescope on the summit. Be prepared for cold weather – even inside, as some of the observatories are air-conditioned to protect the telescopes from the variation in day and night temperatures. The guides have oxygen for people experiencing altitude sickness. The tour ends at 4:30 pm, though you might want to stay near the summit after the tour (maybe hike to the lake or the true summit) in order to watch the amazing sunset. For more information about the visitor center tours, call ☎ 961-2180.

ALTITUDE SICKNESS

Speaking from personal experience, altitude sickness is a serious condition, with symptoms like dizziness, nausea, headache, drowsiness, shortness of breath, loss of balance and muscle coordination. It can lead to more serious conditions like pulmonary or cerebral edema (fluid in the lungs or brain). There is 40% less oxygen at the summit of Mauna Kea than at sea level, which caused one guide to quip, "That's my excuse if I forget something today." Jokes aside, the only cure for altitude sickness is descent to a lower elevation. The staff at the visitor center doesn't allow the following list of people on their summit tours, if this tells you anything: pregnant women, those under 16 (permanent damage can occur to kids whose bodies are still developing), anyone who's gone scuba diving in the last 24 hours (you don't want the bends!), and individuals with heart or respiratory problems. Drinking lots of water before and during a visit to the summit can help prevent altitude sickness.

Sunset at the summit of Mauna Kea is a surreal experience. The sun paints the cloud layer and, in winter, the patches of snow. And, as the sun drops closer to the horizon, domes revolve, doors silently slide open, and machines awaken, solemnly positioning telescopes for the night's observations. (If you have a touch of altitude sickness, it seems incredibly weird.)

The best place to park for the sunset is with the line of cars at the upper parking area of the astronomy hub, obviously facing west. Wear clothing to protect you from the cold wind, including jackets, gloves and hats or you'll end up watching from the front seat of your car, which diminishes the experience. You'll envy tour groups their cups of coffee.

Sunset on Mauna Kea (*Henry H. Hsieh*)

Stargazing

"When I have a terrible need of – shall I say the word – religion, then I go out and paint the stars." – Vincent Van Gogh

The night skies at the visitor center at Mauna Kea are usually clear (about 300 days a year) and ideal for stargazing. With so little light pollution, the brilliance and abundance of stars is overwhelming – keep looking up and you'll probably see at least one shooting star.

Each evening, volunteers (many of them astronomy students at University of Hawaii, Hilo) set up telescopes outside the visitor center from 6-10 pm. Some telescopes are left for anyone to wander up and look at the sky, while others are manned by volunteers periodically making announcements such as, "I have this telescope pointed at Saturn if anyone's interested." On some nights volunteers use special light pointers to give a "tour" of the sky's constellations.

THE WEKIU BUG

When biologists discovered the Wekiu Bug on the upper slopes of Mauna Kea, it contributed to the case against building additional observatories on the mountain. The Wekiu Bug looks like a small beetle to the untrained eye, and is remarkable because it can live in such a harsh environment, feeding on the bodies of dead or dying bugs that have been blown by the wind to Mauna Kea.

Saturday is an ideal day to visit Mauna Kea because, not only is there a guided tour to the summit, there are special programs at night. There are one-hour presentations at 6 pm on the first and third Saturdays of each month. The Universe Tonight, on the first Saturday, discusses recent activities and discoveries taking place at observatories on Mauna Kea. The third Saturday focuses on Hawaiian culture, with lectures on topics such as the Hawaiian lunar calendar. The U.H. Hilo Astrophysics Club hosts the second Saturday of stargazing, and international musicians serenade stargazers on the fourth Saturday of each month. Most importantly, hot drinks like cocoa, coffee and tea are available for a dollar every night of the week.

This is *the* place to be for annual meteor showers, when the Visitor Information Center stays open all night for their "All Night Star Parties." Last year, over 500 vehicles crowded around the visitor center for the November Leonid shower. One employee said, "The next morning it looked like there'd been a rock concert!"

Big Island lights: You many have noticed during your stay on the Big Island that street lights glow orange. These are special sodium lights that emit light on only a single wavelength, making it easy for the observatories to filter the light out of their readings.

"Once you can accept the universe
as matter expanding into nothing that is something,
wearing stripes with plaid comes easy." – Albert Einstein

On Foot

Mauna Kea Summit

Difficulty: Strenuous, due to elevation
Distance: ¼ mile total, up-and-back
Time: 5-10 minutes, each way

A climber celebrates at the summit of Mauna Kea

It may be only a short walk to the true summit of Mauna Kea but, at nearly 14,000 feet, it still requires some lung capacity. That said, it is absolutely worth the wheezes and pants it may require for you to get there. The trail to the summit is just across the street from the U of H 88 mm telescope, down and across a narrow saddle. It should be easily recognizable as it's not only the highest point for thousands of miles, but has a *lele* (offering platform) perched on top. It may be a bit dangerous if there is fresh snow, but we've been up when the snow has turned to ice and it's easy to find footholds in frozen footprints. The feeling on the top will likely leave you giddy, whether from the lack of oxygen to your brain, the unmistakable *mana* (spiritual power) or simply the phenomenal 360 degree view.

Lake Wai`au

Difficulty: Strenuous, due to elevation
Distance: 1.8 miles total, up-and-back
Time: 60-90 minutes

Nestled at 13,020 feet, this is the only alpine lake in the state, and the third-highest lake in the United States. It lies in the Pu`u Wai`au cinder cone, and is fed by the rain and snow that regularly fall on Mauna Kea. What makes it unique, however, is that it doesn't drain. Basaltic lava is generally porous, and

Lake Wai`au (*Henry H. Hsieh*)

cannot hold water for a long time, which is the reason that you don't regularly see pooled water in cinder cones. Over time, layers of ash and silt have accumulated here, making for a more impermeable sedimentary layer. Soon after the eruption that created the cinder cone, scientists speculate, sulfur-laden steam discharged through layers of ash and cinder altering their composition, creating an impermeable, clay-like layer. Rain and snowmelt runs off of this layer and collects in the basin at the bottom of the cone. Scientists dismiss the commonly suggested notion that a layer of permafrost feeds the lake, asserting that the daytime temperatures are too high to sustain it.

Whatever the science of the lake may be, the power of its presence, its history and its cultural significance are undeniable. For those who are open to such things, the area emanates a palpable *mana*, injecting one with a feeling of sacred awe. Though it is small, shallow, and a dingy brown color, it is somehow wildly beautiful. For generations Hawaiians trekked to the top of their world to bring the umbilical cords of their newborn children and deposited theminto the lake to give power to their children.

Lake Wai`au is believed to be the umbilical cord connecting the Hawaiian Islands to the heavens.

The hike to the lake is fairly easy, but it does require some up and down at an elevation over 13,000 feet. Begin at Lot 2, a rough parking area at the big bend in the road as you are approaching the observatories. Take the left road toward Millimeter Valley, then another quick left into the parking area. The trail leaves from the south end of the lot and skirts the western edge of Pu`u Haukea, the large cinder cone directly to the south. Remain on the obvious trail, which is the upper portion of Mauna Kea Trail. (DO NOT follow the rock piles to the west, which will lead to a high headwall with a difficult descent to the lake.) Continue along the trail until you reach a junction, just south of the cinder cone, about ¾ of a mile down the trail. Follow the junction to the right, and over a short rise you should see Lake Wai`au shimmering less than a quarter-mile beneath you. Return the way you came. Remember this area is sacred to native Hawaiians. Do not disturb the lake, or the *ho`okupa* (offerings) left there.

Authors' Note: If you are in top physical condition and have the desire, it is possible to hike the **Mauna Kea Trail**, which leads from the visitor center at 9,300 feet to Millimeter Valley, a short distance from the summit for an elevation change of over 4,500 feet in six miles. Be prepared for cold, wet weather and an oxygen-deprived atmosphere. You can also drive to the summit of Mauna Kea, and hike separately to Lake Wai`au so, unless you crave that hard-earned feather in your cap, you'll probably just want to drive it.

On Snow

Commercial ski operators are not allowed on Mauna Kea, though some people like to carry their planks up and ski down when snow covers Mauna Kea and its cindercones, usually from December through April. If you'd rather not destroy the bottoms of your skis on the crusty "Pineapple Powder," go local-style and slide down on a boogie board. Or, better yet, think again. The staff at Mauna Kea strongly discourages snow recreation because of the fragile environment, cultural significance, and danger involved – it's easy to slam into a patch of rock and really hurt yourself. There are rumors of "a kid on a boogie board who died."

Hawaiian Mythology: Mauna Kea is home to Poli`ahu, the snow goddess and rival to Pele, goddess of the volcano. Snow (*hau*) is her physical manifestation (*kinolau*), just as lava is Pele's.

Where to Stay

The only accommodations in the area are the cabins in Mauna Kea State Recreation Area on the Saddle Road. There are seven cabins, though they aren't always all open, due to a problem with the park's water distribution system. It seems the spring that fed the park for years dried up, which led to the long-term closure of the cabins. For the moment, however, they are open once again. Each cabin has beds, a stove with utensils, hot showers and a toilet. Bring extra blankets or a sleeping bag, as it's chilly year-round at 6,500 feet. The cabins are $35 per night, and permits must be arranged in advance through the Division of State Parks. (See page 52-53 for details.)

Nearby Attractions & Adventures

Saddle Road (Highway 200)

"The real voyage of discovery lies not in seeking new landscapes, but in seeing with new eyes." – Marcel Proust

Saddle Road cuts through a lava desert

The infamous Saddle Road connects the west and east sides of the island along the high saddle that runs between the towering mountains of Mauna Kea and Mauna Loa. It may only be 50 miles long, but it *feels* longer than that. While it is certainly the shortest distance between the two points, it is not necessarily the fastest way from one side of the island to the other (unless you are one of the locals who drives 75 mph without a second thought). The road is nauseatingly twisty, with frequent dips and blind turns.

On the Kona side, the road climbs through verdant ranch lands, with bright green hills and tall eucalyptus trees. Vegetation thins out as you approach Pohakuloa Military Training Facility, where you may encounter long military convoys. There are scuzzy bathrooms and some picnic tables at Mauna Kea State Recreation Area if you need a break. The road then enters a land of cinder cones and lava flows, before going over the hump toward Hilo, where the condition of the road improves as it winds through *o`hia*, ferns and fog.

DRIVE CAREFULLY

Many car rental companies prohibit their customers from driving their vehicles on Saddle Road. This isn't because you need 4WD to navigate the curvy road, but because there are so many accidents here. If you leave from Kona, you'll be tempted (like most locals) to drive down the center of the road, which is freshly paved, instead of in your lane. This leads to obvious problems if another car whips around a turn doing the same thing. In a striking display of how tax dollars are distributed on the Big Island, the entire portion of the Saddle Road in the Hilo district is paved, despite the fact that the bulk of tax revenue is generated Kona-side. But there is hope: The 2006 state budget allots $30 million for the Saddle Road Improvement Project, which would greatly reduce the danger and risk of using the road once it's completed.

On Foot

Kipuka Pu`u Huluhulu

Difficulty: Easy
Distance: 3/5 of a mile, loop
Time: 30 minutes

Located by the hunter sign-in station near the turn to Mauna Kea, the trailhead for Kipuka Pu`u Huluhulu leads to a sweet little loop through native hardwood forest with rewarding views of the nearby mountains and golden cinder cones.

The trail ascends for 10 minutes through a stand of *koa* and the yellow, phallic stalks of mullein to a clearing with views of Hualalai, Mauna Loa and Mauna Kea, as well as the Saddle Road cutting through a lava flow. This is a prime opportunity to catch your breath while snapping photos.

If you have time, finish the loop by continuing on the trail to the left of the clearing, eventually descending through a forest for views of a bubbly lava flow through mossy *koa* trees and some *o`hia*. Though you'll probably be serenaded by native songbirds, you might also be scolded by surprised jungle fowl. There are a few forks that rejoin the trail; at the first, veer left (up) and at the second, turn right.

To get here, park at the hunter station just east of mile marker 28, across from the Mauna Kea Access Road. There is a pit toilet near the trailhead.

A *kipuka* is formed when an older lava flow is surrounded by more recent flows, often leading to a forested "island."

Saddle Road's **Pu'u O'o Trail** (not to be confused with the Pu'u O'o in Hawai'i Volcanoes National Park) is a moderately difficult trail through lava fields to birdwatching forests and Emesine Cave. Visit www.bigislandadventureguide.com for details.

On Wheels

Mana Road/Keanakolu Road

If you have a 4WD vehicle and want to explore one of the most remote areas of the Big Island, which is full of *koa* forests and native birds, you won't want to miss the Mana Road between Saddle Road and Waimea. Though the road is 40 miles long, it is so rough – and you'll want to stop to listen or photograph birds so often – that you should allow between four and five hours to complete the drive.

To access it from Kona, take Saddle Road and turn on the Mauna Kea Access Road at mile marker 28, then turn right 2.1 miles up onto Keanakolu Road. About 4½ miles in, you may be relieved to find yourself on pavement – this sensation will last for about five seconds before you see the sign "Pavement Ends." The road is challenging, but passes through majestic

Negotiating the lava fields requires a 4X4

stands of *koa* trees – the ones with sickle-shaped leaves and twisted trunks and branches – and to the Hakalau Forest National Wildlife Refuge public access point at the Maulua Tract 16.8 miles in (see below). If this is your destination, you'll want to return the way you came, because several miles of the worst part of the road start pretty much halfway in. It's Murphy's Law that the worst part of the road lies in the worst place to break down and find yourself stranded – 20 miles from either end.

While driving the Mana Road, you may be tempted to turn off the radio and listen to the chorus of songbirds above you, or even to stop in the middle of the road and breathe it all in. A good place to do this is a pull-out 15.7 miles from the Kona-side turnoff, in the Piho section of the Hilo Forest Reserve. There's a ladder over a fence here with access to unmaintained trails. But the best part is just standing at the side of the road looking up at the moss-covered trees, watching for flashes of red and yellow honeycreepers and listening to their twittering, buzzing, chirping, squawking, trilling, whistling and pootweeting.

The road on the Waimea side passes through pastureland, and many of the cows – particularly the bulls – are less-than-amused by having to move for humans in a car. Wild turkeys and the striking chukar, a partridge with a black band that leads from each eye to its neck, are common sights here as well. By the time we reach this section of road, either the wiggling rumps of turkeys hustling across the road, the antagonism of the cows or the adrenaline rush at having survived the worst part of the Mana Road has us giggling like lunatics. It's just another fun way to pass time on the Big Island.

BIRDING HOT-SPOT

I`iwi

Hakalau Forest National Wildlife Refuge (☎ 933-6915) was created in 1985, when the US government set aside 32,733 acres of forest on the windward slope of Mauna Kea to protect Hawaii's endangered native birds and their rainforest habitat. The refuge is in a remote part of one of the least visited areas of the entire island, and the birds love it. Hakalau ("many perches") is home to endangered native birds like the *i`iwi* and other brilliant little honeycreepers (as well as the endangered *`apa`ape`o*, the Hawaiian hoary bat). This is also an area where you'll find game birds like wild turkeys, and possibly *nene*, the world's rarest goose (we've seen *nene* alongside the Mana Road in this area).

Public access is limited to the Maulua Tract on weekends. There aren't any hiking trails, so you pretty much drive in a mile or less, park, and look for birds. You'll need to call in advance for permission to enter the area – and to get the combination to unlock the gate. There is an annual Open House, usually the first Saturday in October, which allows the public to visit other areas of the park with tour guides to explain about the refuge and its birds, and view informational displays. Again, you'll need to call ahead. Another option is to book a tour with Hawaii Forest and Trail (www.hawaiiforest.com).

Mauna Loa Road

There is a 17.4-mile road that ascends to 11,150 feet up the northern flank of Mauna Loa, leading to the Mauna Loa Weather Observatory. The road is paved, but it is a single lane that winds up and down many stark lava hills as it climbs toward the observatory. The view of Mauna Kea on clear days is inspiring and may be worth the effort, but there is no visitor's center or services available at the observatory, with the exception of a pit toilet. Altitude sickness can be a problem at this altitude, and you'll want to bring plenty of water and suntan lotion, as the UV rays are intense.

Most people who venture up here are heading to the summit of Mauna Loa along the Observatory Trail, which is an incredibly grueling path that climbs over 2,500 feet in under just over six miles. This is a trail that requires planning, acclimatization and contingency supplies such as extra food and water, clothing, and possibly even shelter. Snow and freezing rain are not uncommon at the highest elevations on Mauna Loa, even in summer, and the high elevation and frequent fog can cause disorientation and poor judgment. Though it seems to be day-hike length, this trail is difficult and dangerous. There is a less arduous, though longer, multi-day backcountry trail that begins at the end of Mauna Loa Road in Hawai`i Volcanoes National Park. Backcountry permits are required.

The road up Mauna Loa is just a few hundred yards east of the Mauna Kea Access Road off of Saddle Road, near the 28 mile marker. Turn south on the east side of Pu`u Huluhulu.

Hawai`i Volcanoes National Park

Ke Akua Wahine o ka pohaku `ena `ena, `eli `eli kau mai!
"Oh Goddess of the Burning Stones, may wonder and awe possess me!" – Hawaiian chant

IN THIS CHAPTER

Few phenomena captivate the human imagination like the volcano, a mountain through which liquid fire from the bowels of the earth explodes to the surface, creating – and sometimes destroying – land. Just as erupting volcanoes inspired awe in ancient Hawaiians for Pele, the tempestuous goddess of the volcano, Hawai`i Volcanoes National Park enchants visitors today.

One of the Big Island's five volcanoes, Mauna Loa, towers nearly 14,000 feet above the park, while Kilauea erupts within it. Kilauea, the world's most active volcano, started erupting in 1983 and hasn't stopped. When it first erupted, a fountain of lava shot 1,532 feet into the air, almost three times the height of the Washington Monument. Over 20 years later, the lava continues to flow – about 175,000 yards flow into the ocean every day. Millions of visitors flock to Hawai`i Volcanoes National Park each year to gape at the steaming craters and drive to "The End of the Road" – so called because the road ends where lava flowed over it – to watch lava pour into the ocean, sending up a massive cloud of steam as it does. But more adventurous visitors, with time for more than a cursory visit, discover even more

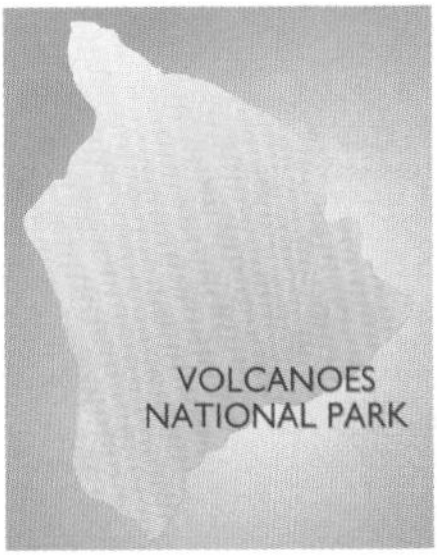

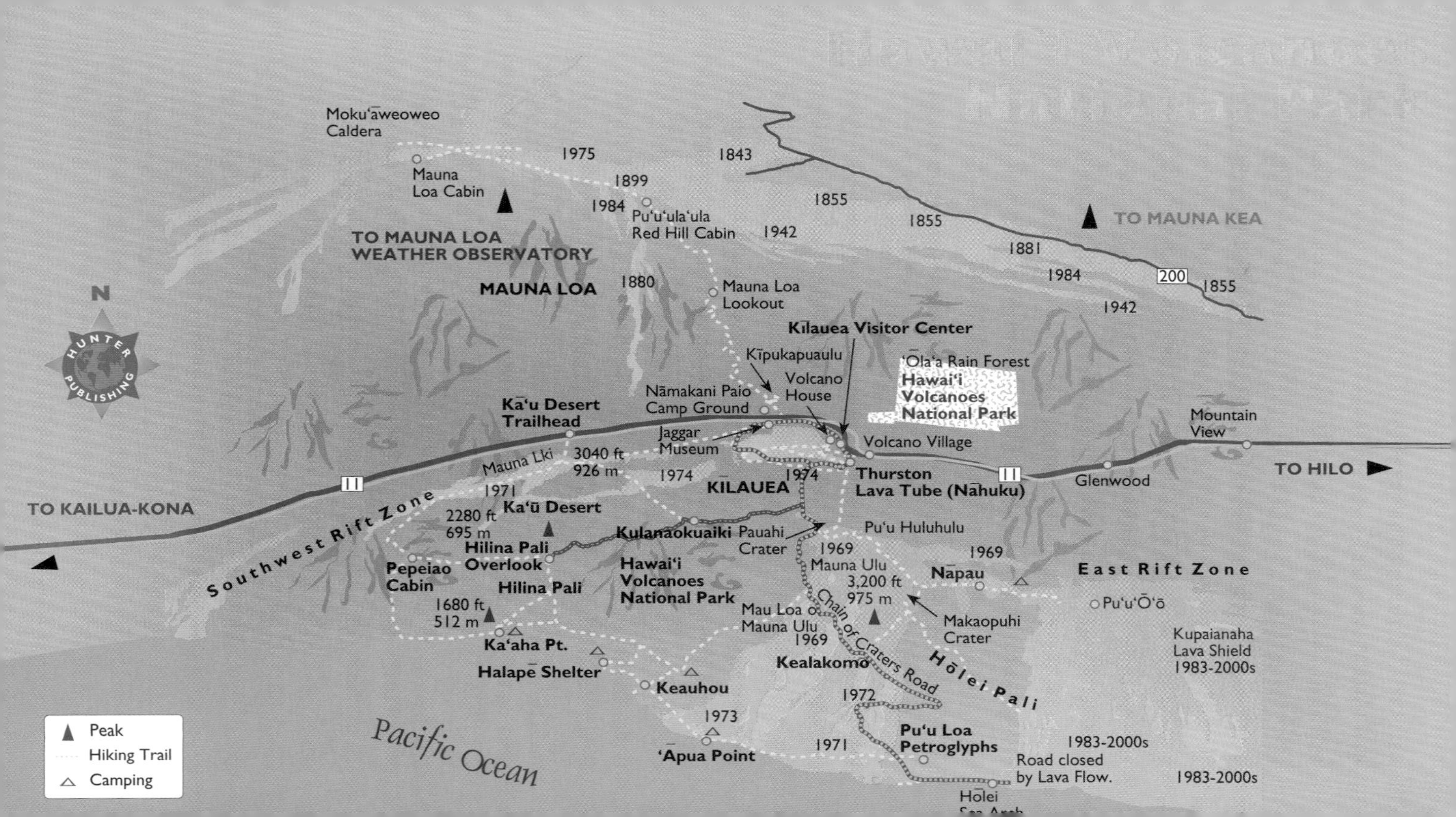
Moku'āweoweo Caldera
Mauna Loa Cabin
TO MAUNA LOA WEATHER OBSERVATORY
MAUNA LOA
Pu'u'ula'ula Red Hill Cabin
Mauna Loa Lookout
TO MAUNA KEA
200
Kīlauea Visitor Center
Kīpukapuaulu
Volcano House
'Ōla'a Rain Forest
Hawai'i Volcanoes National Park
Nāmakani Paio Camp Ground
Ka'u Desert Trailhead
Jaggar Museum
Volcano Village
Mountain View
Glenwood
TO HILO
Thurston Lava Tube (Nāhuku)
KILAUEA
TO KAILUA-KONA
Mauna Lki
3040 ft 926 m
Ka'ū Desert
2280 ft 695 m
Hilina Pali Overlook
Kulanaokuaiki
Pauahi Crater
Pu'u Huluhulu
Southwest Rift Zone
Pepeiao Cabin
Hilina Pali
Hawai'i Volcanoes National Park
Mauna Ulu 3,200 ft 975 m
Nāpau
East Rift Zone
Pu'u'Ō'ō
Makaopuhi Crater
Mau Loa o Mauna Ulu
Chain of Craters Road
Hōlei Pali
Kupaianaha Lava Shield 1983-2000s
1680 ft 512 m
Ka'aha Pt.
Halapē Shelter
Keauhou
Kealakomo
Pacific Ocean
'Āpua Point
Pu'u Loa Petroglyphs
Road closed by Lava Flow.
Hōlei
1975
1843
1899
1984
1855
1942
1881
1880
1974
1971
1969
1972
1973
1983-2000s
N
HUNTER PUBLISHING
Peak
Hiking Trail
Camping

of the park's wonders, developing a lasting appreciation for the majesty of this amazing National Park.

There are over 150 miles of maintained hiking trails in the park. Some of the trails are paved, short and easy, while others traverse lava flows with trails marked only by rock cairns, called *ahu*. Some of the easier ones include a short hike to a collection of petroglyphs, mysterious symbols carved onto lava rocks by ancient Hawaiians. The **Puu Huluhulu hike** passes numerous lava trees, formed when lava swept through a forest and entombed the trees in rock before draining away. An amble through **Kipuka Pualu (Bird Park)**, is a chance to experience a *kipuka* – in this case, an island of old growth forest formed when a newer lava flow surrounded an older one. Here the native hardwood trees – *koa* and *o`hia* that are hundreds of years old – are filled with the songs of native honeycreepers, who flash bright red and yellow as they flit between branches. You'll undoubtedly share the trail with Kalij pheasants, colorful game birds that strut around like they own the forest. While these cocky birds start to seem common in the park, catching sight of an endangered *nene*, the state bird and the world's rarest goose, is a special chance to admire the bird's clumsy grace.

Longer hikes, such as the **Crater Rim Trail**, allow for a visceral appreciation of the diverse beauty of the park, passing by stunning views of the park's major craters like Pele's home of Halema`uma`u, vistas of the Steaming Bluff, through stark lunarscapes of lava deserts, and into lush rainforests. One of the park's most popular hikes is Kilauea Iki, which crosses the floor of the steaming crater. The experience is otherworldly, as is hiking the **Napau Trail** to get close to the Pu`u O`o vent, the opening from which Pele has been spewing lava since 1983.

Keen-eyed hikers in the park may spot Pele's Hair, hair-like strands of volcanic glass, or her tears, small droplets of lava. Cavers with flashlights can venture into the "dark side" of **Thurston Lava Tube**, a way to glimpse the natural tunnel without overhead lights. No matter which adventure you choose, you will feel the power and diverse beauty of nature at Hawai`i Volcanoes National Park.

The nearby town of **Volcano Village** has one of the highest concentrations of bed and breakfasts on the island, and boasts some terrific restaurants as well. There may not be too much in the way of nightlife, but with an art gallery, a high-country golf course and the island's only winery, there's more here than meets the eye.

"Hawaii is paradise born of fire." – Rand McNally

■ Orientation

Located on the southeastern part of the island, Hawai`i Volcanoes National Park encompasses 333,000 acres and the summits of Mauna Loa and Kilauea, the most active volcano in the world.

Ranging in elevation from sea level to 13,677 feet, the park has a wide variety of climates. The Kilauea Caldera (pronounced "KEE-lau-EH-ah") and the visitor center sit at about 4,000 feet. The northwest trade winds blow moisture-rich air up the slopes where it cools, condenses and dumps rain year-round. The average temperature at the visitor center is 69°, and the area received an average of 106 inches of rain per year between 2000 and 2005. That said, rainfall can vary wildly and often does. For example, in January of 2002 and 2004, the visitor center received over 20 inches of rain. However, in 2001 and 2003, the same area got only 2.1 inches. At the end of Chain of Craters Rd, where the lava meets the sea, the temperature will nearly always be in the 80s during the day, and it receives little rain. So, you never really know what you're going to get – you'll want to bring clothes for all types of weather.

The park is on Hwy 11, 28 miles west of Hilo and about 90 from Kailua-Kona, a two-hour drive. From the Kohala resorts, it's nearly as fast to take the Saddle Road to Hilo, though the drive is more taxing that way. However, when returning (or getting an early start), it's better to avoid the Saddle Road.

The entrance to the park is on Hwy 11 between the 28 and 29 mile markers.Latest eruption information is available through the park's information line, ☎ 985-6000, or on the web at http://hvo.wr.usgs.gov/kilauea/update/.

Directional info: We've written the directions the way they're given on the Big Island: *mauka* and *makai*. Turn *mauka* means "toward the mountain," while *makai* means "toward the ocean." This way you'll be sure to turn the correct way no matter how you're headed.

"The thing to remember when traveling is that the trail is the thing, not the end of the trail. Travel too fast and you miss all you are traveling for." – Louis L'Amour

HOW MUCH TIME?

How much time do you need at the volcano? First, keep in mind that it takes at least two hours to drive to the park from Kailua-Kona and the Kohala resorts. Then, it will take you about two hours to circle Crater Rim Dr, and an additional two hours to complete a round-trip of Chain of Craters Rd, taking in the sights along the way. You'll need to factor in more time for hiking and lava viewing, which you will want to do. You could spend a week here and still not see everything (we've tried!).The thing people most regret about a trip to the park is that they don't have more time. Most people are fixated on seeing flowing, red lava, but once they are here they realize how much there is to do. It's a good idea to plan an overnight and, with so many excellent and affordable accommodations in the area, the only reason not to do it is the impulse to stay at the beach the whole time!

■ Geology

Kilauea Volcano (Hawaiian Images)

The entire Hawaiian Island chain was created by a combination of two factors: a submerged volcanic "hotspot," and the steady tectonic movement of the Pacific

Plate. The Hawaiian hotspot is essentially a massive eruption taking place below the tectonic plate that causes the buildup of a volcanic mountain over time. At the same time, the Pacific Plate is moving steadily northwest at about four inches per year. Eventually, these mountains break the surface and become volcanic islands, continually erupting and growing in land mass as they spew magma fed from deep in the earth's core. As the volcanoes move farther off the hotspot, however, their magma reservoirs are no longer refilled after eruptions, and they slowly begin to cool and eventually become extinct. Meanwhile, a new volcanic mountain over the hotspot begins to grow. Each of the Hawaiian Islands was created in this way. The farthest main island from the hotspot, Kaua`i, has extinct volcanoes that have had time to erode in fascinating ways, resulting in the striking topography of the island. On the Big Island, the youngest of the islands, the oldest volcano is Kohala, which makes up the northern coast. It is the farthest away from the hotspot and is the only extinct volcano on the island. The youngest volcano is Kilauea, which is closest to the hotspot and still has an active and intensely hot magma chamber, as it retains a direct magma conduit to the hotspot. It is thought that Mauna Loa and Hualalai no longer have a direct conduit, but still have active magma reservoirs, which will undoubtedly result in future volcanic eruptions.

STILL GROWING: LOIHI

The newest Hawaiian island is the seamount of Loihi, an active volcano about 20 miles off the southeastern coast of the Big Island. Its elevation is about a half mile below sea level. It is directly over the Hawaiian hotspot, and is expected to break sea level some time over the next 10,000 to 100,000 years.

Practicalities

Before You Go: There are no gas stations in the park. The only two are in Volcano Village. Chain of Craters Road drops 4,000 feet over 20 miles as it zigzags down to the sea, so you'll be consuming plenty of fuel. If you are driving back to the Kona side, the last gas station in town closes at 9 pm.

At the park entrance, you'll pay the admission fee, which is good for seven days – keep your receipt if you plan to return! The attendant will also give you a brochure with a map of the park and, if you ask, a list of hiking trails. Admission is $10 per vehicle.

PELE'S CURSE

The staff at Hawai`i Volcanoes National Park receives packages every day from former visitors who pocketed a lava rock they found. The people send back the lava with long letters detailing the bad luck they've experienced since stealing the rock from the park, begging the rangers to return the lava to Pele so she can lift her curse. But the rangers have no way of knowing the proper place for the rocks (they're dumped in a giant heap out back), so there is no guarantee of a reversal of fortune. Curse or no curse, out of respect for Hawaiian culture, it's best to avoid removing anything from the park.

Kilauea Visitor Center (☎ 985-6000, www.nps.gov/havo) is just inside the park entrance area, and is the first stop for most visitors who want to get oriented. There are outdoor exhibits with maps and suggested itineraries if you have only two hours, four or more, and so forth. Rangers and volunteers frequently lead talks and short tours; check the board for event times or ask inside. There are interactive displays, such as the large rainforest diorama where you can push buttons to hear the songs of different endemic birds. The gift shop sells maps, books, posters and other souvenirs. One of the highlights of the center is a 20-minute orientation movie that provides a geological, natural and cultural overview of the park. It traces the history of the island from its genesis 80 million years ago as a rift on the ocean floor to the evolution of over 50 types of honeycreepers from a single finch to the arrival of the Polynesians and the emergence of Hawaiian culture. High production values and spectacular lava footage make this a worthwhile introduction to the park. The film plays on the hour between 9 am and 4 pm in the 200-person, state-of-the-art theater. Open 7:45 am-5 pm.

Junior Rangers. Our National Park system has a cool program for kids that teaches them to become Junior Rangers. At Hawai`i Volcanoes National Park, kids seven-12 can learn about the park and help protect it by becoming Junior Rangers. Potential Junior Rangers should talk to a Park Ranger at the Kilauea Visitor Center, where they'll get an activity booklet that they need to complete to qualify. The possible activities include exploring the park with their family, creating a poster and taking a hike. At the end of the day, after the Park Ranger checks their work and certifies that they have completed the requirements to become a Junior Ranger, the Park Ranger announces their accomplishment over the intercom at the Visitor Center. We've spoken with several Junior Rangers (and their parents) who loved the experience.

"The cure for boredom is curiosity.
There is no cure for curiosity." – Dorothy Parker

Sights

Volcano Art Center (Hawai`i Volcanoes National Park, ☎ 967-7565). Over 300 artists from all of the Hawaiian Islands display their art at Volcano Art Center, adjacent to the Visitor Center. The collection is impressive, including paintings, *koa* bowls and furniture, ceramics, sculpture, drums and Hawaiian quilts. There is a book room with Hawaiian tomes as well as children's books, and other souvenirs are available, such as bookmarks, clothing and quilts.

The nonprofit art center hosts a number of summer programs for kids, including dance recitals at the nearby Kahua Hula, a dance platform for mele (chant) and hula (dance). Please don't climb on the Kahua Hula (unless you are a serious practitioner of hula and use the space to dance), but feel free to visit it by following the short path away from the Visitor Center. With views overlooking Halema`uma`u Crater, home to Pele, it is easy to imagine the inspiration dancers must receive performing here. Volcano Art Center is open 9 am-5 pm daily.

Ti plant

It is appropriate that the Kahua Hula is surrounded by *ti* plants, because the famous "grass skirts" worn in the past by hula dancers are actually made of *ti*. The native plant is traditionally wrapped around offerings to the gods, and Hawaiians believe that if you plant a *ti* tree in front of your doorway, it will ward off evil spirits.

■ Adventures

Eco-Tourism

AUTHOR'S CHOICE ★ **Native Guide Hawaii** (☎ 982-7575, www.nativeguidehawaii.com). We highly recommend an eco-tour with Native Guide Hawaii to anyone who wants to get the most out of their visit to Hawaii Volcanoes National Park, even if you have only one day to spend there. Warren Costa, the owner, is one of the very best guides on the Big Island. Even after spending plenty of time at the park over the years, taking a tour with Warren greatly enhanced our appreciation of this amazing place. A Big Island native, he is a botanist and archaeologist who worked in both capacities at Hawaii Volcanoes National Park. He is also a passionate scholar of Hawaiian culture, and a patient man who can just as easily tell a story about Pele or traditional Hawaiian canoes as he can describe geothermal tectonics in a clear way. He can find and identify Pele's Hair, thin strands of volcanic glas,s and Pele's Tears, lava droplets, sacred `ohelo berries, and other treasures you might have missed. He'll show you places that aren't crowded with tourists and help you understand why they are significant and special. His love of Hawaii, and of sharing it with visitors, is incredible.

Warren limits groups to six people, so each tour is a personal experience tailored to the skills and tastes of the group. His standard Volcano tour could be enjoyed by anyone, including seniors. He can also arrange for "more serious" lava hikes. His other standard tours explore the Saddle Road and the Puna coast, where he lives. Tours include transportation in Warren's van and a delicious local lunch, costing $225 for one person, or $125 a person for parties of two or more. Call for reservations. No credit cards accepted.

In the Air

There are a number of companies offering helicopter rides over the park, including views of the eruption at Pu`u O`o and the area where its lava enters the ocean. Flying over an erupting volcano is an incredible experience. For information, see *Hilo* (p. 431).

On Wheels

Crater Rim Drive

This 11-mile driving tour takes you around the rim of Kilauea Caldera, and it certainly provides the most bang for your buck in the park. If you only have a short time for your visit, this is where you should spend it. You'll be introduced to most of the major volcanic features available in the park, including steaming pit craters, pungent fumaroles and a lighted lava tube. Many of the finest hikes in the park are accessible via this drive as well. You'll also get some tremendous views of the hulking shield volcano of Mauna Loa and, if you're lucky and it's tremendously clear, perhaps you'll even glimpse the summit of Mauna Kea over the northern flank of Mauna Loa.

Sulphur Banks Boardwalk

Sulphur Banks Boardwalk

Many people stop at the overlook, snap a few photos of the Steaming Bluff, and move on. But there's a nice paved trail (one-mile round trip) leading away from the crater rim (opposite the parking area) that provides a more intimate experience. The Sulphur Banks Trail leads through o`hia trees filled with singing birds and lots of steam. There are benches along the way if you want to stop and soak it all in.

HAWAIIAN MYTHOLOGY

Hi`iakaHi`iaka i ka Poli o Pele, the favorite sister of Pele, is an important partner and counterpoint to Pele, as she regenerates the new earth that Pele lays down. Even as Pele destroys existing homes and vegetation with her lava flows, she is creating new land. You can see the handiwork of her sister Hi`iaka in the *kupukupu*, or Hawaiian sword ferns, that poke through lava flows, offering hope of new life. You can also see her in Hawaiian art, curled inside an egg held by Pele, since this is how the sisters arrived in Hawaii.

Steam Vents

It's always fun to be able to viscerally experience volcanic activity, and vented steam is a non-lethal way of doing that. As groundwater leaks into underground hotspots, it's turned to steam and vented here. The steam is relatively non-toxic, so it's okay to let the kids put their hands in to feel the warmth. Be sure to take the path to the crater, as there are vents along the rim that steam down into the caldera on calm days, or blow out dramatically when the wind is up. The more humid the atmosphere, the more steam you'll see.

Thomas A. Jaggar Museum

Named for the volcanologist who founded Hawaiian Volcano Observatory and served as its first director, the Thomas A. Jaggar Museum's biggest asset is the view it fronts of Halema`uma`u Crater, which Hawaiians consider the home of Pele. There are coin-operated binoculars from the lookout. Inside, there are exhibits about seismographs, eruption data gathering and videos of flowing lava. It's interesting and sometimes slightly unsettling to watch the needles on the working seismographs for various park locations – including Halema`ma`u – move with small tremors and earthquakes. Open 8:30 am-5 pm.

VOLCANIC GLOSSARY

■ A`a ("ah-ah") – Slow-moving lava comprised of rough chunks of broken lava blocks called clinkers that roll under an advancing flow like tank tracks, with a dense, pasty core.

■ Caldera – A large circular depression formed when a subterranean magma reservoir loses magma from either an eruption or withdrawal, resulting in a collapse of unsupported land.

■ Cinder cone – A conical collection of ash and cinder piled around a volcanic vent.

■ Fumaroles – Fissures that vent volcanic gas, often with collected yellow crystals of cooled sulfur vapor around the rim.

■ Kipuka ("Kee-POO-kah") – An older lava flow surrounded by a more recent one.

■ Lava – Erupted magma.

■ Magma – Molten rock beneath the earth's surface.

■ Pahoehoe ("pah-HOY-hoy") – Smooth, fluid-looking lava of varying types, such as ropy and entrail.

■ Pele's hair – Long, thin strands of volcanic glass blown into the air by a volcanic eruption.

■ Pele's tears – Small bits of molten lava that cool quickly in the air and form tearlike drops.

■ Pit crater – Formed in the same way as a caldera, these are simply smaller, with a diameter of less than a mile.

■ Rift zone – A crustal fracture caused by the buildup of magma beneath the zone. Eruptive events occur more frequently in rift zones.

■ Scarp fault – A cliff or steep slope formed by movement along a fault.

■ Spatter – Ejected molten lava fragments that congeal and collect on the ground.

■ Spatter rampart – Formed by lava fountained from broad fissures that build walls of accumulated spatter.

■ Tephra – A broad term meaning anything ejected into the air by a volcanic explosion or carried by volcanic gases, such as Pele's hair and Pele's tears.

■ Vent – Openings in the earth from which lava and volcanic gases escape.

"I go to nature to be soothed and healed, and to have my senses put in order." – John Burroughs

Halema`uma`u Crater

Halema`uma`u Crater (*Hawaii Forest & Trail*)

For over a hundred years, ending in 1924, Halema`uma`u Crater (pronounced "HAH-leh-MAH-oo-MAH-oo") was a tumultuous lake of roiling lava that drew adventurous travelers from around the world. After his visit in 1866, Mark Twain invited his readers to "imagine a coal-black sky shivered into a tangled network of angry fire!" In 1924 the crater was half the diameter of its present 3,000 feet and still filled with molten lava, but that year the underground magma source shifted east and lava drained from the crater. The crater walls collapsed into the new void and hot ground water flowed in, causing massive steam explosions that blew out giant chunks of rock. When the eruptions ceased, the floor was 1,200 feet deep. It has since been filled with subsequent lava flows (the last in 1967), and the floor presently stands at about 300 feet deep. A 0.2-mile path leads to an impressive lookout over the crater. The crater floor still steams, and is strewn with evidence of geologic violence. Despite the lack of flowing lava, it is still a sight to behold.

Health Warning: *Park officials warn that people with heart or lung maladies should be careful around areas where volcanic gases are emitted. Halema`uma`u Crater emits about 200 tons of sulfur dioxide per day, a toxic compound that can irritate the throat and eyes or cause fatal heart failure in high concentrations or to those who are susceptible. If anyone in your group experiences discomfort in this area, get them out of the area immediately.*

Southwest Rift Zone

Visitors can explore an interesting series of cracks and gulches caused by the buildup of magma at this stop. Wander toward the rim to catch a view of spatter ramparts on the caldera floor. Farther along this rift zone are eruptive remnants such as lava shields, cinder cones, spatter cones and pit craters accessible via the Mauna Iki hike. This stop is directly downwind of Halema`uma`u Crater, so be sure to pass it by with the car windows up if anyone in your group has cardiopulmonary problems, as the noxious fumes in the air can cause serious harm or death to those who are vulnerable.

HAWAIIAN CULTURE: KINOLAU

Kinolau is the physical manifestation of a Hawaiian god. This concept is very important to remember in Hawai`i Volcanoes National Park, because lava is considered Pele's *kinolau*. It is extremely disrespectful to remove lava rocks, which are thought to have a specific place, or to throw objects into the flowing lava. A Hawaiian told us about his peaceful contemplation of the lava flow being interrupted by the arrival of "mainland college boys" who laughed and chucked a can of SPAM into the flow. This created a choking black smoke and ruined the experience for everyone.

Keanakako`i Crater

Meaning "cave of the adzes" in Hawaiian, Keanakoko`i used to have one of the finest caves for quarrying stone dense enough to make those stone tools. The lava flow of 1877 covered the floor of the crater, and the cave. A 1974 eruption filled the floor with an additional 20 feet of lava. You can still see frozen cascades of black lava spilling over the sides of the crater.

Ancient Hawaiians used **adzes**, or ko`i, as a tool similar to an axe. After sharpening the edges of basalt rocks (like the ones found in Keanakako`i Crater), they fastened them to wooden handles. They used the adzes to fell trees and shape them into canoes, weapons, and household items.

Pu`u Puai Overlook

This small overlook peers into Kilauea Iki Crater above where the eruptive fissures opened in fall of 1959, creating the now-frozen lava lake before you and the towering cinder cone of Pu`u Puai to your left. If you want to see the destruction that laid waste to this area of the rim, you can hike part of the **Devastation Trail** from here.

Thurston Lava Tube

Approaching the Thurston Lava Tube (HTJ)

This is considered a "must see" by park officials and tour bus operators alike, and the site is swarming with eager tourists most times of the day. There are two sections, one that is well-lit and one that requires a flashlight. The Visitor Center offers daily tours of both, or you can visit on your own.

A 20-minute, third-of-a-mile loop trail through the small, lighted portion of the tube and back through the rainforest begins with a descent along a paved walkway into a verdant, bird-filled crater. Listen for the songs of the native Hawaiian honeycreepers as you wind your way down toward the tube. The tube portion of the hike is easy and paved – or at least it was paved at one time. Now, as happens with roads, the pavement is full of potholes that are filled with the water that constantly drips from the walls and ceilings. Lava is naturally porous, and will quickly drain water before it pools, but the same cannot be said of man-made pavement. If you venture into the "dark side" of the tube, you'll notice no standing water. Keep your eyes open or you'll be soaked up to your socks. The tube originally had wondrous stalactites, but over the years tourists have collected them as souvenirs and they are now gone. The lit portion of the trail is only a few hundred yards, entering at the crater and exiting through a skylight (collapsed ceiling). At that point, those with flashlights can venture another several hundred yards to the end of this portion of the tube, where it ends at a "breakdown," a cave collapse.

In the Lava Tube (*Hawaii Forest & Trail*)

The entire tube is actually nearly 30 miles long, ending at the sea, but there are many collapses that prohibit a full journey. If you tour the "dark side" of Thurston Lava Tube with a park ranger, he will provide flashlights and inform participants about the history and geology of the tube. The dark side is certainly fun to explore, but less so with 50 people. There is an interesting time when everyone is instructed to turn off their lights and "feel the pure darkness." Expect a crying baby to make this impossible. Still, it's an instructive tour and fairly entertaining. Consider bringing your own flashlight and making your way to the back of the tube once the bulk of the tour has left.

"All my life through, the new sights of nature made me rejoice like a child." – Marie Curie

Kilauea Iki Overlook

Kilauea Iki, the small crater within the larger Kilauea Caldera, epitomizes the instability of the volcano, its black, steaming floors a reminder of the magma bubbling somewhere deep beneath your feet. Encircled by lush, steep cliffs, the crater floor displays the crusted remains of a lava lake created during spectacular eruptions in November and December of 1959, one of the park's most stunning displays. New vents opened on the south side of a thousand-year-old crater and began spewing lava high into the air. The lava fountain reached heights of 1,900 feet, filling the crater with molten lava and piling volcanic debris on the southwest rim of the crater. The resulting cinder and spatter resulted in the creation of Pu`u Puai, which means "gushing hill," the striking red cinder cone on the west side of the crater. The vent is visible at the base of the cinder cone, and can be seen up-close during the Kilauea Iki hike, one of the park's best trails. Don't miss this one!

What's the difference between a **crater** and a **caldera**? A crater is smaller, with a diameter of less than one mile; a caldera's diameter is greater than a mile.

Chain of Craters Road

"We must not cease from exploration." – T.S. Eliot

Along the Chain of Craters Road (HTJ)

Many people exit Crater Rim Drive to follow Chain of Craters Road to the lava-viewing spot at the End of the Road – literally the end, since lava flowed right over it. The road passes by numerous craters – hence the name – and descends through 30-year-old lava flows until it terminates at sea level. Science buffs will be interested in the forces that created this unusual topography. The rift zones of Kilauea are areas of geologic weakness that are created by inflating the reservoir beneath Kilauea Caldera. As these rift zones develop, magma takes the path of least resistance, which means that, presently, the magma beneath the summit of Kilauea is flowing out to the East Rift Zone, resulting in flank eruptions. Most recently, these flank eruptions have been occurring at Pu`u O`o Vent. However, before this vent opened up and began erupting in 1983, Mauna Ulu was the main vent for this magma. Chain of Craters Road followed the East Rift Zone until it was inundated by lava during the Mauna Ulu eruptions from 1969-1974. Since then, the road has been rebuilt, but from the trailhead at the Mauna Ulu parking area (where you can see the old road disappear into the lava) the road now turns away from the rift zone and crosses two massive Mauna Ulu flows, turning towards the coast and descending by way of Holei Pali.The stops along the upper Chain of Craters Road are scars of the rift zone. There are several old craters to peer into, though there is little evidence of recent activity until you reach Mauna Ulu.

Hot Lava: The temperature of lava is around 2,000°F, comparable to molten steel.

Hilina Pali Lookout

At the end of the single-lane, snaking Hilina Pali Road you'll encounter a small lookout, but the views are better from just down the trail a short distance. Hilina Pali is a fault scarp, a steep slope created by earthquakes along a fault line, and a trail leading into the backcountry traverses the cliff on its way to a coastal trail. There are lots of *nene* (the state bird) in this area, so keep your eyes open and don't drive too fast. Unless you've maxed out on everything else to do in the park, or you're on your way to the trailhead, you shouldn't feel compelled to wander out here. Kealakomo picnic area provides a better view and is much more accessible.

Kealakomo

Known to locals as "Pizza Hut" for its roof design, this picnic pavilion is a great spot for a pause. At 2,000 feet, the weather is warmer than at the summit, but not as hot as it is just down the road at sea level. The site sits atop Holei Pali, a steep slope – and fault scarp – where the lower land area has dropped during large earthquakes. During the last major earthquake here in 1975, a 7.2 magnitude tremor caused the land to drop a full five feet at the pali (cliff) and over 10 feet at the shore in some places, creating a tsunami that caused loss of life in the park (see below).

Changing Lava Flows: Keep in mind that nature is fickle, and the lava flows are constantly changing. Call the eruption hotline at ☎ 985-6000 (or check online at http://hvo.wr.usgs.gov) and bring binoculars in case the flow is more distant when you visit.

1975 HALAPE TSUNAMI

Thirty-two campers, including a scout troop, were spending the night at Halape, a backcountry campground at Hawai`i Volcanoes National Park, when they were awakened by an earthquake during the night of November 29, 1975. A second earthquake soon followed with a magnitude of 7.2, generating a tsunami that quickly knocked the campers off their feet. Before they could catch their breath, a second wave inundated them, carrying them 100 yards inland to a pre-existing crack, where they endured wave after wave, the highest over 40 feet. One person was carried out to sea and never seen again, while another was battered to death in the crack. Miraculously, the 30 others survived.

End of the Road

Hot lava up-close (Hawaii Forest & Trail)

Virtually everyone who visits Hawai`i Volcanoes National Park wants to "see lava." Without hiring a private guide or joining a tour, the main option is to drive to the End of the Road and hike to the lava-viewing point, where you can witness the lava flowing into the ocean. Visit during the day to see the large plume of gas and smoke, or get there around sunset in order to see the glowing lava and orange smoke in the darkness. As of this writing – the flows are always changing – visitors drive to the end of the road (at least, as close as they can get behind the long line of parked cars) and then hike for about a half-mile over *pahoehoe* (smooth) lava. On November 28, 2005, a 44-acre lava bench collapsed into the ocean, providing an unobstructed view across the water to the entry point. It's rapidly filling in, though, so be sure to check with rangers at the Visitor Center to find out where the current best viewing area is (they usually have a map), and what time the sun will set. Be sure to bring a flashlight to help you find the reflectors that mark the trail at night (and to keep you from hurting yourself by hiking in the dark).

SAFETY TIPS

■ We met a former park ranger who had us rolling with laughter as she told us about some of the foolish behavior she'd witnessed at the End of the Road, from women attempting to hike over lava in high heels, to the man who set his shoe on fire by kicking the lava (when the flow was much closer than it is now). If you don't want to be the butt of jokes – and more importantly, to keep yourself safe – here are some important suggestions:

■ Bring a flashlight. You'll be hiking out at night, after all, and it's very easy to turn an ankle on lava if you don't watch your step. You'll also want a flashlight to explore the "dark side" of Thurston Lava Tube.

■ Wear closed-toe shoes, preferably hiking boots.

■ Layer your clothing – it can be quite hot or quite cold in different parts of the park, and can rain at any time so bring a waterproof jacket or other wet-weather gear.

■ Bring sunscreen and wear a hat – there's not a lot of shade in newer lava fields.

■ Carry and drink plenty of water.

■ Stay on marked trails – crater rims are unstable, cracks abound, and a`a cuts. Volcanic gas is toxic. Always follow the rock piles, or ahu.

■ Remember to leave only footprints, and take only photos! The land is protected by Federal law, and is sacred to Hawaiians. You don't want the government or Pele after you!

The holes in the ground surrounded by railings (and unfortunately, often filled with trash) are **tree molds**, formed when lava flooded an o`hia forest. On contact with the trees, the lava burned the trees but left behind an imprint, or mold. Unlike the lava trees rising from the ground that you'll see elsewhere in Volcanoes, as well as at Lava Tree State Monument in Puna, tree molds were formed because the lava didn't drain. So, looking down at the base of the tree mold, you can see where the ground was before the lava flow.

"The moment one gives close attention to anything, even a blade of grass, it becomes a mysterious, awesome, indescribably magnificent world in itself." – Henry Miller

On Foot

Devastation Trail

This is a fun little half-mile hike to Pu`u Pua`i, also known as "Fountain Hill" and "Eruption Hill." It's the deposit of volcanic debris (cinder, pumice and spatter) from a 1959 Kilauea Iki eruption, forming downwind of the lava fountains that sprayed 1,900 feet high. After winding through a landscape of cinders and sparse vegetation with a few stands of o`hia and ferns, and fantastic views of Mauna Loa on clear days, the trail ends at a lookout over Kilauea Iki. The hike there and back takes 30 minutes tops.

NENE

The Hawaiian state bird is the nene, an endangered Hawaiian goose. They are most likely descended from very lost Canadian geese. The webbing on their feet is greatly reduced, a necessary adaptation to walking on lava. Seeing nene at Hawai`i Volcanoes National Park is a treat. There were once tens of thousands of them on the slopes of Mauna Loa. By 1944, however, there were fewer than 50 birds left – the introduction of goats and ranching destroyed much of their habitat, mongooses and feral pigs devoured their eggs, and hunters shot them out of the sky. They became extinct on Maui. Thanks to captive breeding programs and federal protection, there are a few hundred nene alive today. They are darling, and you'll want to get close if you see one, but please don't feed the nene as it makes them accustomed to cars and unafraid of roads (there are plenty of "nene crossing" signs throughout the park). As the saying goes, "A fed nene is a dead nene."

Kipuka Pualu

Kipuka Pualu

The one-mile loop trail through Kipuka Pualu, also called Bird Park, is a lovely little trail for anyone who wants to experience an old-growth native Hawaiian rainforest. A *kipuka* is essentially a lava island, formed when an older lava flow is surrounded by more recent flows. Often this leads to isolated stands of vegetation, as in the case of Kipuka Pualu. This is a special little enclave of forest, with trees that are hundreds of years old. Because of Bird Park's location within the National Park, *koa* trees have prospered (i.e., not been chopped down), and it is fantastic to be able to look up at the sky and see the silhouettes of sickle-shaped *koa* leaves. (There are numerous *koa* trees to the right of the sign at the trailhead that will help you identify them.)

Native birds like the *kipuka* are here too, and this is the place to catch a glimpse of a yellow or red honeycreeper, and cross paths with numerous *kalij* pheasants, sometimes strutting like tightrope walkers over mossy logs. Their songs fill the forest, and the cacophony of birdsong here at dawn is deafening. About halfway through the hike, there's a small lava tube that you can peek into. About 200 yards from the lava tube, there is a spur trail to the left that leads to large old-growth trees. Another 200 yards alomg the main trail, you'll find an o`hia tree on the right with a hollow crevice; the tree is thought to be 500 years old.

Akiapola`au, a Hawaiian honeycreeper

Did you know? Tree rings do not form in Hawaii because there is no significant change of seasons. That makes it difficult to determine the age of the trees.

"There are only two ways to live your life. One is as though nothing is a miracle. The other is as though everything is a miracle." – Albert Einstein

Kilauea Iki

Difficulty: Moderate

Distance and type: 3.5 miles or 5.5 miles, loop

Time: 90-120 minutes

If you only have time for one hike in Hawai`i Volcanoes National Park, this should be it. Hiking across the steaming crater floor of Kilauea Iki is a thrilling experience. You can hike it as a 3½-mile loop from the Kilauea Iki Overlook or Thurston Lava Tube parking lot, but we prefer to leave from the Devastation Trail trailhead. It only adds about two miles and provides a chance to spend time on the trail without other hikers.

At the trailhead, instead of heading on the Devastation Trail, take the trail over crunchy cinder to Byron Ledge, heading towards Kilauea Caldera and a looming Mauna Loa with

Kilauea Iki

Pu`u Pua`i on your right. You might think it can't get any better, but there's a whole lot more. After 0.6 miles you'll veer right at the **Byron Ledge Trail** toward **Halema`uma`u Trail** and **Kilauea Iki Trail** through dense forest. Note that some of the o`hia trees have aerial "roots" that look like brooms, which are used to capture moisture for the tree. And don't be surprised if a kalij pheasant darts across your path!

Following signs for Kilauea Iki, you'll start climbing for views of the crater and the vents below – there are well-placed railings to prevent you from becoming so captivated by the view that you tumble off the ledge. The steep green *pali* (cliffs) contrast with the black and copper crater floor, with a grayish line marking the trail through the steam vents.

From the Thurston Lava Tube parking lot area (a convenient place to use the public restroom if nature calls), the trail descends though a beautiful canopy of hapu`u ferns. Then you're at the crater floor, facing a trek through an otherworldly moonscape. There's a sign reminding people to refrain from building rock piles – that is because the rock cairns, or ahu, are the trail markers you'll follow to the other side.

This is the meat of the hike. To be in the middle of a steaming crater, surrounded by forested pali filled with chirping birds, is to know the awesome power of nature and the diversity of America's National Parks. It seems that whenever we're down here it starts to drizzle, and the steam becomes thicker, sometimes obscuring the far side of the crater. (Don't forget to bring a waterproof shell!) The hike leads toward Mauna Loa and a side of the crater with more fissures and fumaroles (another reason to hike it in this direction, as well as the fact that many group tours hike in the opposite direction). Climbing out of the crater, there's a short but steep trail that levels off at a bench, a perfect place to stop for a snack. Then you'll reenter the o`hia forest and retrace your steps back to the trailhead, rewarded once again with views of Kilauea Caldera.

Byron Ledge/Halema`uma`u Trail

Difficulty: Moderate

Distance and type: 7 miles, loop

Time: 2-3 hours

A great combination hike for those who have a little more time, this hike combines the o`hia forests along the Byron Ledge, as well as a satisfying zigzag across the floor of Kilauea Caldera. The hike starts alongside the Devastation Trail trailhead, where you'll enjoy an awesome view of Pu`u Pau`i at the top of the trail. Then the trail drops down into the trees on the ledge. Take the left fork toward the Halema`uma`u Trail. There are a few makeshift lookoutas long the way that allow good glimpses of what's to come on the crater floor. It's an eerie feeling to venture out onto the crater floor on frozen lava, leaving the trees behind. (Lava freezes at much higher temperatures than water.)

You'll pass through several lava flows as you go, specifically those of 1974, 1971, 1885, 1954 and 1982. A little more than halfway across the crater you'll enter the 1982 flow area. You'll know you're there when the lava you're walking on becomes "shelly" – that is, thin, crusty lava that breaks easily. This is due to the high temperature and gas content, which resulted in bubbly lava that solidified that way. The trail is more difficult to follow here, as the *ahu* (rock cairns that mark the trail) tend to blend into the landscape, but you must remain on the trail since areas that look stable might easily collapse. Notice the rough spatter ramparts that built up during the eruptions along the floor. These occurred on April 30, 1982, lasted for 19 hours, and then ceased. This was the last eruption in Kilauea Caldera. Just past here is the fork to the Halema`uma`u Crater lookout. If you haven't been here yet in your car, be sure to take a look. If you have already glimpsed the crater from that angle, consider approaching the crater view farther around the rim. Just be aware of the surface cracks that indicate when a chunk of the rim is preparing to shear off onto the steaming floor below.

The return trip heads back toward the Volcano House, the large red building visible on the northeastern arc of the rim. You'll pass across many more lava flows, but this time the trail will become easier as you close in on the Waldron Ledge. There are numerous steam vents along this leg of the trail. When you reach the vegetation on the other side, follow the sign back toward Byron Ledge and prepare for the one uphill portion of the hike. If you still have some gas after the ascent, consider striking out along the Kilauea Iki Trail from here, climbing the far wall, then returning to the Devastation Trail trailhead along the Crater Rim Trail. If you're not up for that, just keep your eyes peeled for the trail back up to your car. This trail can also be started from Volcano House or the Halema`uma`u Crater overlook.

Crater Rim Trail

Difficulty: Moderate
Length and type: 11 miles, loop
Time: 4-6 hours

Along the Crater Rim Trail

This is an 11-mile loop around the rim of Kilauea (technically it should be called the "Caldera Rim Trail"). It's a great alternative to driving the Crater Rim, as you'll get more of a feel and appreciation for what the area is like, with incredible views of the various craters while hiking in varied terrain, from desolate lava flows to lush rainforests. Be sure to bring plenty of water and a waterproof jacket (you'll pass through all kinds of weather, so layer your clothing). The loop starts in front of Volcano House, where you get a panoramic view of what you are about to circumnavigate and an instant reminder to stretch. The paved path to the right, toward the Steaming Bluff, leads through happy forested areas filled with chirping birds and the stench of sulfur (don't breathe too deeply). Heading toward the Jaggar Museum, you'll have stunning views of Kilauea, with Mauna Loa to your right. There's a particularly enchanting lookout in a stand of *koa* trees.

You might want to visit the restroom at the museum because you'll be entering over six miles of the most isolated segment of the trail. As you continue on the trail just past the parking lot, take a moment to pause and enjoy the view of Halema`uma`u. This is a sacred spot to Hawaiians, where they made (and make) offerings to Pele, who, they believe, lives in the crater. The trail gets less obvious from here, so be sure to follow the *ahu* (rock piles). The landscape becomes starker as you progress past the Ka`u Desert Trail to the Southwest Rift, where signs will direct you away from the cracks. It's human nature to want to stand at the edge and peer in, but remember that the rims are unstable. Stick to the trail, and it will lead to safe vantage points.

The trail descends into rust-colored cinder as well as lava flows, and the terrain really feels like a lunarscape. Wind can be gusty here, which adds to the feeling of isolation. This is a good time to consider the millions of people who visit Hawai`i Volcanoes National Park each year, and how few of them have walked the trail you are hiking. You might not see another person on this section of the trail.

Just before outlooks for Keanakakoi Crater, which was a valued quarry to ancient Hawaiians for basalt stones to make adzes, you will be treated to a welcome view of a vibrant kipuka, a section of older lava teeming with life. It's almost startling to hear birdsong again. Pass through the gate – be sure to close it to keep out feral pigs! – and be sure not to turn an ankle in the last bit of lava field.

Turning into the o`hia forest is a reward that wouldn't feel as special if you hadn't first experienced miles of desolate landscape. You might want to identify plants, trees and birds on the flip side of the park's map – it seems they're all here. This is also a great place to plop down and enjoy a lunch break.

After a nice long amble through the rainforest, you'll rejoin the masses at Thurston Lava Tube. Unless you're pressed for time, you should probably visit the tube later, or you'll break the spell of the hike. This is a major tour bus stop, after all. The trail continues at the far end of the parking lot toward the similarly crowded Kilauea Iki Overlook, then skirts the crater for fantastic views. (Be sure to do the Kilauea Iki hike, too!)

The Crater Rim Trail continues for views of Kilauea and Halema`uma`u and soon you'll see a sign that you are 1.0 miles from the Volcano House and Park Headquarters. Yeah!

You cross a paved road that cracked up in the 1983 Mauna Loa earthquake, a temblor that registered 6.6 on the Richter Scale. Gaze across Kilauea at the Waldron Ledge Lookout, and head on to Volcano House, making sure to read Mark Twain's description of what the caldera looked like when it was filled with molten lava.

Mauna Iki

Difficulty: Moderately difficult

Length and type: 5.5+ miles total, up-and-back, or 8.8 miles as an end-to-end with a drop off and pick up

Time: 2-3 hours for the up-and-back, 3-4 hours for the end-to-end

One of the rarely hiked trails in the park, Mauna Iki is a diamond in the desert. Taking in two deep pit craters, jagged vents, and a large lava shield, this hike is fantastic. It's usually done as an up-and-back trail from Hilina Pali Road (as described here) but can also be trekked as an end-to-end from the Ka`u Desert Footprints trailhead on Hwy. 11 to the Hilina Pali Road trailhead. This way is ideal and allows you to view all of the features, but it requires that friends or family with less trail lust drop you off and pick you up. One way or another, the up-and-back portion is wonderful. Begin at the trailhead just past Kulanaokuaiki Campground along Hilina Pali Road. As with many of the hikes in the park, you'll start your trek in the ohi`a trees. In a short time, however, the vegetation will thin out and you'll be heading across old pahoehoe flows. As you descend a short, steep pali (cliff), the twin-summit of Pu`u Koae comes into view. Forging northwest, you'll enter the 1974 Kilauea flow and soon after encounter two deep pit craters and a gaping, drooling cinder cone. The western crater has a deep black pahoehoe ooze flowing into it, a lava cascade frozen in time. Pause for reflection, or try to figure out how to capture both positive and negative elevations in a photo – but don't walk right up to either pit crater rim. The rims are undercut and crumbly. There are signs to remind you of this important fact. Return the way you came, or add extra mileage as noted below.

On the Mauna Iki Trail, a pit crater fronts a cinder cone

If you continue on toward the closest peak of Pu`u Koae, you'll enter a severe, devastated landscape. Little grows here, and few folks pass this way to appreciate these lesser known but marvelous features. Your only friends will be the koa`e kea, the white-tailed tropic bird, tracing elegant arcs in the naked sky. About two miles farther on, you'll begin to climb the Mauna Iki shield, the summit of which provides the only glimpse of the ocean you can find in the area. A mile downhill from there brings you to the footprints shelter, and three-quarters of a mile farther dumps you out on Hwy. 11. We've experienced some dizzying sulfur dioxide fumes on this hike, blowing downwind from Halema`uma`u Crater, so keep your nose peeled, so to speak.

WHITE-TAILED TROPIC BIRD

With their long white tails sailing beautifully behind them, the *koa`e kea* are often seen in the craters around the park, starkly contrasted against the black, wasted topography. They are primarily sea birds, but are drawn to the cliffs of this volcanic land to nest and breed.

"Thoughts come clearly while one walks." – Thomas Mann

Pu`u Huluhulu

Difficulty: Moderately easy
Length and type: 3 miles total, up-and-back
Time: 60-90 minutes

Pu`u O`o vent

On a clear day, this hike offers rewarding views of the smoking Pu`u O`o vent, source of the current lava flow. On days when it's socked in, you can still enjoy hiking over two lava flows from 1973 and 1974 that left numerous lava trees on the landscape, as well as sections of rainforest.

The trailhead starts at the Mauna Ulu parking lot on Chain of Craters Road. Follow the *ahu* (rock piles) across the lava flows. The trail is also marked by reflectors for people who hike it at night to see the fiery glow in the Pu`u O`o vent. Be sure to look for lava trees, formed when lava poured into an *o`hia* forest. The lava hardened around the trees before incinerating them and draining away, leaving hollow tubes where the trees once stood.

Lava plume from Pu`u O`o vent

You might feel a surge of happiness when the trail veers away from the stark features of the lava flow and enters a lush, forested cinder cone. You'll climb 300 feet in about five minutes before you arrive at the summit of Pu`u Huluhulu, where you can peer out at Pu`u O`o and

Mauna Ulu, and into the verdant crater below. Stairs lead to the lookout point, which has arrows that point to landmarks like the Puna Rift. You may want to swat at the "lava flies," or helicopters, that buzz overhead.

The hike takes a little over an hour, and is not particularly difficult except that you need to watch your step to avoid cracks, particularly at night, when it should take much longer because you're paying even more attention to where you step.

PACIFIC GOLDEN PLOVER

Like the humpback whales, these birds (called *kolea* in Hawaiian) travel from Alaska in the winter and head back in the summer. Unlike the whales, the plovers reach speeds of 60 miles per hour and can make the trip in two days. Also, while the humpbacks come to Hawaii to give birth before returning to Alaska to gorge on the abundant summer krill, plovers come to Hawaii to feed and return to Alaska in the summer to nest.

Mauna Ulu

Difficulty: Moderate

Length and type: 3.5 miles total, up-and-back

Time: 90-120 minutes

The view from Pu`u Huluhulu provides a nice look at the bulging Mauna Ulu shield, a volcano that spewed vast amount of lava that can be gawked at on the way down Chain of Craters Road. It's presently quiet, and provides quite a thrill for those willing to make a small uphill addition to the Pu`u Huluhulu hike.

The rim of Mauna Ulu is a rough jagged hole in the wasted earth. Steam still pours from its mouth, proving there are still hotspots below the surface. The five- to 10-minute hike to the top isn't difficult, but the shelly pahoehoe (smooth) lava that you must traverse can make your blood pressure rise like lava in your veins: as you walk, the lava sounds hollow – because it is. There are numerous small lava tubes up the side of the hill, and possibly even larger ones, and areas where the thin, crusty lava has clearly crumbled underfoot. That should inspire you to tread lightly. Once on top, admire the view, but stay clear of the rim. Resist the urge to peer directly down into the guts of the volcano, or it may swallow you up.

To get there, proceed past the turnoff to Pu`u Huluhulu for about 200 yards. Then turn right and walk up the hill. You may see a spray-painted 'T' symbol, indicating a vague trail that is marked only by the occasional stripe. It does provide some comfort knowing that others have traversed this route, perhaps indicating that it is more stable than other routes. Then again, maybe it is worn and ready to cave in. Seriously.

Rainforests: More than 90% of Kilauea's surface has been covered by lava in the past 1,100 years, yet there is a remarkable amount of rainforest. This is due to the 17 feet of fog drip and rainfall that nourish the park each year, enabling a forest to mature in as few as 400 years.

Napau Crater

Difficulty: Difficult

Length and type: About 16 miles, up-and-back

Time: 6-8 hours

Permission: A free permit is required and available at the park's visitor center

This is probably the most intense hike in the park – the only trail in the park that will allow you to walk right up to Pele herself at the Pu`u O`o vent (if the trail is open). The source of the current eruption has been spewing molten earth, ash and poisonous gas since 1983, and it is a wonder to behold. Even from a distance it is thrilling, but to actually approach it is a gift. The trail will also take you past (and possibly up to the rim of) the Mauna Ulu lava shield, bring you face-to-face with the second-largest crater in the park, and introduce you to some of the most twisted lava trees in the park.

The hike begins from the Mauna Ulu parking lot and trailhead. A mile in brings you to the Pu`u Huluhulu spur trail, for vistas in all directions and possibly a glimpse of your ultimate objective smoldering in the distance: Pu`u O`o. Back on the trail, a few hundred yards farther you have the option to take a short detour up Mauna Ulu. That will give you a glimpse into the smoldering vent that spewed massive amounts of lava in the late 60s and 70s, completely covering the original Chain of Craters Road. The trail roughly follows

Rainforest on the way to Napau Crater (Hawaii Forest & Trail)

this road, which, upon its completion in 1928, connected Crater Rim Drive with Makaopuhi Crater. The road was later expanded to Kalapana in 1964, but it didn't last too long. The Mauna Ulu eruption of 1969 buried it.

As you arc around the base of Mauna Ulu, you'll arrive at Alae Crater, a relatively small *puka*, but a fierce, steaming hole in the ground nonetheless. It is a great example of why you shouldn't stand on the rims of pit craters. Notice the huge cracks around the rim and the mighty chunks of earth poised to heave off onto the spent pile below. From here you'll wander over the lava flow of 1973 as you descend about 500 feet over the next 1½ miles on your approach to Makaopuhi Crater.

Makaopuhi Crater is a massive double-pit crater dating back 500 years. It is nearly a mile wide and a half-mile across. A 1972 Mauna Ulu lava flow poured into the crater, destroying a portion of the rich rainforest that covers the rim and half of the crater floor. This black and green contrast is striking. If you're getting hot at this point, take heart, as the trail is about to plunge you into the forest. You'll be tracing nearly 180 degrees of the crater rim on your way to Napau Crater. The forest is a welcome respite, either from the heat or the rain (probably the latter). Huge *hapu`u* ferns tower overhead, and you'll likely be greeted by a symphony of native honeycreepers.

About 1¾ miles after you enter the forest, you'll arrive at some stone ruins and a sign informing you that this is the former site of an old *pulu* factory. The coiled, emerging fronds of the tree ferns that surround this area are covered with a silky fluff, called *pulu*, which protects the young shoots. Hawaiians used to embalm their *ali`i* (royalty) in *pulu*, but westerners saw another use for it. Between 1867 and 1884, over four million pounds of *pulu* were exported as stuffing for mattresses and pillows. Unfortunately, pulu doesn't hold its loft and quickly turns to dust. The forester C.S. Judd put it this way in 1927: "when new, (the pulu-stuffed mattresses and pillows) are admirable, but after the thread-like cells had broken down, the mattresses became lumpy and an old pulu pillow was just as comfortable as a bag of very fine sand."

SULFUR DIOXIDE

Pu`u O`o vent belches out 2,000 tons of this toxic gas each day. While its more benign relative hydrogen sulfide is responsible for that "rotten egg" smell, sulfur dioxide is a compound that can cause anything from minimal discomfort in the nose, throat and lungs, to more serious complications like lung and heart failure. Just as it's recommended that those with heart problems, or lung ailments, such as asthma, forego a stop at the Halema`uma`u Crater lookout, hikers on the Napau Trail should be wary of getting too close to Pu`u O`o in case the winds shift – I was once chased out of the area in just that situation!

A short distance past the pulu factory, the trail splits, with a spur trail going to the Napau Crater Lookout. It is worth the five-minute detour, even if you intend to go the whole way. Pu`u O`o now stands less than three miles distant; it dominates the horizon, its dark hulking mass filling your vision. It is worth hiking to this point even if the trail beyond is closed. However, if it is open, you are in for an incredible treat.

Return to the trail junction and head toward Napau camp. There are only a handful of primitive campsites here, and a pit toilet. It rains here constantly, and the threat of noxious fumes is high, but if it's too difficult to hike in and out, this makes a tolerable base camp for venturing to the base of Pu`u O`o the following day. A bonus of staying the night here is the chance to see boiling lava reflected in the clouds above the vent.

Proceed past the camp to where the trail begins to descend; you'll see a stunning collection of lava trees. They appear as ghoulish, twisted figures, like fanciful circus dwarves melted by the will of the earth. With the vent steaming in the distance, it is a foreboding site. The trail drops to Napau Crater floor directly down a 1972 *a`a* flow. There are few switchbacks, so watch yourself as the footing is awkward and it's difficult to keep your eyes on the trail as Pu`u O`o spews in front of you. The crater last erupted from the fissures on the northern end in 1997, so it is very much alive and threatening. The crater is about a half-mile across, and from there each rise brings the vent closer into view. You may want to take this opportunity to put some aloha into your heart, and perhaps touch the *o`hia lehua* blossoms to curry favor with Pele, since it is her favorite flower. The trade winds carry the plume of toxic gas to the south of this position, but it seems awfully close, and you will likely be very much aware that a sudden and slight change in wind direction could kill you.

Finally, you will crest the last rise and Pu`u O`o sits before you, belching death and molten earth. Around you the world is devastated and mean: fissures vent gas, cinder is littered at your feet. For our fellow *Lord of the Rings* nerds, it will seem like the incarnation of Tolkien's Mordor, and you're standing at the base of Mt. Doom. Luckily you don't have to climb it! The "trail closed" signs will likely be between about 2½ miles from the Napau camp, depending on current vent activity. Obey them. Venturing farther is foolhardy. Pu`u O`o has collapsed in the past, and will collapse again, probably sooner rather than later. Soak in the raw power of the creation of earth, then return the way you came, giving thanks to Pele for favoring you with life.

On the return trek, it's shorter to take the Kalapana Trail to the Naulu Trail down to the picnic pavilion at Kealakomo. If you can't arrange for a pick up, it will likely not be too difficult to hitch back up Chain of Craters Road back to the Mauna Ulu parking area. The trail follows various Mauna Ulu eruptions, occasionally offering a glimpse of the old road, where the lava spared it. It's bizarre to see signs of civilization among so much devastation. Whichever way you choose to return, this hike is unforgettable!

VOG VS. LAZE

VOG is formed when volcanic gases such as sulfur dioxide combine with atmospheric elements such as moisture and dust to create a visible haze that can irritate people with lung maladies. LAZE, or lava haze, is formed when lava dumps into the ocean. Hydrochloric acid is created by the vaporized seawater and is carried off by the steam plume, often resulting in acid rain along the Ka`u Desert and other areas downwind. The steam plume also carries tiny fragments of glass that can cause scarification in the lungs.

Pu`u Loa Petroglyphs

Pu`u Loa Petroglyphs

This is a "don't miss" hike. Many people race past it on the way to the End of the Road, but that is a mistake. It's only a .7-mile hike over *pahoehoe* (smooth) lava (follow the rock piles, or *ahu*) to a boardwalk that leads you through lava covered with petroglyphs, the mysterious symbols drawn by ancient Hawaiians. The collection is impressive, and it's easy to understand why they might have chosen this beautiful spot to gather and create petroglyphs. At the moment, a visit to the petroglyphs is even more incredible because it has views of the lava entering the water (this is a hike for daytime only). Please remember to stay on the boardwalk and do not touch the petroglyphs.

Ka`u Desert Footprints

The access to the area is from a trailhead outside of the park's road system. On Hwy 11 by mile marker 38, look for the Ka`u Desert trailhead. From here, it's about ¾ of a mile to a small shelter where there are footprints captured in volcanic ash, the product of a smothering eruption from Kilauea in 1790.

People have varying ideas of whose footprints these are, but the park contends that they are those of an army regiment belonging to King Kamehameha the Great's enemy, Keoua (see below). The shelter contains a small rectangle of mud containing a few vague footprints, but there are many more outside. As the constant winds blow the sand around, more footprints are revealed. Sometimes they seem to be everywhere; other times it's as if they don't exist. Be careful if you do find them, as they are easily destroyed. Many have been lost to the ages already by vandalism.

A mile farther will bring you to the summit of the Mauna Iki lava shield, with a remarkable view of various volcanic features to the east and the steep *pali* (cliff) leading to a sliver of the ocean. It's worth the time if you have the energy and the water.

KAMEHAMEHA & KEOUA

In the year 1790, Kamehameha I was attacking Maui and O`ahu in his bid to dominate all of the islands, but he still had not vanquished his final enemy on his home island. Keoua was the son of the dead ruler of the island, and his army raided Kamehameha's lands in east Hawai`i, burning homes and destroying fish ponds. Kamehameha returned from O`ahu to fight him, but their battles ended in stalemate. Then, as Keoua and his men – along with their wives and children – were returning to their homelands in Ka`u, they passed close to Kilauea as an eruption filled the sky with ash and burning cinder. The front and rear groupings of the procession miraculously survived, but they discovered their comrades in the middle group had become corpses, frozen in their last dying acts. Some were found embracing their wives, noses touching in a final act of love. Soon after, Keoua accepted Kamehameha's invitation to the initiation of his new war temple in Kohala, Pu`ukohola, and was killed.

"I do not seek. I find." – Pablo Picasso

Where to Stay

Volcano House (Hawai`i Volcanoes National Park, ☎ 967-7321, www.volcanohousehotel.com, 42 rooms $95-$225). The long history of this hotel began when Benjamin Pitman, Sr. built a grass house on the edge of Kilauea Crater and gave it the obvious name, Volcano House. Travelers from around the world would stay and marvel at the fabulous view. Mark Twain visited in 1877, and declared about the existing structure: "neat, roomy, well furnished and a well kept hotel." Well, that is no longer the case.

Volcano House lobby

What was once an elegant gem on the rim of the world's most active volcano, is now a remnant of things past. Overpriced, worn down, poorly maintained – these are the terms that best describe the current incarnation of the Volcano House.

We would have given the Volcano House a "Tourist Trap" box, but the view... well, it *is* a terrific view. $$-$$$

See page 65 for an explanation of the hotel $ price codes.

Kilauea Military Camp (Hawai`i Volcanoes National Park, ☎ 967-8333, www.kmc-volcano.com). For active or retired military personnel and their families, the Kilauea Military Camp offers an affordable military resort. Loaded with amenities such as a bowling alley, tennis courts and a fitness center, this place is hard to beat for military folks. Some guest cottages have in-room Jacuzzis and fireplaces. Prices are based on rank, with higher ranks forking over more dough.

Namakani Paio Cabins (Hawai`i Volcanoes National Park, ☎ 967-7321, www.volcanohousehotel.com, 10 cabins, $50). Located adjacent to the national park campground, these cabins (owned by the Volcano House) are an affordable accommodation option. With one double bed and two single beds, each cabin sleeps up to four people. Unfortunately, the provided bedding is light, so you'll still need to bring a sleeping bag or extra blankets. There's no kitchen, but each cabin has a basic grill and picnic table outside. The bathroom, with hot showers, is communal. Located *mauka* off of Hwy 11 between mile markers 31 and 32. $

Camping

Namakani Paio Campground. With sites clustered among the tall eucalyptus trees and a grassy expanse, the national park's main campground is a bargain for the price: free with paid admission to the park. It isn't overflowing with amenities (there are no showers) and it can sometimes get crowded when the park decides to close half of the sites for restoration, but you can't argue with what you don't pay for. There are cold-water restrooms, a few fire pits, grills and a picnic pavilion. Located *mauka* off of Hwy 11 between mile markers 31 and 32.

Kulanaokulaiki Campground. This national park campground is within the park, several miles down lonely Hilina Pali Road., on the edge of the Ka`u Desert. There are eight primitive sites with picnic tables, but no fire pits, grills or running water. There *is* a pit toilet. You park at the lot and lug your gear to your chosen spot along a short loop trail. There are basic camping pads, a few of which are comprised of concrete slabs with a few inches of dirt thrown on for comfort, making it pretty difficult to stake your tent. Previous visitors have left logs and rocks to tie down on the pads, but you'll want to tie off to your picnic table or a tree, since the wind can be vicious here. You'll likely find some solitude here, but little else. The location is decent if you're going to head out on the Mauna Iki trail, or you want to spend a night before forging into the backcountry on the trail at the end of Hilina Pali Rd. A sign on the bathroom door warns of night rats. Free with park admission, seven-days-per-month limit. To get there, turn west on Hilina Pali Road off of Chain of Craters Rd about two miles from Crater Rim Dr. The campground is five miles down on your right.

Where to Eat

Volcano House Restaurant (Hawai`i Volcanoes National Park, ☎ 967-7321). You know how usually when you eat in those revolving restaurants at the top of skyscrapers the food is not great but you're paying top dollar for the view? That's what's going on a Volcano House Restaurant – its view of Kilauea is one of the most phenomenal in the world, but the food is not so good. You can fork out for a mediocre breakfast or lunch buffet, or really pay for an à la carte dinner menu at night when you can't even see the crater. A picnic on the wall outside would be more enjoyable. Open for breakfast 6:45-10:30 am, lunch 11 am-2 pm, dinner 5:30-9 pm daily. $$$$

Volcano House Restaurant

Volcano Village

The tiny village of Volcano is the commercial hub for this creative, artistic community and the park. It is on the north side of Hwy 11, just east of the park entrance. There are several access roads into the village between mile markers 28 and 25.

The **Post Office**, on Old Volcano Road near Kiawe Kitchen, is open 7:30 am-3:30 pm Mon-Fri, 11 am-noon Sat.

Kilauea General Store (Old Volcano Rd, ☎ 967-7555). One of the two gas stations in town is in this little complex, along with the Lava Rock Café and quilt shop. The store has basic groceries, beer and smokes, but also has an ATM and sells firewood. They make an attempt to offer some produce, but don't expect too much. Gas pumps close at 9 pm. Open 7 am-7:30 pm daily.

The Volcano Store (Old Volcano Rd, ☎ 967-7210) sells gas and general merchandise, with drinks, ice cream, alcohol, some groceries, a few produce items, over-the-counter medicines and a big selection of orchids and other tropical flowers. Gas pumps close when they do (sometimes by 6:30 pm). Open 5 am-7 pm daily.

Where to Shop

Kilauea Kreations (Old Volcano Rd, ☎ 967-8090, www.kilaueakreations.com). Located behind the Kilauea General Store, Kilauea Kreations is a "can't miss" for quilters and anyone interested in local crafts. Half of the store is devoted to quilting supplies such as fabrics, Hawaiian quilt kits, coconut buttons, books, fat quarters, as well as completed Hawaiian quilts. The other portion of the store is a souvenir shop, with kids' books, stuffed toys, cards, lava photos, *koa* bookmarks and other crafts. Open 9:30 am-5:30 pm daily.

Volcano Garden Arts (19-3834 Old Volcano Rd, ☎ 985-8979, www.volcanogardenarts.com). Brainchild of artist Ira Ono, this is a high-quality art gallery housed in a 1908 farmhouse made of redwood. Some of the fun and funky art available includes ceramics, tea sets, paintings, pit-fired masks (which you will see on properties all over Volcano), pug sculptures, photos, prints, jewelry, Christmas ornaments, vases, and "candle nests." There are gardens on the three-acre grounds, another gallery and a studio in greenhouses out back. Best of all, they have plans for a vegetarian café and tea pavilion that should open soon. Open 10 am-4 pm Tues-Sun.

Where to Stay

My Island B&B (19-3896 Volcano Rd, ☎ 967-7216, www.myislandinnhawaii.com, six rooms and six houses, $70-$145). If you want to be adopted by a pair of welcoming grandparents while you're in Hawaii, you won't want to miss My Island B&B, a friendly operation run by Gordon and Joann Morse for over 20 years. Despite being in their late 70s, the Morses still get up every morning at 5:30 am to cook breakfast for up to 58 people and serve it in the cozy front room of a house built in 1836 by Connecticut missionaries, the Lymans (of the Lyman Museum in Hilo). Gordon entertains the guests with his gregarious nature, urging kids to read the vast collection of *I Spy* and *Calvin and Hobbes* books, or telling their parents to help themselves to one of the over 100 choices of tea, making sure they pick the mug that "speaks" to them. Mrs. Morse bustles in the kitchen making apple pan dowdy, homemade jams, and slicing papaya to top with lime, pineapple and chopped macadamia nuts.

Their daughter Kii manages the place, helping guests find their rooms in one of the six houses on the property, which includes tropical gardens of orchids and anthuriums, or around town. Each room is different (though all have TVs), and are simple, clean and comfy, sometimes with a "Little House on the Prairie" feel. The Morses have shared a bathroom with their guests in the main house for 22 years! That's when you know you're family. The spacious residential houses available are a ridiculous bargain, with two bedrooms, a big living room with a stove, dining room, full kitchen, and large windows with garden views. $$-$$$

See page 65 for an explanation of the hotel $ price codes.

Volcano Country Cottages (Old Volcano Rd, ☎ 967-7960, toll free ☎ 888-446-3910, www.volcano-cottages.com, four cottages $95-$120). This collection of well-thought-out cottages is an excellent and affordable find among the glut of B&Bs in and around Volcano Village. With a total of four cottages scattered around the heavily-forested property, it's hard to go wrong with any of the choices. Those blessed with manual dexterity will enjoy the Artists' House, which not only has a full kitchen and two bedrooms, but also includes an artist easel, paper and fine pencils and pastels. The Ohelo Berry Cottage is the coziest of the offerings, with just a kitchenette and a single queen-sized bed. But the old school lanai and its proximity to the hot tub more than make up for its diminutive size. The two newest "cottages" are actually more like single-family homes ditched out in the *o`hia* trees and ferns, with wraparound lanais, full kitchens, dining rooms and living rooms, but with only a single bedroom and a futon. One of the great things about this place, though, is the choice by the owners to forego TVs, instead opting for board games, books and views of the rich vegetation outside. It's also in a very convenient location in the heart of Volcano. $$

AUTHOR'S CHOICE ★ **Hale Ohia** (☎ 967-7986, toll free ☎ 800-455-3803, www.haleohia.com, eight rooms incl. three cottages, $95-$179). We meet a lot of returning guests of Hale Ohia, an immaculate property on three acres. The main residence was built in 1931 and has a distinctive cedar turret. For 30 years, the designer of Lili`uokalani Gardens in Hilo acted as the caretaker for the property; needless to say, the grounds are beautiful. Owner Michael Tuttle has created a B&B with an eclectic vibe. There are different styles in each room or cottage that seem – should we coin a phrase? – rustic chic. For example, Cottage No. 44 is built in a 1930 redwood water tank with a two-sided, see-through fireplace, so that you can enjoy the blaze from either the bedroom or the mahogany living room.

Hale Ohia

Hale Ohia is an ideal option for guests seeking privacy, since a breakfast of fresh bread, fruit, juice and coffee is brought to each room instead of shared in a common area. There are no TVs or phones in the rooms, through there is free wireless Internet use, flashlights, umbrellas, irons, tea kettles, hair dryers and an outdoor Japanese hot tub. Some have kitchenettes, most have stained glass windows. The Ohia Cottage has a full kitchen and sleeps up to 10 people. This is a peaceful place to relax after a day of exploring the park. $$-$$$

Kilauea Lodge (Old Volcano Rd, ☎ 967-7366, www.kilauealodge.com, 12 rooms, $150-$190, two houses, $175-$185). An upscale encampment right on Old Volcano Rd in Volcano Village, the Kilauea Lodge provides cushy accommodations with 12 rooms in three *hales* (cottages), and two homes in separate locations in Volcano Village. Several of the rooms have their

Kilauea Lodge

own woodburning fireplaces, and Hale Aloha has a large, well appointed common area with TV, couches and comfy chairs clustered around a fireplace. Located out in the garden, which features some fine examples of important Hawaiian plants like *ti*, is a hot tub *hale*. A beautiful full breakfast is served every morning in the dining room and is included in the room rate. $$$

Volcano Rainforest Retreat (☎ 985-8696, toll free ☎ 800-550-8696, www.volcanoretreat.com, four cottages, $140-$260). Though the intent of Kathleen and Peter Golden, the owners, is to create a serene environment in their B&B nestled in the rainforest, we found it created something we call "architectural lust." A master carpenter has created four unique wooden cottages on the property, as well as other structures; Hale Nahele is octagonal, the Sanctuary is a hexagon. Amenities differ for each space, though most have TV sets (no cable, but movie libraries), lists of local massage therapists who will come to the property, and propane or wood-burning stoves. Breakfast includes mac-nut muffins, fruit scones, yogurt, granola, rice and soy milk, coffee and tea.

Volcano Rainforest Retreat, Bamboo Guesthouse

There is a New Age sensibility to the grounds, which are dotted with prayer flags, and in the décor, which has Asian influences such as Japanese lanterns. Kathleen is a Reiki practitioner and counselor, and there is a Tuesday night Buddhist meditation from 7 to 9 pm in the Gathering Place, which includes a dharma talk and tea. There are day- and weekend-long retreats at other times throughout the year. $$$$

Where to Eat

Thai Thai Restaurant (Old Volcano Rd, ☎ 967-7969). Thai food fans love this place, with an extensive menu of classic Thai noodle dishes, soups, salads, rice and appetizers. Curries can be spiced mild, medium, hot or "Thai hot." Open 4-9 pm nightly. $$-$$$

Lava Rock Café (Old Volcano Rd, ☎ 967-8526). While other local restaurants close between lunch and dinner, Lava Rock Café doesn't, which is probably the best reason to come here. For basic grub, it's just fine, though don't get your heart set on a specific dish or drink because they tend to run out of things. You can get *loco moco* (a bowl of rice, topped with a hamburger or other meat smothered in gravy and topped with a fried egg), pancakes (with sinful *liliko`i* or guava butter) and omelettes for breakfast as well as "magma mini-meals" like biscuits and gravy. Lunch includes plate lunches, fajitas, fried chicken, stuffed baked potatoes, soups, "tsunami salads" like taco, tuna or shrimp and crab, burgers, or "seismic sandwiches." You can access the Internet with their computers at $4 for 20 minutes. Open for breakfast 7:30-10:30 am, lunch 10:30 am-5 pm daily. $$

For an explanation of the $ price codes, see page 55.

Kilauea Lodge and Restaurant (Old Volcano Rd, ☎ 967-7366, www.kilauealodge.com) is the "splurge" option in Volcano. With rustic chandeliers, rich wood tables, cedar vaulted ceilings, windows with garden views, pictures of flowing lava illuminated by track lighting and miniature lamps on each table, the Lodge is a classic. The chef/owner Albert Jeyte bought the property in 1986 after his work as a make-up artist ended when *Magnum P.I.* went off the air and he didn't want to return to Germany. His recipes haven't changed much over the years and reflect a German influence; the sautéed mushrooms are rather soupy but pleasant, with a strong flavor of wine and scallions. This is the place to come for exotic meats, as the menu includes dishes with veal, antelope, rabbit, lamb, ostrich and, of course, Hawaiian seafood. Ask your server for the laminated diagram detailing the components of the International Fireplace of Friendship, in which stones from 32 countries (from places like the Acropolis and Mt. Vernon) and coins from around the world are embedded. Open 5:30-8:45 pm nightly. $$$$

AUTHOR'S CHOICE ★ **Kiawe Kitchen** (Old Volcano Rd, ☎ 967-7711). The service is spotty, there's usually a wait, and the restaurant is drafty. But the gourmet pizzas from the wood-burning oven and just about everything else on the menu are so delicious that we once ate here four nights in a row. We might have been camping in the rain, but it didn't matter when we could escape to Kiawe Kitchen and grilled asparagus, hot soups, thin crust pizza and a bottle of wine. It goes without saying that we'll be back. Open for lunch noon-2:30 pm, dinner 5:30-9:30 pm daily. $$-$$$

Entertainment

There are often community activities and educational events in Volcano. Check the newspaper for upcoming events.

Cooper Center (☎ 967-7800). This is the venue for many community events and the location of Farmers Market on Sundays (8-9:30 am) with produce, prepared food, books and other wares. There are themes for each Sunday, such as "meet public officials" on the second one of each month. The market is generally picked clean by 8:30 am.

Volcano Winery (☎ 967-7772, www.volcanowinery.com), at the end of Pi`i Mauna Drive, is the only vineyard on the Big Island. Most of the grapes used in the wines at Volcano Winery are grown on the property (weather permitting), primarily Chardonnay and Pinot Grigio grapes. The wines tend toward the fruity side, and there are some unusual offerings like the Hawaiian Guava, made by fermenting guava, as opposed to adding flavorings, and the Macadamia Nut Honey Wine. There are free tastings in the gift shop, where knowledgeable employees can talk about the wines at great length. Open 10 am-5:30 pm 365 days a year.

Adventures on the Links

Volcano Country Club (Pii Mauna Dr, ☎ 967-7331, www.volcanogolfshop.com, $63.50 includes cart, $51 twilight rate after 12 pm). Located adjacent to Hawai`i Volcanoes National Park, it's cold and wet, but at over 4,000 feet your ball really flies up here. The frequent precipitation keeps the course green and allows balls to hold pretty well. The course is fairly wide open, though you may find yourself in the *o`hia* trees on several holes if you're not careful. There's little water to contend with, but the many bunkers are ill-tended, stuffed with various plant life, which causes variable consistency. Better to just take a drop closer to the hole! It can get a little mucky with all of the rain up here, and the dearth of cart paths means there are sometimes nasty ruts in the fairway. You might as well take a drop from them, too, while you're at it. When it's clear, you'll catch some gorgeous views of Mauna Loa. The pro shop has little in the way of equipment, but is stuffed with shirts and hats emblazoned with a cool logo that tells your buddies back home that you've been golfing on a volcano. Keep your eye out for wild turkeys, Kalij pheasant and the endangered *nene*.

Volcano Country Club (www.teetimeshawaii.com)

To get there, turn *makai* from Hwy 11 on Pii Mauna Dr, just west of mile marker 30.

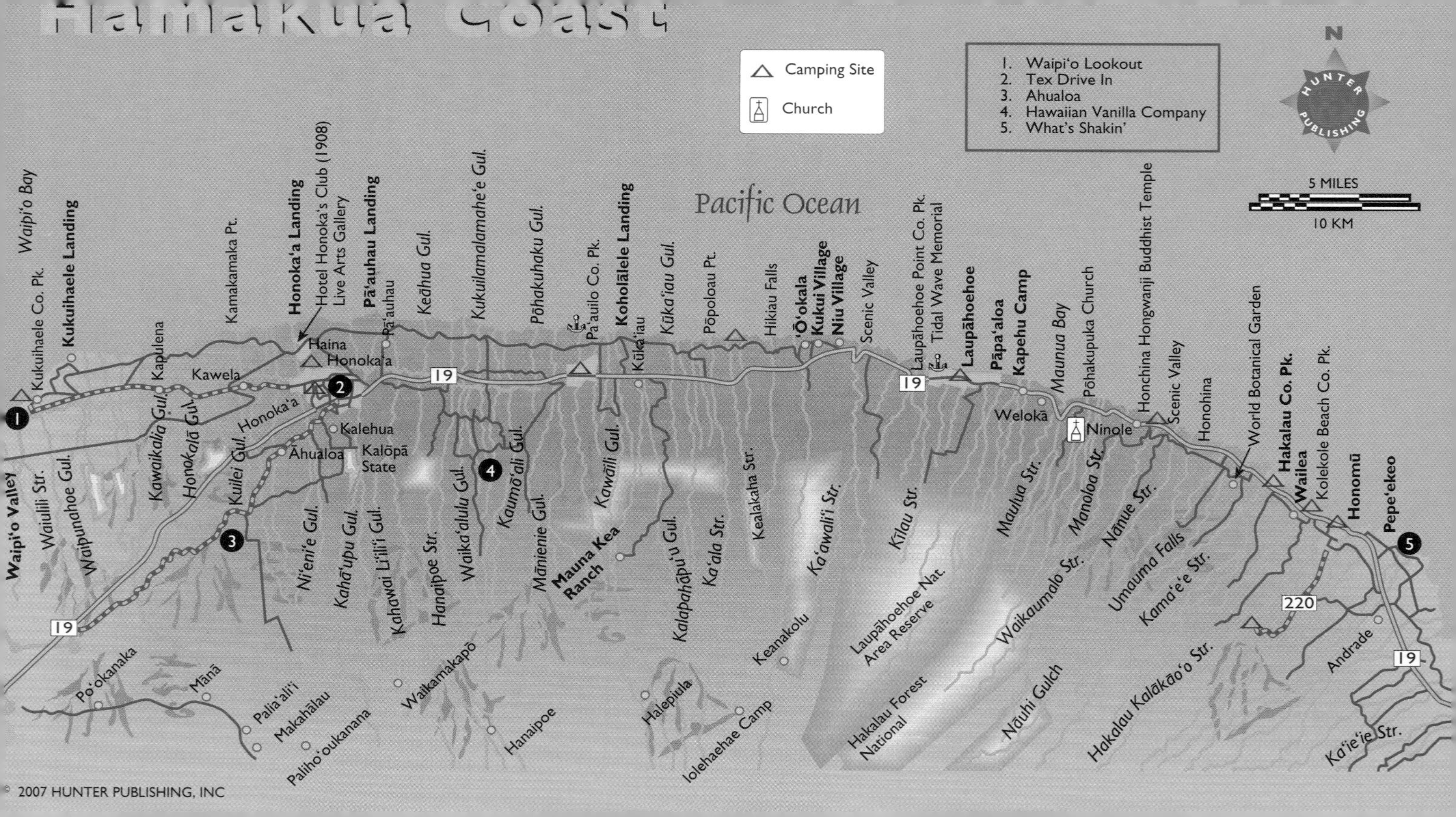
Hamakua Coast
Camping Site
Church
1. Waipi'o Lookout
2. Tex Drive In
3. Ahualoa
4. Hawaiian Vanilla Company
5. What's Shakin'
5 MILES
10 KM
N
HUNTER PUBLISHING
Pacific Ocean
Waipi'o Valley
Waipi'o Bay
Kukuihaele Co. Pk.
Kukuihaele Landing
Waiulili Str.
Waipunahoe Gul.
Po'okanaka
Kawaikalia Gul.
Kapulena
Honokalā Gul.
Kawela
Mānā
Kuilei Gul.
Honoka'a
Kamakamaka Pt.
Palia'ali'i
Makahālau
Paliho'oukanana
Ni'eni'e Gul.
Āhualoa
Honoka'a Landing
Hotel Honoka's Club (1908)
Live Arts Gallery
Haina
Kahā'upu Gul.
Kalehua
Kalōpā State
Honoka'a
Kahawai Li'ili'i Gul.
Pā'auhau Landing
Pā'auhau
Waikamakapō
Hanaipoe Str.
Keāhua Gul.
Waika'alulu Gul.
Kukuilamalamahe'e Gul.
Kaumō'ali Gul.
Hanaipoe
Mānienie Gul.
Pōhakuhaku Gul.
Mauna Kea Ranch
Pa'auilo Co. Pk.
Kawāili Gul.
Koholālele Landing
Kūka'iau
Halepiula
Kalapahāpu'u Gul.
Kūka'iau Gul.
Ka'ala Str.
Pōpoloau Pt.
Iolehaehae Camp
Kealakaha Str.
Keanakolu
Hikiau Falls
'Ō'okala
Kukui Village
Ka'awali'i Str.
Niu Village
Scenic Valley
Hakalau Forest National
Laupāhoehoe Nat. Area Reserve
Kīlau Str.
Laupāhoehoe Point Co. Pk.
Tidal Wave Memorial
Laupāhoehoe
Pāpa'aloa
Weloka
Maulua Str.
Kapehu Camp
Nāuhi Gulch
Waikaumalo Str.
Maunua Bay
Manoloa Str.
Ninole
Pōhakupuka Church
Nānue Str.
Hakalau Kalākāo'o Str.
Umauma Falls
Honchina Hongwanji Buddhist Temple
Kama'e'e Str.
Scenic Valley
Honohina
World Botanical Garden
Hakalau Co. Pk.
Wailea
Kolekole Beach Co. Pk.
Andrade
Honomū
Ka'ie'ie Str.
Pepe'ekeo
19
220
© 2007 HUNTER PUBLISHING, INC

Hamakua Coast

IN THIS CHAPTER

If you enjoy lush tropical rainforests, picture-perfect waterfalls, black sand beaches and guava-scented breezes, then you won't want to miss the Hamakua Coast. Driving the coast is an adventure on wheels, and it's sure to dazzle.

It rains a lot on this side of the island (usually late afternoon or at night), creating lush greenery and gleaming rainbows. There are botanical gardens and beach parks, easy hiking trails through Hawaiian forests and scenic drives to lookouts over dramatic coastlines and gulches filled with vine-wrapped trees, often with the bright orange blossoms of African tulip trees adding dashes of color to the mix.

The Hamakua Coast is home to the much-photographed Akaka Falls and Umauma Falls, the legendary Hawaii Tropical Botanical Garden and former sugar towns with unique, affordably priced souvenir shops and an "Old Hawai`i" feel. Sit on a street corner or in a café and "talk story" with a local. You might learn of their favorite picnic spot along a stream, or a hidden beach. These are the kinds of people who compare Kailua-Kona to Waikiki and Las Vegas – they can't tolerate the stress of "big city" traffic.

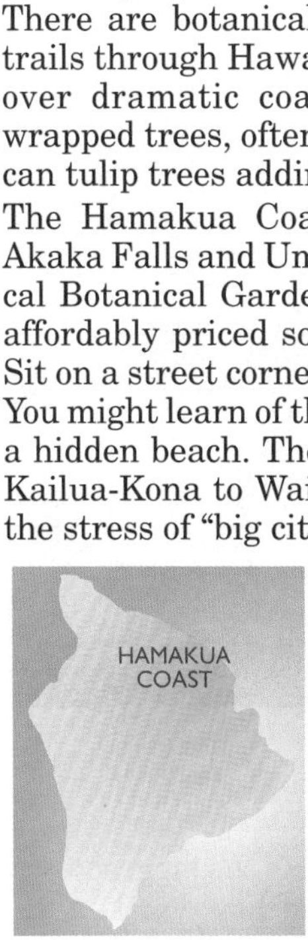

The centerpiece of this magical part of the Big Island is the **Waipi`o Valley**. The island's second-most popular attraction (after Hawai`i Volcanoes National Park) is spectacular; as one visitor gasped to her husband, "This is the Hawaii we've been looking for!" Verdant green *palis* (cliffs) with waterfalls cascading over them to pools a thousand feet below, the Pacific Ocean crashing onto a black sand beach, gushing streams, flowers and rainbows... this is the Hawaii we've all been looking for.

TAKE YOUR TIME

Allow at least a full day to explore the Hamakua Coast. It's less than 40 miles long so many visitors think they can speed through it. That's missing the point. There are so many backroads, trails, waterfalls and vistas that beg for a closer look (or a picnic) that you won't want to rush. We learned this the hard way years ago on vacation with our family. On our last day, we all piled into a van on Kona-side with the goal of visiting Hawai`i Volcanoes National Park. But once we reached the Hamakua Coast, we felt the need to stop or detour so frequently that we spent the entire day on the coast – and we never made it to the erupting volcano. Take our advice: the Hamakua Coast is a region to be savored.

Hamakua Coast (Hawaiian Images)

Honoka`a

With a population around 2,200, Honoka`a is the biggest town on the Hamakua Coast – an indication of how low-key the area is. When the last sugar mill finally closed in the mid-1990s, the town needed to find new sources of income. These days, Honoka`a looks to industries like tourism to keep the economy viable. The town's proximity to the Waipi`o Valley – eight miles away – doesn't hurt at all.

Honoka`a (Hawaiian Images)

This is a tranquil town. Shortly after one resident praised Honoka`a as a place with a "relaxed, village feel, where people still gather to talk story," we saw and heard a young local boy strolling down the street while strumming his ukulele. It doesn't get much sweeter than that.

Many proprietors on the Hamakua Coast operate on the relaxed "Hawaiian time," so business hours are more of a guideline than a rule. (We asked one woman if her store was closed on certain days, and she laughed and said, "Yeah, whenever I take my days off.") Also, many restaurants do not accept credit cards or personal checks, so keep a supply of cash with you, or plan on visiting ATMs while on the Coast.

Practicalities

Honoka`a has two **ATM** machines in front of banks on Mamane St, several **gas stations** and a **post office** (45-490 Lehua St, at the corner of Mamane).

The **hospital** and **emergency room**, Hale Ho`ola Hamakua, is at 45-547 Plumeria St (☎ 808-775-7211).

The public **library** at 45-3380 Mamane has public **restrooms** (most businesses do not), and free events for children such as pre-school story time. Closed weekends.

The **TKS Supermarket** (45-5002 Lehua, across from the post office) sells groceries and alcoholic beverages. There is no cash back on debit card purchases. Open 7:30 am-8 pm Mon-Sat, 8 am-6 pm Sun.

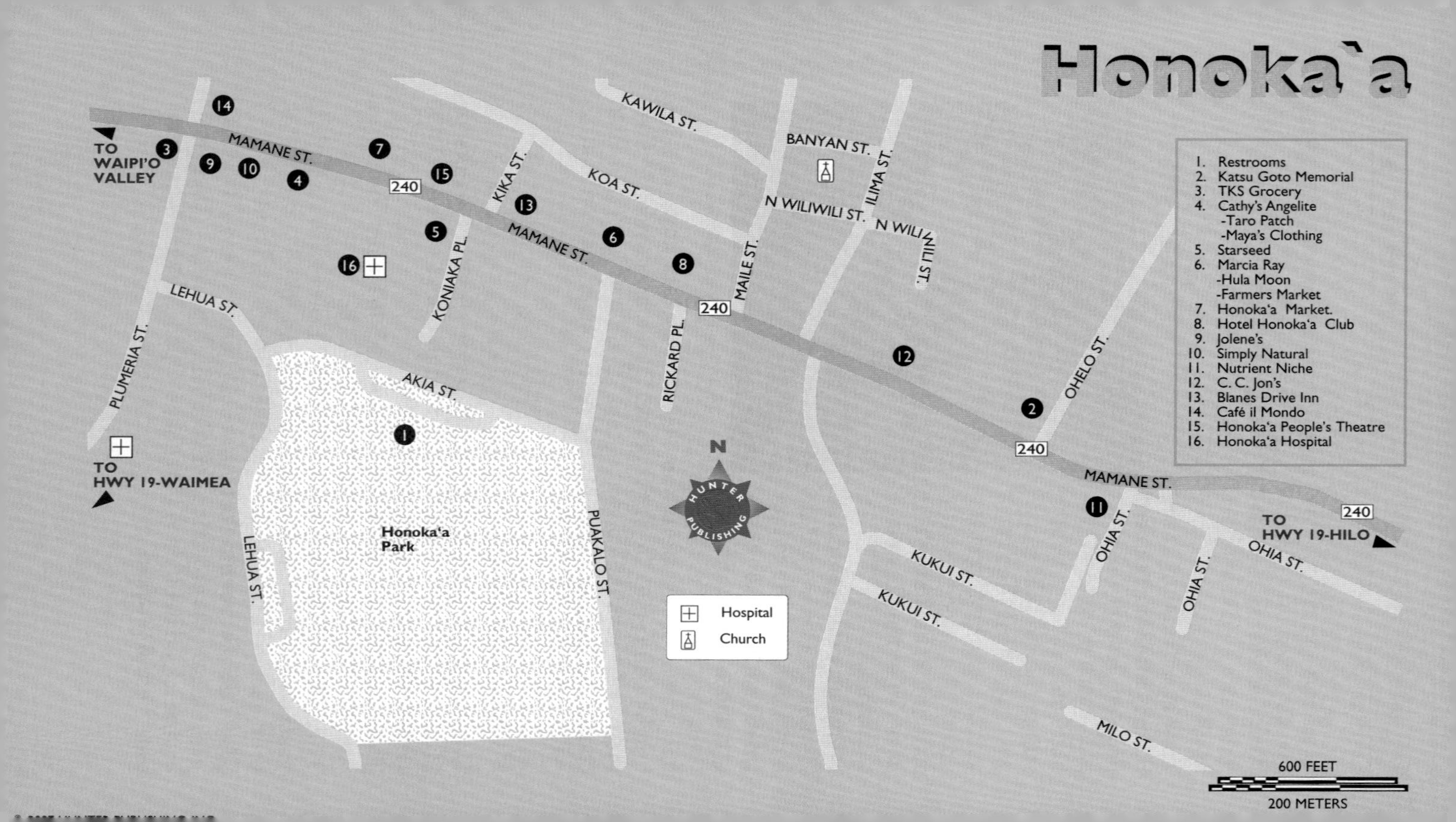
Honoka`a
1. Restrooms
2. Katsu Goto Memorial
3. TKS Grocery
4. Cathy's Angelite
-Taro Patch
-Maya's Clothing
5. Starseed
6. Marcia Ray
-Hula Moon
-Farmers Market
7. Honoka'a Market.
8. Hotel Honoka'a Club
9. Jolene's
10. Simply Natural
11. Nutrient Niche
12. C. C. Jon's
13. Blanes Drive Inn
14. Café il Mondo
15. Honoka'a People's Theatre
16. Honoka'a Hospital
TO WAIPI'O VALLEY
TO HWY 19-WAIMEA
TO HWY 19-HILO
MAMANE ST.
240
KAWILA ST.
BANYAN ST.
KOA ST.
KIKA ST.
N WILIWILI ST.
N WILI
WILI ST.
ILIMA ST.
MAILE ST.
KONIAKA PL.
RICKARD PL.
LEHUA ST.
PLUMERIA ST.
AKIA ST.
PUAKALO ST.
OHELO ST.
OHIA ST.
KUKUI ST.
MILO ST.
Honoka'a Park
N
HUNTER PUBLISHING
Hospital
Church
600 FEET
200 METERS

There is only one **area code** for the entire island: 808.

Honoka`a Park consists of a baseball diamond, gymnasium, tennis courts, a soccer field and best of all, public **restrooms**. Turn *mauka* from Hula Moon on Puakalo Street; it's a block up at the corner of Akia St

The **Honoka`a Farmer's Market** takes place on Saturdays from roughly 10 am-2 pm in front of Marcia Ray Art Studio. It's so small that if you aren't looking for it, you'll probably drive right past it. There are a few tables under beach umbrellas with local produce, plants and flowers like orchids, tuberose and sunflowers for sale.

There is no door-to-door mail service – everyone has a post office box – so many people in Honoka`a don't know their physical address. It isn't even on business licenses. Fortunately, the majority of the town's businesses are clustered within two blocks on Mamane Street, so it is easy to find the shops and restaurants we include.

Where to Shop

Honoka`a and other towns along the Hamakua Coast offer unique souvenirs at a fraction of the price you'd pay at resort areas in the Kohala Coast or Kona. For many more shops, visit www.bigislamdadventureguide.com.

**Honoka`a Marketplace** (45-3586 Mamane St, ☎ 775-8255). This excellent store sells a range of souvenirs, such as calabash, candles, a chessboard with Hawaiian warriors and *ali`i* (royalty), prayers like the Lord's Prayer and the Serenity Prayer translated into Hawaiian, sarongs, guava jelly, understated "Alohawear," and books. Quilters will love this store's "handpainted" quilts with colorful Hawaiian scenes, quilt kits for traditional Hawaiian quilts (recognizable by a pattern that includes a "snowflake" with pineapples or flowers in its design), and pillow covers. Open 9:30 am-5:30 pm Mon-Sat, 9:30 am-4 pm Sun.

Kama`aina Woods (45-469 Lehua, ☎ 775-7722, www.hulihands.com). There is a large cage with Easter-egg-colored canaries to entertain kids while their parents browse the beautiful carved goods in the gift shop, or watch artists carve wood in the studio. The artists primarily use local hardwoods like *koa, milo* and *kou* to create $1,500 bowls, $7 door stops and everything in between. The bowls, frames, bracelets, cutting boards and even visors with hardwood brims are gorgeous. The bestsellers are the moon-shaped wine stands and "huli hands" for tossing salads. It's worth the walk midway down the steep hill behind the post office. Open 9 am-5 pm Mon-Sat.

Taro Patch (45-3599 Mamane, ☎ 775-7228, www.taropatchgifts.com) is a fun souvenir shop with a range of goods, from campy hula girl dusters and books like *Pidgin to da Max* to Hawaiian perfumes such as "Island Plumeria," wooden spoons and art. They've been in business for over a decade now, so they must be doing something right! Open 9:30 am-5 pm Mon-Sat.

Mohala Pua (45-690 Pakalana St on Hwy 19, ☎ 775-9800). This nursery ("garden center"), next door to Tex Drive In (which offers coupons for Mohala Pua), features tropical plants and trees, as well as gardening books, tools and ornamentation like tiles, wind chimes, pots and baskets. There are cuttings for local plants that you can take back to the mainland. The staff will also ship floral arrangements and leis to the mainland; their photo album of custom-made funeral wreaths is quite touching. Open 9 am-5:30 pm Sun-Thurs, 8 am-5:30 pm Fri/Sat.

Adventures

On the Links

Hamakua Country Club (☎ 775-7244). This semi-private nine-holer is about as unpretentious a golf experience as you're going to find. Your $20 greens fee gets you all the golf you can play in a day. Just stick your cash in the drop box and grab a scorecard. The privileges of membership appear to be that you earn the right to boisterously talk story with your clubmates. That, and use of the "practice area," a small slab of grass by the parking lot limited to "Members Only." The course is short but well maintained, and you can play in your *slippahs* or even barefoot.

From Hwy 19 turn *makai* between mile markers 42 and 43, then bear left on the frontage road about 100 yards until you come to the small parking lot.

Where to Stay

Hotel Honoka`a Club (on Mamane next to Blanes, ☎ 775-0678, www.hotel-honokaa.com, 22 rooms $50-75, incl. five dorm rooms $18/pp). This is the only hotel on Mamane. Even if you aren't staying here, you might want to stop by – manager Annelle is a font of information. There's even a sign for "Visitor Info" in front of Hotel Honoka`a Club, which is now a hotel sans club – sadly, there is no bar in town. It's a pity, because the former club room has a beautiful wood bar and booths. Rooms are basic – you get what you pay for. She also sells showers for $7, if you've just hiked out of Waipi`o and need to hose off. If you sleep in the dorms in D5, the roosters will wake you up. Check in from 4 -8 pm only. $

See page 65 for an explanation of the hotel $ price codes.

Waipi`o Wayside B&B Inn (between mile markers 3 and 4 on Hwy 240, *makai* side, ☎ 775-0275, toll free ☎ 800-833-8849, www.waipiowayside.com, five rooms, $95-$170). This is a casual B&B run by Jacqueline, who calls herself "the grandma of the B&Bs." There is a common area with a big television and lots of movies and books, a shared deck with a hammock and gazebo with a distant ocean view, as well as of palm, plumeria, African tulip and citrus trees. Breakfast is mostly organic. Despite the name, there are no views of the Waipi`o Valley, though the 1½ acre grounds are beautiful in their own right. Family reunions and weddings are held here. Cat-friendly, no smoking. $$-$$$

Luana Ola B&B (45-3474 Kawila, ☎ 775-1150, toll free ☎ 800-357-7727, www.island-hawaii.com, two cottages, $125). This charming B&B is nestled in the side streets of Honoka`a, where homes have lush yards with fruit trees, chirping birds and ocean views. Luana Ola is no different. A footpath through a small lily pad pond leads you from the driveway to the owners' residence. Breakfast includes organic citrus, mango and papaya grown on the property. The two comfortable cottages have satellite TV, kitchenettes, A/C, a queen-sized bed and a futon – and a big balcony overlooking the ocean. Guests who stay a week get one night free, and there is a "substantial discount" for a month-long visit. $$

Where to Eat

Simply Natural (Mamane St, ☎ 775-0119). A cockatiel named Bernie welcomes you to this artsy snack shop, where smoothies are the main attraction (along with the colorful mural of Hawaiian women on a lanai that covers one wall), though owner Elizabeth, reluctant actress in local flick *Night Marchers II*, touts the Hilo Homemade Ice Cream she serves as "the best on the island." She has breakfast temptations like taro banana pancakes and veggie sandwiches for lunch. Wi-Fi Internet service is available. Open 8 am-4 pm Mon-Sat, 8:30 am-12:30 pm Sun. $

For an explanation of the $ price codes, see page 55.

AUTHOR'S CHOICE

Café il Mondo (45-3626-A Mamane, ☎ 775-7711). You can smell this casual, Italian eatery as you approach it – just follow your nose and you won't be disappointed. Café il Mondo is a Slow Food establishment, a part of the growing national movement encouraging people to slow down and enjoy their meals, particularly with food made from local, natural ingredients. Use of such quality ingredients leads to fresh, delicious items such as pesto flavored with Big Island macadamia nuts. Try it in their signature calzones, or on a nine-inch pizza ($10.50-$13.25) with a thin, flaky crust (larger pizzas available to go). The garlic focaccia is terrific, and the salads have interesting dressings like miso and oriental sesame. The café also has tasty sandwiches before 5 pm, espresso and tart, fresh-squeezed lemonade. Alcohol is BYO, and there is a $2-$5 corkage fee. Open 11 am-8 pm Tues-Sat. $$

Café Rendezvous (Mamane St, ☎ 775-9230). This crêperie is fabulous. The new café has a few tables on a lovely lanai with a view of the ocean framed by avocado trees, a perfect place to sip an espresso (or another drink from their extensive coffee menu), mango juice or a ginger mint iced tea. The crêpes are exquisite. We like to order one savory crêpe, such as the Swiss cheese, and one sweet, say the Pomme Cannelle with caramelized apples and cinnamon, and share. The chef lived in France for 20 years and her daughter, the server, studied there during college. Open 10 am-4 pm Sun, Mon and Thurs, 10 am-9 pm Fri-Sat. $-$$

Tex Drive In (45-690 Pakalana St on Hwy 19, ☎ 775-0598, www.texdrivein.com). Up on the main highway, this fast food joint is another local hot spot, with a drive-through window for "Ono Kine Food" and a bustling lanai. The menu includes local *grinds* like plate lunches, sandwiches, burgers, saimin, spam loco and curry stew. The main attraction, though, is the *malasada* selection. Malasadas are Portuguese donuts that give Krispy Kremes a run for their money. These warm, rectangular donuts are coated with sugar and come plain (90¢) or with fillings like chocolate cream. There's a big window where you can watch them being made. $

Entertainment

Honoka`a People's Theater (45-3490 Mamane St, ☎ 775-0000) shows one movie at 7 pm Tuesdays and Wednesdays, and a different one Fri-Sun. There is an old Super Simplex projector in the lobby that's worth a look. This is the kind of theater that plays jazz instead of commercials before the feature film. We found out the hard way that some seats are comfortably padded and some are wooden, so be sure to check!

Kukuihaele

The small village of Kukuihaele is reached by heading northwest on Hwy 240 out of Honoka`a, then bearing *makai* on the loop road which rejoins the highway just before it ends at the Waipi`o Valley Lookout. There isn't much to the village aside from an assortment of attractive B&Bs, as well as the Waipi`o Valley Artworks and the currently closed Last Chance Store. Many tours into and above Waipi`o Valley begin at one of these two places.

Sights

Waipi`o Lookout

Even people making a mad dash through the Hamakua Coast to get somewhere else have to stop here – you don't ignore the Waipi`o Valley. This lookout, down a short paved path with handrails, provides a view of the steep green *pali* (cliff) that separates Waipi`o from Waimanu Valley, waves rolling onto the black sand beach, and the lush six-mile valley below. There are four picnic tables under a roof if you want to stop for a snack, though they are very close together.

Where to Stay

AUTHOR'S CHOICE ★

Hale Kukui Orchard Retreat (48-5460 Kukuihaele Rd, ☎ 775-7130, toll free ☎ 800-444-7130, www.halekukui.com, three cottages, $180-195). Seventeen years ago, Hale Kukui ("House of Light") was a sugarcane field, but owners Bill and Sarah McCowatt had the foresight to clear the land and plant fruit trees on the four-acre property. The trees liked their new environment, and now there are around 20 kinds of fruit trees, such as pumelo, starfruit, lychee, and avocado – guests can pick all the fruit they like for only $5 per stay. It is a tranquil setting with awesome views of the Waipi`o Valley, not only from the lookout on the property, but from the jet tubs on the deck of each cottage! There are also ponds where guests (and owners) like to swim. This isn't the kind of luxury that includes bellmen or room service, but it's the kind that leads to low blood pressure. $$$

**Waipi`o Lookout** (45-5516 Waipi`o Road., ☎ 775-1306, www.waipiohi.net, one apt, $85). Owners Phyllis Tarail and Joel Cohen were vacationing at the property in 2000 and were so

enchanted by the area and the home that they bought it before the end of their stay. The visitors' abode consists of a one-bedroom that can accommodate up to three visitors, a fully-equipped kitchen and a lanai with views of the Waipi`o Valley (though not as good as the view from the owners' home above). Every room has a view, even the bathroom. $$

Where to Eat

Waipi`o Valley Artworks (48-5416 Government Main. Rd, ☎ 775-0958, www.waipiovalleyartworks.com). This gift shop has a small snack bar with sandwiches and pre-scooped ice cream, homemade banana bread, chips and sodas. Souvenirs include carved bowls, ceramics, kids' books, area books, art, jewelry and local CDs, including several by one of our favorite Hawaiian musicians, "Iz" (Israel Kamakawiwo`ole, check out *Facing Future* for good island vibes). A number of horseback, ATV and van tours leave from this store, so bottled water is a little overpriced. If you are backcountry camping in Waimanu Valley, you can arrange to park there overnight – it's more secure than the trailhead ($7.50-$15). Open 8 am-5 pm daily.

Waipi`o Valley

"Look deep into nature, and then you will understand everything better." – Albert Einstein

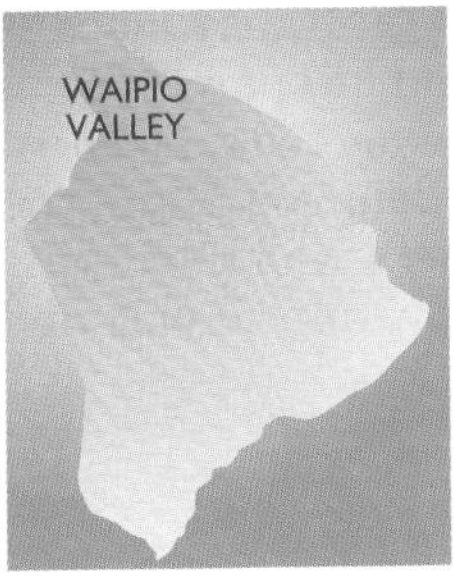

Close your eyes and picture the greenest, lushest Hawaiian valley of your dreams, flanked with ribbon waterfalls, overgrown with ancient tarot fields and fruit trees, cut by a picture-perfect stream that spills into the heavy surf at a quintessential black sand beach and inhabited by wild island horses. Then, open your eyes at the Waipi`o Valley Lookout. Notice the difference? There isn't one.

Orientation

IN THIS CHAPTER

Waipi`o Valley is eight miles northwest of the town of Honoka`a along Route 240. Proceed past the turnoff for the town of Kukuihaele. You'll reach the end of the highway at Waipi`o Lookout.

The descent into Waipi`o is along a precipitous, snaking road that drops nearly 1,000 feet in less than a mile. While the incline of nearly 45 degrees in some places makes for a fun amble down into the valley, it also makes for a brutal trudge back up. However, sympathetic folks on their return drive are usually kind enough to offer a ride. Only 4-wheel-drive vehicles can make this descent. Not only is it foolhardy to try it in a 2-wheel-drive car, there is a massive fine for attempting it. Most rental car agencies forbid taking their vehicles down this road.

Background

Waipi`o Valley, which literally means valley of "curving water" is also known as the "valley of the kings." The *ali`i* of old chose to live in this valley, where some estimate the population was as high as 50,000 people. Kamehameha the Great was hidden in Waipi`o Valley after his birth to save him from regicide. Many *heiaus* (religious temples) were built in the valley over the years, the most sacred of which was Paka`alana, a place of refuge, similar to the still existing Pu`uhonua O Honaunau on the south Kona coast, where the condemned could try to flee and escape death. If they made it to one of these sanctuaries, their lives would be spared. Additionally, many important Hawaiian legends took place in Waipi`o Valley, including the death of the demigod Maui, the savage midnight walks of the Night Marchers, and the taking of a wife by Lono, Hawaiian god of fertility, rain, music and peace.

LEGENDS OF THE FALLS

The Waipi`o Valley (Hawaiian Images)

The names of two of the waterfalls that cascade into Waipi`o Valley relate to ancient Hawaiian legend. **Hi`ilawe Falls**, the crown jewel of the valley, took its name from an ancient chief. As he was dying, his *leis* and loin cloth were taken from him and placed on the cliffs of the valley, where they became the flowers and vines we see today. His body was transformed into a boulder on the highest precipice of the valley, and his ghost was changed by the goddess Hina into water that crashed against the valley floor and turned to the mist that floats over the valley to keep an eye on all the people of Waipi`o.

On the west side of the valley is **Nanau`e Falls**, named after the "shark-man" of Waipi`o Valley. On the advice of his father, the shark god Ka-moho-alii, his mother raised him as a vegetarian. All was well until he got his first taste of meat. Soon after, local fisherman began disappearing. Then, as he grew bolder, Nanau`e would challenge his friends to swimming competitions from which they would never return. Finally, as suspicion grew, the kapa cape that he would never remove was ripped off of him by a fellow taro worker, and there for everyone to see was the shark mouth that had grown on his back. He managed to escape into the river, then out to Maui where he continued his carnivorous ways, and finally to Moloka`i, where he was discovered, pulled limb from limb and burned to death.

The late 1800s saw an influx of immigrants from China, and the valley was developed with many homes, as well as churches, restaurants and schools. However, the population dropped dramatically when the inhabitants moved to higher ground following the huge tsunami of 1946 that, amazingly, took no lives in the valley. Some attribute this to the *mana* (spiritual power) of the many great kings who are buried in the high cliffs that surround that valley and assure that no harm will come to those that dwell there.

Today the population has dwindled to fewer than 50 people, mostly taro farmers and throwback, alternative-lifestyle folks living "off the grid."

Sights

Waipi`o Beach is a wave-battered slice of black sand, backed by ironwood trees, and inhabited by wild horses. A waterfall – which you can't see from the lookout – plunges off a *pali* (cliff) near the water, making it an exquisite place to visit. Locals flock to the beach after work when the surf is up, some to test their skills and others to relax and soak in the shocking beauty of the valley.

The Waipi`o Valley & Beach

Waipi`o Stream splits the beach, and many visitors don't venture to the western side where there is better sand and more privacy. If you are tempted to, be very careful crossing the stream. Take one of the driftwood sticks near the bank to help you stay on foot. It may be advisable during higher water to cross farther upstream where the water is slow and you can swim across. The experience of getting halfway across, then feeling your feet start to slip out from under you in the swift water, is not only life threatening, but more effective than a quadruple shot of espresso to get you going in the morning.

To get to the beach, bear right at the fork when the road into the valley reaches the floor, and follow the rough road for a half-mile until it hits the beach.

Safety Tip: Flash floods are unfortunately common in the northern valleys of the Big Island. If it's raining hard, do what the locals have figured out over the years and stay topside. If you're already down in the valley and faced with crossing a swollen stream, patiently wait for the waters to subside. It shouldn't take too long (a few hours) due to the relatively small size of the watershed, and it's a lot more pleasant than waiting in a doctor's office.

Kaluahina Falls

Waterfalls abound in Waipi`o, and it seems there's a new one around every corner. Waterfall walks include the short trip around the eastern seaside *pali* to Kaluahina Falls, which is the site where Kevin Costner made landfall in his much-panned film *Waterworld*. Of less dubious importance, it's a beautiful ribbon of water that either spouts wildly onto the seaside rocks, or dribbles in thin cascades down the deep green cliffs, depending on the recent rainfall. To access Kaluahina Falls, simply walk down to the beach and look to your right. You can't miss it. Waiulili Falls is just a bit farther on down the *pali* to the east. You can reach this waterfall during low tides, or when the surf is mellow, but watch for rogue waves. As one former Waipi`o Valley resident told us, they have a saying down there that summarizes the tendency for things to be washed away by floods or waves: "Here today, gone to Maui." For a hair-raising waterfall adventure, see the trail description to the base of Hi`ilawe Falls below.

For a seldom-viewed glimpse into the back of Waipi`o, cross Waipi`o Stream to the western side of the beach, and ascend the unmistakable "Z" trail visible along the western *pali*. This is the trail to Waimanu Valley (see box below), which is not a day hike, but a short trip up the trail provides an excellent vantage point that few visitors get to see.

THE NIGHT MARCHERS

Hawaiian legend contends that on certain nights of the year, ghosts of warriors wander along set paths from battlefields back into the underworld. If any mortal views the procession, they will be quickly filleted by the phantom soldiers. An entrance to the underworld in the cliffs above Waipi`o Valley accounts for the presence of the Night Marchers in the valley.

In 2000, local filmmaking twins Blake and Brent Cousins made a *Blair Witch*-style movie about a documentary crew that ventures down into Waipi`o for concrete evidence of the Night Marchers, and never return. The film was successful enough to warrant a sequel – *Night Marchers II: Return of the Ka`ai.* More info at www.nightmarchers.com.

Adventures

On Foot

While Waipi`o Valley snakes for miles into the back of the North Kohala Mountains, most of the land is trailless and on private property, so it's best to focus your wanderings on the first mile or two around the bay.

Don't drink the water! That is, not without first treating it with water purification tabs or boiling it vigorously. All streams in and around Waipi`o and Waimanu Valleys are exposed to feral and domesticated animals (and humans!) on higher ground whose waste generates leptospirosis and giardiasis, either of which can ruin your vacation (as well as the weeks and months that follow). FYI, water filters are futile against leptospirosis.

Hi`ilawe Falls

Hi`ilawe Falls

Difficulty: Difficult
Distance and type: 1 mile round-trip, out-and-back
Time: 90-120 minutes

This exhilarating – but treacherous – hike is to the base of the achingly beautiful Hi`ilawe Falls, which plummets a total of about 1,600 feet, first cascading 300-400 feet into an upper pool, then sliding and tumbling down the face of the cliff the rest of the way. Hi`ilawe Falls is actually a twin falls, with Hakalaoa Falls usually dry due to an irrigation diversion on the topside of the valley. There is a plan to restore the water to Hakalaoa Falls, but, as with all bureaucracies, the process is painfully slow. Sometimes a trickle of water is present, while at other times it is a waterless ghost clearly visible next to the flowing falls of Hi`ilawe.

The trail to the falls is unmaintained, rough, and non-existent in some places. Plan to spend plenty of time in the stream, perhaps even swimming. That means you'll want a waterproof bag with you, unless you decide to leave your camera behind, which would be a shame. The road from the top side splits when it reaches the valley floor, with the road to the beach forking off to the right. Follow the valley fork until just before it crosses through the first stream. The trail to the base of the waterfall begins on the left side of the road, just before the stream. *Look closely.* The trail is there, under some trees, running over a small knoll and into the jungle. The trail starts near Hi`ilawe Stream just three-quarters of a mile below the falls. That doesn't sound far, but due to the difficulty of the trek, that is a misleading distance. A trail exists for most of the way, but it can be difficult to follow, and you will have to deviate into the stream to get around obstacles or pick up the trail on the opposite side. The stream bed is slippery and rocky, so hiking poles or felt-soled shoes are helpful. For full details on this hike, visit www.bigislandadventure.com.

Ecotourism

Hawaiian Walkways (☎ 775-0372, toll free ☎ 800-457-7759, hawaiianwalkways.com). If you want a guided hiking tour, Hawaiian Walkways offers a "Waipi`o Waterfall Adventure." This company, based in Honoka`a, was named "Tour Operator of the Year" in 2002 by the Hawaii Ecotourism Association, and the guides' knowledge of Hawaii's natural and cultural history. This 4.5-mile hike skirts the rim of the Waipi`o Valley – 1,000 feet above the valley floor – with stops to swim in waterfall pools and to picnic. It is rated a moderately difficult hike, though guides will adjust their pace and itinerary to accommodate different skill levels. There is a two-person minimum, 10 maximum, hike that costs $95/pp and leaves at 9 am each morning. The tour includes light packs, walking sticks, rain gear, lunch and drinks. Hawaiian Walkways also conducts hiking tours on other parts of the Big Island, and can arrange custom tours.

On Water

With a waterfall cascading off a *pali* (cliff) near the beach, the surf spot in the Waipi`o Valley has to be one of the most beautiful in the world. (You'll want to check it out even if you don't surf!) The water is tumultuous at Waipi`o Bay, and the local surfers dig on it. They say it can break like Waimea on the north shore of O`ahu. There is a nasty riptide just off the beach that can pull you in three directions at once, so this spot is only for the experienced. Swimming here is nearly always unadvisable.

It is possible to kayak the break here, as well as to paddle Waipi`o Stream. Additionally, a sea kayak adventure to the neighboring valleys to the west is possible, but at press time there were no longer any rentals available in or around the valley. To get here, make a hard right near the end of the road into the valley when you can.

On Horseback

There's something indescribably peaceful about meandering across the Waipi`o Valley floor on horseback, under monkeypod trees and through streams to get to incredible views of the valley's waterfalls. It's also nice not to have to hike down (or up) the steep road into the valley – a van escorts you into and out of the valley. Most tours in the valley request reservations 24 hours in advance (though if you have the money, they seem to be able to find a way to squeeze you in at the last minute). There is usually an age requirement (no small children) and a weight limit (under 230 lbs).

Waipi`o Na`alapa Stables (☎ 775-0419). We like these guys because they're a simple operation, with guides who are very familiar with the valley. Ours grew up in Waipi`o, and regaled us with stories of how, as kids, they kept busy by organizing canoe races, or jumping on wild horses as teens. A 2½-hour tour across the valley floor is $85/pp.

**Waipi`o on Horseback and Taro Farm** (☎ 775-7291). This tour is similar to the Na`alapa tour, except there is a stop at a working taro farm. The tour is also $85 and lasts 2½ hours so, if you're eager for maximum horse time, it might not be for you. Then again, if you're interested in the main ingredient in *poi*, the farm tour will appeal.

**Waipi`o Ridge Stables** (☎ 775-1007, www.waipioridgestables.com). This organization offers the choice of a 2½-hour tour along the valley rim, for views from the top of Hi`ilawe Falls ($75/pp), or you can continue on for a tour lasting five hours that leads to a "hidden" waterfall, where you picnic and swim ($145/pp). There are few better feelings than swimming in a waterfall's pool – it makes you feel alive. After all, that's why you came here, isn't it?

On Wheels

Waipi`o Valley Wagon Tours (☎ 775-9518, www.waipiovalleywagontours.com). This is a great family tour, as a mule-drawn wagon splashes through streams on the valley floor. The tour lasts 1½ hours, can accommodate up to 10 guests, and runs three times daily Mon-Sat. Adults $45, kids $22.50, under three free.

Waipi`o Valley Shuttle (☎ 775-7121, www.waipiovalleytour.com). This is a four-wheel-drive van tour in the valley to a fish pond, taro patches and waterfalls that takes 1½ hours. $45/pp, $20 kids under 11, with a two-adult minimum. Tours leave Mon-Sat at 9 am, 11 am, 1 pm and 3 pm.

There are ATV tours with views from above Waipi`o Valley but that do not drive into it. Riders must be at least 16 years old.

ATV Ranch Ride (☎ 877-775-7291). This is an all-terrain tour for people with some experience on ATVs. The 2½-hour guided tour travels on a 260-acre ranch (tours 9:30 am and 1:30 pm). $100/pp. No wheelies or donuts.

Kukui ATV & Adventures (☎ 775-1701). Ride B is the shorter, two-hour tour ($100/pp), while Ride A is three-four hours and includes a picnic at a waterfall ($145). Ride B leaves at 9 am and 1 pm; Ride A leaves at noon. Riders should have experience driving a car.

■ Where to Stay

Over the years there have been several accommodations on the floor of Waipi`o, including the famous Waipi`o Treehouse and Tom Araki's hostel. Unfortunately, the Treehouse went bust and Tom Araki died in 2000 at the age of 90, leaving nowhere to stay in the valley. Additionally, there used to be several public camping areas, but due to the massive popularity of the campsites and the fact that toilets were never installed, the situation grew quite messy over the years. The state got wind of this, so to speak, and closed the valley to all camping. There is still state-sponsored camping in Waimanu Valley (see box below).

WAIMANU VALLEY

Waimanu Valley (Hawaiian Images)

The intriguing "Z" trail that streaks up the western *pali* of Waipi`o Valley is the beginning of the **Muliwai Trail**, a rough-and-tumble trail to Waimanu Valley. While it is less than three miles to Waimanu as the crow flies, you don't fly like a crow. The trail rises 1,200 feet from the floor of Waipi`o, drops into 12 gulches (some as deep as 500 feet), is wet, muddy, poorly maintained, and the final 1,200-foot descent of the nine-mile trail is death-defying in the wrong weather. That said, if you wish to go, plan on spending at least one night in the backcountry (for which you'll need a permit, see *Camping*, p. 52-53). Don't even think about trying to hike this in one day. Waimanu Valley itself is startlingly similar in appearance to Waipi`o, but is only about half the size and uninhabited. It's a jewel to behold, if you can make it. For day-trippers, traveling up the "Z" trail a bit is a great way to achieve a less photographed view of the valley than from the lookout on the opposite side of the valley. The views of the falls are especially nice.

■ Kalopa State Recreation Area

This 100-acre park, at about 2,000 feet, provides a leafy respite from the hustle and bustle sometimes found Kona-side. The rain forest contains a bounty of upland native trees, particularly *ohi`a,* as well as non-native species such as eucalyptus, ironwood and tropical ash, the latter having been planted by the Civilian Conservation Corps in the 1930s for erosion control purposes. The forest provides sanctuary for several interesting bird species, including the *`io*, the endangered Hawaiian hawk and the *auku`u*, or night heron, which forages in the gulches for frogs and crayfish.

`Io

Auku`u

Adventures on Foot

The hiking here is limited to about five total miles of trails. Up by the cabins there's a 0.7-mile nature loop with signs to help you identify some of the tree species. The trailhead for the other trails is a little obscure. It's just before the road splits to either the cabins or the campsites. Alternatively, you can begin your hike immediately at the entrance to the park where there is a sign for hunters explaining the maximum number of animals that they're allowed to drag out of the forest. However, if you start there, keep in mind that you are on the horse-rim trail, which is poorly marked in some places.

Kalopa Trail Network

Difficulty: Moderate

Length and type: 2-4 miles, loop

Time: 1-2 hours

Starting from the intended trailhead, proceed 0.3 miles to a dry streambed. Take a peek over the edge and marvel at the trees and massive boulders that have been thrown around like pebbles by the rushing water. Watch for flash floods. The trail resumes across some boulders and tree roots several feet up on the other side of the streambed. At that point, the rim trail skirts Kalopa Gulch, which, along with the other gulches in the area, was created by the glacial melt from Mauna Kea in the Pleistocene era. Two spur trails – **Blue Gum Lane** and **Silk Oak Lane** – head back to the **Jeep Road** that will in turn lead back to the trailhead. These trails can be difficult to follow, but if you're lucky and the trails have been recently maintained, you'll be able to follow colored flagging in the trees which will reliably lead you where you want to go. At the end of the rim trail, you have the option of returning along the Jeep Road or continuing on along the rim trail. This trail can be a little difficult to keep track of, too, but follow the fence until you pick up the trail again and it heads back into the forest.

There is a tremendous amount of lush, green vegetation along these hikes, from towering trees to thick, arcing ferns. When the *o`hia* trees are blooming with the red puffs of *lehua* flowers, this hike is particularly enjoyable. All in all, though, it doesn't provide a classically Hawaiian experience: no jaw-dropping views of the volcanoes, no plunging waterfalls. It's a great place to spend a morning, but unless you're an avid hiker or a hopeless tree nerd, you shouldn't feel like you've missed the opportunity of a lifetime if you can't jam this site into your busy vacation schedule.

Where to Stay

The facility provides restrooms, a picnic pavilion, several cabins and three "campsites." The campsites cost $5 per night, and consist of small pavilions with a concrete floor, upon which campers are, in fact, expected to pitch their tent. Since camping on a slab of concrete is not terribly comfortable, the caretakers seem to expect and tolerate tents pitched on the soft, green grass right next to the pavilions. Additionally, there are four cabins available for rent. Each can accommodate up to eight people, and includes beds, bedding, towels and showers. The cost of the cabins is $55 per night. Permits are required for both the campsites and the cabins. Reservations can be made in advance; however, the permits must be picked up in person at the state offices in Hilo (see *Camping*, p. 52-53).

■ Pa`auilo

Pa`auilo, a small settlement today, was the end of the line for the Hamakua Consolidated Railroad because the funds never came through to extend it all the way to Honoka`a.

Agritourism

Hawaiian Vanilla Company (43-2007 Pa`auilo Mauka Road, ☎ 776-1771, www.hawaiivanilla.com). That's right – agri-tourism. The Hawaiian Vanilla Company, the only commercial vanilla grower in the United States, is tucked away above sleepy Pa`auilo. It might seem odd until you learn that vanilla comes from an orchid – and after all, the Big Island is the Orchid Isle. There are weekly events to enhance the visit: "Vanilla Tasting and Presentation" is held at 3 pm every Mon and Tues ($10 includes refreshments such as vanilla bean ice cream, vanilla tea, banana bread and vanilla lemonade); "Upcountry Tea" on the second Saturday of every month ($29/pp, advance reservations required); and the "Hawaiian Vanilla Experience Luncheon," a gourmet, multi-course affair 12:30-2 pm on Wed and Thurs ($30/pp, advance reservations required). The tasting room has high ceilings with giant windows. The gallery and gift shop is open daily from 1-5. The vanilla lotion smells heavenly and supposedly wards off mosquitoes, though we still find DEET more effective.

Pa`auilo (Hawaiian Images)

To get there, turn *mauka* at the sign from Hwy 19 for Pa`auilo (between mile markers 37 and 36), then left at Pohakea, which also has a sign for the Vanilla Co.

The Big Island is the world's largest producer of **orchids**, thanks to the rain-fueled lush conditions on Hilo-side.

Laupahoehoe

Laupahoehoe, or "Leaf of Lava," is a town of a few hundred residents in another former sugar town. The dramatic coastline here, with waves crashing onto lava outcroppings, will have you reaching for your camera.

LAUPAHOEHOE POINT

Hawaiian legend explains the formation of the lava coastline at Laupahoehoe Point as a fight between two of the island's goddesses. When Pele, goddess of volcano and fire, noticed that Poli`ahu, snow goddess of Mauna Kea, was garnering more attention when they were sledding, she became jealous. She caused a volcanic eruption to push Poli`ahu back to the summit of Mauna Kea. But, once she was at a higher elevation, Poli`ahu fought back by creating a shower of snow on the molten lava, forcing Pele's lava through Laupahoehoe Gulch and into the ocean.

Practicalities

There is one **gas station** in Laupahoehoe, the only one between Honoka`a and Hilo on the Hamakua Coast. The **Minit Stop**, on Hwy 19, is open from 5 am-11 pm, and sells the usual mini-mart goods, as well as Maui Fried Chicken (the aroma is a little hard to take at eight in the morning).

Laupahoehoe (Hawaiian Images)

Sights

Laupahoehoe Point. A monument stands "in memory of those who lost their lives in the tidal wave" on April 1, 1946, when a tsunami triggered by earthquakes in the Aleutian Islands swept 24 schoolchildren and teachers to their deaths at Laupahoehoe Point. The tsunami, the worst natural disaster in the history of the state, caused deaths throughout the

Hawaiian Islands, but the Big Island's Laupahoehoe and Hilo were hit the hardest. There is also an educational board with photos of the deceased and newspaper clippings about the disaster.

Laupahoehoe Train Museum (36-2377 Mamalahoa Hwy by mile marker 25 on Hwy 19, ☎ 962-6300, www.thetrainmuseum.com). The volunteer-run Laupahoehoe Train Museum, in an old railway company home, has a short movie with old train footage as well as artifacts and photos about the Big Island's railroad history. There are toy trains on the front porch that kids can play with. Adults $4, open 9 am-4:30 pm Mon-Fri, 10 am-2 pm Sat-Sun.

HAWAI`I CONSOLIDATED RAILWAY

Hamakua Coast

The original adventure on wheels along the Hamakua Coast was the Hawai`i Consolidated Railway, which at one time ran all the way from Hilo to Pa`auilo. The sugar industry was already booming in Hawaii when the United States granted duty-free status on sugar imports from the islands. This influx of money and demand necessitated a rail route along the rough Hamakua Coast. The railway was used by both industry and tourists until the 1946 tsunami destroyed several bridges and key infrastructure points. The railway was abandoned, though much of the route, including several scenic bridges, is where the highway exists today.

Note: There is no access to Hakalau Forest Natural Wildlife Refuge, though the refuge land stretches into this area. For information on the refuge and entry, see the *Mauna Kea/Waimea* chapter.

Camping

Your only option for spending the night in Laupahoehoe is to pitch your tent at Laupahoehoe Point Beach Park. The ocean waves get pretty showy down on this scenic spit of land, and if you camp too close to the rocks your tent may get wet. Use your rain fly (which is probably a good idea anyway, since it tends to rain on this side of the Big Island), but don't forget to wash it off with fresh water when you get home to keep it from corroding.

The best campsites are on the northern side of the park where there are picnic tables and sites tucked among the trees. If you can, try to avoid camping in the spot adjacent to the boat landing. There's a really bright street light there, and it also seems to attract local partiers at all hours of the night. In fact, unless you don't need the sleep, it's probably better to plan to camp here during the week, avoiding the weekends.

Permits are required, cost $5 per adult per night, and must be picked up at the county parks office in Hilo (see p. 52-53).

Where to Eat

Back to the '50s Highway Fountain (35-2074 Old Mamalahoa Hwy, ☎ 962-0808). This lively '50s nostalgia restaurant has great ambiance and pretty good food with very reasonable prices, serving dinners like spaghetti with garlic bread, a 10-oz NY steak, and a Mahi filet burger. Shakes, floats and banana splits round out the meal. For $1 more, you can add fresh Laupahoehoe grilled mushrooms – they are phenomenal. There are black and white checkered floors, a jukebox that cranks '50s tunes (co-owner Larry often sings along), cut-outs of James Dean and Marilyn Monroe, and mannequins dressed in poodle skirts. The bathroom is a shrine to Betty Boop. A sign above the entrance reads, "Tourists treated same as home folks" – the photos and letters from happy tourists are a testament to this. Don't forget to sign their "guest book" by sticking a pin in your hometown on their map on the wall. Open 7 am-7 pm Tues-Sat, 8 am-2 pm Sun. $

Adventures on Wheels

World Botanical Gardens/ Umauma Falls (*Mauka* at mile marker 16 on Hwy 19, ☎ 963-5427, www.wbgi.com, adults $9.50, teens 13-17 $5, kids five-12 $2.50, under five free). This park is largely unspectacular, especially when the Hamakua Coast offers so much breathtaking foliage for free. In its defense, it is a young park that is still developing (they are soliciting "share owners" to invest). There are some placards identifying plants – check out the yellow-flowered *kalamona*, or "scrambled egg tree." But the gardens have an ace in their hand: a view of the stunning Umauma Falls. The three-tiered waterfall is what you want a Hawaiian waterfall to look like, and is reputed to be one of the most beautiful waterfalls in the state. Most people think this justifies the price of admission.

Pea hen

Umauma Falls

Tip: Visit Umauma Falls early in the day so that you can avoid shooting into the sun.

The World Botanical Gardens also offer a paved rainforest walk that is wheelchair-accessible for about 10 minutes until the half-mile "rainforest extension," which has loose rocks and gravel. There isn't much shade in the extension, which climbs

Orchid

above the Honopueo Stream and follows it, but the views of the ocean on the way up are spectacular. Take the extension if you're on Hawaiian time or want to get the most bang for your buck – bring water and bug repellent. The extension ends at the road that loops back to Umauma Falls, a great excuse to take one more look (20-minute walk back to the car). Open 9 am-5:30 pm daily.

KEIKI (CHILDREN'S) FUN

There is a children's maze in the World Botanical Gardens next to the registration hut, in the Garden. It's easier than the maze Harry Potter had to navigate for the Triwizard Tournament, but a parent should hold their child's hand in the maze because it is a challenge, about the size of a football field (adults can see over the shrub "walls.") Make the first left in the maze or, as one employee put it, "You're lost forever. " When you return to registration, they give free fruit and drinks.

Nearby Attractions & Adventures

Scenic Detour

Despite the fact that this chapter is oriented from north to south, we would recommend doubling back on some scenic detours, like this one, to ensure that you don't miss any views while on your detour.

From the registration area of the World Botanical Gardens, turn right (north) and cruise along the **Old Mamalahoa Highway** for a beautiful drive through viney gulches and across old bridges, meandering through pastureland and into tropical forests. At one point, you'll drop into a gulch with a verdant canopy so dense that it surrounds the road like a tunnel into the Garden of Eden.

You'll also pass the old **Honahina Cemetery**, possibly the most beautiful site for a cemetery in the world, surrounded by the bright-orange blossoms of African tulip trees and a distant view of the Pacific Ocean. The road travels to swimming holes and beckoning streams, and eventually leads to the very scenic **Waikaumalo Park**, where monkeypod trees line the banks of a gorgeous stream, another ideal picnic spot. If it weren't for the bold red signs warning of leptospirosis, one would be unable to resist a swim. Rejoin Hwy 19 just past the park a bit north of mile marker 19. As with the rest of the Hamakua Coast, wear insect repellent if you get out of the car for a closer look – the mosquitoes in the area are voracious.

Hakalau

Little is left of the once thriving town of Hakalau, located *makai* between mile markers 15 and 16 on Hwy 19. This area was a hotbed of action during the sugar years, and some of the structures still stand, including the Hakalau Theater, which is now the post office. Other structures from that era haven't survived as well.

Hakalau (Hawaiian Images)

Wailea

This is a very slow, quiet settlement – most inhabitants are in their 80s or 90s. It's a peaceful place in another gorgeous spot along the Hamakua Coast. It's fun to take a slow roll through the town and get a sense of what all the locals around here call "Old Hawai`i." The best way to approach Wailea is to turn north up the gulch when leaving Kolekole Beach Park. The fruit trees, vines and flowers give way to the old town buildings as you climb out of the gulch.

Where to Stay

Akiko's Buddhist B&B (☎ 963-6422, http://alternative-hawaii.com/akiko, $55-$85). Zen practitioner Akiko says of her B&B, "It's a place to come to be quiet and experience Old Hawai`i." There is a range of accommodations, from dorm-style rooms with a common kitchen area, a monastery where silence is observed from 6-6 am, or the real find: two solar-powered cottages in a banana grove. Meditation "sits" are open to the public ($5 suggested *dana*), and take place for an hour each morning at five, and also from 7-8 pm on Tues, Thurs, and Fri. Akiko also owns the adjacent I. Motonaga Garage Art Gallery, where special events like concerts are held. (Check her website for upcoming events.) $-$$

See page 65 for an explanation of the hotel $ price codes.

Camping - Kolekole Beach Park

Even if you aren't camping, Kolekole is a beautiful place for a picnic (there are two tables for just this purpose). It sits on a lovely little stream fed by a low, rushing waterfall near the mouth, feeding into the ocean, where locals surf. The surroundings are so lush that signs warn, "Beware of falling coconuts." You'll see it from the bridge between mile markers 15 and 14 along Hwy 19 – turn *mauka*.

Camping is on the broad expanse of lawn. Permits are needed from the county office in Hilo. Rates are $5 per person per night (see *Camping*, p. 52-53). This park gets a little rowdy on weekends; we were advised by the county official who issued our permits not to leave our tent unattended during the day "just in case."

Fines for littering run between $500 and $1,000 along the Hamakua Coast – an extra incentive to keep the area beautiful.

Honomu

"Everybody needs beauty as well as bread, places to play in and pray in, where nature may heal and give strength to body and soul." – John Muir

Honomu is another former sugar mill town with a sleepy demeanor – business hours here are really iffy. The town has a main drag along Hwy 220, with businesses catering to the tourists that flock to the nearby Akaka Falls State Park, a "must see" on the Hamakua Coast. There are some interesting shops in town. Visit www.bigislandadventureguide.com for more details.

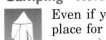

Honomu (Hawaiian Images)

Sights

Akaka Falls State Park

A short loop trail (0.4 miles) down and up mossy stairs takes you to lookouts for Kahuna Falls and the graceful Akaka Falls, which plummets 442 feet down a *pali* (cliff) to a pool below. A ribbon of white water hurls over the sheer jade wall, breaking along crags and creating a misty effect – all the beauty you expect from Hawaii. If you're short on time (or breath), just walk to the Akaka Falls lookout. The view of Kahuna Falls is somewhat obscured by an awkward angle and dense foliage. Still, we've never met a waterfall we didn't like.

To get here, turn *mauka* between mile markers 13 and 14 on the main highway in Honomu onto Hwy 220 and follow it until it deadends after 3¾ miles at the parking lot for Akaka Falls State Park. There are public restrooms here.

Where to Stay

The Palms Cliff House Inn (☎ 963-6076, www.palmscliffhouse.com, eight rooms, $250-$395). This is a luxurious Victorian property. All eight guestrooms are ocean-facing with lanais, and the deluxe ones have fireplaces and Jacuzzis that overlook the ocean. It's

The Palms Cliff House Inn

beautifully landscaped and decorated; in fact, weddings and high teas are regularly held here. A gourmet breakfast is included in the cost, and guests can opt for special packages, such as "Hot Hawaiian Nights," which includes rose petals on the bed, champagne, candles and chocolates. Children under 12 are not allowed. $$$$

Where to Eat

Woodshop Gallery and Café (☎ 963-6363, www.woodshopgallery.com) is part-gift shop, part-café. The gift shop offers framed art, wooden bowls and furniture as well as hunks of *koa* in case you want to try your hand at carving. The café has *ahi* and taro burgers, sandwiches, smoothies and creamy Big Island Ice Cream. Open 10 am-5:30 pm daily. $

Lisa's Pizza and Deli (☎ 963-5252). If you need a pizza fix, look no farther. Lisa serves up big slices of NY-style pizza ($1.90, toppings $.45) with a smile. She also serves whole pies ranging from Greek to Mega Meat, as well as wraps, deli sandwiches, burgers, dogs and fries. We're fans. Open 11 am-7 pm Sun-Thurs, Fri/Sat 11 am-8 pm. $

Nearby Adventures & Attractions

Adventures on Wheels

Pepe`ekeo Four-mile Scenic Drive

This mandatory detour begins *makai* between mile markers 7 and 8 on Hwy 19 and loops you back north just south of mile marker 11 on the main highway. The drive is crammed with delights, from the hikes to the gardens to the *ono grinds* at the end. Don't miss this.

Adventures on Foot

Onomea Bay

Difficulty: Easy to Moderate

Length and type: ½ mile, out-and-back, or a 1-mile loop

Time: 30 minutes

Onomea Bay

The Onomea Bay trail system comprises a short and lovely walk down to a glittering bay snuggled into the rocky, windward coast. Onomea Stream escapes from the green valley and empties lazily into the bay. A palm-covered outcropping that was once the site of a small fishing village is battered ceaselessly by the tumultuous waters. This is essential Hilo-side Hawaii.

Access to the Onomea Bay trail system has been limited due to ongoing legal fights between the state and the owner of the Hawaii Tropical Botanical Garden, but the issue seems to have finally been resolved. There are now two access points: one from the north and one from the south.

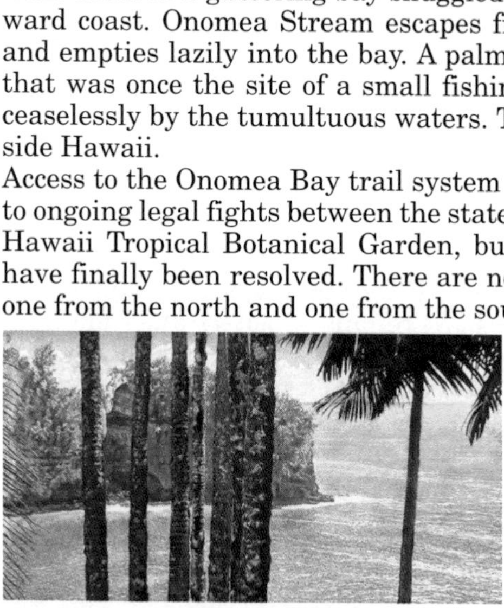

Onomea Bay

Both trailheads for the easy, rewarding hike are found along the Four-Mile Scenic Route. From the south, you will arrive at the southern trailhead in about a mile. Park on the shoulder where there are probably several cars already parked.

The southern trail leads immediately down about 100 feet to a small cove with a gravel beach. Notice that even on relatively

Onomea Bay *(Hawaiian Images)*

calm days the tides are fiercely pulling at each other. Return to the trail and make your way through the network of chain link fences and warning signs that flank the trail through the botanical gardens property. This is an apparent fallout from the negotiations that led to the public being allowed access to the bay, but not the gardens (at least, not without paying the $15). If you come during business hours you will probably encounter a guard who's there to ensure that you don't enter the garden without forking over said admission.

Proceed past the guard until you come down a slight dip in the trail at Onomea Stream. To your left is a beautiful little swimming hole, complete with an awesome split waterfall: a perfect piece of Zen paradise. Be aware of the leptospirosis in the water. (A very nasty infection results, with fever, chills and vomiting. Trust us: you don't want to take this home as a souvenir.) To your right is the "beach" and landing at Onomea Bay. On the south side you can still see where Onomea Arch stood before it crumbled, after thousands of years, during an earthquake in 1956. Directly out in front of the bay are the twin rocks – two lovers, according to legend, who volunteered to give their lives in order to protect the bay from attacking war canoes.

The trail continues on the other side of the stream. Depending on the tide and the recent rains, you can either ford the stream directly, or you may be able to proceed down to the beach, then pick your way across rocks and hop to the other side without getting wet. The trail ascends and you get your first view of the next inlet, and the fantastic lava outcropping. It was here that the little fishing village of **Kahali`i** once existed; it was one of the first landing points for cargo ships on the Big Island. The ships would anchor in Onomea Bay, and large laden-down rowboats would transport the cargo to shore. Donkeys would then haul the cargo up to the road along the old Donkey Trail. Later, when sugar was king, the Onomea Sugar Company had a major presence here. The Onomea Sugar Mill was once right behind where the visitor center of the tropical garden stands today. Conversely, sugar was brought down to be loaded on the ships via the Donkey Trail.

By the 1930s the Hamakua railroad made this landing unnecessary, and the 1946 tsunami destroyed most of what remained of the village of Kahali`i. The valley was largely abandoned until purchased by the developers of the botanical garden in the late '70s.

From here, either head back the way you came, or complete a loop by continuing along the trail as it ascends straight up the hill for a quick 150-foot elevation gain. You will rejoin the road just to the north of the botanical gardens. This is also the alternative trailhead. Your car will be a half-mile south of the parking lot. It's downhill and an easy walk or jog, but you may just talk one of the garden attendants into giving you a lift in his golf cart.

Hawaii Tropical Botanical Garden (27-717 Old Mamalahoa Hwy, ☎ 964-5233, www.hawaiigarden.com). Hawaii Tropical Botanical Garden sparkles – and it smells great. Plan to spend an hour or two here. There is a steep 150-foot-long trail into the Gardens, but this doesn't stop the busloads of senior citizens that flock to the exquisite site (once inside, the trails are paved and fairly level, and there are plenty of benches throughout the park). There are various trails with well-marked plants – over 2,000 species from rainforests around the world – and many views of Onomea Bay. The Orchid Garden is very popular; we also love the Heliconia Trail, since we're fans of "hanging lobster claw," and the Torch Ginger Forest. In fact, there are numerous trails worth exploring here. There are caged macaws in the bird aviary when the kids get bored, and a carved *tiki* of the war god Ku. They ship tropical flower arrangements to the mainland. Admission is $15 for adults, $5 kids six-16, children under five free. Open 9 am-5 pm daily, last admission at 4 pm.

AUTHOR'S CHOICE

What's Shakin' (27-999 Old Mamalahoa Hwy, Pepe`ekeo, ☎ 964-3080) is a perfect reward after hiking the Onomea trails and visiting the Hawaii Botanical Tropical Garden. The not-so-secret ingredient at this smoothie and sandwich stand is fresh, succulent produce. Their smoothies ($5-$5.50) are fantastic, made with fresh frozen tropical fruit and 100% fruit juices – no ice, no sherbet, no added sugar. Wow! The Groovy Guava is one of our favorites – guava, banana, strawberry and apple juice. The food is great, too – stick with a meal that highlights the produce like the Designer Bagel sandwich, instead of something like nachos. They also sell their fresh produce; we've seen people buy a giant avocado and eat it with a spoon at one of the tables on the lanai. The jovial staff creates specials that reflect the vibe of the place, such as the "May you be blessed all year" taco duet, or the "You are a beautiful person" pastrami sandwich. Open 10 am-5 pm daily. $-$$

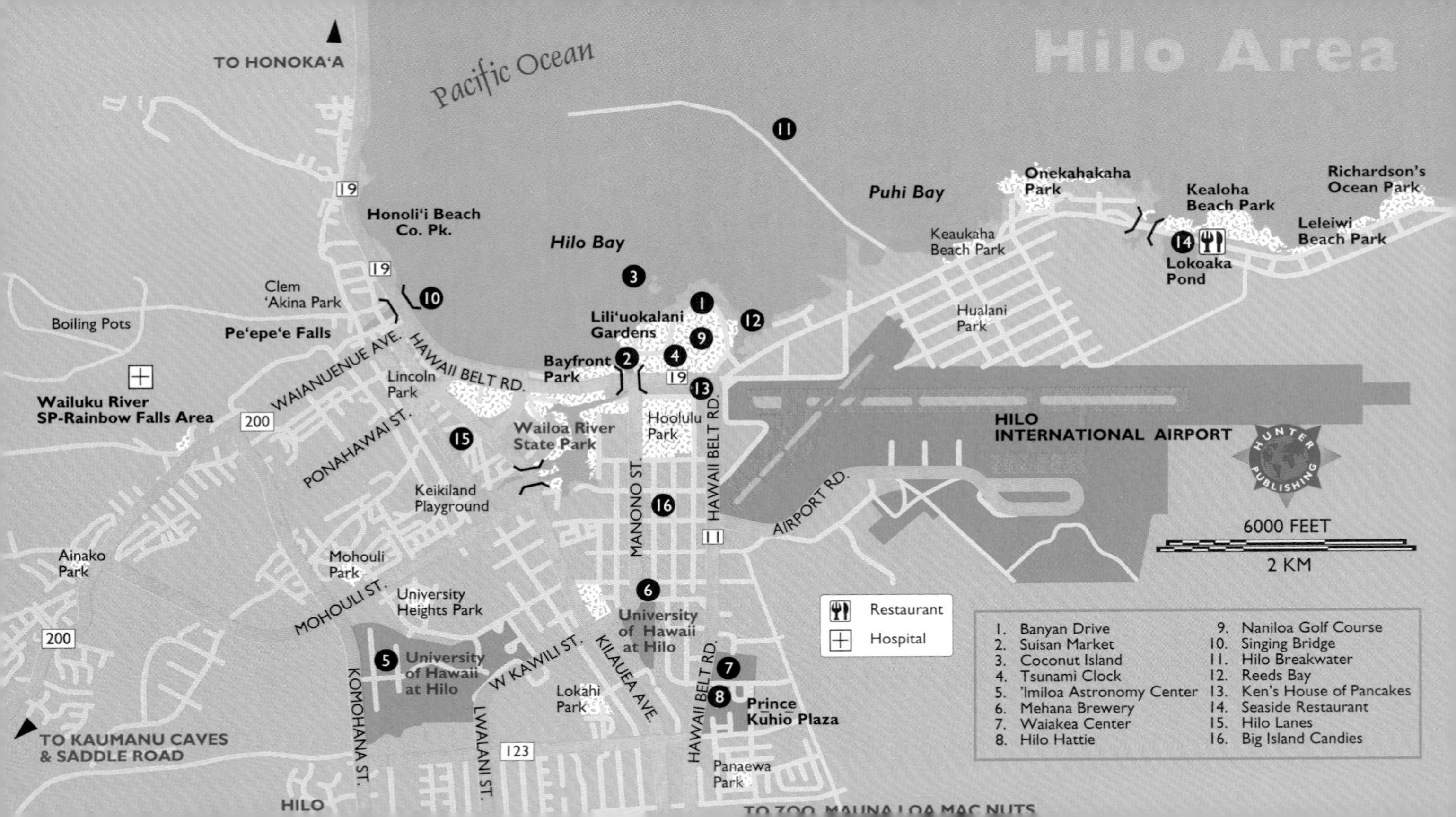

Hilo Area
Pacific Ocean
TO HONOKA'A
Honoli'i Beach Co. Pk.
Hilo Bay
Puhi Bay
Onekahakaha Park
Kealoha Beach Park
Richardson's Ocean Park
Leleiwi Beach Park
Keaukaha Beach Park
Lokoaka Pond
Hualani Park
Clem 'Akina Park
Boiling Pots
Pe'epe'e Falls
Wailuku River SP-Rainbow Falls Area
Lili'uokalani Gardens
Bayfront Park
Lincoln Park
Wailoa River State Park
Hoolulu Park
HILO INTERNATIONAL AIRPORT
HUNTER PUBLISHING
6000 FEET
2 KM
WAIANUENUE AVE.
HAWAII BELT RD.
PONAHAWAI ST.
MANONO ST.
AIRPORT RD.
Keikiland Playground
Ainako Park
Mohouli Park
MOHOULI ST.
University Heights Park
University of Hawaii at Hilo
W KAWILI ST.
KILAUEA AVE.
Lokahi Park
Prince Kuhio Plaza
Panaewa Park
KOMOHANA ST.
LWALANI ST.
TO KAUMANU CAVES & SADDLE ROAD
HILO
TO ZOO, MAUNA LOA MAC NUTS
Restaurant
Hospital
1. Banyan Drive
2. Suisan Market
3. Coconut Island
4. Tsunami Clock
5. 'Imiloa Astronomy Center
6. Mehana Brewery
7. Waiakea Center
8. Hilo Hattie
9. Naniloa Golf Course
10. Singing Bridge
11. Hilo Breakwater
12. Reeds Bay
13. Ken's House of Pancakes
14. Seaside Restaurant
15. Hilo Lanes
16. Big Island Candies

Hilo

IN THIS CHAPTER

Hilo ("HEE-low"), the largest town on the Big Island, is the seat of county government and a major port for Hawaii. But for most people, Hilo is synonymous with rain. Receiving about 130 inches of rain a year and 277 days with rain, Hilo has the dubious honor of being the rainiest city in America. While all this precipitation might seem like a deterrent for some, it has had an incredibly positive impact in shaping the town. The local bumper sticker, "Hilo: Where Rain Reigns," is not a complaint but a badge of pride. For, in addition to creating vibrant, lush foliage and ideal conditions for growing things, the rain has kept development pressures at bay – which has helped keep the cost of living more reasonable as well. Hilo is an authentic Hawaiian town that has retained its soul.

It's also a town of survivors. Hilo has been slammed by more tsunamis than anywhere else in Hawaii, losing many lives, homes and businesses on the crescent-shaped Hilo Bay in 1946 and 1960. Hilo's **Pacific Tsunami Museum** reminds visitors about the past tsunamis while educating them to help prevent future tragedies. The tsunamis also led to the conversion of the bayfront into green space, and its many public parks, like **Lili`uokalani Gardens**, have led to its nickname "City of Gardens."

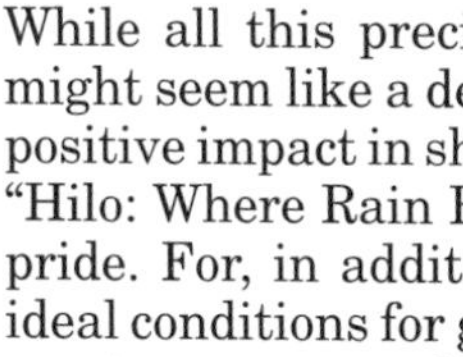

All that rain is great for farmers, too. Hilo and its surrounding area is one of the world's largest producers of orchids, many of them available for purchase at the fantastic **Hilo Farmers Market**,

Banyan Drive

along with other tropical flowers, luscious produce and local goods at ridiculously cheap prices.

When the sun does peek through the clouds, Hilo is glorious. The leaves of trees glisten in the many parks and in the mighty banyan trees along **Banyan Drive**, planted years ago by locals and celebrities like Babe Ruth. The rainforest around the gulches at Boiling Pots in **Wailuku River State Park** sparkles, but the site that benefits the most from the sunshine is **Rainbow Falls**, where rainbows circle the mist in the gulch that surrounds the powerful waterfall. On especially clear days, **Mauna Kea** looms above the town. These are the moments and days when Hilo smiles.

Naturally, Hilo has plenty of indoor activities for rainy days, such as art and cultural centers, performing arts theaters, a dollar movie theater and museums. The newest museum, the $28 million **`Imiloa Astronomy Center of Hawai`i**, has over a hundred hands-on exhibits about astronomy and Hawaiian culture. For a nature-based indoor activity, there's **Kaumana Cave**, formed by an 1881 lava flow that threatened Hilo. And, of course, Hilo has plenty of shopping and wonderful restaurants to distract everyone from the weather. Visitors interested in experiencing "real Hawaii" will want to spend some time in Hilo.

■ Orientation

Located on the east coast of the Big Island, Hilo sits at the edge of the rainy eastern slopes of Mauna Kea. It is accessible via the Hawaiian Belt Road, known as Hwy 19 from the north or Hwy 11 from the south. Hilo can also be reached via the Saddle Road, which splits the high ridge between Mauna Loa and Mauna Kea. The quickest way to Hilo from Kona or the South Kohala

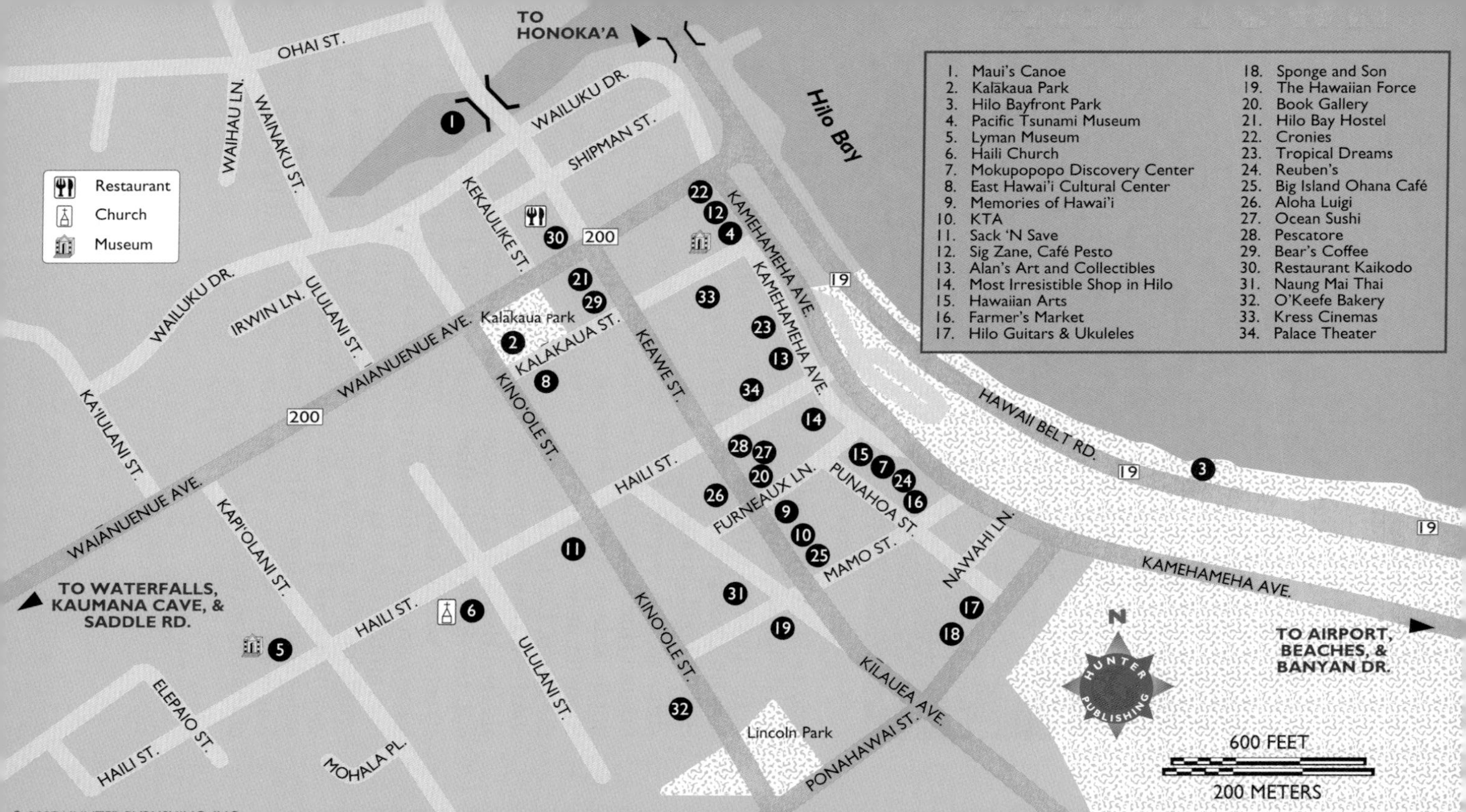

1. Maui's Canoe
2. Kalākaua Park
3. Hilo Bayfront Park
4. Pacific Tsunami Museum
5. Lyman Museum
6. Haili Church
7. Mokupopopo Discovery Center
8. East Hawai'i Cultural Center
9. Memories of Hawai'i
10. KTA
11. Sack 'N Save
12. Sig Zane, Café Pesto
13. Alan's Art and Collectibles
14. Most Irresistible Shop in Hilo
15. Hawaiian Arts
16. Farmer's Market
17. Hilo Guitars & Ukuleles
18. Sponge and Son
19. The Hawaiian Force
20. Book Gallery
21. Hilo Bay Hostel
22. Cronies
23. Tropical Dreams
24. Reuben's
25. Big Island Ohana Café
26. Aloha Luigi
27. Ocean Sushi
28. Pescatore
29. Bear's Coffee
30. Restaurant Kaikodo
31. Naung Mai Thai
32. O'Keefe Bakery
33. Kress Cinemas
34. Palace Theater
Restaurant
Church
Museum
TO HONOKA'A
Hilo Bay
TO WATERFALLS, KAUMANA CAVE, & SADDLE RD.
TO AIRPORT, BEACHES, & BANYAN DR.
OHAI ST.
WAIHAU LN.
WAINAKU ST.
WAILUKU DR.
SHIPMAN ST.
KEKAULIKE ST.
IRWIN LN.
ULULANI ST.
WAIĀNUENUE AVE.
Kalākaua Park
KALĀKAUA ST.
KINO'OLE ST.
KEAWE ST.
KAMEHAMEHA AVE.
HAWAII BELT RD.
HAILI ST.
FURNEAUX LN.
PUNAHOA ST.
MAMO ST.
NAWAHI LN.
KA'IULANI ST.
KAPI'OLANI ST.
ELEPAIO ST.
MOHALA PL.
KĪLAUEA AVE.
PONAHAWAI ST.
Lincoln Park
200
19
N
HUNTER PUBLISHING
600 FEET
200 METERS

Aerial view of Hilo (*Hawaiian Images*)

resorts is either Saddle Road or Hwy 19 via the Hamakua Coast. Locals have their preferences, but it will essentially take the same amount of time. The highway will make you less nauseous than the relentless curves on the east side of Saddle Road, however.

Hilo, with a population of around 45,000 residents, sits around Hilo Bay, with the historic downtown clustered on the north side of town. Generally, downtown is defined by Kamehameha Avenue on the east, Waianuenue Avenue on the north, Kinoole Street on the west and Mamo Street to the south. Wailoa River State Park separates downtown from eastern Hilo due to the tsunamis of 1946 and 1960 that wiped out the buildings in that stretch. Beyond the downtown streets, which follow a basic grid pattern, the rest of Hilo's streets are perpendicular or parallel to the bay. Since the city arcs around the circumference of the bay, this can cause some confusion for newcomers. Essentially, Hwy 19 follows the oceanfront all the way out to Richardson Ocean Park several miles east of town. The belt road resumes on Hwy 11 as Kanoelehua Avenue, which intersects Hwy 19 at Ken's House of Pancakes. Got that?

Hilo Mornings. The prevailing weather pattern in Hilo (and on the rest of the island) is sunshine in the morning, with clouds moving in during the afternoon. So, even if you're a night owl (like us), you might think twice about sleeping too late!

Practicalities

There is only one **area code** for the Big Island: 808.

There are plenty of **ATM** machines around Hilo, including at the First Hawaiian Bank at 120 Wainuenue, Hawaii National Bank next door to the Pacific Tsunami Museum and in the S. Hata Building that contains Café Pesto (where there are also public **restrooms**).

Likewise, **gas stations** abound in Hilo, including the 24-hour Tesoro at the corner of Ponahawai and Kamahameha, the 24-hour Chevron in the Waiakea Center on Hwy 11 and Makaala St Gas in Hilo is cheaper than anything you'll find Kona-side, so fill it to the brim while you're here.

What's in a name? Hilo, literally "to twist," refers to the first night of the Hawaiian lunar calendar, when there is a tiny sliver of moon visible. Many believe that Hilo was named after this moon phase because of its crescent-shaped bay. Others say that King Kamehameha the Great named the town Hilo because during one of his visits there, his servants secured his canoe by twisting *ti* leaves into rope.

The main **police station** is at 349 Kapiolani St. The **Hilo Medical Center** (☎ 808-974-4700) is at 1190 Wainuenue St, close to Rainbow Falls. They have a 24-hour emergency room.

The Hilo downtown **post office**, in the imposing courthouse at 154 Waianuenue Ave, is open 8 am-4 pm Mon-Fri, 12:30-2 pm Sat. The **Hilo Main Post Office**, at 1299 Kekuanaoa St by the airport, is open 8 am-4:30 pm Mon-Fri, 9 am-12:30 pm Sat.

There are public **restrooms** at the **Hilo Public Library** (300 Waianuenue Ave, ☎ 933-8888), which is open 11 am-7 pm Tues-Wed, 9 am-5 pm Thurs and Sat, 10 am-5 pm Fri. The library has brochures about the landmark stones in front of the building (see *Sights*).

Abundant Life Natural Foods (292 Kamehameha Ave, ☎ 935-7411) is a health food store in downtown Hilo that carries not only groceries, bulk food and supplements, but books, cards, candles, ceramics, wooden bowls and other gifts. It is also home to **Natural Foods Café**, dedicated to supporting local and organic food producers. The café has smoothies (many made vegan with soy milk), five kinds of veggie burgers ($6.50), half- and whole sandwiches like pesto grilled cheese ($3.75/$6.50), plus soups salads, bagels and other goodies. It's all good here. The Café is open 8:30 am-5:30 pm Mon, Tues, Thurs, Fri, 7 am-5:30 pm Wed and Sat, 10 am-4 pm Sun. $-$$ Store open until 7 pm daily except 5 pm Sun.

There are several grocery stores in Hilo, including the downtown **Sack 'N Save** (250 Kinoole, ☎ 935-3113), which is open daily from 6 am-11 pm.

KTA Super Store (321 Keawe St, ☎ 935-3751), downtown with ample parking off of Mamo St, is a fully-stocked grocery store, also carrying beer, wine and liquor. Open 7 am-9 pm Mon-Sat, 7 am-7 pm Sun.

Mo`oheau Bus Terminal (329 Kamehameha Ave). The Hele-On intra-island buses stop here, as well as the cruise ship shuttles. They also have an information booth with flyers and a staff. Most importantly, there are fairly well maintained public restrooms, though sometimes unsavory characters linger in the vicinity.

YOGA & MASSAGE

A wander through downtown Hilo makes it pretty clear that Hilo is the center of these practices on the Big Island; every third window seems to advertise massage services. Whether you are interested in becoming a yogi yourself, or simply having your muscles massaged, Hilo is a great place to try it. And it's certainly more affordable than the resort spas located Kona-side.

■ Sights

"Suffering makes you deep. Travel makes you broad. In case I get my pick, I'd rather travel." – Judith Viorst

Even if you aren't staying at one of the many hotels on Banyan Drive, you'll want to check out the beautiful street lined with majestic banyan trees. At the base of the trees, there are signs noting who planted each tree and when; Amelia Earhart planted her tree on January 6, 1935. At the start of the drive

Banyan tree

heading east, you'll notice a few trees that don't have the usual brown wooden signs – one of them has a special plaque created by the County of Hawaii to honor Franklin Delano Roosevelt, who planted his tree July 25, 1934 (Richard Nixon's 1962 planting just has the standard wooden sign).

Banyan Trees

It may look like the Indian banyan trees on Banyan Drive (and elsewhere around the Islands) have vines hanging from them, but they are actually aerial roots. When the roots make contact with the ground, they grow into the earth, creating supportive trunks so that the tree can continue to spread. One of the world's broadest spreading trees, there is a legend that Alexander the Great once camped under a banyan tree that sheltered his army of 7,000 men.

Naha and Pinao Stones (300 Waianuenue Ave). On the lawn of the Hilo Public Library sit two large stones. The larger of the two, lying horizontally, is the Naha Stone. The 3½-ton stone is said to have been brought to Hilo in a canoe by the chief of Kaua`i and was used to determine royal heirs: young males were placed on the stone and those that sat quietly were considered royalty, while those that cried were denied the royal claim. King Kamehameha is said to have overturned the Naha Stone, proving the prophecies that he would one day conquer all of the islands. The smaller stone is thought to be the original entrance pillar to the Pinao Temple where the Naha Stone was kept. A brochure with more information about the stones is available at the front desk in the library.

Naha and Pinao Stones

Maui's Canoe. Legend holds that the demigod

Maui was traveling while his mother, Hina, who lived in the huge cave (still visible today) behind Rainbow Falls, rebuked her suitor. The suitor reacted by damming the river beneath the falls in an attempt to drown her in revenge. Maui came to her rescue in his canoe, and came ashore with such force that his canoe was forever jammed into the rocks of the Wailuku River. He saved his mother, and the curious can see his canoe from the bridge across the river on the northern end of Keawe St. Look upstream and you'll see the canoe-shaped rock wedged into the rapids.

Kalakaua Park. Located on the corner of Waianuenue and Kinoole, Kalakaua Park is named after the Merrie Monarch, who was a frequent visitor to Hilo. A statue of the king was dedicated in 1988 and stands below a huge banyan tree. The small park also contains a reflecting pool and marble war memorial containing names of locals killed in World War II, Korea and Vietnam. In the southwest corner of the park sits a sundial with a faded inscription on it. Standing in the pouring Hilo rain, struggling to make out the inscription, we've wondered what in the world Hilo needs a *sundial* for anyway. For the record, it says, "This sundial was erected in the Fourth Year of the reign of King Kalakaua, AD 1877, Hilo, Hawaii."

"Hula is the language of the heart, and therefore the heartbeat of the Hawaiian people." –

THE MERRIE MONARCH

King David Kalakaua

King David Kalakaua (reigned 1874-1891) was the final king of the Hawaiian Kingdom, and during his time he became the first king to sail around the world, fought against foreign interests in Hawaii, and was responsible for the resurgence of hula, which had been banned by missionaries in the 1820s. He was known as the Merrie Monarch for the joy he took in the arts. Known as the "Olympics" of Hula, Hilo's Merrie Monarch Festival is named in honor of King Kalakaua.

Hilo Bayfront Park. Even if it's raining, it's pleasant to stroll through Hilo Bayfront Park, past the black sand beach, canoe houses for various local canoe clubs, palm, monkeypod and ironwood trees, gazing at the surf. Airplanes landing at the airport can pass really close overhead. FYI, the public restrooms are in the powder blue structure near many of the canoe houses.

Monkeypod tree in Hilo Bayfront Park

Suisan Fish Market

Suisan Fish Market (85 Lihiwai St, ☎ 935-9349, www.suisan.com/market). This picturesque fish market on Hilo Bay at the mouth of the Wailoa River has been operating since 1907. The famous early morning fish auction no longer takes place here, but inside they still sell fresh whole fish and fish cuts, as well as a wide array of seafood concoctions, including several types of *poke* (raw fish salad), kimchee, smoked marlin and other assorted sea foods. The selection is generally best earlier in the day, as many locals frequent the market and snatch up whatever looks good. You can have your fresh fish fried up at the adjacent café, then take a short wander over to Lili`uokalani Park for a picnic. Open 8 am-5 pm Mon-Sat.

Lili`uokalani Gardens (BIVB)

**Lili`uokalani Gardens**. Just past the Suisan Fish Market, you'll find a beautifully manicured park named for Queen Lili`uokalani, the last reigning monarch of the Kingdom of Hawaii. On the bay, Lili`uokalani Gardens has picturesque bridges over duck ponds, mini-pagodas, benches and picnic tables. There are many artifacts in the park that are gifts from Japanese people to the residents of Hilo. For instance, there are boats near the tea room that were donated by the people of Nago City, Okinawa to the people of Hilo "to bridge the friendship" between them. Many current residents of Hilo, as well as those who lived in Shinmachi, the section of Hilo that was destroyed by the 1960 tsunami, are of Japanese descent.

Coconut Island (BIVB)

Coconut Island. There is a pedestrian bridge leading from Lili`uokalani Gardens over part of Hilo Bay to little Coconut Island, which has great views of downtown Hilo across the bay. There is a notable palm tree with markers showing water levels for different tsunamis that rolled over Hilo.

Coconut Island (Hawaiian Images)

Hilo is called the "**City of Gardens**" because so many residential areas on the waterfront were converted to green space after the 1960 tsunami killed 61 people. Hilo also lost 96 people to the devastating 1946 tsunami. For safety reasons, homes are now built farther from the shoreline.

Wailoa River State Park. This is a grassy park that stands out because of its arched bridges and several important sights. A sign marks the site of Shinmachi, a largely Japanese settlement that was hard-hit by the 1960 tsunami. There is an eternal flame burning at the **Hawai`i County Vietnam Memorial**, where palm trees are planted above wreathed plaques for local veterans. The **Wailoa Center** (open 8:30 am-4:30 pm Mon, Tues, Thurs, Fri, 12-4:30 pm Wed) exhibits local art, such as woodwork (admission is free). A gilded statue of King Kamehameha is a tribute to the Hawaiian monarch who united the Islands under his rule.

Waiakea Social Settlement Clock. This clock, located *makai* on Kamehameha just east of Manono St, was the only landmark that withstood the 1960 tsunami. Its hands point to 1:04 (am), the time the tidal wave struck (though a plaque there claims they point to 1:05). On a recent visit, a wizened man was working diligently to remove weeds around the base of the clock. He told us that he was 38 when the tsunami swept through the neighborhood. "I lost my father to the tidal wave," he said before returning to his labor of love.

Pacific Tsunami Museum (130 Kamehameha Ave, ☎ 935-0926, www.tsunami.org). Any place brimming with docents who can relate harrowing stories of how they narrowly cheated death when giant waves destroyed their town can inspire even the most reluctant museum-goer. The exhibits here include pictures of the massive destruction tsunamis have inflicted on Hilo town and the Big Island over the years, as well as an impressive number of videotaped interviews with survivors, some heroic and inspiring, others poignant and heart-rending. The museum is in an old bank building with solid concrete walls and a bank vault theater which has survived tsunamis itself. This may help comfort you while you are taking in the exhibits and your eye wanders out the door and across the street to where waves are exploding high over the bay-front breakwall.

Hilo has sustained more tsunami damage than any other area of the Hawaiian Islands. For the first 65 years of the 20th century, Hilo experienced tsunamis of over one meter/3.28 feet every five years on average. The tsunamis of 1946 and 1960 destroyed much of the town and killed 157 people. Those lovely green parks in central Hilo used to be bustling urban centers, destroyed completely by the two devastating events. The museum is open 9 am-4 pm Mon-Sat. General admission is $7, seniors $6, students $2, children five and under are free.

The bright yellow **tsunami sirens** that you see on the Big Island and throughout the state are tested at 11 am on the first working day of each month. So if you hear sirens wailing at that exact time, don't panic – though you may want to check the radio or TV to make sure it is just a test. If you hear a siren any other time, feel an earthquake while on the beach, or see the water suddenly recede, immediately head inland to higher ground. Surfers should not attempt to surf the tidal wave, which doesn't break like a normal wave.

Lyman Museum and Mission House (276 Haili St, ☎ 935-5021, www.lymanmuseum.org), a Smithsonian affiliate, is the kind of place made for grade school field trips (we've toured it with 60 students, as a matter of fact). The museum started with the Mission House, the home of New England missionaries David and Sarah Lyman, which was built in 1839. If you're interested in old houses, take a tour (the only way to

The Mission House

get inside) at 10, 11 am, 1, 2 or 3 pm.

The adjacent Lyman Museum was essentially built to showcase David Lyman's extensive shell collection. It's an impressive display that also includes a number of sparkly minerals, some of which are illuminated by a black light in the "glow in the dark minerals" exhibit. Other parts of the museum educate visitors about the ecology and culture of Hawaii. One room has dioramas of different climactic zones and the plants and animals you'll see there. Another houses artifacts of some of the cultures that contributed to Hawaii, with dresses from the Philippines, Chinese flu remedies and so on. You can watch a fascinating video about a lava flow that covered a Big Island town in the 1980s called "Kalapana: Death of a Hawaiian Village." You can spend plenty of time here on a rainy day. Open 9:30 am-4:30 pm Mon-Sat, general admission $10, seniors $8, kids six-17 $3, students $5.

Ho `ona `auau. "Gain wisdom."
– sign at the Mokupapapa Discovery Center

Mokupapapa Discovery Center (308 Kamehameha, ☎ 933-8195, www.hawaiireef.noaa.gov/center, 9 am-4 pm Tues-Sat). Right on the main drag of downtown Hilo, the Mokupapapa Discovery Center has displays about remote coral reefs in the Northwestern Hawaiian Islands, which few people ever see. Signs, written in English and Hawaiian, inform visitors of facts like this one: there are five times as many fish on the remote reefs than around the main Hawaiian Islands. Yeah! If you have any love of the inhabitants of the ocean, you will probably want to quit your job and become a researcher there.

There are a few tactile exhibits that will delight kids, like the simulated Pisces submersible (which can plunge to 6,000 feet below the surface), where visitors can try to pick up rock samples with robotic arms, like scientists do. It's hard! There's also a small aquarium with tropical fish, and a non-narrated video of fish, turtles, seals, sharks and dolphins set to soothing music. It's hard to believe it's free!

The Haili Congregational Church, which was founded by the Lymans, is noted by a tourism marker on Haili Street because it was founded in 1824. The **Haili Church Choir** is one of the oldest and most widely acclaimed church choirs in Hawaii, and was inducted into the Hawaiian Music Hall of Fame. There are 11 am Sunday services. The pink church diagonally across the street is **St Joseph's**, a Catholic church with beautiful stained glass windows that was built in 1919.

`Imiloa Astronomy Center of Hawai`i (600 Imiloa Place, ☎ 969-9700, www.imiloahawaii.org). If you're wondering what the three metal (titanium) cones are that loom above the UH-Hilo campus, you've spotted `Imiloa, a $28 million complex that opened in February of 2006. Funded primarily by NASA, `Imiloa ("Exploring new knowledge") has the admirable goal of educating the public about "the connections between the rich traditions of Hawaiian culture and the groundbreaking astronomical research conducted at the summit of Maunakea." (Note: Maunakea is the original spelling of Mauna Kea.)

To achieve this goal, the 40,000-square-foot complex has a planetarium, 3-D movie (sit in the front row while you "explore space"), videos and interactive exhibits. Everything is translated into English and Hawaiian. The scope is a little overwhelming. There is a video presentation that you won't want to miss. The Planetarium show is another must-see – plan your visit around when the show will take place (they are fiddling with show times at the moment).

There are a lot of astronomy exhibits with things for kids to touch – you know this will be a major stop on the school field trip circuit (another goal of `Imiloa is to inspire Hawaiian children to pursue careers in science). We found the key is to hold down some of the buttons until the display starts working. Ask a volunteer for help if you have any questions. There are some goofy "rides," like the cosmic taxi ride with a driver who speaks with a Pidgin inflection and jokes that he drove too close to the moon and put a new crater in it. Fun! To mirror the astronomy exhibits, there is a lot of information about Polynesian navigation, which is guided by nature rather than mechanized instruments. You can spend some time here. Admission $14.50, kids four-12 $7.50, children under four free. To get here from downtown Hilo, head *mauka* on Wainuenue Ave for a mile, then turn left on Komahana St Proceed for about 1.5 miles, then turn left at Nowelo St Parking can be found at the second left. Open 9 am-4 pm Tues-Sun.

"I have no special talents. I am only passionately curious."
– Albert Einstein

■ Where to Shop

First Fridays: On the first Friday of each month in Hilo, many downtown shops, museums and restaurants are open later than usual, with special incentives such as sales, live music and other entertainment.

AUTHOR'S CHOICE ★ **Basically Books** (160 Kamehameha Ave, ☎ 800-903-MAPS, www.basicallybooks.com) carries a lot more than books, though there are plenty of those, particularly about Hawaii and travel. There are tons of quality maps for Big Island areas, as well as booklights, compasses, key chains, magnets, journals, cards, lighters, soaps, lotions, tiles, garden stakes, calendars, shell necklaces, bookmarks, swizzle sticks, trays, umbrellas (with fun designs like a giant sunflower), stickers, CDs, kids' puzzles and globes. As one local said, "It's where I go to buy gifts to send to my sister in Texas, something more unusual than what you'd find at Wal-Mart or Longs." The owners also own Petroglyph Press, in the back of the store, which is a printing center where customers can make copies and fax. Open 9 am-5 pm Mon-Sat, 10 am-4 pm Sun.

Orchidland Surf Shop (262 Kamehameha Ave, ☎ 935-1533, www.orchidlandsurf.com), open since 1972, is a great surf shop packed with apparel and boards. For rash guards, board shorts or t-shirts, this is the place. They have a selection of new and used boards in the back of the store, and rent boards for $20 a day. Open 9 am-5 pm Mon-Thurs, Sat, 9 am-6 pm Fri, 10 am-3 pm Sun.

Touched by Angels (300 Kamehameha Ave, ☎ 969-9915) sells a variety of unique gifts, particularly the gorgeous, locally made *koa* canes carved into spirals. There are New Age gifts such as dream catchers and rocks, and birthday cards that tell you what the day of your birth means (people born on the 24th are characterized by integrity, and on the 2nd by harmony, apparently a sign that you can trust your authors!). Kids (and a few soccer moms we know) will enjoy the large selection of Ty stuffed animals, and kids may want to shell out for a real shark tooth. Open 10 am-5 pm Mon-Sat, 11 am-3 pm Sun.

The Grove Gallery (302 Kamehameha Ave, ☎ 961-4420, toll free ☎ 866-657-0400, www.thegrovegallery.com). Home to quality local art such as paintings, photography, *koa* carvings, jewelry and Hawaiian quilts, The Grove Gallery also caters to shoppers looking for souvenirs like t-shirts made from bamboo and whimsical clocks with the numbers in a jumble at the base and the slogan, "Who cares?" Definitely worth a look. Open 10 am-5 pm daily, closing at 3 pm Sun.

Book Gallery (259 Keawe St, ☎ 935-4943), with a nice selection of Hawaiian travel guides and Hawaiian-related books, is another fine resource for literature in Hilo. They also carry a hefty amount of children's books and toys, making this an excellent stop if your little one is getting a little antsy with all the rain pounding on the windshield. They have parking around back so you don't have to parallel park on Keawe St. Open 9 am-5 pm Mon-Fri, 9 am-3 pm Sat.

AUTHOR'S CHOICE **Hilo Farmers Market** (www.hilofarmersmarket.com). Each Wednesday and Saturday "from dawn till done," the tarped area at the corner of Mamo Street and Kamahameha Avenue explodes with color for the Hilo Farmers Market. This is one of the best farmers' markets we've ever seen. There is so much beautiful, locally grown produce sold for ridiculously cheap prices – four papayas for a dollar?!? – and great deals on tropical plants and flowers like orchids, proteas, bird of paradise and anthurium, as well as *lei*. There are other vendors interspersed, selling baked goods, tamales, Thai iced tea, smoothies and macadamia nuts.

Flowers are cheap at the Farmers Market

Across the street, the market is more like a flea market, with clothing, hand-beaded jewelry, bags, tarot readers, *koa* bowls, sarongs, pickled mango, sauces, kava, raw honey, and war clubs adorned with sharks' teeth. Locals know a good thing when they see it, so the paths between the stalls are packed with shoppers. Over 120 vendors sell their wares here – the place is hopping!

The big days are Wednesday and Saturday, but some of the produce and flower vendors are here daily, in case you visit on an off-day. There are other shops near the market selling t-shirts, woven hats and mats.

AUTHOR'S CHOICE **Sig Zane Designs** (122 Kamehameha Ave, ☎ 935-7077, www.sigzane.com). Sig has been designing clothes in Hilo since the mid-'70s, and he's approaching mastery of the art of alohawear. Each garment has a native Hawaiian plant worked into the design to achieve their goal of honoring the land and culture of the Big Island of Hawaii. These aren't throwaway *luau* shirts, but skillfully

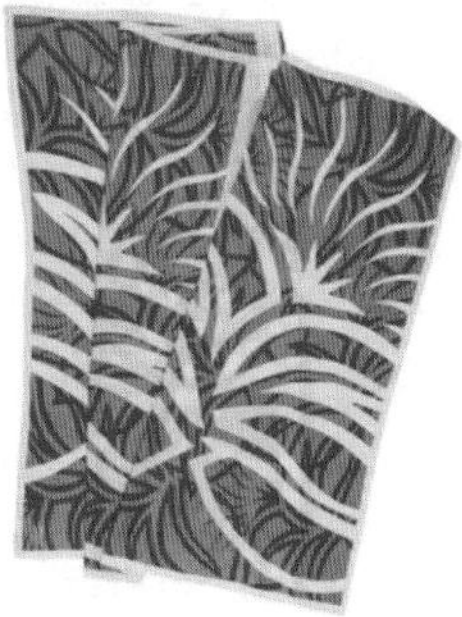

Sig Zane pareu

designed and produced apparel of premium price and quality. Open 9:30 am-5 pm Mon-Fri, 9 am-4 pm Sat.

Hilo Guitars & Ukuleles (56 Ponahawai St, ☎ 935-4282, www.hiloguitars.com), as the name implies, sells the stringed instruments, and a large selection at that. They also carry a few other instruments like violins, banjos, and mandolins. Even if you don't play, you can appreciate their beauty. Open 10 am-5 pm Mon-Fri, 10 am-4 pm Sat.

Ka Huina Gallery (128 Kilauea Ave, ☎ 935-4420, www.kahuina.org). There is some really cool art at the Ka Huina Gallery, an art and music co-op where nine local artists with diverse styles and backgrounds pitch in for rent to display their unusual paintings, mirrors, murals and other work, and discuss art with interested visitors. Located at the intersection with Mamo, this is also a place to come on Friday nights for poetry readings that start at 7 pm and are sometimes followed by live music. Open 10 am-4 pm Mon-Sat and some Sundays.

AUTHOR'S CHOICE ★ **Hilo Surfboard Co.** (84 Ponahawai St, ☎ 895-1489, www.hilosurfboardco.com) is a store with a cool motto: *E he`enalu me ka ho`ihi*, which means "Surf with respect." The owner Scott conscientiously carries boards by major shapers as well as local ones, with a variety of prices to keep locals happy. They also offer board repair. If you're looking to buy a board in Hawaii, be sure to check this place out. Open 10 am-5 pm Mon-Sat, until 3 pm Sun.

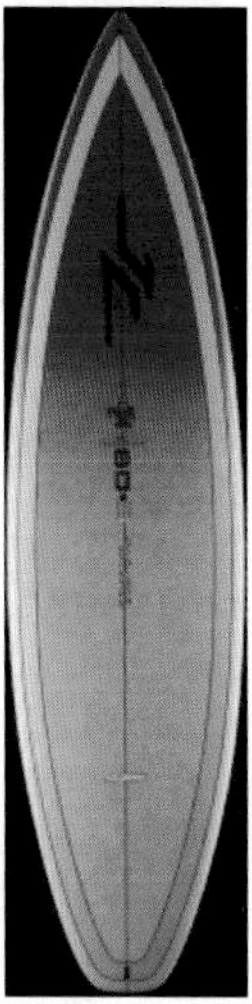

Mehana Brewery (275 E. Kawili Street, ☎ 934-8211, www.mehana.com) is Hilo's only microbrewery. These are the folks that brew special beers for the Roy's restaurant chain. There is a small tasting room where you can decide for yourself if Hilo water does indeed make better tasting beer. Hops snobs may not be impressed, but if you're after clean, crisp beer, drink up. You can buy six packs here, as well as t-shirts, hats, pint glasses and other Mehana merchandise. You may find yourself wishing they had an actual pub so you could drink a pint and munch on nachos (hint, hint). To get here from downtown Hilo, follow Kamehameha Ave east past Wailoa River State Park, and turn right on Manono St, just over the Wailoa River bridge. Follow Manono St for 1.1 miles and take a left on East Kawili St. The brewery will be a half-block on the right. The tasting room is open from 9ish until 5:30 pm Mon-Sat.

"Beer is proof that God loves us and wants us to be happy."
– Benjamin Franklin

Waiakea Center (northern corner of Hwy 11 and Makaala St) is a strip mall with a 24-hour gas station as well as **Office Max**, **Wal-Mart**, **Ross**, a food court (see the outstanding Hilo Bay Café in *Where to Eat*), **Borders** (☎ 933-1410, open 9 am-9 pm Sun-Thurs, 9 am-10 pm Fri- Sat) and **Island Naturals Market and Deli** (☎ 935-5533, open 8 am-8 pm Mon-Sat, 9 am-7 pm Sun), a natural food grocery store that also sells sandwiches, salads and smoothies. Hilo Hattie is prominently located on the street in front of the mall.

Hilo Hattie (111 East Puainako St, ☎ 961-3077, www.hilohattie.com) bills itself as "The Store of Hawaii," and it definitely has a presence on all four of the main islands. Started in 1963, Hilo Hattie has grown into the world's largest manufacturer of "Hawaiian and Island lifestyle products" (though check the label – your aloha shirt was actually manufactured in Asia). It's famously cheesy, but loved for the greeters who welcome guests to the store by placing a free *puka* shell necklace around their necks. This is kitsch at its finest. We bought matching tacky, hot pink aloha outfits and fake leis here to wear for Halloween on the mainland and have made a lot of people chuckle when so costumed. There are some more tasteful clothes, as well as mugs, plastic pineapple pitchers, video postcards, books, and all kinds of souvenirs. Open 8:30 am-6 pm daily, including holidays.

Prince Kuhio Plaza (southern corner of Hwy 11 and Makaala St) is Hilo's indoor mall, complete with a movie theater (**Prince Kuhio Stadium Cinemas**, show times at ☎ 961-FILM), ATM machines, food court and tons of national retail shops like **Payless**, **GNC** and **Radio Shack**. There's a small video arcade called Tilt, and one food stand definitely worth visiting: **Maui Tacos**. The mall is open 10 am-9 pm Mon-Fri, 9:30 am-7 pm Sat, 10 am-6 pm Sun.

Info on many more shops in Hilo is online at www.bigislandadventureguide.com.

Adventures

On the Beach

Chances are that you aren't in Hilo for the beaches, but east of town, there are plenty of beach parks along a four-mile stretch of road with "shoreline access" signs pointing toward the ocean, and "evacuation route" signs pointing away from it. Even if you aren't up for a swim, you may want to picnic at one of the parks.

KID FRIENDLY **Onakahakaha Beach Park** is Hilo's beach park for kids, with an enhanced breakwall for protected swimming and a lifeguard just in case. This is a big picnic beach, with pavilions for just that purpose, restrooms, showers and kids hollering, "Auntie! Uncle!" An added bonus of the park is that it's close by Hilo Homemade Ice Cream – just head east toward Kealoha Beach Park and stop in for the creamy treat everyone loves.

"Our greatest natural resource is the minds of our children."
– Walt Disney

Kealoha Beach Park

This beach park's location, across from the Seaside Restaurant, was pounded by the 1946 tsunami. These days you'll find *honu* (green sea turtles) swimming and basking here – as always, remember to stay at least 15 feet away from them. There is a yellow ladder that leads to protected snorkeling with a white sand bottom, so you might get a chance to see the *honu* while you're swimming, which is always a rush. There is a lifeguard stand, restrooms, and a covered picnic area here.

Dela Cruz Shave Ice Truck plies the beach parks along this stretch, offering cold refreshment to beachgoers in need. In addition to shave ice (or "ice shave," as it's sometimes called in Hilo), the truck carries ice cream, candy, chips, hot dogs, saimin and 60¢ pork hash.

Lele`iwi Beach Park

Lele`iwi Beach Park (www.shorediving.com)

There are lots of fishponds at the scenic Lele`iwi Beach Park, as well as lava rock outcroppings and signs to beware of falling coconuts. There are covered picnic tables here. If you have your dive gear and conditions permit (no swell or heavy rain), this is a good spot for a shore dive. The park's gate is open 7 am-8 pm.

Richardson Ocean Park

Richardson Ocean Park (www.shorediving.com)

Richardson is renowned for having the best snorkeling in Hilo. It consists of a small black sand beach in a grove of coconut palms and *hala* trees. The police outpost for the "Aquatics Division" is here, as well as public restrooms, showers and a lifeguard. This is a good body boarding or surf spot during high surf advisories.

Surfing

"Only those who will risk going too far can possibly find out how far one can go." – T.S. Eliot

Surfing is big in Hilo, not just in terms of popularity but also due to the giant winter swells. The steady northwesterly trade winds create huge surf that the locals eat up like so much *poi*.

Honoli`i

Honoli`i

We hope we won't be pummeled by Hilo surfers for pointing out this surfing hot spot. When the surf's up, surfers and spongers flock to Honoli`i even if it's pouring down rain! There is a great vantage point at the top of the stairs leading down to the black sand beach, where a cold river flows into the ocean. (Paddle out fast to the warmer salt water!) This is a gorgeous spot with a long line of parked cars.

SURF LEGEND: EDDIE AIKAU

The phrase "Eddie would go" appears on bumper stickers and is used by big-wave surfers as a testament to Eddie Aikau, a Hawaiian surfer and Oahu lifeguard known for his skills in the water, and confidence in them – the surf might be huge, but Eddie would go. He died in March of 1978 during the second voyage of the canoe Hokule`a, when it capsized and he tried to save his crewmates by paddling on his surfboard for help. The crew survived, but Eddie was never seen again. His legendary status was immortalized in the book *Eddie Would Go*, by Stuart Holmes Coleman.

There are a lot of breaks here that allow different levels of surfers to share a large expanse of waves. You'll see spongers (body boarders), grommets (short boarders), *wahine* (females) and long boarders coexisting in a rare display of socialism. Of course, it's probably just because there's enough real estate here to keep them off of each other's waves.

To get here, head north towards the Hamakua Coast and turn *mauka* after a few miles at Nahala Street. Then turn left at the T on Kahoa. **Important note:** Drive slowly – this road is narrow and to exit, locals often drive out in reverse.

Bayfront

From the north end of the Bayfront Highway you can watch locals tackle monstrous waves from shore. When it's really raining, you can barely make them out as they battle the rollers like dark ghosts in the fog. They enter right by the Singing Bridge where the Wailuku River meets the bay. It gets murky here after a downpour (read: often) which is when sharks like to come to the river mouths to feed on scraps that are washed out to sea. Locals say that hammerhead sharks breed in the bay, too. When we asked one local surfer how he deals with this threat while surfing here, he shrugged and said, "I just try not to think about it." Okay.

Diving

Nautilus Dive Center (382 Kamehameha Ave, ☎ 935-6939, www.nautilusdivehilo.com). Hilo-side doesn't have the incredible visibility for diving that Kona-side does, but there are still plenty of swim-throughs, fish and turtles out there if you want to scuba dive. You can rent gear with Nautilus Dive Center, or head out with them for shore or boat dives. They also offer certification classes and repair services, and rent snorkel gear ($6/day), wetsuits ($10/day) and boogie boards ($8/day). Open 9 am-4 pm Mon-Sat.

> **Warning:** If you plan to dive in Hilo, you should keep in mind that many locals and dive instructors Kona-side warn against it, because of the dangerous downcurrents. You'll need to be an experienced diver, and stay alert.

On the Links

Naniloa Golf Course (120 Banyan Drive, ☎ 935-3000, www.naniloaresort.com/golf.htm, 9 holes $25, 18 holes $45, carts extra). This place was shut down temporarily as the new owner of the Naniloa Resort debated what to do with it. It is scheduled to reopen again soon with a renovated club house. The course is green enough, thanks to the Hilo rain, and the design is straightforward. At the time of writing, bunkers were full of grass and the course needed some TLC. The Naniloa Volcanoes Resort website says there are 18 holes here, but there are really only nine. You will need to play the course twice to achieve a full round. You're better off at the Muni.

Hilo Municipal Golf Course (340 Haihai St, ☎ 959-7711, $29 weekdays, $34 weekends). Referred to by locals as "the Muni" and owned and maintained by the county, this is an impressive local course that's just right for the average player. The course has no sand, but there's a lot of water and the setting of the course up above Hilo is just lovely. The fairways can get muddy after it rains, but that also makes it easier to hold the elevated greens. There's also a lighted driving range here which is open until 8:30 pm. Greens fees are good for all-day play. Carts are extra.

In the Air

Several companies offer helicopter flights that depart Hilo Airport and fly over Hawai`i Volcanoes National Park to the eruption at Pu`u O`o and the area where its lava flows into the ocean. This is a spectacular experience – a bird's eye view of an erupting volcano provides a thunderbolt of adrenaline. And there's no other way to see it.

There are often discounts for booking online through the company websites.

AUTHOR'S CHOICE ★ **Blue Hawaiian Helicopters** (☎ 961-5600, toll free ☎ 800-786-BLUE, www.bluehawaiian.com). Safety and the quality of vehicle maintenance are particularly important for tours involving helicopters, so you'll probably want to fly with the best. In this case, it's Blue Hawaiian. The company has multiple tours on the Big Island as well as Maui and Kaua`i, has received numerous awards for its safety and technician standards, and is the choice of film crews for movies like *Jurassic Park*. Pilots are often decorated veterans of the military.

Each helicopter seats six people, and they'll weigh you when you check-in at the airport to plot the flight's weight distribution (there's a "comfort seat charge" if you weigh over 250 pounds). After a safety briefing, you board the helicopter and put on headphones that not only minimize the noise from the rotors but enable you to hear the commentary from the pilot. You won't hear a word as you buzz around the Pu`u O`o vent, gaping at the bubbling pots of lava and swirling clouds of gas. We thought it was worth every penny. The "Circle of Fire plus Waterfalls" tour is 45-50 minutes and costs $198 a person.

Paradise Helicopters (☎ 969-7392, www.paradisecopters.com). The company's claim to fame is that they have two-way communications between the pilot and passengers, so that you can ask questions while you're in the air. There is the option to upgrade to the "Doors-Off Experience," which involves removing the helicopter doors so that passengers can feel the heat of the eruption. The "Doors-Off Experience" lasts 50 minutes and costs $212; the standard "Volcano and Waterfall Tour" also lasts 50 minutes but costs $175. Prices include tax.

Note: Scuba divers should remember to wait 24 hours from their last dive before taking a helicopter tour.

Sunshine Helicopters (☎ 882-1223, toll free ☎ 800-622-3144, www.sunshinehelicopters.com) has been offering helicopter tours since 1985. The owners, Ross and Anna Scott, are self-described "army brats" who met in high school and married soon after. Ross is a decorated Vietnam veteran who was a senior pilot and platoon leader by the age of 25. Their "Formations of Pele" tour lasts 50 minutes and costs $190.

Photography Tip: Taking pictures through a reflective window of a helicopter can be a frustrating experience. Darker clothing will cause less reflection, though you might need long sleeves! Your best option is to hold the camera as close as possible to the window.

Where to Stay

The truth is, there is no really nice hotel in Hilo. Banyan Drive, the waterfront hotel hub, could be much improved with some massive renovations... but it would take a lot of time and money to bring these places up to speed. You won't find the resort atmosphere you might expect if you've stayed in South Kohala or Kona. You might not even find an elevator. So try to think of Hilo hotels as economical accommodation, or opt for a B&B. We've included a few here. For more options, visit www.stayhawaii.com.

See page 65 for an explanation of the hotel $ price codes.

Hilo Bay Hostel lobby

Hilo Bay Hostel (101 Waianuenue Ave, ☎ 933-2771, www.hawaiihostel.net, 11 rooms for up to 50 people, $20 dorm beds, $50-$60 private rooms). We've stayed lots of times at this inviting hostel with a prime location in downtown Hilo, in the historic 1911 Burns Building. Rooms are situated around a central common area with hardwood floors and warm wood accents, a TV, info boards and computers where the public can surf the Internet for $5/hour. There's a common kitchen and a downstairs "garden patio" with tables and chairs for socializing near the colorful murals and potted plants. Rooms have high ceilings and fans. $

Aerial view of Arnott's

Arnott's (98 Apapane Road, ☎ 969-7097, www.arnotts-lodge.com, dorm $20, rooms $42-$67, can accommodate "at least 100 people"). Arnott's is a backpacker hostel, with shuttles to downtown, free bicycle use, inexpensive tours to places like Volcanoes (available at a higher rate to the public), and bonuses like a free pizza and beer party on Saturday nights. There are shared kitchens in the male and female dorm areas, and a co-ed dorm. There's also a tented area with lots of tables to hang out and talk story. There's a lawn area where guests can pitch a tent for $10 per person. $

GOOD VALUE ★ **Dolphin Bay Hotel** (333 Iliahi St, ☎ 935-1466, toll free ☎ 877-935-1466, www.dolphinbayhotel.com, 18 rooms, $89-$129) is a motel-style hotel, but it's clean, with a friendly staff and an amazing garden on the property with a little stream and a gravel trail through lush foliage; as a sign warns, "Caution! Falling Breadfruit!" This is an ideal base for Adventure Guide readers who want an affordable place to crash each night after exploring Volcanoes or the Hamakua Coast. There is a light breakfast of coffee, fruit and pastries served "until everyone's gone." This place has a lot of return guests. $$

Dolphin Bay Hotel

AUTHOR'S CHOICE ★ **Bay House B&B** (42 Pukihae St., ☎ 961-6311, toll free ☎ 888-235-8195, www.bayhousehawaii.com, three rooms, $120) is run by a super-friendly couple, Tina and Tom. They met in Costa Rica when she was in the Peace Corps and he was in medical school. They opened their bed and breakfast in 1997, with a lanai from which you can see and hear the surf of Hilo Bay, and a hot tub that overlooks the water. Rooms have Hawaiian quilts on the beds, TVs, plants, and wood floors and furnishings. Continental breakfast includes baked items, cereals, hard boiled eggs, fruit, and juice. There is no minimum night stay. This is a great deal. $$

Bay House B&B

Naniloa Volcanoes Resort

Naniloa Volcanoes Resort (93 Banyan Dr, ☎ 969-3333, toll free ☎ 800-367-5360, www.naniloaresort.com, 325 rooms, $105-$230, suites $500-$800). Built in the '60s as a premier resort, and located on a spectacular piece of prime real estate, it's hard to imagine a more complete fall from grace. Dilapidated, dingy and unattractive, the only real hope this "resort" has is that the new owner is required by the terms of the purchase to invest $5 million over the next three years to renovate the place. $$-$$$$

Hilo Seaside

Hilo Seaside Hotel (126 Banyan Drive, ☎ 935-0821, toll free ☎ 800-560-5557, www.hiloseasidehotel.com, 135 rooms, $110-$130). A rambling motel with a confusing layout, the Hilo Seaside Hotel couples reasonable value with a quality location on lovely Reed's Bay. All rooms contain two double beds with fairly thin, worn mattresses, a mini-refrigerator, cable TV and AC. The rooms are kept clean and the centrally-located pool will be popular with the kids. Parking is very limited, and you may be required to park on the street or down at the beach park where break-ins may occur. A decent restaurant is on-site, serving breakfast, lunch and dinner. $$-$$$

Ice Pond: Right by Reed's Bay on Banyan Drive, what appears to be a deep incursion of the bay is actually a spring-fed lagoon with shockingly cool water. If the humidity of Hilo proves too much, wander over in front of the Hilo Seaside Hotel or Harrington's restaurant and take a flying leap for instant refreshment.

Uncle Billy's

Uncle Billy's (87 Banyan Drive, ☎ 935-0861, toll free ☎ 800-442-5841, http://www.unclebilly.com/hb.html, 144 rooms, $89-$114). Love it or hate it, Uncle Billy's (both in Hilo and in Kona) does a lot of business. We've always had good luck here, but the last time we were waiting to check in, the couple in front of us were insisting on a refund and leaving early because they couldn't stay another night. Many of the rooms have kitchenettes, and most rooms overlook the garden courtyard which is filled with octopus trees, ginger, ferns, *tiki* torches and a bubbling stream. The birds gather here at dawn and dusk and make a crazy racket, but it's kind of nice. The wing of standard rooms overlooks the parking lot, which is definitely less attractive. The lobby is vintage Hawaiiana, with *tiki* themes and wicker furniture. The towels are thin, the elevator always seems to be broken, and a large cockroach may cross your bedroom floor. If that's going to freak you out then this is not the place for you. However, if you're willing to take a chance and you get a good rate, you might have a nice stay. Amenities include a pool, cable TV and A/C. There is no high-speed Internet access available. $$

Hilo Hawaiian (71 Banyan Drive, ☎ 935-9361, www.castleresorts.com/HHH/, 286 rooms, $155-$205, suites, $235-$405). While the formerly grand hotels of Hilo's Banyan Drive have been run down across the board, the Hilo Hawaiian remains the best of the bunch. Clean and well-run with excellent service, this is our choice for a large hotel in Hilo. Built in 1975 and renovated in 1993, the hotel lobby and restaurant retain some of its '70s charm while elements of the guest rooms are renovated on an annual

Hilo Hawaiian

cycle, resulting in a more modern feel. All rooms have A/C, mini-refrigerator, coffee maker, cable TV and most rooms have some sort of broadband Internet access available. The ocean-view rooms have awesome vistas across Hilo Bay, and all the way to Mauna Kea when it's clear. There is ample parking here, as well as a pool, gift shop, massage, a coin-op laundry and one of those old-school ice cream vending machines where you open little doors to grab your ice cream sandwich or fudgesicle. The Waioli Lounge just off the lobby serves up a full bar and *pupus*, and features live music on the weekends. The Queens Court is famous for its buffets, and has both a faithful local and a tourist following. $$$-$$$$

Where to Eat

There are a lot of great restaurants for a range of budgets in Hilo, and they're all less expensive than Kona-side. It's probably because Hilo has to cater to locals as well as tourists, and word of mouth is the best advertising there is.

For an explanation of the restaurant $ price codes, see page 66.

Café 100 (969 Kilauea Ave, ☎ 935-8683). There are a lot of local "drive in" joints in Hilo with the usual inexpensive, Hawaiian comfort food – mix plate lunches, loco moco, saimin and burgers – but Café 100 is the granddaddy of them all. Established in Hilo in 1946 – then destroyed by the tsunamis in 1946 and 1960 – Café 100 is famous for its loco moco, offering around 20 different kinds. They aren't afraid to improve upon the traditional loco moco: a bowl of rice, topped with a hamburger or other meat smothered in gravy and topped with a fried egg. If this is a dish that appeals to you, go find one custom-tailored to your tastes at this Hilo institution. Menu hotline at ☎ 935-MENU. Open 6:45 am-8:30 pm Mon-Thurs, until 9 pm Fri-Sat. $

Big Island Pizza (760 Kilauea Ave, ☎ 934-8000, www.bigislandpizza.com) serves up pies with a crisp, chewy crust, fresh ingredients and an array of gourmet toppings. They pride themselves on using quality ingredients like 100% olive oil, roasted garlic, and Italian sausage. Their homemade marinara is simmered with herbs and spices to give it pizzazz, though you can also have pesto, alfredo or barbecue. Then they create inspired combinations of pizzas (or you can build your own), such as the Country Club, with artichoke hearts, Italian sausage, feta cheese and mozzarella, or the Blue Shroom, with portabello mushrooms, roasted onions, bleu cheese, aged Parmigiano-Reggiano and bacon crumbles. Take-out and free delivery – perfect for rainy nights when you want to stay in. Open 11 am-9 pm daily. $$

Nichols Public House (776 Kilauea Ave, ☎ 934-8782). Hilo finally has a quality pub in Nichols, which opened at the end of 2005. During our first visit to Nichols, as we complimented the bartender on the tasty mushrooms stuffed with olives, breadcrumbs, sweet onions and three kinds of cheese, an excited Hilo resident named Paul proclaimed, "Isn't the food great? I've eaten here 13 days in a row. Come back in a week and it'll be 21 days!"

There are crazy offerings on the menu, like "Pitcher and a Pound" – a pitcher of any beer they pour and a pound of chicken strips ($21), wings ($21), fries or onion rings ($17). If you get the fries, make it extra-decadent and order a side of the Welsh cheese. More dignified dishes, such as salads, a Ploughman's lunch, and shepherd's pie, grace the menu. There is live music here some weekends, when over 100 people squeeze into the pub. Open daily 11 am-2 am. $$

AUTHOR'S CHOICE

Reuben's (336 Kamehameha Ave, ☎ 961-2552, $$). This colorfully dingy restaurant has been our favorite Big Island place for Mexican food over a decade. Once you start eating at Reuben's, it's hard to stop. The menu has 44 combo plates, including such standards as tacos, quesadillas and chimichangas, as well as more local preparations such as fresh fish tacos. The cheese enchilada and chile relleno combo is a sure bet, or branch out and try the Enchiladas Verdes do Jaibo, which consists of crab enchiladas, green chile sauce, avocado and sour cream. Whatever you order, expect a sizzling hot plate of gooey, cheesy goodness. The tequila selection is impressive and moderately priced, and they offer island-style margaritas like *liliko`i* and guava. They pour with a heavy hand, so be sure you don't have to drive all the way back to Kona before ordering one. 11 am-9 pm Mon-Fri, 12-9 pm Sat $$

Ken's House of Pancakes (1730 Kamehameha Ave, ☎ 935-8711). "Ono Grinds...Anytime!" proclaims Ken's House of

Pancakes, where the entire gigantic menu is available 24 hours a day. Woohoo! Opened in 1971, it's the only 24-hour restaurant in Hilo. This is a bustling diner with orange vinyl booths and counter stools, friendly, efficient waitstaff and as they say, *ono grinds* (delicious food). Can we get a "broke da mouth?" Ken's is always garnering awards and praise from its grateful public, like Best Breakfast on the Big Island. Choices include omelettes (three eggs or egg substitute), waffles, loco mocos, French toast, pancakes, eggs and pork chops, vegetarian benedict, burgers, sandwiches, *saimins*, salads, stews, dinner plates, milk shakes, ice cream floats, plenty of "meatless" and "healthy choice" options, syrup like maple, papaya, "kokonut" and guava... not to mention that there are all-you-can-eat nights. This place can satisfy just about any cravings. $-$$

Island seafood risotto

Café Pesto (308 Kamehameha Ave, ☎ 969-6640, www.cafepesto.com) is loved by tourists and locals alike. Larger than the original Café Pesto in Kawaihae, South Kohala, the ambiance of the café, with high ceilings and an open kitchen, is highly conducive to a good time. And the food is great, a sort of Hawaiian-fusion-meets-Italian cuisine. If you can somehow pass up the gourmet calzones and pizzas that are baked in an *ohia* wood-fired oven, you can opt for pastas and risottos like the "hibachi style" chicken risotto, or the fresh catch of the day with coconut macadamia fettuccini alfredo, Thai vegetable slaw, and mango-liliko`i sauce. You also can't go wrong having a meal of appetizers and salads (the Volcano Mist salad gets us every time). Cap it off with a cappuccino from the espresso bar and a dessert like the crême brulée with fresh fruit preserves and you won't want to eat again for a week (yeah, right). There is usually live music here on Sunday afternoons. Open daily 11 am-9 pm, until 10 pm Fri-Sat. $$-$$$

O'Keefe Bakery (374 Kinoole St, ☎ 934-9334). With an extraordinary variety of breads and baked goods, this is *the* place to pick up a loaf of something yummy for a few days spent camping at the volcano or a week in a condo. With such baked delicacies as garlic sourdough, black pepper cilantro wheat, and mac-nut pesto foccacia, it's hard to go wrong here. For *ono* pastries, try the mango turnover or cinnamon pull-apart. Folks also flock here for picnic sandwiches. Try the chicken mac-nut salad on Russian rye, roast beef and cheddar on an onion hoagie, or spicy curried tofu on miller's wheat. Also serving good coffee, espresso and fresh-brewed iced tea. Open 6 am-5 pm Mon-Fri, until 3 pm Sat. $

The Seaside Restaurant

The Seaside Restaurant (1790 Kalanianaole Ave, ☎ 935-8825). If based upon the popularity and the word-of-mouth of the locals, this place would win best restaurant in town. Don't be fooled by the unpretentious ambiance, as several selections of fish are pulled straight from their adjacent fish ponds, which are operated in the ancient Hawaiian tradition, so they are always absolutely fresh. Choices from the aqua culture ponds include mullet wrapped in Ti-leaf and steamed with lemon and onion, and crispy fried *aholehole*. Ocean fish are also offered here, as well as chicken, steak, lamb and a token veggie dish. All dishes include a dinner salad, vegetable and rice or pasta. Reservations highly recommended. Open for dinner 5-8:30 pm Tues-Thurs, Sun, 5-9 pm Fri and Sat. $$-$$$

GOOD VALUE ★ **Aloha Luigi** (264 Keawe St, ☎ 934-9113), while primarily an Italian eatery, also serves up a sizeable selection of Mexican favorites. With a convenient location right on Keawe St in downtown Hilo, this is a great place to catch a quick bite. The counter service is efficient and friendly, and in no time you'll be enjoying a thick slice of Sicilian pizza with a garlicky Caesar salad loaded with crunchy croutons and an inordinate amount of freshly grated parmesan. Other Italian selections include eggplant parmigiana, five cheese lasagna, and an Italian sausage, pepper and onion wrap. The eggplant parm and Caesar salad wrap is one of the most inspired creations we've ever eaten. Yum! On the Mexican side of the menu, choose from three handmade corn tortilla tacos with fillings such as salmon, carnitas or tofu-bean mole, or try one of their giant burritos. They also serve a "brunch," featuring huevos rancheros, frittatas and the like. Open 9 am-4 pm Tues, Wed, Thurs and Sat, 9 am to 7 pm Fri. $-$$

Hilo Bay Café (315 Maka`ala St #109, ☎ 935-4939). If you've left downtown Hilo and are lost in the strip mall world at Waiakea Center, do not despair! Hilo Bay Café is tucked into a corner by the food court, an oasis of upscale comfort in an otherwise generic and bleak mall setting. OK, maybe that's overly dramatic, but that's how we felt the first time we stumbled across this foodie haven, just looking for a place to grab a happy hour drink. Somehow we ended up ordering a cheese course of three specialty cheeses served with thinly sliced apples and topped with walnuts – an act of decadence to lift our spirits after a day of slogging around in a downpour. Things got even better when the couple next to us gave us their crusty bread because they were on the Atkins Diet. In the words of Homer Simpson, "Woo-hoo!" Hilo Bay Café uses local and organic ingredients to create fusion dishes like blackened pork tenderloin with risotto cake, guacamole and ancho chile sauce, or vegan coconut-crusted tofu with curried coconut sauce, sautéed vegetables and jasmine rice. There are wine pairing suggestions with every entrée. You might want to start with an appetizer like Guinness onion rings with balsamic ketchup and garlic aioli, but don't forget about the desserts like coffee cheesecake with chocolate espresso beans. Lunch has sandwiches like eggplant marinara with fresh mozzarella and parmesan, or crab cake with organic arugula and sweet chili mayonnaise on a coconut bun. This restaurant really is out of place in a mini-mall. Open 11 am-9 pm daily. $$-$$$

Hilo Bay Café

Restaurant Kaikodo (60 Keawe St ☎ 961-2558) is Hilo's fine dining option, and it's a standout. The owners are art collectors, and their taste is reflected in the chic décor, with blown glass lamps and Japanese lanterns in the high-ceilinged restaurant. Everything we've eaten here has been

Restaurant Kaikodo

spectacular. Mushroom lovers should try the Hamakua mushroom teppanyaki, an appetizer of clam-shell, Portobello, shiitake and trumpet mushrooms in garlic, roasted onions and truffle essence. And how's this for a filet mignon preparation: grilled to order with roasted garlic and herbed mashed potatoes, roasted tomatoes, grilled avocado, Kentucky bourbon sauce and blue-cheese butter or béarnaise? Even the women's bathroom is impressive, with aqua glass bottles and a matching sink. Open for lunch 11 am-2 pm Mon-Fri, dinner 5:30-9 pm daily, till 10 pm Fri and Sat.The lounge is open "till close," and becomes a trendy club that sometimes has a DJ. $$$$

Tropical Dreams (174 Kamehameha Ave, ☎ 935-9109, www.tropicaldreamsicecream.com), in the Art Deco-style Kress building, features "superpremium" (18% butterfat) ice cream served by the cone or cup. It's as creamy as you could ever want. Note the interesting soda fountain in the eating area, a remnant of the Kress five-and-dime that was located here for nearly 50 years before closing its doors in 1980.

For info on many more Hilo restaurants, visit www.bigislandadventure.com.

Entertainment

Palace Theater (38 Haili St, ☎ 934-7777, www.hilopalace.com) was built in 1925 as the largest theater in Hawaii outside of Honolulu. It has survived two major tsunamis. The theater shows indie flicks, documentaries, plays and hosts concerts

Palace Theater

from well known acts. Movie tickets are $7 for general admission.

GOOD VALUE ★ **Kress Cinemas** (174 Kamehameha Ave, ☎ 935-6777). The marquis outside the Kress discount movie theater advertises a matinee price of 50¢, $1 after 2 pm. A buck! You can pay a dollar to watch the scene from your favorite movie if don't have time to watch it all! But most families stay for the whole show, *grinding* popcorn and nachos (regular cinema prices) and laughing out loud or shrieking in horror – this is a fun place to feel the vibe of an audience during a movie. There are video games in the lobby of the historic building. Because of the rock-bottom price, we expected this to be a scary place with a lot of shady characters and were pleasantly surprised; it just seemed too good to be true. If it's a rainy evening in Hilo, this is a nice option to have. As our friend Steve likes to say, "What the f*&%, it's only a buck!"

UHH Theatre (200 W. Kawili St, ☎ 974-7310, http://performingarts.net/Theatre). The 600-seat performing arts theater for the University of Hawaii at Hilo hosts over 150 performances a year, from lectures by guest speakers to concerts, dances and plays. The shows are performed by students as well as national acts. Tickets are available online, or through the box office noon – 6 pm Mon-Fri.

Hilo Lanes (777 Kinoole St, ☎ 935-0646) is a vintage '60s bowling alley with 40 wooden lanes and no electronic scoring. Because it is a family establishment, signs warn bowlers to avoid using profanity. There is no alcohol here, but there is a small diner with inexpensive burgers and snacks, and an arcade where you can play video games or shoot pool. It's a unique place, where the slogan is "Let the good times roll." Open 11 am-10 pm daily, until 11 pm Fri and Sat.

Shooters Bar and Grill (121 Banyan Dr, ☎ 969-7069). With motivation such as daily drink specials, Shooters retains a faithful following of hard-partying locals who groove long into the night here. A stage, DJ booth, pool tables and foosball assure things rarely slow down once they get going. Open 3-2 am Mon-Wed, Thurs-Sat, until 3 am.

Nearby Attractions

Waterfall Way. For a short but spectacular drive that brings you to three magnificent waterfalls, head straight out of downtown Hilo on Waianuenue Ave ("rainbow water" in Hawaiian). First try and discern the prismatic effect at Rainbow Falls, before stopping at the Boiling Pots for a view of Pe`epe`e Falls, then round out the drive with a hike to some lovely pools at Wai`ale Falls.

It's not hard to guess how Rainbow Falls got its name

Rainbow Falls is beautiful in the rain, but if possible, go when the sun breaks through the clouds so you can see the rainbow circling the mist in the gulch. Wow, is this place ever pretty! The stairs and wheelchair ramp to the right have views of the falls but not where they make contact with the water below, so for your best photos, snap away from the lower railing. Follow the walkway to the left for fantastic views of the top of the falls and, often, the rainbows. Don't forget to take off your sunglasses or the UV filter will make the rainbow invisible! You may be tempted to continue into the banyan trees to pick your way down the steep, slippery slope to the top of the falls for a photo op, but keep in mind that people die doing just that from time to time when a flash flood catches them unaware. Follow Waianuenue Ave out of downtown Hilo and look for the sign to Wailuku River State Park and Rainbow Drive.

Pe`epe`e Falls & Boiling Pots. Also in Wailuku River State Park, the Boiling Pots are a series of pools connected by a subterranean flow; the surging water makes the pools appear to boil. There is a simple lookout that provides a view from above. From the lookout you can also see Pe`epe`e Falls, but you'll notice an inconvenient green wall in your way from catching a perfect photo. To the right of the lookout, there is a trail down to the Boiling Pots. From there, some adventurous souls rock hop to the far side of the river to reach the base of the falls. If the water is low enough this may be an option, but keep in mind that people drown here doing that. There are public restrooms here. Follow Waianuenue Ave. about 1½ miles past Rainbow Falls, then turn right on Pe`epe`e Falls St.

Pe`epe`e Falls

**Wai`ale Falls**. Yet another gushing torrent on Hilo's Wailuku River, Wai`ale Falls is easy to view from the bridge that crosses the river. You might want to think twice about leaping to the pool below, as the concentration of flowers and wreaths on the bridge are testament to the fact that jumpers don't always make it. However, there are some terrific pools up above the falls that are perfect for splashing around in. See *Adventures on Foot* below.

Mauna Loa Macadamia-Nut Visitor Center. These folks process 35 million raw macadamia nuts a year from their 2,500-acre orchard! Tourist buses head straight for the company's visitor center, where guests can watch a video narrated by "Mac, your Nutty Buddy," while factory workers toil below. Visit Mon-Fri if you want to see the factory operational. Visitors grab handfuls of nuts and chomp on them while they browse the shop for boxes of Mauna Loa products, as well as – bewilderingly – gold jewelry and other non-macadamia related souvenirs. To get here, drive just over five miles from Hilo on Hwy 11, and turn left on Macadamia Drive. ☎ 545-8046, www.maunaloa.com. Open 8:30 am-5 pm daily.

Did you know? Macadamia nuts must drop to the ground before they are harvested or the flavor won't be right. It takes 300 pounds of pressure per square inch to crack the hard shells.

Kaumana Caves. Free caves! Almost four miles up Rt. 200 from Hilo, you'll find Kaumana Caves Park. Be very careful crossing the street from the parking area to the cave entrance as cars come screaming around the corner and appear out of nowhere. The *puka* (hole) itself is very beautiful, choked with vegetation and root systems. A bright yellow staircase delivers you to the two entrances, and unless you are wildly claustrophobic you should at least descend and ponder the large cavernous opening to the right.

Kaumana Caves

Like many other caves on the Big Island, Kaumana is wet. Water drips not only around the entrance, but deep inside as well, especially during one of the frequent soaking rains. Roots from above work through the lava shell and dangle like wet hair from the ceiling, adding a certain lost world quality to the trek. The lava tube is a product of the 1881 flow from Mauna Loa that threatened Hilo and stopped just short of it. The two cave entrances here are the product of a roof cave-in, so it is the same lava tube with two ways to explore it. While the entrance to the right is more interesting, the cave to the left is more fun to explore. A short distance into the left tunnel, still within daylight, you will encounter a shelf. The top closes off quickly, and the bottom requires a short squeeze through a three-foot opening. Once down and through, the tunnel opens into a 30-foot-high wall that runs for 10 minutes before encountering the first rock fall. You can continue on from there.

Tip: Modern cavers bring a minimum of three light sources with them. You should carry at least one backup, even if you're just going in for a short distance. The lava in these lava tubes is incredibly sharp and will easily injure you if you are groping blindly for the entrance because you dropped your flashlight and broke the bulb. Long pants, gloves and a helmet are also advisable.

All in all, there are about five miles of explorable lava tubes here. Don't bring just one flashlight; bring a backup too. Caving (cavers don't like to be called spelunkers) is much more relaxing if you have ample backup in the event of a broken light. Also, make sure you have supportive foot wear. The most dangerous aspect of caving here is the potential for turning an ankle, or getting a foot stuck and falling in the wrong direction until you hear a soft crunch!

There are public restrooms near the entrance to the cave, but they are some of the grottiest of "maintained" bathrooms on the island. They've even been immortalized at Urinal.net. Check 'em out: www.urinal.net/kaumana_caves/.

PELE & PRINCESS RUTH

The Kaumana Caves were formed by an 1881 lava flow stemming from an 1880 eruption of Mauna Loa. When the flow got within a mile and half of Hilo and residents felt helpless, Kona's Princess Ruth Ke`elikolani camped out at the base of the flow after entreating Madame Pele to stop the lava, offering her distilled spirits, red silk scarves and a lock of her hair. The story says that when she woke the next morning, the lava had hardened and Hilo was saved!

Shortbreads from Big Island Candies

Big Island Candies (585 Hinano St, ☎ 935-8890, toll free ☎ 800-935-5510, www.bigislandcandies.com). If you have a sweet tooth, do not miss Big Island Candies. As you walk into the candy factory (and retail store), you are handed a small cup with samples of goodies like shortbread and a "crunchy" – mac nuts and potato chips in milk chocolate. Inside, you can sip a free cup of 100% Kona coffee while you watch factory workers hand-dip shortbread into chocolate. There are many more free samples scattered around the store, like chocolate-covered mint brownie cookies, or butter-free lavender cookies. These folks like to dunk things in chocolate, even rice crackers. Do your kids a favor and let them loose in the candy store. To get here from downtown Hilo, follow Kilauea Ave south past the Waiakea fish ponds, then turn left on Kekuanaoa St for about half a mile, then turn left on Hinano St. Free admission. Open 8:30 am-5 pm daily.

White tiger at the zoo

Pana`ewa Rainforest Zoo (☎ 959-9233, www.hilozoo.com). Because this is in a rainforest that receives more than 125 inches of rain each year, you'll find animals from similar habitats here. The approach to the zoo is an attraction in itself, since the beautiful driveway is lined with palm trees, and the parking lot is surrounded by monkeypods. The zoo itself is a little worse for wear, with faded signs and not too many butterflies in the butterfly house, but hey, it's free! The zoo houses exotic birds like macaws, poisonous frogs, sloths, iguanas, and energetic monkeys. Peacocks roam the grounds. But the centerpiece is a white Bengal tiger named Namaste. He lives in a large enclosure with a banyan tree and a hill; he frequently climbs up and paces near the walkway. It's a thrill to be so close to a tiger! You may want to reach out and pet his fur as he rubs against the chain link fence, but you'll think again if you see him lunge for an errant peacock – he kills one every month or so, according to one zoo keeper. He is fed at 3:30 pm each day, so he gets antsy around feeding time. Then he's put into a small enclosure to eat, where he stays for the rest of the night, so be sure to visit before then. The zoo is off of Hwy 11, south of Hilo. Turn right on W. Mamaki St just after the four mile marker and follow the signs. Open 9 am-4 pm daily, with a petting zoo Saturdays from 1:30-2:30 pm.

Adventures on Foot

Wai`ale Falls

Difficulty: Moderate
Distance and type: 4/10 mile total, out-and-back
Time: 20 minutes, round-trip

Many visitors to Hawaii arrive with images of tropical waterfalls and plunge pools splashing around in their heads. It's true that there are few things more pleasant than spending a hot afternoon frolicking in cool, tumbling pools surrounded by thick, green jungle. The top of Hilo's "waterfall way" provides quick access to such a place, but be warned: the trail is not particularly easy, especially after a rain, and once you arrive at the pools the area can be quite dangerous when the river is high.

Follow Waianuenue Ave straight up from downtown Hilo. The trailhead is just over the bridge on the left-hand (upstream) side. The trail is often muddy, clogged with vegetation, and there are several spur trails that lead down steep, slippery paths to other destinations. On top of that, the trail splits the top of a high, narrow ridge with steep drops on either side, though the drops may be hidden by plants and trees. It's only about a 10-minute hike up to the pool area, but once you are there, pick your way carefully. The lava has many hand and foot holds, which make for easier walking, but there is still ample opportunity to slip into fast water and find yourself making an unwanted trip down the falls.

The best pools are about 200 yards upstream from the top of the falls. These are created by the split of the river that gives way to the spur that displays the fabulous triplet of waterfalls on your right as you enter the clearing. There are more pools farther upstream, which may be possible to reach if the water is low enough. That said, it may be impossible to reach any pools if it has been raining heavily upstream. If that is the case, simply appreciate the view, which is impressive, and enjoy the sound of the rushing, falling water, keeping in mind that there are people in cities using machines to create that very sound to relax and fall asleep.

"Certainly, travel is more than the seeing of sights; it is a change that goes on, deep and permanent, in the ideas of living." – Miriam Beard

Puna

"Anyone who keeps the ability to see beauty never grows old."
– Franz Kafka

IN THIS CHAPTER

It is impossible to forget that you are living on a volcano in Puna. Located in the east rift zone of Kilauea, virtually every part of Puna has been covered by lava in the last 400 years. There are daily reminders of the close proximity of the erupting volcano: steam vents provide natural saunas; beaches are made of jet black volcanic sand; not-so-distant billows of steam signal where the current lava flow from Pu`u O`o reaches the ocean. In 1990, seven years after Kilauea began its ongoing eruption, Madame Pele unleashed her power on the village of Kalapana, destroying nearly every home in the area, and burying it under 50 feet of lava.

In Puna, there is no question that the Earth is a living thing, and that Nature calls the shots. As such, Puna has attracted the most eclectic transplants to the Big Island – at least, it has the highest concentration of them. Euphemisms and other attempts to categorize these residents abound; bohemian, Californicated, hippie, and '60s throwbacks are common. It's true that this is a region that hosts New Age retreats, where *pakalolo* (marijuana) farmers and artists live, where residents gather for jam sessions and puppet shows, where the phrase "clothing optional" is not uncommon. But the diversity here cannot be pigeonholed or classified. Perhaps it's best left at this: Puna residents are anything but boring.

One thing "Punatics" have in common is a love of the area's beauty, as it is full of natural wonders. Many of the roads

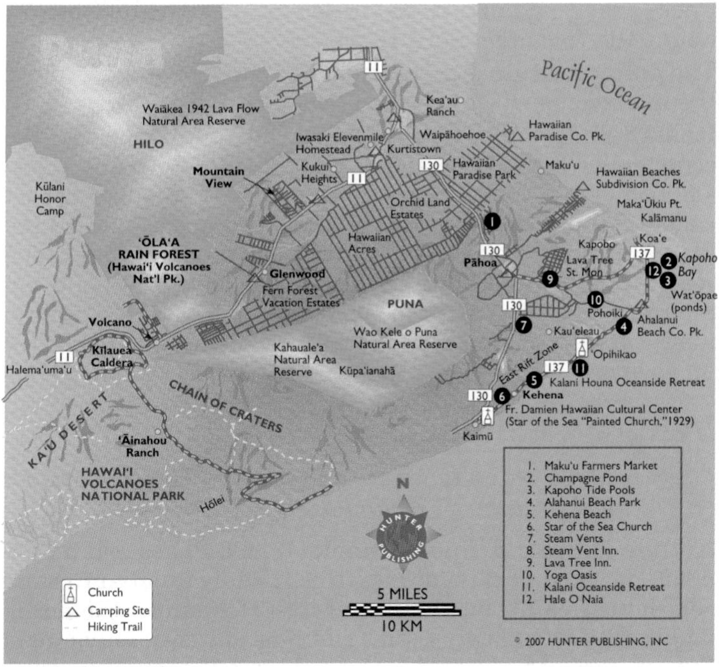

pass through "tree tunnels," where sunlight filters through a lace canopy until the road opens to views of the surf pounding against a rugged lava coastline. Locals soak in geothermal "hot ponds," snorkel in the extensive Kapoho tidepools, and sunbathe naked at the black sand beach at Kahena. The rainforest that surrounds the lava molds of *o`hia* trees at Lava Tree State Monument seems enchanted. The name Puna means "spring," a spring of water, of life, and it fits.

Kea`au

Primarily a crossroads town between Puna, Hilo and Volcano, Kea`au possesses a small but dense commercial area to service the locals who live in nearby subdivisions.

Practicalities

Don't forget: There is only one area code for the entire island – 808.

There are two **gas stations** in Kea`au. The Shell is open 24 hours, the 76 station until 10 pm.

The **police station** is across from Kea`au Shopping Center at the intersection of Old Volcano Road and Pili Mua St.

Kea`au Shopping Center** (16-586 Old Volcano Road) is the commercial hub of the town, with the **Post Office** (open 7:30 am-4 pm Mon-Fri, 10 am-noon Sat), a supermarket called **Puna Fresh Foods** (☎ 966-9316, open 7 am-10 pm Mon-Sat, till 9 pm Sun), a natural food grocery store called **Kea`au Natural Foods (☎ 966-8877, open 8:30 am-8 pm Mon-Fri, 8:30 am-7 pm Sat, 9:30 am-5 pm Sun), a laundromat, a hardware store, two local food restaurants, an ATM and a sports bar.

Where to Shop

"Every time I see an adult on a bicycle, I no longer despair for the future of the human race." – H.G. Wells

Aikane Bicycle & Sport Shack (16-566 Pahoa Rd, ☎ 966-6060). Located next to Verna's, this friendly family-run store sells bikes (mainly mountain and cross) for adults and kids in addition to skateboards, and running and swimming gear. Repair services available. Open 11 am-6 pm Mon, Tues, Thurs, Fri, 9 am-3 pm Sat.

Where to Eat

You can find the usual inexpensive local grinds at **L&L Drive In** and **Hiro's Place** in the Kea`au Shopping Center, and at **Verna's Drive In** nearby on Pahoa Road.

Charley's Bar & Grill (Kea`au Shopping Center, ☎ 966-7589, www.charleysbar.com) is a sports bar by day; there's a small dance floor with a stage for live music at night (Thurs-Sat). Charley's serves standards like burgers, sandwiches and lots of fried food, plus breakfast on Sunday mornings. Portions are generous and the quality is somewhat better than you'll find at similar establishments. Appetizers like chicken fingers, jalapeno poppers, *poke* and fried zucchini sticks are served until 11 pm Thurs-Sat. Free pool on Tuesdays. On nights with live music, no *slippahs* allowed. Open 11 am-11 pm Mon-Thurs, 11 am-2 am Fri-Sat, 9 am-9 pm Sun $$

Pahoa

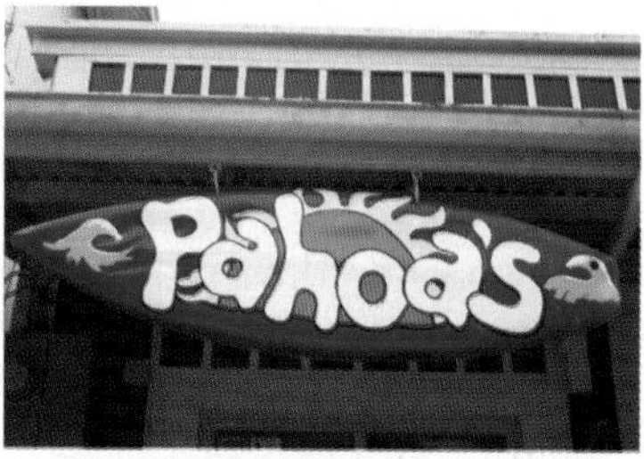

Pahoa may be smaller than Kea`au, but it is the heart of Puna, with restaurants and shops that reflect the area's diverse interests. The postings on Pahoa bulletin boards give you a taste of what the region is like: a High Vibe astrology workshop; a free reggae gathering; a potluck hosted by a raw vegan bodybuilder; an upcoming interactive arts festival organized by the local Burning Man affiliate; a missing-person poster. Most of the businesses listed here are on Pahoa Village Road, which runs right through town.

Practicalities

The **gas station** at the N&P Mart is open 5 am-8 pm daily.

There are **ATMs** at the Bank of Hawaii and First Hawaiian Bank, which sometimes has a security guard.

Island Naturals Pahoa (Pahoa Village Rd, ☎ 965-8322) is a natural food grocery store with a deli case, as well as a hot bar with vegetarian dishes that is open until 6 pm. They also sell beer and wine. Open 7:30 am-7:30 pm Mon-Sat, 8 am-7 pm Sun.

THEFT

The warning you hear in Puna starts to sound like a broken record: Don't leave valuables in your car. Pahoa and its surrounding area have a considerable problem with drugs, including ice (crystal meth), so car break-ins are common. Some locals will play down crime in the area, with anecdotes like "The key's been stuck in my car's ignition for four years and nobody's taken it yet!" But everyone is not so lucky, particularly if they have a rental car. So one more time for the record: Don't leave valuables in your car, including your trunk.

Where to Shop

Pahoa has plenty of funky, offbeat shops. For details, visit www.bigislandadventures.com.

Rite of Passage Surf (15-2950 Pahoa Village Rd, ☎ 965-2345) is Pahoa's newest surf shop, with new and used boards, kayaks, skateboards, and clothes. Owners Brock and Frank also own Kona Boys in Kealakekua, where they offer surf lessons and kayak tours. Open Wed-Sun 10 am-6 pm.

Puna Style (15-1403 Pahoa Village Rd, ☎ 965-7592) has the largest inventory of funkadelia in Pahoa, with island-inspired dresses and shirts, woven bags and Indian purses, cloth mermaid dolls, wind chimes, sarongs, candles, kids' puzzles, stickers, fairy statuettes, and jewelry among its offerings. Open 10 am-5 pm Mon-Tues, 10 am-6 pm Wed-Sat, 9 am-2 pm Sun with a half-hour lunch break at some point each day.

MAKU`U FARMERS MARKET

Maku`u Farmers Market has supplanted the Pahoa Farmers Market (Sundays in the parking lot behind Luquin's) as the market hot spot. Held in a big parking lot on Highway 130 north of Pahoa, Maku`u has stalls selling the usual food, produce, and flowers, as well as art, tiles, honey, fresh juices, surfboards, clothing, glass, massage, tiles and miscellaneous thrift items. The line at the Mister D's Ono Steaks van gets long around lunchtime. The market takes place Sundays from 8 am-2 pm, with a scaled-down version on Saturdays.

"If you are lucky enough to find a way of life you love, you have to find the courage to live it." – John Irving

Located outside of Pahoa proper at the corner of Hwy 130 and Old Pahoa Road, the **Pahoa Marketplace** is a strip mall with a grocery store, the Malama Market, a 24-hour Aloha gas station, and a few stores worth mentioning (see below).

Jungle Love (15-2660 Keaau-Pahoa Rd, Pahoa Marketplace, ☎ 966-7775) is the best hippie clothing store on the island, with silks from India, colorful sundresses, funky jewelry, art and cards by Puna artists, bags and incense. Prices are low. Open 9 am-6 pm Mon-Sat, till 4 pm Sun.

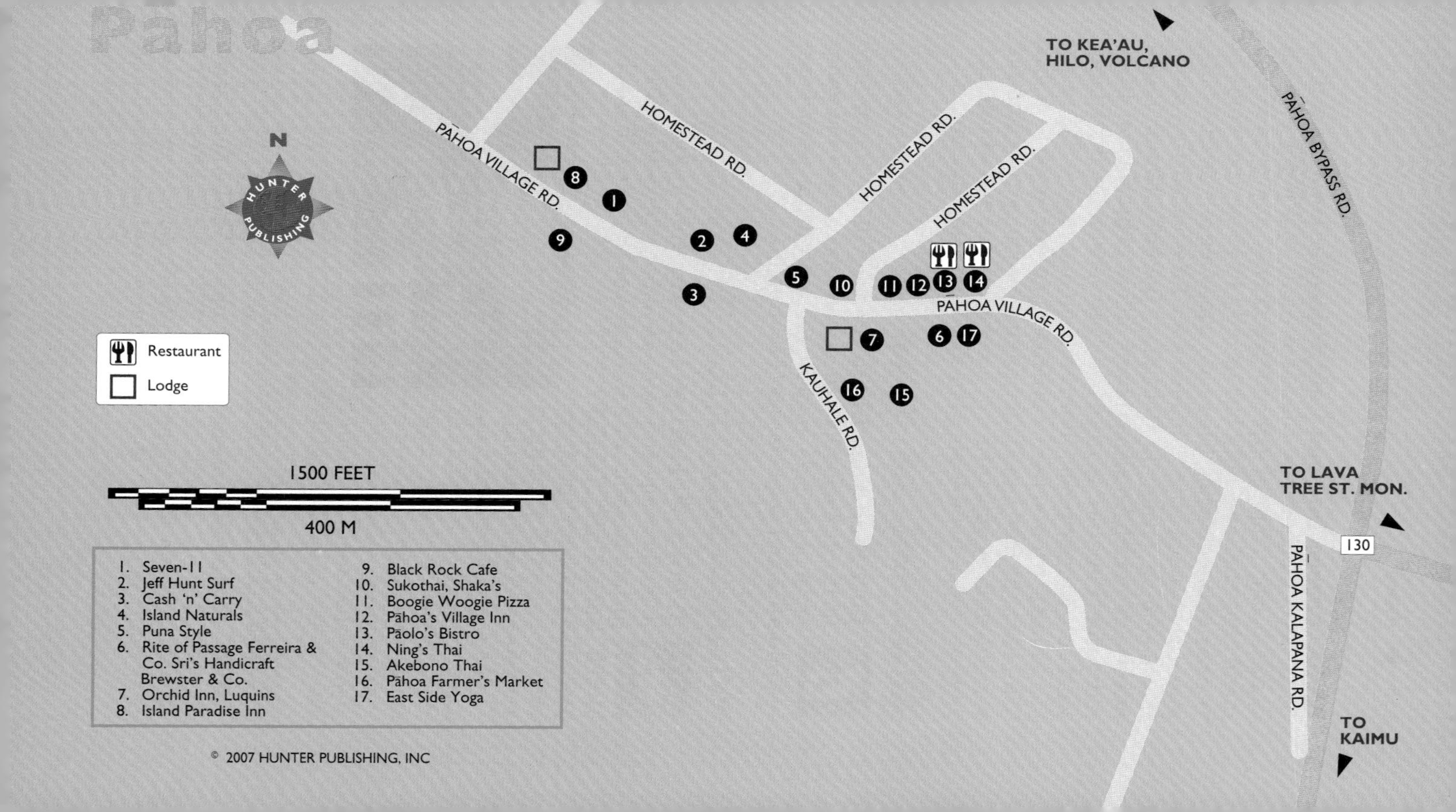
Pahoa
TO KEA'AU, HILO, VOLCANO
PĀHOA BYPASS RD.
HOMESTEAD RD.
HOMESTEAD RD.
HOMESTEAD RD.
PĀHOA VILLAGE RD.
PĀHOA VILLAGE RD.
KAUHALE RD.
TO LAVA TREE ST. MON.
130
PĀHOA KALAPANA RD.
TO KAIMU
N
HUNTER PUBLISHING
Restaurant
Lodge
1500 FEET
400 M
1. Seven-11
2. Jeff Hunt Surf
3. Cash 'n' Carry
4. Island Naturals
5. Puna Style
6. Rite of Passage Ferreira & Co. Sri's Handicraft Brewster & Co.
7. Orchid Inn, Luquins
8. Island Paradise Inn
9. Black Rock Cafe
10. Sukothai, Shaka's
11. Boogie Woogie Pizza
12. Pāhoa's Village Inn
13. Pāolo's Bistro
14. Ning's Thai
15. Akebono Thai
16. Pāhoa Farmer's Market
17. East Side Yoga
© 2007 HUNTER PUBLISHING, INC

Aloha Outpost Internet Café (Pahoa Marketplace, ☎ 965-8333, www.alohaoutpost.com) is a really cool place with an espresso bar, Tropical Dreams ice cream, and a sandwich menu that changes daily but usually includes five kinds of vegetarian sandwiches. There are trippy murals on the walls, and a back room with computers for Internet surfing or in-house gaming. Owner LaMont plays his Puna Nation Radio at the café, which he also streams online to provide an alternative for "Punatics" to the usual radio fare on the Big Island, with dub, chill, trip hop, funk, ambient and reggae. There are community events here such as open-mic poetry nights Thursdays at 6:30 pm. The café also provides copy and fax services and, by appointment, notary, graphic and web design services. Open 6 am-9 pm Mon-Fri, 7 am-9 pm Sat-Sun. $

Adventures with Yoga

East Side Yoga Shala (Pahoa Village Rd, ☎ 965-0010). It seems like there's always something going on at East Side Yoga Shala, with drum workshops, acupuncture and yoga classes ($12 drop in).

Where to Stay

Island Paradise Inn (☎ 990-0234, www.islandparadiseinn.com, 15 units, $39-$49). With a prime location in Pahoa, across the street from the Black Rock Café, Island Paradise Inn is an unbelievable bargain for budget travelers. Run by bubbly Ophelia and her son Steven, each room has a different decoration scheme and includes a sink, microwave, refrigerator, stove or hot plate, coffee maker, toaster, rice cooker, cable TV and ceiling fan. $

Where to Eat

Note: Most of the restaurants in Pahoa don't serve alcohol, though many are BYO, sometimes with a corkage fee. Being able to bring your own wine or beer really helps keep the cost of dining in Pahoa affordable, though the prices are already much lower than you'll find Kona-side.

AUTHOR'S CHOICE ★ **Paolo's Bistro** (333 Pahoa Village Rd, ☎ 965-7033). If you're the kind of person who loves fresh-made pasta, head straight to Paolo's Bistro for authentic Italian food. The restaurant is intimate, with only eight tables, dim lighting, Hawaiian art hung haphazardly on the walls, wooden floors, lazy ceiling fans and curtained windows. A local musician, perhaps a classical guitarist, sometimes serenades diners, creating a comfortable environment, particularly when it is raining. The menu, like the restaurant, is small, but with pasta, meat and fish dishes, as well as salads and fabulous appetizers like the gnocchi with tomato cream sauce. Entrée prices include a delicious bowl of vegetarian minestrone soup. Chef/owner Paolo Bucchioni could charge a lot more money for the quality food that he serves. BYO, with a $5 corkage fee. Open 5-9 pm Tues-Sun. $$

Sukothai Restaurant (15-2923 Pahoa Village Rd, ☎ 965-5449). Food-wise, Sukothai Restaurant is the better Thai option in Pahoa, with more flavor than Ning's. It has all the classic curries, noodle dishes, fried rice, and spicy entrées, like eggplant with tofu, beef, pork or chicken. The soups are really popular, from Tom Yum to the coconut chicken soup. The small restaurant has booths and tables covered with Thai silk, local art on the walls, and fresh cut flowers on each table. BYO. Open noon-9 pm daily except Wednesday. $-$$

LOCAL'S PICK ★ **Luquin's Mexican Restaurant** (Pahoa Village Rd, ☎ 965-9990) is a big restaurant and it's always hopping – easily the most popular restaurant in Puna. With respectable Mexican food, light, non-greasy chips, fresh salsa with a kick, and margaritas that blessedly don't overdo the sour mix, it's a solid bet for a fun night out in Pahoa. Vegetarians will love the option of having tofu tacos, flautas and enchiladas. There are 19 combination platters, mixing and matching standards like enchiladas, tacos, chile rellenos, and burritos, as well as carne asada, fajitas and carnitas. There's also an espresso bar called "Café Ole" and ice cream sundaes. Open for breakfast 7 am-11 am, lunch and dinner 11 am-9 pm daily. $$

AUTHOR'S CHOICE ★ **Pahoa's Village Café** (15-2941 Pahoa Village Rd, ☎ 965-7200). Easily recognized by the colorful sign painted on three surfboards out front, they serve "island influenced mainland fare" made from scratch. It's really good, as any place that serves fresh-squeezed juice usually is. The ambiance is inviting; on the walls in this brightly lit space are fans with nature scenes on them, as well as paintings by local artists. There are woven mats on the floor, and upbeat music wafts through the room. Eggs are served all day, with build-your-own omelette ingredients like bacon, avocado, cheeses, black olives and sausage. Waffles, crêpes and pancakes are served until 11 am, after which time the menu adds burgers on hoagie rolls, BLTs with turkey and Swiss, hot pork sandwich smothered in gravy, and a veggie hero with Brie. There are also salads, coconut shrimp, and other inspired options. They have an excellent selection of hot sauces for you chili heads. Yum! BYO. Open 7 am-2 pm Wed-Sun. $-$$

Entertainment

Shaka's (15-2929 Pahoa Village Rd, ☎ 965-1133) is a new bar (replacing the one shut down for dealing drugs) with live entertainment. There's a dance floor in the front room, and booths and tables in the back room, which is less intense, with a safari tent feel and a mellow vibe. The crowd on St Patrick's Day makes for some interesting people-watching, to say the least. The party can go late here.

Nearby Attractions & Adventures

AUTHOR'S CHOICE

Native Guide Hawaii (☎ 982-7575, www.nativeguidehawaii.com). One of the very best guides on the Big Island happens to be a Puna resident who leads small groups on eco-tours of the Puna Coast. Warren Costa, the owner and guide of Native Guide Hawaii, is a Big Island native who has worked as a botanist and at Hawai`i Volcanoes National Park (his tour there is terrific). He is a passionate scholar of Hawaiian culture with a soft-spoken demeanor – he's an all-around cool guy. Tours include transportation in Warren's van and a delicious local lunch. They cost $225 for one person, or $125 a person for parties of two or more. Call for reservations. No credit cards accepted.

Lava Tree State Monument

Lava trees

In the late 18th century, a lava flow from Kilauea poured into the rainforest and *o`hia* grove at what is now Lava Tree State Monument. On contact with the trees, the lava cooled and left hollow "tubes" or casts where the trees were. Today you can stroll through the forest, which is once again a lush rainforest but filled with lava trees. It has a vaguely mystical quality, as if Hobbits might be just around a corner. One area on the short trail has a group of lava trees reminiscent of Stonehenge. Also note the giant fissure to the right of the trailhead, which is estimated to be a thousand feet deep. The presence of *pukas* (holes) like these helped the lava drain out of the area.

There are some benches and a picnic table in the park, but you'll want to wear extra bug repellent if you plan to linger. There are also public restrooms. To get here, travel east on route 139 from Pahoa through a tree tunnel until you get to a small wooden sign for the monument, where you'll turn left. Veer right at the Y to the parking lot. Admission is free.

HAWAIIAN MYTHOLOGY: O`HIA & LEHUA

According to Hawaiian legend, the volcano goddess Pele became enamored of a handsome mortal named O`hia, who was in love with his beautiful girlfriend Lehua. When O`hia rejected Pele's advances out of loyalty to his girlfriend, she was outraged and turned him into a gnarled tree. Lehua was stricken with grief, and the gods took pity on her and transformed her into the red *lehua* flower of the *o`hia* tree, reuniting the couple. So now if you pick a *lehua* blossom from an *o`hia* tree, it will rain like tears, because you have separated the lovers.

LOCAL PEST: COQUI FROGS

Coqui frogs, a Puerto Rican frog named for its chirp of "Koh-KEE," are introduced pests that have infested Puna and many other parts of the island. They are bad news for Hawaii's endemic birds, which compete with them for spiders, crickets and flies. The foliage of Lava Tree changes from time to time after the area is sprayed with citric acid in an attempt to kill the coqui frogs there. But listen to the chirps around you and you'll know these efforts are in vain – the noise can reach up to 70 decibels, as loud as a vacuum cleaner. In other coqui populations around the island, the noise can reach 80-90 decibels, comparable to a lawn mower.

Steam Vents

On Highway 130 directly across from mile marker 15, there is a pullout between signs for a "Scenic Point." You'll find there's not much there, except for empty cars. What's going on? The answer: steam baths. Follow the trail from the parking area and randomly pick some forks. There are several baths through here, ranging from single-person *pukas* to multi-person party rooms. Local folks have brought in ladders to access the deeper baths, and benches to make others more comfortable. Bring a towel to drape over your head to corral the steam. You'll likely see locals toting a canvas that they'll toss over the roof of a bath to more effectively steam a whole room. It's a lot of fun, very relaxing, and you'll probably see a few naked people. Maybe you'll be one of them!

Where to Stay

Lava Tree Inn (☎ 965-7441, www.lavatreetropicinn.com, five rooms $80-$130, one two-bedroom cottage $165). With a great location in central Puna adjacent to Lava Tree State Park, staying in the Lava Tree Tropic Inn is like visiting a friend from the Old World. Host Irene Grunfeld is a Hungarian transplant with a welcoming, laid-

Lava Tree Inn

back style that will make anyone feel right at home. The inn has an unpretentious, lived-in feel that melds perfectly with Irene's personality. The grounds are fantastic, choked with jungle vegetation, beautiful flowers and fruit trees. Free-range chickens roam the yard and provide fresh eggs. A pleasant veranda outside the back door is stuffed with chairs for relaxing, while two of the upstairs guestrooms share a large lanai that looks out into the trees. Breakfast consists of tropical fruit, fresh baked bread and Hungarian cheese spread. A comfortable meditation room is available to guests for hanging out, reading books from the library or watching DVDs. There is a computer for guest use, and WiFi throughout the house. $$-$$$

See page 65 for an explanation of the hotel $ price codes.

Room at the Steam Vent Inn

Steam Vent Inn & Health Retreat (13-3775 Kalapana Hwy, ☎ 965-2112, www.steamventinn.com, three rooms, suggested donation $150-$350). Located near (and on) the natural steam vent saunas that are heated by Kilauea, the Steam Vent Inn used to be a pretty basic accommodation. But it has been transformed by its new owners, Len and Jackie Horowitz. Dr Leonard Horowitz is a controversial, best-selling author of over a dozen books, including *Emerging Viruses: AIDS & Ebola – Nature, Accident or Intentional?* He is a vastly intelligent, fascinating person to talk to; it's worth a visit to the Steam Vent Inn just to meet him and learn about his passions.

He and Jackie run the Inn as a "nonprofit educational nondenominational spiritual healing ministry," and they let nature do the teaching. Their 29-acre property has ocean views, organic gardens, trails through rainforest, a 250-foot-deep sinkhole, a lava tube, anthurium trail, a lava-heated hot pond, and two lava-heated steam saunas, with tiled benches for meditation, and showers to cool off while you sweat out your toxins; as the owners say, it's "purgative and restorative." Plans include a dozen "jungalows," bungalows in the jungle, and a rainbow color therapy trail – throw a switch at night and walk through the rainbows in the naturally occurring steam. Existing rooms are in a spacious home; trim that runs the length of the house is adorned with paintings of tropical fish. There are televisions without cable, but with VCRs and educational videos. As a health care expert, Dr Len also offers various therapy treatments by donation, such as biofeedback and health counseling. Because the Inn is a nonprofit, instead of rates there are "suggested contributions."

RED ROAD

Many of Puna's natural wonders are found along Red Road, Highway 137. It was nicknamed Red Road because it was originally paved with red cinders. Much of it was repaved with black asphalt, but you can see the original color along the sides of the road. (Locals were amused that when they decried the paving of Red Road, officials responded by offering to paint it red.)

Attractions & Adventures

Cape Kumukahi

Puna residents are famous for inhaling a variety of substances, and one of their finest offerings is the fresh air! The northeast trade winds blow in from one of the least populated areas of the world and land at Cape Kumukahi, the easternmost point in the state. The air here is some of the purest to be found anywhere. A testing station adjacent to the light beacon measures the amount of pollutants in the air, providing data for scientists to monitor the impact of human activity on global pollution.

As Hwy 137 comes to a T at the Red Road, head straight across the road down the rough 2WD track out to Cape Kumukahi and its light beacon. The light beacon was erected in 1934 as a signal for ships and planes arriving in the islands from the east. It is situated on top of a unique pair of concrete pads, which bookend a layer of sand in order to withstand the frequent earthquakes in the area. The over-active seismic activity is due to its location within the east rift zone of Kilauea. The 1960 eruption of Kilauea that destroyed the town of Kapoho flowed all the way out to the light beacon, destroyed the outbuildings and orchard of the lighthouse keeper, then split into two streams, sparing the light by only a few feet.

Champagne Pond

This is another one of the natural gems that make Puna such a unique place. Wedged between a rough lava flow and a subdivision, Champagne pond is a placid, geothermally heated pool right at the edge of Kapoho Bay. *Honu* (sea turtles) like to gather here, as do residents and tourists who don snorkel gear to get a better glimpse of these gentle creatures. The clear water is usually warmer near the back,

Champagne Pond

where a ladder and landing provide better access to the people in the subdivision. Even if there aren't any *honu* around, this is still a lovely place to relax, soak and let the day go by. Be aware that the bottom of the pool is rough *a`a* lava, which can easily cut up your feet. Reef shoes are recommended.

The 4WD road to the Champagne Pond begins at the southern end of the parking lot for the light beacon on Cape Kumukahi. Follow the road from the parking area for 1.2 miles. You'll encounter the most brutal part of the road in the first 100 feet. After 1/10 of a mile, turn right, then take a quick left. There are forks leading left and right along the way, but as long as you remain on the widest, clearest road you'll hit the beach at Kapoho Bay. Turn right at the beach and you'll find the pond over a low hill.

Wai`opae Tide Pools ("Kapoho Tide Pools")

Locals and tourists alike flock to this aquatic wonder to explore the countless pools teeming with underwater splendor. A wide oceanfront area contains a large network of shallow pools that support an astounding amount of marine life. Almost like a barrier reef, a shallow shelf breaks the waves well offshore, allowing the stunted waves to wash into the pools. This shallow water holds one of the widest arrays of corals we've ever seen in the Hawaiian Islands. There is also an abundance of tropical fishes through here, as well as eels, many of which are juvenile. Yes, eels are *even cuter* when they're babies!

Kapoho Tide Pools

It's possible to spend hours snorkeling from pool to pool here, though you may find yourself high and dry between some of them. The downside is the posted health advisory warning visitors that the waters frequently fail water quality tests and advising swimmers to wash themselves thoroughly when finished. We would advise that, too. Unfortunately, there are no facilities here, so you'll have to find a shower elsewhere. The largest, most popular pool is definitely not the most exciting. Explore some of the outer pools to glimpse the coolest stuff, but be sure to watch out for the currents. When the tide is on the move, the flow in or out of some of the pools can be intense. To get here, turn *mauka* off of the Red Road between mile markers 8 and 9 onto Kapoho Kai Dr. Follow this street for one mile as it slips into the Vacationland subdivision. At the last street, turn left on Wai Opae and park on the street in the designated area.

"To live is so startling it leaves little time for anything else."
– Emily Dickinson

Ahalanui Beach Park

Ahalanui Beach Park

This is the most accessible of the volcanically heated "hot ponds" in the area. Locals of all stripes love this spot, and gather to soak, hang out and talk story. The setting under swaying palms and alongside crashing waves is blissful, making this a great place to unwind. The water temperature is usually only slightly warmer than body temp, so it feels nice even on warm days. It's possible to find warmer areas by moving around the pool, and the spot where the ocean enters the pool is always the coolest. Folks seem to enjoy snorkeling here, but the visibility is generally poor, there are no corals and only a few fish. The most interesting occurrence to witness under water is when a wave washes over the sluiceway and brings in a school of small, silvery fish. Showers and fresh water are available, and there are usually port-o-potties. The park is between mile markers 9 and 10 on the Red Road (Hwy 137).

Isaac Hale (Pohoiki)

While this county park is on the beautiful Pohoiki Bay, there isn't too much in the way of amenities here. It primarily serves as the area boat ramp, surf spot and general hangout spot for locals, many of whom aren't always particularly welcoming to tourists. Camping is permitted here with a county permit (see p. 52-53), but without potable water, electricity or park security, this isn't an attractive option. There is a small volcanically heated pool a short walk down the path to the right of the boat launch, but the access is through private property. There are so many other warm ponds in the area that reaching this one is probably not worth the "stink eye" you'll receive from the locals.

Isaac Hale Beach Park

Surfing Hot Spot: The most popular surf spot in Puna can be found just north of Isaac Hale Beach Park. Drive just past the park on the Red Road and you'll likely see a bustle of surf activity. Waves break over a very shallow reef which makes this site only for seasoned riders. It breaks all year long.

MacKenzie State Recreation Area

We'll just come out and say it: MacKenzie is creepy. It's a shame, because the area is so beautiful, with surf pounding against 40-foot lava cliffs, spraying into the air, and leaving behind ribbon waterfalls on the rocks. Still, the presence of an emergency call box is a red flag that maybe something shady is going on here. In fact, it was installed after the kidnap, rape and murder of Dana Ireland in the 1990s, which occurred nearby. Theft and drug deals are more prevalent than violent crime, but it's probably safe to visit only during the day. There is a state campground at MacKenzie, but take the advice a local resident gave us, "Just don't camp there."

Kehena Beach

Anything goes at Kehena Beach, a beautiful black sand beach and gathering place for Puna's many free spirits. It's a clothing-optional beach where you'll see more sarongs than beach towels, and signs of joy like senior women dancing and leaping in a circle, happy dogs digging holes and plenty of nudity, like a naked man walking around in nothing but yellow swim fins. A lively drum circle takes place every Sunday

Kahena Beach

afternoon. Keep in mind that swimming conditions can be rough here.

It's a bit of a scramble down a steep lava trail descending about 75 feet to reach the beach. Park either in the small lot or along the side of the road just south of the 19 mile marker on Hwy 137 (There's plenty of loitering up here, so be sure not to leave any valuables in your car.) There are no facilities, so pack in what you need. The trailhead starts *makai* about 50 feet from the parking area next to a sign covered with graffiti.

Kalapana

Before 1990, Kalapana was a Hawaiian fishing village, where native Hawaiians had lived for generations near Kaimu Beach, one of the most famous black sand beaches in the world. The small community expanded in the 1970s when the kama`aina (long-time residents) were joined by malihini (newcomers), mainly haoles from the mainland attracted by the beauty of the area, the relatively inexpensive real estate, and the aloha in the community – most of them helped build each others' houses.

When Kilauea began erupting in 1983 – as it still is – lava crept toward the village, but for years residents held out hope that their town would be spared. By 1990, the flow from Kupainaha vent threatened the entire area. Only one structure was relocated, Star of the Sea Painted Church, which was moved just 45 minutes before the lava flow sealed off the road. One by one the lava consumed homes (and another church) in its path, and residents watched as their houses and businesses burned. The lava buried not only Kalapana under 50 feet of lava, but the beautiful black sand beach at Kaimu as well.

Former road in Kalapana

Walking over the lava to the beach is an emotional experience to which people have varying reactions. Some feel awe at the power of nature, or anger that the volcano destroyed the island's best black sand beach and the peaceful community that lived around it instead of, say, a strip mall. Some feel hope when they spy fern shoots peeking through cracks in the lava, or the coconut palm saplings that former residents planted along the shoreline. One way or another, it's a powerful reminder that nature cannot be controlled.

The eruption

The hike over pahoehoe lava to "the new Kaimu Beach" begins at road's end, at a parking lot with a few basketball nets, a stand for raw honey, Uncle Robert's house, and a Verna's Drive Inn (great if you need fries or an ice cream sundae to perk you up). The hike is a third of a mile and takes about 15 minutes. Follow the metal poles, then turn inland when they end and head to the palm shoots by the shore. Watch your step, as there are many cracks in the lava (hiking sandals are better than slippahs). But don't forget to look up to see the steam plume from the lava flow entering the ocean off to your right – the flow may have shifted, but it's still flowing.

A visit to Kalapana will really hit home if you see the movie, *Kalapana: Death of a Hawaiian Village*. Filmed over the seven years while the lava threatened and ultimately destroyed the town, it is a heart-wrenching account of the disaster. Hilo's Lyman Museum screens it for visitors; as a volunteer said, "They just kept filming it right till it took their houses!"

"Carve a tunnel of hope through the dark mountains of disappointment." – Martin Luther King, Jr.

Star of the Sea Church

Star of the Sea Church being moved to a safe location (photo by D. Weisel 5/4/90)

Want to see the church that was rescued from Kalapana? Head to Star of the Sea Church, esteemed for its painted interior. The small Catholic church was built in 1927 and painted by Father Everest Gielen to create the impression of being in a much larger, classic Catholic cathedral. The barrel-vaulted ceiling is relatively high while the images and arched lines there assist in the mirage. In 1964, a new painter added another dimension to the interior with a painting behind the altar that creates the appearance of a long hall. The style is noticeably different, but it's the most effective image in the building. The parish was started by Father Damien, who left before the church was built to oversee the leper colony on Molokai. The original location of the church was two miles farther west in Kalapana, but church and community members heroically rallied to

Interior of the Church

move the church out of the flow of lava during the 1990 Kilauea eruptions that covered nearly the entire area. Today the church has been deconsecrated and is maintained by the generosity of its many visitors. Open 9 am-4 pm daily.

Another Puna town was destroyed by a Kilauea eruption in recent history: **Kapoho**. The homes, community center and church of the village were claimed by lava in 1960, with most of the destruction complete by January 27, 1960. Kapoho and Kalapana should serve as reminders that Mother Nature is fickle, especially in Puna.

Where to Stay

Yoga Oasis (Pohoiki Rd, ☎ 965-8460, toll free ☎ 800-274-4446, www.yogaoasis.org, four rooms with shared bath $100, three cabins $145, camping $60, single rates available). The name says it all. The owners, Star and Heywood, are yoga practitioners and former acrobats who have created a simple haven where they can practice yoga with their guests, in a retreat on 26 acres of rainforest. The yoga studio is awesome, on the second floor of the main building with inspiring views of the jungle. The space is 1,400 square feet of high ceilings, a gymnastic spring floor (making beginner inversions easier), wood paneling and just about any yoga prop you could ever need.

There are numerous options for accommodation, including four simple rooms with shared bath, covered camping platforms, and three secluded "cabins" with screen walls so that you are really aware of the surrounding rainforest. There are a lot of thoughtful touches to the property, like the intricate Balinese frames that grace most doorways. The entire facility is solar-powered. Massage and body treatments are also available. Rates include a two-hour morning yoga class, a scrumptious breakfast (usually organic) and wireless Internet. This is an authentic retreat run by authentic people. $-$$$

Kalani Oceanside Retreat (Opihikao, ☎ 965-7828, toll free ☎ 800-800-6886, www.kalani.com, 47 total rooms in a lodge, tree houses, and cottages, $110-$260; camping also available). Kalani is known around the Big Island as a sort of New Age empire, the king of the retreat circuit. And it's true: this sprawling retreat center offers simple, comfortable accommodation, thoughtfully prepared food, a resort-style pool and hot tubs, and massage services interwoven with New Age capitalism. Accommodations seem a little overpriced for their rustic quality, including screened, rather than glass, windows and a bit of a bug problem.

The food in the cafeteria is popular with guests, and includes many vegetarian options as well as fish and chicken. The retreat offers a variety of "Wellness Services," including Hawaiian *lomi lomi* massage and watsu (water shiatsu). This is an excellent place for large groups, though their presence can overwhelm the independent traveler. Vacation packages are available that are a much better deal, and include all meals, daily programs and some treatments. One point of contention: while the entrance to the center is indisputably across the street from the ocean, none of the grounds are actually adjacent to the ocean in any way. Hence, the "Oceanside" name is misleading. $$$

Hale O Naia master suite

Hale O Naia (Kapoho, ☎ 965-5340, www.hale-o-naia.com, three rooms $85-$175). Of all of the B&Bs on the Big Island, few are situated so seductively on the ocean. Tucked into a calm swimming cove on Kapoho Bay, Hale O Naia has a location worth drooling over. All three rooms have a view through the palms over the bay, where multiple surf breaks etch the ocean with bright white waves. Two of the rooms are comfortable but small, and share a bath with a Jacuzzi tub. The Master Suite, on the other hand, is the ultimate indulgence, with a king-sized bed, his-and-her baths, and a perfect lanai overlooking the perfect view. The house itself is airy and sunny, just what a Hawaiian home should be. Other amenities include an in-house cedar sauna, a six-person hot tub on the shore, and kayaks and snorkel gear for exploring the cove. Prices include a large continental breakfast, which one guest told us is "fan-freaking-tastic, and I'm a gourmet chef, so I know."

Nai`a ("NAI-ah") is the Hawaiian word for "dolphin."

Along Highway 11

Where to Shop

AUTHOR'S CHOICE ★ **Akatsuka Orchid Gardens** (between mile markers 22 and 23, ☎ 967-8234, www.akatsukaorchid.com). You don't have to be a resident of the Orchid Isle to love the diversity and beauty of orchids. The folks at Akatsuka have developed 2,000 orchid hybrids, and over a thousand of them are on display in their greenhouse, which is open to the public. They sell books, starters and cuttings that you can bring back with you (unless your state prohibits it – the labels are marked if that is the case). Because it's a tour bus stop, there are clean public restrooms and a gift shop. Next to the door, they give free orchids and bobbie pins for your hair. They also ship orchids to the mainland. Open 8:30 am-5 pm daily.

Akatsuka Orchid Garden

Adventures Underground

Kazumura Cave Tours (Glenwood, ☎ 967-7208, www.fortunecity.com/oasis/angkor/176/). At over 40 miles, Kazumura Cave is the longest known lava tube in the world. It is also the world's deepest cave, dropping over 3,600 feet from its beginning near Hawai`i Volcanoes National Park down to Paradise Park in lower Puna. The portion of the cave that is accessible through the family-run Kazumura Cave Tours is still pristine, and they take great care to keep it that way. The tours are given in Glenwood, which is just a short distance from the national park, making it a convenient side tour to augment your experience at the volcano.

They offer three different tours, all of which are terrific bargains and well worth the time. The shortest, Lava Falls ($10 per person), takes two hours and follows the tube "upstream," climbing four lava falls, the highest of which is 16 feet. Lava falls are dramatic sights, created when molten lava spills over a ledge into a plunge pool below. Other features include lavacicles, lava straws, dribble spires, lava plunge pools, lava blades and tube-in-tubes. You'll have to take one of the tours to find out what all of that stuff is! The guide has incredible knowledge of the cave, and will jam your brain with as much information as you can handle. The second tour ($15 per person) follows the same route but goes farther, taking four hours round-trip to the Pit Room, where you'll see a mind-boggling cave formation that defies description. There are no tight squeezes along these tours, and the grade is mild. Upon special request, they also offer a third tour, which is an all-day affair that requires climbing and ropes experience since there are several rappels necessary to descend into the Sexton Maze. The first two tours require 24-hour advance notice, while the Maze Tour requires a week's advance booking. The cave entrance is on private land, so remember to call and schedule a reservation first.

Where to Stay

The Butterfly Inn (Kurtistown, ☎ 966-7936, toll free ☎ 800-54MAGIC, www.thebutterflyinn.com, two rooms, $65, also work exchange cottage). For over 20 years, The Butterfly Inn has been a safe, comfortable and affordable retreat for female travelers. Located on an acre of land with all sorts of tropical plants, fruit and mac nut trees, the inn is a unique place to recharge. "They're my sisters – every woman that walks through the door is treated like a friend and welcomed with aloha," says Patty, who runs the inn with her partner Kay. The two rooms are simple and clean, and share a bright blue kitchen, common area with a dining room table and big windows overlooking the backyard, and a living area with a TV, stereo, guitar, books, board games and tarot cards. Outside, there is a Jacuzzi, steam room and outdoor shower. Former guests – an international group of women from all walks of life – have filled stacks of books with letters and drawings thanking Patty and Kay for their wonderful experience at the inn. $

Spa at the Butterfly Inn

Ka`u

I mohala no ka lehua i ke ke`ekehi `ia eka ua.
"The lehua blossom unfolds when the rains tread on it."
– Hawaiian proverb

IN THIS CHAPTER

It all began here – the first Polynesian landed in the Hawaiian Islands in Ka`u. Sometime around 300 AD, they ended their long canoe voyage, guided by currents and celestial navigation, coming ashore at this southernmost part of the island chain. Probably their first steps on Hawaiian soil were near Ka Lae (South Point), the southernmost point in the United States (if you exclude Puerto Rico).

Today, Ka`u is a sparsely populated, rural region that has withstood most developmental pressures so far. It has some interesting adventures for the intrepid traveler. Ka Lae is a chance to see the dramatic coastline where, surprisingly, there is no fanfare at the bottom tip of the US, just a chance to see fishermen reeling in big ones from the currents below. Nearby **Green Sands Beach**, whose olivine component lends it a light green hue, is a reward for adventurers willing to scamper through jagged lava to bask on its unearthly sand – in fact, the mineral olivine is found on the moon.

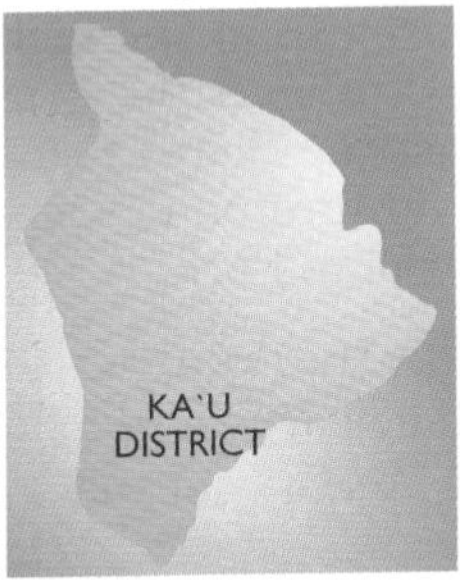

Punalu`u Black Sands Beach** is a basking and nesting ground for *honu* (turtles), whose endangered status makes them off-limits for touching but not photographing. Other special places in Ka`u include **Wood Valley Temple, a Tibetan Buddhist retreat center, and **Kula Kai Caverns**, one of the world's

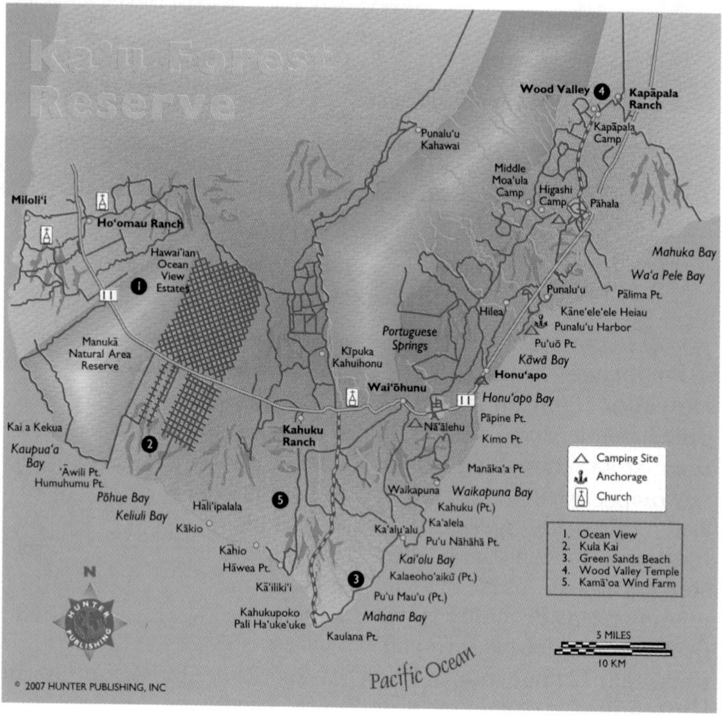

largest lava tubes. These are some of the surprises you'll find in Ka`u – you will feel like you're on a completely different island down here.

Orientation

The **Mamalahoa Highway** (Hwy 11 and Hawaii Belt Road) is the transportation lifeline through Ka`u ("Kah-OO"). It forms a basic horseshoe as it enters the area from the lush vegetation of South Kona, dips into the arid Ka`u desert as it swings past the South Point turnoff, then reenters the verdure as it veers north again toward Hawai`i Volcanoes National Park.

We've written the directions the way they're given on the Big Island: *mauka* and *makai*. Turn *mauka* means "toward the mountain." *Makai* means "toward the ocean."

Manuka State Park

Manuka State Wayside Park was developed between the mid-1930s and -50s as a "wayside for travelers to rest and relax," according to a small monument near the parking lot. A forestry work crew cleared eight acres of forest land, and then planted 48 species of plants native to Hawaii and over 130 species of exotic plants. It's a sort of oasis after the scrub-like vegetation at the start of the district. There are also public restrooms here.

Be respectful of the Hawaiian grave in front of the parking lot by giving it a wide berth – do not step on it.

Manuka State Park

Adventures on Foot

Manuka Nature Trail

Difficulty: Moderately easy
Distance and type: 2 miles, loop
Time: 1-2 hours

Manuka Trail

This well-maintained, two-mile loop trail offers a pleasant peek into the 25,000-acre Manuka Natural Area Reserve. There's a decent guide leaflet available at the trailhead that will help you identify many species of local trees and vegetation. Ohi`a dominates most of this hike, but you'll be introduced to many more endemic species, as well as important Polynesian imports such as *ti* and *kukui*. There's also a volcanic pit crater about ¾ of a mile in. The trail rises from 1,800 ft to 2,200 ft, so it will get your blood pumping. The final quarter-mile is over ankle-buster lava; take your time and make sure you have sensible footwear. The literature suggests you allow two to three hours for the hike, but one to two hours is all you'll need, unless you're going to try to memorize all of the different trees. You won't be tested later. Bring bug dope.

Camping

There's a camping pavilion here that's just straight up unappealing. Between the bugs and the proximity to the highway, you're better off camping elsewhere. Permits are available through the state (see *Camping*, p. 52-53).

ROAD TO THE SEA

With the promise of two black-and-green sand beaches, rugged coastline and few people, the Road to the Sea has been drawing more and more visitors down its difficult track in recent years. This, of course, somewhat defeats the purpose, as it is harder to find solitude here than in the past. This is undoubtedly what led some disappointed tourists to comment to us during our last trip down here that it "just wasn't worth it."

Ocean View

Many Ocean View residents commute to Kona for work, braving several hours in the car each direction because of the much less expensive real estate and rental prices in this last bastion of affordability on the sunny side of the island. There are a number of subdivisions nestled into a lava flow in the community, including H.O.V.E. – a central commercial hub with a distinct edge. "Ice," or crystal methamphetamine, is a problem here, bringing other problems like burglaries and some sketchy driving (no lights, speeding backwards, etc.). So stay alert – one resident of several years says the secret is not making eye contact with anyone, a sad concept that is very out of place on the Big Island.

There is one terrific adventure here – caving in one of the world's largest lava tubes – which is safely located in a gated community.

Practicalities

There is only one **area code** for the entire island: 808.

The **post office** (☎ 929-7593) is open 9 am-noon, and 12:45-4 pm Mon-Fri, and 9 am-1 pm Sat. Located next to the post office, **Ocean View Market** sells groceries and alcohol from 7:30 am-7:45 pm Mon-Sat, 8 am-6 pm Sun. **Kahala Gas** is open 8 am-8 pm Mon-Sat, 8 am-8 pm Sun.

Adventures Underground

Goat Cave

Kula Kai Caverns (☎ 929-9725, www.kulakaicaverns.com).The second-largest network of lava tubes in the world is found in the southwest rift zone of Mauna Loa beneath Ocean View. Much of this 1,000-year-old cave sits on private property and is run as Kula Kai Caverns. Several tours of varying lengths are offered, but once you're in the cave you'll realize the longer the better. This is the kind of subterranean beauty that excites one's sense of adventure, wondering where the next bend in the tunnel will lead.

Lighted interpretive trail

Not only is the geological aspect of the cave fascinating, but there is a rich historical and cultural heritage here, too. An experienced guide points out gourd cradles that former dwellers used for collecting water to support life in the harsh Ka`u Desert, as well as the ashes of the kukui nuts they used to light their way, petroglyphs, and discarded goat bones. You may even see the lava glob that looks like Bob Marley. The guide's knowledge and passion for the cave is impressive.

For those who are a little leery of confined spaces, there is a 30-minute lighted walk through the yawning, high-ceilinged cavern at the main entrance. Often people don't really know how they'll feel until they are in the cave, and they can opt for the longer tour once they're inside if they feel comfortable. (Occasionally, though, claustrophobia overcomes someone and they turn and bolt for the exit.) Lights, helmets, knee pads and drinks are included for your caving pleasure. This is a hot spot for professional cavers (modern cavers refuse to be termed "spelunkers") around the world, who come to survey the network; maps near the company's yurt label sections with enticing names like "Jewel Box," "Great Hall," and "Chocolate Factory." We highly recommend this tour. Half-hour tours cost $15, longer tours start at $65 per person.

KUKUI NUTS

Polynesians brought and planted these when they came to Hawaii. They are known as "candlenuts." Their high oil content causes them to burn slowly and evenly, thereby providing light for a sustained period of time. Candlenut's oil also acts as a laxative or purgative when consumed in excessive amounts, providing a medicinal use in days gone by. Today, highly polished kukui nuts are most often seen as leis in souvenir shops around the Islands.

Where to Stay

Leilani Bed and Breakfast (92-8822 Leilani Parkway, ☎ 929-7101, www.whenworkisplay.com/leilanibsb, three rooms, $75-$85). A spacious, screened-in common area provides a relaxing centerpiece to this unique B&B. A lava-rock waterfall gurgles away while you have breakfast, read a book, or commune with the two Jackson's chameleons that blend into the lava wall. The three guest rooms are sophisticatedly rustic, thematically decorated, and adorned with art that the hostess has created herself. An outdoor barbecue area is a nice place to relax or enjoy dinner. There are three large pukas (in this case, volcanic pit craters) on the property that are well worth exploring, one of which is heavily forested and over 100 yards deep. Continental breakfast, including tropical fruit and pastries, is included. $$

Where to Eat

Ocean View Pizzaria (525 Lotus Blossom Lane, ☎ 929-9677). This casual, brightly lit pizza joint was a pleasant surprise, with good pizzas at inexpensive prices ($12 for a small that is big enough for two people). The broken pinball machines and plastic tables belie the quality food – plus anytime we can choose between pesto and marinara sauce we get excited. Not too much cheese, fresh toppings, a satisfying crust – and you can BYO. Open 11 am-7 pm Sun-Thurs, until 8 pm Fri and Sat. $-$$

You have to love a place that has "Life is short, eat dessert first!" on the cover of their menu. **Desert Rose Café** is the nicest dining option in Ocean View, with indoor seating as well as an outdoor lanai. The sautéed mushrooms in butter sauce will whet your appetite for their plate dinners like teriyaki strip steak or tofu veggie stir fry. Burgers are made with a special blend of ground beef patted by hand, and you'll probably want to use your garlic bread to wipe clean your bowl of shrimp scampi pasta. Desert Rose Café serves house wines by the glass or bottle, sometimes only available in the 1½-liter size – or there is a $10 corkage fee. It can be creepy to go to the public bathroom, located down a set of stairs and past the post office. Open daily for breakfast 7 am-11 am, lunch 11 am-5 pm, dinner 5-8 pm (dinner until 9 pm Fri-Sun). $$-$$$

■ South Point

Known in Hawaiian as Ka Lae (the point), this is the southernmost tip of the island chain, which also makes it the southernmost point in the United States. You would think that it would be crowded with souvenir trinket stands, but it's

South Point

refreshingly devoid of this – even of a marker denoting "The Southernmost Point in the USA." Instead, it has been allowed to remain a pleasant place populated with fishermen and people like you, who are naturally curious about it.

It is widely thought that this is where the first wave of Polynesians landed from the Marquesas or Society Islands (1,500-2,000 miles south of Ka Lae) around 300 AD. As such, the area has been included in the National Registry of Historic Places.

The road down begins between mile markers 69 and 70 on Mamalahoa Hwy, about five miles west of Wai`ohinu. Turn makai. It's a decent, two-lane road until you pass the Kama`oa Wind Farm, about five miles in. They've picked a great location: the wind usually howls through here, as evidenced by trees bent at 90-degree angles. This alternative energy facility has been snatching energy out of the air since 1986. Its 37 Mitsubishi windmills produce enough electricity to supply 7,000 homes, saving 25,200 barrels of oil per year. That's when it's operating at full capacity, though, and the last time we passed through here none of the windmills were operational.

A half-mile past the wind farm, the road narrows to a single lane. Drive with aloha: pull over for other people and they will do the same for you. At precisely 10 miles from the highway, the road splits. The right fork leads 0.6 miles down to South

South Point (*Hawaiian Images*)

Point and some abrupt cliffs. This is a good place to park if you don't have a 4WD; just watch out for the large *puka* (hole) at the northern end of the parking area. Peek over the edge for a glimpse of the sea surging and retreating into the hole below.

There are some hoists here that are used to raise and lower small boats, but it seems like a pretty tricky proposition most days. The hoists have ladders at the bottom which seem to invite you to launch off the cliff and simply climb out using the ladder. But be wary! The current could suck you straight out to sea. On extraordinarily calm days you may see people doing this, or perhaps snorkeling. We suggest you wait for one of these days to actually see others who aren't meeting their end here before you even consider it.

There will likely be many fishermen around, as the currents that converge around Ka Lae create an exceptionally bountiful fishing ground.

Walk south along the cliffs to a point demarcated by a small sign, to view some ancient Hawaiian canoe moorings. In the past, resident fishermen drove holes into these cliffs to secure their canoes while fishing, to avoid being sucked away by the currents. Some of the holes are still visible. They are marked and numbered, but you have to hunt around a little bit to find them.

Continue south down to the light beacon, and locate the low lava wall that runs down to the sea. At the end of this wall is South Point, though it isn't marked as such. A few hundred yards farther on there is a small *heiau*, Pu`u Ali`i, which marks an ancient Hawaiian burial site. There are 4WD roads here that will take you around to the boat launch, which is the trailhead to Green Sands Beach, though it's probably better to go the way described below in order to preserve the area's tranquility.

HOKULE`A

It is incredible to consider that ancient Polynesians were able to sail around and settle the Polynesian Triangle (formed by Hawaii, New Zealand and Easter Island) without the use of modern instruments such as a compass. Instead, they relied on natural indicators from the sun, moon, stars, winds, tides, swell directions and birds. Some scholars found this accomplishment too hard to believe, insisting that ancient Polynesians drifted to the islands by accident. So in 1973, several Hawaiians, including renowned artist Herb Kane, founded the Polynesian Voyaging Society to refute this assertion. Kane designed a replica of an ancient voyaging canoe and, on May 1, 1976, the crew of the vessel Hokule`a shoved off for Tahiti to retrace the traditional migratory route – without using instruments. Thirty-three days later, Hokule`a was greeted in Papeete, Tahiti by 17,000 people – over half the population. The success of the voyage spurred a resurgence of Polynesian cultural pride and renewed the ancient bond between its people. Since then, Hokule`a has sailed over 100,000 miles of the Polynesian Triangle without the use of instruments, indisputable proof of the astounding feat of ancient Polynesian navigators. For more information, visit www.pvs-hawaii.com.

"The question is not what you look at, but what you see."
– Henry David Thoreau

Green Sands Beach

Green Sands Beach is one of those geological wonders that showcases nature's wild imagination – a pale yellow-green beach with aquamarine water, framed by a Salvador Dali-esque monolith. Because you need to scamper down lava to access the small beach, there are no waitresses serving daiquiris or hotels marring the skyline; it's just a thing of beauty in the middle of nowhere.

To get here from South Point, double-back 0.6 miles to the fork in the main road, and follow the alternate fork (or if you're coming from the main road, take the left fork). There will probably be a sign for the "Visitor's Center," a place that doesn't actually exist. Follow this road around until you get to an area marked as parking for Green Sands Beach. You can park here, but it's easier to simply park with everyone else down by the boat ramp.

From Kaulana Ramp, a 2¼-mile dirt road leads to the beautiful Mahana Bay, otherwise known as Green Sands Beach. The beach is surrounded by high bluffs, which make for a dramatic look, as well as seemingly difficult access. Look for the sign asking you not to take any sand from the beach (and please don't). It won't look like a feasible way down, as

Green Sands Beach

there's a short climb down to a ledge, but there are hand- and foot-holds in the lava and it's easier than it looks. Don't chicken out. It's worth it to rest down there after the hot hike, take a soak in the strikingly blue water (on calm days) or ponder the specks of olivine in a handful of sand. The road is drivable for those with 4WD, but walking isn't too bad either. Allow a good 45 minutes, and *bring water.* There is no shade on the trek, and no concession stands at the beach.

Olivine is peridot: When you're at Green Sands Beach, pick up some sand and examine it in your palm. Do some of the light green granules look like tiny peridots? That's because they are! Peridot, the birthstone for August, is the French word for olivine, the mineral that gives Green Sands Beach its color and name.

Wai`ohinu

After driving past lava fields splashed with hardy *ohi`a* trees and their fuzzy, red and white blossoms, you enter a lush green valley that is home to Wai`ohinu. This sleepy community was once a center for sugar and ranching; notice the rock walls that kept the cattle from entering family yards as they were herded to marinas to be hoisted onto ships. It is a relaxed village with some wonderful accommodation options.

Sights

"Travel is fatal to prejudice, bigotry, and narrow-mindedness." – Mark Twain

Mark Twain Monkeypod Tree

A sign marks the monkeypod tree that Mark Twain planted in 1866. It was largely demolished in a hurricane in 1957 but you would never know it – it has regenerated into a beautiful umbrella of a tree.

Before he became famous, Mark Twain (a pseudonym

used by Samuel Clemens) traveled to Hawaii in 1866 as a correspondent for the *Sacramento Union*, touring Oahu, Maui, and the Big Island. His enchantment is recorded in *Mark Twain's Letters from Hawaii,* where he refers to Hawaii as "the loveliest fleet of islands that lies anchored in any ocean."

Where to Stay

AUTHOR'S CHOICE ★

South Point Banyan Tree House (corner of Mamalahoa Hwy and Pinao St, ☎ 929-8515, reservations ☎ 715-355-0244, www.southpointbth.com, one house, $165, two-night minimum). We love this place, a one-of-a-kind hideaway whose owner is a laid-back Jimmy Buffett personality you can't help but like. His spacious suite, tucked up in the lofty embrace of a massive banyan tree, has a stereo, TV/VCR, full kitchen with gorgeous mango wood cabinets, washer/dryer, a plush queen-sized bed and a wrap-around deck with a hot tub. A portion of the roof is transparent, allowing you to lie in bed and watch the leaves play in the wind. You'll find a bottle of wine waiting for you on the kitchen counter, and some sodas and beer in the refrigerator. This place is perfect for romantics. $$$

South Point Banyan Tree House

Macadamia Meadows Farm Bed and Breakfast (☎ 929-8097, toll free ☎ 888-929-8118, www.macadamiameadows.com, five rooms, $69-$129, stay five nights and get one night free). While this is a working macadamia nut farm, the rooms

Macadamia Meadows Farm B&B

are spacious and immaculately kept, and the tennis court and pool remind you that you are on vacation in Hawaii. All rooms include a coffee maker, microwave and refrigerator, and have been recently renovated. The Punalu`u Black Sand Beach room is especially agreeable, and boasts a gorgeous queen-size teak canopy bed. The dining room is in the main house, a large ranch-style home with an immensely high ceiling and a wide lanai that looks out over the orchard. Free range chickens wander the property to keep the bugs down and make pesticides unnecessary, providing for a healthier product. Your hosts will give you a tour of the plantation and fill you in on anything and everything you ever wanted to know about macadamia nuts. Breakfast is included. $-$$

The Rainbow Cottage at Margo's

Margo's Corner Bed and Breakfast (☎ 929-9614, www.margos-corner.com, one cottage, $90, one suite, $130 plus $30 per person after two people, two-night minimum, several campsites, $30 per person). The novel and unpretentious accommodations provided by Margo have made this a popular destination for all kinds of folks. Outside, cats laze around on their own network of bridges and poles, while kaleidoscopic color splashes are found around every corner. The Rainbow Cottage is no exception, with a chromatic mandala blazed on the wall above the bed and a prism of colors in the rafters cut across a blue-sky ceiling. The Adobe Suite accommodates up to six people in three beds tucked into soft adobe arches, and includes a sauna. Several camping pads are available outside, but the lawn is also open for pitching a tent. The gay-friendly establishment has a natural food store on the premises which Margo operates on a non-profit level for those in the community. Rates include a full breakfast and dinner, mostly organic and vegetarian. $-$$

■ Na`alehu

Key West, Florida may be the southernmost town in the continental US, but the southernmost town in the entire United States is Na`alehu. As such, nearly every business in the small town claims to be the southernmost of its kind – you'll find the southernmost bar, restaurant, bakery, market, etc. It's a small settlement with a slow pace of life – a pleasant stop on your way to or from the volcano.

Practicalities

Note: All of the Na`alehu businesses listed are located along Highway 11/Mamalahoa Highway.

There is a **76 gas station** open 5 am-10 pm Mon-Fri, 6 am-10 pm Sat and Sun. The **post office** is open 8 am-4:15 pm (closed lunch 1-2 pm), 8 am-10 am Sat. **Island Market** (☎ 929-7527), the "Southernmost Market in USA," is a grocery store open 8 am-7 pm Mon-Sat, and 9 am-6 pm Sun.

Don't miss **Na`alehu Theatre**, a local landmark easily recognized by the picture of the turtle painting on its roof.

Where to Shop

Jackie's Plantation House (95-5586 Mamalahoa Highway, ☎ 829-8134, www.jackiesgiftsandworldtravel.com). Jackie Dunn, a retired school teacher and "world traveler," sells a variety of gifts, sometimes brought back from her trips abroad – she also leads vacation tours to places like China. The store is crammed full of Americana too, like the large selection of Beanie Babies and her clothing and luggage designs. This must be one of the last places in the country where you can still buy penny candy! Open 10 am-5 pm Mon, Wed, Fri and Sat.

The small **Ka`u Farmers Market** is held on Wednesdays and Saturdays from 8 am-noon on the lawn of Ace Hardware, with produce, plants, jewelry and other goods for sale.

"Age does not protect you from love. But love, to some extent, protects you from age." – Anais Nin

Where to Eat

**Punalu`u Bakeshop and Visitor Center** (95-5642 Mamalahoa Highway, ☎ 929-7343, www.punaluubakeshop.com). This place fills Ka`u's need for a tour bus stop – clean bathrooms, gift shop, snack foods and Hawaiian sweetbreads from "the southernmost bakery in the US." It also has a small – but free! – botanical garden, basically some labeled trees ranging from a giant banyan to a sapling noni. Sandwiches come in a plastic container, even if you're eating there. There is pleasant outdoor seating underneath two gazebos. The visitor center consists of a small information wall near the bathrooms. Open 8 am-7 pm Mon-Sat, 9 am-6 pm Sun. $

Hana Hou Restaurant (95-1148 Na`alehu Spur Road, ☎ 929-9717) is the place to eat in Na`alehu – you guessed it, the "southernmost restaurant and bakery in the USA." It's a pleasant eatery in an old plantation house, with vintage café tables and chairs and origami swans hovering in mid-air. The portions are large – as one server said proudly, "No one leaves here hungry!" Try the "porker" omelette – three eggs with bacon, tomato, shitake mushrooms and Swiss cheese, served with rice, toast or cornbread (the breads here are pure comfort food). Open 8 am-3 pm Mon-Wed, 8 am-9 pm Thurs-Sun. $$

Camping

Whittington Beach Park

Whittington Beach Park, *makai* between mile markers 60 and 61, is known for the nearby large *pahoehoe* (smooth lava) tide pools, which have a few coral heads and small fish. Camping by county permit (see *Camping*, p. 52-53) is on grass where you can hear the waves crashing on the lava. We've camped here twice. The first time, we slept well, interrupted only once by the heart-stopping screeches of feral cats. The second time, we arrived at our campsite a little before 10 pm and found a woman smoking ice from a glass pipe and carving a tombstone. The eerie "chink, chink" of her chiseling echoed throughout the campsite, and we were so unnerved that we drove all the way back to our apartment in Kailua-Kona. Maybe that's why there aren't usually many tents here.

However, there is hope for the future of the park. In a victory for Ka`u residents, the tract of land adjacent to Whittington Beach Park, Honu`apu, was purchased from developers at the end of 2005 and will become an expanded county park – protected from future development.

Whittington Beach *(Hawaiian Images)*

■ Punalu`u

At the moment, Punalu`u, a former sugar port, is home for a smattering of people. But a proposed housing development would add up to 2,000 homes, permanently altering the face of the area by adding over 3,000 new residents and putting additional strain on the turtle habitat. Public meetings with the developers, Sea Mountain Five, have been heavily attended by locals opposed to the project. Perhaps Punalu`u will be as successful in withstanding developmental pressures as other areas of Ka`u.

Green sea turtles (*honu*) get their name from the color of their body fat, which is green from the seaweed (*limu*) they eat. They do not reach sexual maturity until they are about 25 years old. Adults can weigh up to 270 pounds!

Punalu`u Black Sand Beach (Hawaiian Images)

Punalu`u Black Sand Beach Park

The jet black volcanic sand sparkles in the sun at this small beach, which is a nesting ground for green sea and hawksbill turtles (*honu `ea*). There are signs warning visitors to keep at least 15 feet from the federally-protected turtles that come to the shore to bask in the sun or lay their eggs. Still, this beach is on the map for tour buses, and the beach can be overrun with people scrambling to take photos of the turtles that sometimes seem too daunted to come ashore – which leads visitors to snorkel after them.

Respect the signs and give the turtles space, or we will disrupt their habits and drive them away. And don't be afraid to holler "Fifteen feet!" at anyone who violates the law!

At low tide, check out the tide pools and the fresh water springs that gurgle into them. Taste it and you'll know it's salt-free!

Did you know? There are fewer than 30 nesting hawksbill turtles in the state of Hawaii. The endangered turtles were hunted to the point of extinction for their beautiful exterior shell, whose mottled coloring known as "tortoise shell" became very popular in the fashion industry. They nest primarily between May and October.

Camping

Camping at **Punalu`u Black Sand Beach Park** is by county permit (see *Camping*, p. 52-53). There are some wide open grassy areas and several pavilions where locals tend to party, especially on weekends. We found ourselves camped in the midst of one raucous party that was not even broken up by the cop car that circled the lot around 10 pm, when the lights are supposed to go out (they didn't) for quiet time. We thought it was pretty amusing, but the little family camping near us was fairly traumatized in the morning. Expect to be woken up early by day trippers coming to gawk at the *honu*. There are public restrooms and showers here.

■ Pahala

Practicalities

Pahala's commercial complex is on Kamani Street (where you turn *makai* off Highway 11 at the sign for Pahala) and Pikake Street. There is an **ATM** at the Bank of Hawaii, a **post office** (open 8 am-4 pm Mon-Fri with a lunch break from 12:15-12:45 pm), a **grocery store** (Mizuno Store open 6 am-7 pm Mon-Fri, 7 am-5 pm Sat, 8 am-noon Sun) and clean public **restrooms** behind Tex Pahala.

Ka`u Hospital (☎ 808-928-8331) is right on Highway 11 at the turn for Pahala. The entrance to the hospital and emergency room is on Kamani Street.

Where to Stay

Wood Valley Temple and Retreat Center (☎ 928-8539, www.nechung.org, nine rooms for up to 15 people $75, or dorms for $40). If you have even the slightest interest in Tibetan Buddhism or meditation, you must stay at this very special place. Nestled on 25 acres in the beautifully forested Wood Valley, Nechung Dorje Drayang Ling ("Immutable Island of Melodious Sound") is a Buddhist temple and retreat center with daily meditations and weekend classes. Visiting lamas sometimes teach here as well. In fact, Wood Valley Temple (its local nickname) was dedicated by the Dalai Lama in 1980, who visited again in 1994 to address 3,500 people.

The serene grounds are highly conducive to finding inner calm, and many groups reserve time here for retreats, sometimes filling the original meditation hall with massage tables or yoga mats. Rooms are simple, with a large screened lanai and common area where guests can cook, or gather to play guitar or talk.

Wood Valley Temple

One of the caretakers says that because their resident lama is away in India, pressures of day visitors (normally welcomed on weekends for a *dana* of $5) are putting a strain on their resources. So if you would like to visit, please reserve a room here. You will be glad that you did!

There is also a library with spiritual books, and a Temple Store with Buddhist items, including an awesome poster of the Dalai Lama visiting Kilauea during his 1980 visit (the photo is also on their website).

Essentially, if you are in need of a peaceful retreat, Wood Valley Temple should be your destination.

Where to Eat

Tex Pahala (☎ 928-8200). Like the famous Tex Drive-Inn of Honoka`a, Tex is known for it *malasadas*, or Portuguese donuts, sugary confections without a hole. You can see them made in a window while you wait for a plain one, or one filled with gooey treats like Bavarian cream. Tex also serves milkshakes, and burgers, wraps, Portuguese soup, breakfasts and plate lunches. Open 7 am-7:30 pm daily. $

Hawaiian Glossary

a`a . . . jagged lava
ahu . . . stone cairns that mark hiking trails
A hui hou . . . until we gather again
ahupua`a . . . traditional land division
`aina . . . land
akamai . . . smart
akua . . . god
ala . . . road
ali`i . . . royalty
aloha . . . greeting meaning welcome or goodbye; love
a`ole . . . no
`aumakua . . . protective diety
E komo mai . . . welcome
hale . . . house
hana . . . work
haole . . . foreigner, Caucasian
hapa . . . half, part
he`e nalu . . . surfing
heiau . . . religious structure
hoaloha . . . friend
hoku . . . star
holoholo . . . take a walk or ride for fun
holua . . . ancient sled
honi . . . kiss
honu . . . green sea turtle
honu`ea . . . hawksbill turtle
hukilau . . . group net fishing
hula . . . traditional Hawaiian dance
huli . . . to turn; when a canoe or kayak flips over
ipo . . . sweetheart
imu . . . underground oven used to cook luau pig
kahili . . . feathered standard of Hawaiian royalty
kahuna . . . expert Hawaiian with a skill
kai . . . sea water
kalo . . . taro
kalua . . . method of cooking in an imu
kama`aina . . . longtime resident of Hawaii
kanaka . . . native Hawaiian
kane . . . man
kapa . . . cloth made by pounding bark
kapu . . . forbidden, "no trespassing"
kaukau . . . food, eat
keiki . . . child
ki`i . . . carved statue of diety
kipuka . . . an older lava flow surrounded by a younger one
koa . . . native hardwood tree
kohola . . . whale
kokua . . . help

kona . . . . . . leeward side
kumu . . . . . . teacher
kupuna . . . . . . grandparent, elder
lanai . . . . . . patio, verandah
lau . . . . . . leaf
lauhala . . . . . . leaf of hala tree, woven into mats and hats
lele . . . . . . jump
lei . . . . . . flower necklace
limu . . . . . . seaweed
lolo . . . . . . crazy
luau . . . . . . feast
mahalo . . . . . . thank you
mahina . . . . . . moon
makai . . . . . . toward the sea
malama . . . . . . care for
malihini . . . . . . newcomer
mana . . . . . . spiritual power
mano . . . . . . shark
mauka . . . . . . toward the mountains; inland
mauna . . . . . . mountain
mele . . . . . . song, chant
menehune . . . . . . Hawaiian leprechaun
moana . . . . . . ocean
nalu . . . . . . wave
nene . . . . . . Hawaiian goose
niu . . . . . . coconut palm
nui . . . . . . very much
`ohana . . . . . . extended family
ohi`a . . . . . . gnarled tree with red powderpuff flowers, called lehua
`okole . . . . . . rear end
Okole maluna! . . . . . . Bottoms up, cheers
ono . . . . . . delicious
pahoehoe . . . . . . smooth lava
pakalolo . . . . . . marijuana
pali . . . . . . cliff
paniolo . . . . . . Hawaiian cowboy
pau . . . . . . done, finished
poi . . . . . . taro paste
pua . . . . . . flower
puhi . . . . . . eel
puka . . . . . . hole, cave
puke . . . . . . book
pupu . . . . . . appetizer
pu`u . . . . . . hill
wa`a . . . . . . outrigger canoe
wahine . . . . . . woman
wai . . . . . . freshwater
wikiwiki . . . . . . hurry, quick

Index